Globalization and the Post-Creole Imagination

A JOHN HOPE FRANKLIN CENTER BOOK

Christopher Cozier, *The Castaway* (2005), ink on paper, detail from the Tropical Night Series

GLOBALIZATION
AND THE
POST-CREOLE
IMAGINATION

Notes on Fleeing the Plantation

MICHAELINE A. CRICHLOW
with PATRICIA NORTHOVER

DUKE UNIVERSITY PRESS *Durham & London 2009*

Printed in the United States
of America on acid-free paper ∞
Designed by Jennifer Hill
Typeset in Minion Pro by Keystone Typesetting, Inc.

Library of Congress
Cataloging-in-Publication Data
appear on the last printed page of this book.

For "SPA" & GEORGE & SARAH

CONTENTS

Where are your monuments, your battles, martyrs?
Where is your tribal memory? Sirs,
in that gray vault. The sea. The sea
has locked them up. The sea is History.[1]

Even in dreams I will submerge myself
swimming like one possessed
back and forth across that course
strewing it with sweet smelling
flowers
one for everyone who made the journey.[2]

THIS BOOK IS an intervention into discussions of Caribbean sociocultural practices gathered under the rubric of "creolization," which express, as Michel-Rolph Trouillot suggests, processes of "selective creation and cultural struggle." These discussions by and large have tended to treat creolization as critical to the forging of sociocultural relationships, identities, and freedoms in the Caribbean and by extension Plantation America. In engaging with the discourse, my argument hinges on a project designed to redirect the terms of the creolization debates in ways that speak to the journeys toward the refashioning of self, times, and places in the intertwinement of global and local processes. In particular, the text endeavors to displace the notion of creolization outside its original setting, in order to explore its circuits in the dense seas of present histories-in-the-world. I do not seek, however, to jettison the *idea* of creolization's *rhizomic rootings* in the Caribbean but rather wish to treat the construction of those groundings relationally.[3] That is, as articulations of spaces and peoples, whose places of enunciation and sociocultural practices have been sited within a global frame entangling, so to speak, modern power and its subjects, as contesting yet inseparable autonomies. This repositioning of the discourses on "creolization" opens up the possibility of exploring the Caribbean, unencumbered by what Irit Rogoff calls "three really burdensome models: the impositions of geography, of geographical location; the nation-state and local identity; and the legacies of colonialism that established a binary opposition with colonial powers."[4] Thus, rather than reconfiguring exhausted debates about "Creole" identity per se, constructs which are inescapably enmeshed in essentialisms and secreted from a perspective on "culture" as possession and end product, the approach here is to explore identity as "something profoundly incoherent," as well as critically pragmatic, by locating the Caribbean's experiences as an entangled site and a portal. Seeing creolization in this fashion requires a vision of such torn experiences as "liminal states" and a "limbo gateway," as Wilson Harris suggests, burdened with the possibilities that spatial thresholds offer for experiencing liminal transformation.[5] Indeed, it is through this violent ritual of crossing that those whose lives have been staked in the present seek to remake the incoherencies of cosmologies of presence, through a more or less open ended forging of new world processes, contingent on a politics of space and place, indeed, contingent on "une poétique de la Relation."[6]

Creolization processes are thus read here as symbolic refractions of a particular mapping of the present, to borrow Stuart Elden's concept, and the ontological media for renegotiating the incoherencies of presence (absence) and for navigating space and place. However, lest we forget, people journey through such seas of history not as free floating signifiers but rather as real "bodies," culturally rooted and routed, in substantive contexts of power enfolding performatives of time and space. In the text, this node of articulation of space and place is traced to the projects of modern power, *viz* "modern governmentality," that seek to delimit, control, determine, and direct "scenes of presence," as Derrida suggests, and "spaces of hope," as Harvey intimates.

In the frontispiece, the provocative drawing *The Castaway* (detail from the Tropical Night Series), by the Trinidadian artist Christopher Cozier,[7] gestures to the idea of such processes of articulation and liminal movement in states of incoherence. It conjures movement (a change of place, position, or posture; or a particular instance or manner of moving), yet there hangs an eerie stillness of the image, an unfathomable denseness of being-in-the world. A torrent of questions is set loose by the image, whose meaning can only be discovered by a journeying of the imagination. Imagine, then, the swimmer, partially submerged, enfolded by the sea, conducting the world, it would seem at the price of his impalement by it, yet can this enable "the rhythm of the swift and slow of human doing itself"?[8] Is there a politics, or even a poetics, of sacrifice entailed in the quest for place? Can creolization avoid incoherence? Is it a prisoner of the Middle Passage? Is movement conditional on violence? Is being-in-the-world unthinkable without the weight of the map, mapping the site of presence/place, yet never able to reveal any essential essence of identity; leaving opaque the mystery of living, life, the figures of self? "What is the what" exactly here?[9] Where exactly is it? The image, a puzzle, becomes a labyrinth of space, time, power, and place. Or so it seems. Our wonderment leads us to Brathwaite's *Emigrants:*

Where to?
They do not know.
Canada, the Panama
Canal, the Miss-
issippi painfields, Florida? Or on to dock
at hissing smoke locked
Glasgow?[10]

But the blurred spectral antique map can only faintly represent places and spaces of geographies. What map of Africa or India, or the world, should become staked for Caribbean New World movements? The figure too is blurred, it hovers with its arm askance almost beneath the surface, unconnected to no One, no "Other," yet in connection to some thing, and located, betwixt and between, in the seas of subterranean history. Which citizenship, what memories, what subjectivity, what "space," "place," "mode of dwelling," or "homing" is being articulated then in this liminal state—a state that is simultaneously being vaguely situated and almost fully sub-merged, marginal?

The image thus resonates powerfully with ideas calling for an articula-tion. This text hopes to provide such an articulation by teasing out, analyt-ically and empirically, the complexities of living in, as well as through, "the world," as mediated by space, place, and time. There is much ground to be traveled here, then, which this text wishes to facilitate. Drawing inspiration from varied sources, the text will thus put forward arguments on thinking creolization anew yet through terms evocative of the incoherence of identity and culture, its instrumentality and its weight, all of which are argued to be creatively worked through and articulated by human beings "exercising existence," as Mbembe reminds us.[11] This perforce, as argued in the book, takes the form of a journeying, or crossing, which paradoxically roots and routes our densely inscribed subjects through seas of history and obscure mappings of the present; through ineluctable rites of Middle Passage and its liminal spaces exciting dreams, memories, hopes, and the post-Creole imagination of opaque futures. Indeed, this book takes very seriously the work of the artist and the image, which Christopher Cozier suggests conveys the critique that "conventional notions of history are limited by a fixation on place and ownership like a fixation on fact and text, as distinct from oral and visual."[12]

These wonderings and meditations on this work of art have thus helped bring forth the arguments of this text, which rework literary, artistic, sociological, historical, hermeneutic, political, economic, ethnographic, and philosophical insights into an analysis of the sociocultural practices of Caribbeans and other citizens of the present space of the global world. The book also presents its discussion of creolization through an engagement with key social theoretical accounts of the relation between structure and agency, as the reworking of notions such as habitus, space, and place strives to do, without losing sight of the making and remaking of the fields and basis of spatial being in the world.

The book emerged from chapter 4 and my thinking about the Lucians group and their peculiar carnivalesque performances within and outside the nation-state and worked outward to include other concerns and inquiries about Caribbeans in the world and the world in the Caribbean. I was trying to understand the kind of protest discussed in that chapter that seemed so different. And it was happening in a place where I had partly grown up. I really wanted to write about how small places like the Caribbean encompassed larger worlding processes from a more personal perspective. I savored memories of Konte dancing on moonlit nights, drummings, dancings, and spirit possessions;[13] about an elevated Pons Te Te (Bridge of Tits), where barebacked women washed their clothes in the river below, slapping, and pounding them hard against the river rocks. As romantic and even as premodern as this sounds, those women reflected a modern condition of the "rural" Caribbean, the unavailability of pipe-borne water in a very "modern" place—indeed, a place which has been modern since the eighteenth century, given the protoindustrialized mechanics of slave plantations. And in hindsight, the dancing was the very act of remaking space and asserting a particular identity, injecting a different self.

The idea of creolization provided just the hook I needed to reformulate arguments about "exercising existence" beyond the modern sites of the plantation, the enduring focus of creolization studies. My interlocutors were scholars grappling with and interrogating creolization's universalization and its translatability outside of the region, especially in view of its Caribbean ideological and cultural exclusions of Indo-Caribbeans, but also of others deemed profane and vulgar. While creolization has been popularized in relation to Caribbean forms of modernity originating with plantation and slavery generally, giving rise to cultural forms in worlds made anew in the Americas, it seemed to me that one could justifiably argue that creolization was a process that transcended an emphasis on its originary places, populations, and spaces. This became a crucial optic of the text. Its argument was then more fully framed around three processes: creolization generalized, creolization historicized, and creolization dynamized. Indeed, generalizing the creolization process beyond any plantation, and historicizing it as Trouillot demanded, also contained within it the seeds and outcomes of creolization as a *dynamized* process. This step, I believe, should help get us beyond the romanticization of creolization's politics and peoples, especially those considered primarily "peasant folk" who often become the central figures of the production of "Caribbean culture" (that is, if we wish to reclaim a history that was at once Caribbean but also truly worldly).[14]

The groundwork for this sort of theorizing, or alternative historical interpretation, if you will, had already been considered in a previous work, *Negotiating Caribbean Freedom*. But I was fortunate to be working on a project on critical development and globalization with my friend and colleague Patricia Northover.[15] We drew upon some of these ideas and pulled them into this creolization manuscript. Patricia's disciplinary training in economics, as well as her interdisciplinary interests in philosophy, social theory, and postcolonial development and theory, combined well with my own historical sociological training and eclectic interests in literature, social theory, and postcolonial studies by way of poststructural reasonings. The result is the jointly produced model of creolization dynamized, fully addressed in chapter 2. Undoubtedly, this collaboration enabled a firmer grounding of the notion of creolization as an emancipatory practice, working into its theorization notions of history as spatialized and space as historicized. My ethnographic and historical interpretations of the lived experiences of Caribbeans, which constitute the text's body, are framed by this model.

The manuscript, originally titled "Globalization and the Postcreole Condition: Notes on Fleeing the Plantation," gave way to a focus on imagination. How do people imagine their "condition" and address the location of their culture within the ineluctable structures of power they encounter? How do they seek to get beyond these positions which work to shape their subjectivities? What sorts of spaces allow for the vital movements which facilitate their "selective creation(s) and cultural struggle," the core of creolization? These questions suggestively point to creolization's specificity as well as its universality.

The recognition that such cultural struggles were located within social habituses but not determined by them led to considerations of the notion of *fleeing* and *homing*. "Fleeing the plantation" appropriately captures the idea of the nondeterminism of social being, as well as of agency and imagination. "Fleeing the plantation" incorporates two dimensions: first a call to creolization scholars to treat the plantation as a site that was approached differently according to the imaginations of those who were trapped there; second, the need to make a strategic shift to understand the processes that all these miraculous projects of the enslaved entailed. And also to gesture to those projects in the post-post-emancipation period, a period that somehow rarely seemed to elicit discussion within the frame of creolization. It was as if the process of creolization had reached a dead end, where there was no need anymore to grapple with the structures and strictures of controlling powers. I felt that we needed to break up this kind of temporal and spatial dwelling, because creolization practices themselves were ongoing and varied expressions of mobile strategies that went beyond the plantation. "Fleeing the plantation" thus represented, or sought to capture, a sense of an ongoing journey, or crossing, that one sought to make in the pursuit and homing of modern freedoms. This dual and paradoxical aspect of "rooting *and* routing," of "staying *and* fleeing," of "re/membering *and* for/getting," needed to be given further analytical and empirical attention, in order to better illuminate the multivalent nature of the creolization process itself.

And so the book promotes not only the accretion of diverse empirical detail to support the case for fleeing the plantation, analytically, historically, and metaphorically. It also seeks to generate a perspective on the imagination of Caribbeans and those in the world who, like Caribbeans, find themselves grappling with modern power's projects in novel and distinct ways.

This book was written in several locations made possible by several grants. At the University of Iowa (UI) in Iowa City, I received two Arts and Humanities Initiative grants, three Old Gold Awards, international travel grants, and a career development award, in the form of leave, to research these ideas. Support from the Ford Foundation, via the UI Crossing Borders program, facilitated travel to the Caribbean, Europe, and later the Pacific. In Amsterdam I first started putting together thoughts on migration for a different project but one with similar themes. There I was hosted graciously by Lucea Nankoe and Ellen Ombre. I hung out at the Frontline restaurant, watching the comings and goings of Africans and Caribbeans, where I ate curried duck, a Surinamese recipe which, the owners said, was prepared with imported Surinamese ducks! In St. Lucia I collected data from the Folk Research Center and the National Trust. In Trinidad, rare manuscripts in the library of the University of the West Indies, St. Augustine, particularly the West Indian Collection, proved useful for understanding the Peoples National Movement (PNM) nationalist project. In Kingston, the staff of the African Caribbean Institute, the UWI main library, the West Indian Collection, and the Sir Arthur Lewis Institute of Social and Economic Studies (SALISES) Documentation Center were welcoming (have always been) and supportive. There, Omar Davies, Clare Forrester, Annie Paul, Marcia Sepaul, Carmen Tipling, and Enid Walters (Miss Gladly) provided strong friendships and dinners, conversations, contacts, and intellectual openness. And I cannot forget young Sarah Northover, whose playfulness proved essential for my overall well-being. In Durham I polished the manuscript and in my upper-level classes, on nationalism and diaspora, I floated many of these ideas, sometimes surreptitiously and tentatively, other times openly. Along the way, I've presented some of these ideas at conferences and workshops as well, receiving invaluable suggestions: from the University of Chicago's Globalization Graduate symposium; the University of Iowa's Crossing Borders conference; the Caribbean, Diaspora and Atlantic Studies colloquium at UI; the Davenport Museum in Iowa during the lecture series for the exhibition of the work of the Haitian artist Edouard Duval Carrié; the Sir Arthur Lewis Community

College in St. Lucia and their sixth formers; Duke University's sociology department; the "Rethinking Caribbean Culture" conference in Barbados; the Caribbean Studies Association's annual meetings in Belize and Brazil; the UWI Jamaica conference commemorating the work of Sir Arthur Lewis, the Nobel Laureate and St. Lucian, and his epic *Theory of Economic Growth*; and the "African Diasporic Knowledges" conference in Cape Town, South Africa. I benefited tremendously from feedback I received in these places.

The revision of the text coincided with my participation in a Duke University reading group from a collaborative project, "Race, Space, Place: The Making and Unmaking of Freedoms in the Atlantic World and Beyond," with colleagues Sean Metzger, Ara Wilson, Maurice Wallace, Patricia Northover, Alexis Gumbs, Matthew Smith, Ishtar Govia, and Johanna Cross.[16] All the readings were useful, especially the interdisciplinary reflections on the work of Henri Lefebvre and Nikolas Rose, and helped to stimulate a development of our perspectives on space, place, time, and modern governmentality.[17]

My colleagues and friends Anny Curtius, Carolle Charles, Charles Carnegie, Mary Lou Emery, Sean Metzger, Guha Shankar, and Tanya Shields read sections of the manuscript and offered useful suggestions. Jerry Wever and Betty Rodriguez, UI graduate students, provided helpful feedback and pointed me to relevant literatures. Very detailed and fine-grained comments offered by the readers of a coauthored paper for a volume on ontology were especially useful in rethinking our conceptualization of the arguments and clarifying the models.[18] Also the astute comments of the anonymous readers helped in the reshaping and clarifying of key aspects of the text's arguments. I appreciate the encouragement I received from Reynolds Smith, the Duke University Press editor, and his assistant Sharon Torian, who believed in the project and stuck with it, as did my AAAS colleagues at Duke.

Needless to say, the cooperation of research subjects, mentioned throughout the text, especially Lucians and gens anglaises, is the text's foundation. From their cooperation comes a plea that underscores the arguments of this book—that is, that we begin to think of conducting our politics in a more open and less parochial manner, given that our cultural practices and histories bespeak a broader and more pluralized provenance. I dedicate this book to the global people of the Caribbean and its beyonds.

GLOBALIZATION AND CREOLE IDENTITIES
The Shaping of Power in Post-Plantation Spaces

The unity is submarine.[1]

Stitches on time.[2]

CREOLIZATION, TREATED here as a historicized process of *selective creation and cultural struggle*, is this
book's central concern. Such a view of creolization, salient
for apprehending Caribbean sociocultural configurations
within the region, is also critical for understanding their
contexts: that is, the plural uneven temporalities and spaces
that constitute nation-states' and subjects' histories. Saskia
Sassen's term "frontier zones," characterized by "regulatory fractures" or "informal sectors," captures these uneven
temporal pluralities that constitute nation-states' histories.
For as Sassen rightfully notes of globalization, and as David
Harvey notes of postmodernity,[3] the existence of plural
temporalities culminates from the partiality of the imposition or incorporation of economic structures and symbolic
practices. Partiality is an enduring condition of all human
systemic endeavors.

Partiality constituted within a whole and a whole constituted within these partialities invite one to conceive of creolization and globalization as *projects*. As such, as Nicholas

Thomas suggests, they draw "attention not towards a totality such as culture, nor to a period that can be defined independently of people's perceptions and strategies, but rather to a socially transformative endeavour that is localized, politicized and partial, yet also engendered by longer historical developments and ways of narrating them."[4]

Seen from these perspectives, Caribbean histories and cultural processes are multidirectional, making for complex postcolonial creolization processes. Creole citizens in the Caribbean have always negotiated and maneuvered within intertwined histories of diverse but linked places constituting the world economy/society, and they have done so often from their local transnational vantage point. For *staying* or *dwelling* involves imaginative movement.[5] In other words, all such kinds of movement of Caribbeans takes place within an unequal register of a Westernness, more or less received and selectively engaged, rather than lived as a fully quotidian experience. Consider Richard Price's essay "The Dark Complete World of a Caribbean Store," which marvelously describes a Martiniquan store/rum shop. Price states:

> During July 1983, the store stocked some 213 items or brands. And of these 84% were imported from outside Martinique, from 31 countries and from every continent except Australia. Toilet paper and garlic from Italy, condensed milk and hair rollers from Switzerland, bathing trunks from Thailand, sardines from Morocco, orange drink from Israel, underpants from Spain, chewing gum from Denmark (where did they get the chicle?) raisins from Greece.[6]

The shelf contents of the rum shop certainly demonstrate a high end cosmopolitanism, "proof" of the Caribbean-Western problematic of which much has been written. Even so, insofar as such a shop has not itself been undermined by the new expanding supermarket, it services a particular Caribbean and inhabits a particular temporality, dominated by the coordinates of a kind of capital and culture different from the dominant one of today. Thus, it is a moment no less structured by the world positionality of Martinique which at once facilitates and is the outcome of a different Creole experience, another kind of modern than others of the region and outside of it.[7] This was palpably clear to me in 1990, when I conducted research there on land use and tenure. I stayed with a smallholder's family, consuming at its board all the paté du monde, participating in their passion for the

Tour de France, and almost losing my life as a passenger in Louis's fast Peugeot car! That sort of smallholder Creole life was worlds apart from that other Caribbean, those of the Windward Islands, Martinique's neighbors: Dominica, St. Lucia, St. Vincent, and Grenada, the constituent parts of my study.[8] Neither was the smallholder life in Martinique similar to that among land reform workers/settlers in Jamaica, where I studied in the late 1970s, researching land reforms under Democratic Socialism. These working people, who were "working for capital," to use Michel-Rolph Trouillot's apt phrasing, occupied an entirely different position in the world,[9] not very well supplied or stocked, much of their own stock, like the Martiniquans, originating from elsewhere, and proferring a differently flavored dwelling/migratory movement.

The "creolization" process outlined and theorized in chapters 1 and 2 is thus best understood as an ongoing dynamic within complex open systems. What new and different conditions influence its contemporary practices of the inner and outer exercising of existence? Are the semiotics of "inequality and struggle" mobilized in the production of local cultures now? Specifically how and in what context is power being exercised; who is in and who is out, and how are imaginings of citizenship now being negotiated? How is agency, *or rather agential power,* being measured or "weighed up" and how is it being expressed, tempered, and structured? On the whole, how concretely does Caribbean creolization, as a process of selective creation and cultural struggle, find expression in this postcolonial, neoliberal economic era? These are considerations that are substantially engaged at the theoretical and methodological level in chapters 1, and 2, but such questions and concerns are also central to the subsequent essays' open-ended empirical inquiries. Chapter 1 addresses the generalizations that can be made about the creolization processes that take us beyond the plantation. Chapter 2 offers a methodology rooted in those observations about creolization's genesis and evolution that facilitates an understanding of the process implicated in the making of place, and in creating spaces for the expression of particular forms of agency, as open and dynamic. Creolization grasped as a dynamized process further facilitates an engagement with theories of social change, making for their linked but specific articulations.

In chapter 3, "Decentering the 'Dialectics of Resistance' in the Context of a Globalizing Modern: Afro-Creoles under Colonial Rule," framed by Lila Abu Lughod's insightful essay about resistance,[10] I assert that Afro-Creoles under primarily British colonialism, particularly its later interventions, interwove modern ideas about development, such as export agriculture, with notions of "respectability" within their specific Creole practices. These helped to reposition Afro-Creoles within local sociocultural and economic hierarchies and facilitated access to non-plantation-derived globalized sites of material and ideological production. In such a situation, particularisms and universalisms blend strategically and mutually, constituting uneven and manipulable textures to the fabric of modern Caribbean life. Aníbal Quijano's and Immanuel Wallerstein's concept of "flight to modernity" underscores the futuristic devices that inhere in the strategic Creole apparatuses of survival, or dwelling in the present, throughout the Americas.[11] It is understandable that the quest for a collective and an individual desire for *respectability* is ordered according to general sociocultural and economic tendencies obtaining within the world economy. Without this framework it would be difficult to comprehend the changing interpretations of a certain notion of respectability such as that which dominated up until the 1960s for a significant section of the population.

The current restructuring of the (more or less) moral economies of smallholders throughout the region further insinuates the global coordinates of a revitalized neoliberal world economy into the locales of the Caribbean.[12] The intertwinement of the economic and the cultural are manifest in Creole forms, not simply in a materialist way that privileges economic concerns but as intersecting, mutually constituting spheres composed through the double movement practices of governmentality, in much the same way as feminists argue that the so-called public sphere is constitutive of the private and vice versa.[13] Nowhere is this more striking than in the area of informal economic activity, where questioning Creole practices is remobilized for various purposes.[14] Informalization, a generic phenomenon of centers and margins of capital accumulation within the world economy, has become more intensified, especially in nonagricultural employment, although much of this informalization process can be tied to processes of "rural othering" describing a cultural politics embedded in the distancing of capitalist social relations from its feudal traditions.[15] The informal sector accounts for more than half of nonagricultural employment in Latin America and the Caribbean and as much as 80 percent in parts of Asia and Africa and is responsible for 83 percent of new jobs in those regions. It is estimated that economically active women compose the majority of informal sector workers. But women's participation in the informal sector is underrepresented statistically, because much of their work is home-based and not quantified.[16]

Caribbean women (like Filipinas and other third world women) seek work in many places, though the experience of patriarchy globally leads to a different framing or rationalizing of this need for employment. Operating under a Confucian patriarchy, Filipinas frame their "duties" in terms of patriotic and religious obligations, emphasizing their marital status as wives or as mothers. Women in the Caribbean, on the other hand, operating under a different patriarchal principle wherein the circumstances of indentureship and slavery have made the idea of the working woman an acceptable, necessary fact,[17] generally outperform men yet go under- or unrewarded. In the higher echelons of the governing and corporate world, no justification is needed, no heroizing of women, given the history of women working outside the household. Among third world women, patriarchy undergoes enormous transformation given the structural adjustments imposed by powerful organizations and states within the interstate system of the world economy, and it is a fact of life that both women and men must travel to work. Such a practice may even be considered a virtue,[18] even though such travel is facilitated directly or indirectly, by state policies.

On the recommendation of a U.S.–based Jamaican academic, Orlando Patterson,[19] then Jamaican prime minister P. J. Patterson announced his government's intention to solidify formal arrangements with the United States to import skilled Jamaicans.[20] Citing the cost of the uncontrolled exodus of Africans from the continent (roughly 20,000 professionals annually), costing African countries US$4 billion a year, he stated that his government was not restricting movement:

> People are free to come and go, but what we do intend is to provide a sufficiency of trained people that we have enough to satisfy our needs and when countries like America want some—because we are the best nurses and the best teachers—we can say to them we have a pool that is available. And we are inviting the United States to enter into a partnership with us in that regard and not wait until we have trained the people and pounce on them and leave us the poorer.[21]

Despite these imaginative movements of staying or dwelling in creolization processes, analysts intent on distinguishing Caribbean cultural processes insist that creolization studies must primarily involve attention to unequal power, considering that in many Caribbean states these miraculous cultural phenomena were spawned in enormously conflictive master-slave, black/white relationships. Nigel Bolland, for instance, argues:

> The Creole-society thesis needs a general theoretical framework, incorporating dialectical theory, for the analysis of social and cultural change. Roger Bastide, the French sociologist-ethnologist, articulated such a general framework within which he studied the African religions of Brazil. He stressed the connections between religious beliefs and activities and the conflicts in the wider society, in particular the relation between religious ideologies and practices, on the one hand, and the issues and relations of domination/subordination on the other. For Bastide, the process of cultural change is not to be understood as the clash of "cultures," but rather as the activities of individuals who are located in institutions and differentiated by power.[22]

The dialectical relationship is stressed as an analytical technique illuminating the contentious local elements pivotal to the production of Afro-American culture. However, the nature of the dialectical processes embedded in the experiences of creolization is complex, ambivalent, fractured, and open ended. Indeed as Steve Pile argues, "Resistance cannot be understood as a face-to-face opposition between the powerful and the weak, nor as a fight that takes place only on grounds constituted by structural relations—because other spaces are always involved: spaces that are dimly lit, opaque, deliberately hidden, saturated with memories, that echo with lost words and the cracked sounds of pleasure and enjoyment."[23]

Creolization processes cannot therefore be simply read through conflictual, economistic, binaristic, or deterministic scripts as I have endeavored to argue, but rather through the exercises of a cultural politics expressed in the conducts of modern governmentality, as discussed in chapters 1 and 2.

THE PROJECTS OF CREOLIZATION

Advanced as a way of getting beyond a static ethnographic description preoccupied with retentions and survivals a la Herskovits,[24] and intent on revealing the creative processes at work in the midst of "modernity's inaugural regime of violence," to use Herman Bennett's apt phrasing,[25] the projects of creolization embraced fundamentally the cultural practices of

Afro-Creoles in a specific location, primarily the plantation, leading analysts to privilege a certain idea of rural space as the quintessential site of original "culture-building."[26] This preoccupation deserves the criticisms that it spawned, no less the ideological exclusions that it propagated. A number of analysts have highlighted the notable silences that inhere in the practice of Creole identity in the Caribbean, the production and privileging of a certain Afro-Creole sensibility, and the marginalizing of others, notably, but not solely, Indo-Caribbeans.[27] The political project of nation building, and the rationalities of decolonization, which bestowed full citizenship on all, belied palpable exclusions. Generating a Creole identity was an ideological project for the imagining of a particular kind of community.[28] "This ideological project of nationalism has been "the bonding agent of Caribbean society."[29] These efforts to bind, control, define, and localize Creole cultures of the region, a project which is still actively under way in a number of territories, have been well documented.[30]

Consider the objective of Trinidad and Tobago's Best Village Competition: to create a national community, by giving a space and a say to "*the small man* of the country who has been for so long a citizen in name only, who was expected in the past to conform with decisions, and had no opportunity to take part in the formulation of decisions."[31] It was a PNM (People's National Movement) project to protect the national community against foreign influence through the projection of local "folk culture." As a government minister put it presciently nearly forty years ago,

> In an age when the wireless and more recently the television tend to dominate the leisure hours of the more sedentary among our citizens, there is the danger that our powers of self-expression in all things cultural may become inhibited. In addition, the constant struggle to maintain and improve our standards of material well-being may restrict or even obstruct our endeavours in matters of cultural significance.[32]

Susan Craig noted the heavy PNM mobilization in Trinidad and Tobago and the direction of the Best Village Competition in the 1970s when it flourished, and concludes:

> The most striking feature of the village councils throughout Trinidad and Tobago is their *composition*. In all but two of the districts observed, Belle Garden (Tobago) and Felicity (near Chaguanas) the core of the

village council activists were also active members of the PNM and over 35. Where the population was predominantly African, for example John John, women outnumbered men in the councils where it was almost homogeneously Indian (for example, Spring Village), women are seldom seen at such meetings. In areas of mixed racial composition, where Indians form the majority of the population, the village council members were usually Africans, with very few, if any, Indians (for example, Rio Claro, Balmain, Couve (when the village council existed), St. Margaret's Village/Claxton Bay).[33]

Accounting for the composition of the village councils, Craig avers:

Firstly some of the persons who formed the village councils in the late "forties" and early "fifties" have remained in them over the years, dominating such activity as is undertaken. These were, everywhere, the people who later joined the PNM, many of them becoming important party activists and country councillors. Men like Councillor Fuentes (Rio Claro), ex-Councillor Mylan Meschier (Mayaro), Luther Nelson (Fyzabad), Victor Barclay (Princes Town), Desmond Baxter (Balmain), spring readily to mind. Not only have the early village council members been prone to join the PNM, but also, as shown above, the PNM have been explicitly urged to join and influence the village councils.[34]

What Craig does here is to disclose the specific ways in which state elites mobilized notions of culture, misrecognizing or simply ignoring differences and contestation over the meaning of Creole citizenship. Revealed also is the hegemonic restructuring of popular notions of uniqueness, spooled around ideas about the national, the community, and self-development, then threaded through internalized notions of what it is to be Trinidadian and who is better placed to be an authentic one. Such control techniques are intrinsic to the ways in which communities are imagined. In order for them to perform a certain national labor, communities need the active collusion of the popular to see in and through a particular optic that has become the "commonsense" for most Caribbeans in much the same way that the ideology of racial democracy works for most Brazilians.[35] While the nationhood project oftentimes imparts a Fanonian psychological cultural boost to people said to be "without histories," as has been noted by several analysts, it also restricts and silences alternative imaginings, leading, perhaps, to the torrent of current perceptions that the seams of the project of nation building have come apart. Both for the Caribbean and elsewhere, criticism of the nation-state's objectives and styles has intensified across various sociocultural divides.

Framing and elaborating on aspects of these projects of nation building and indeed nation undoing, chapter 4, "Power and Its Subjects in Postcolonial Performance," examines how young, urban, middle-class youth yank at the already fragmented state-managed Creole project, utilizing its techniques and assumptions, grafting on-to them parodic devices developed in other parts of the Americas to critique culture, economy, elite knowledge, and politics and to unsilence some of its elitist assumptions. These performances typify the complex nature of postcolonial Creole imaginations. Through popular cultural forms, performers ambivalently question the projects of the postdevelopmental state. The chapter recomposes the issue of creolization within the context of the demise of the "embodied histories"[36] of state developmentalism, highlighting the changing nature of state power and the sociocultural opportunities available on a global level to resuscitate and reevaluate the nation in conjunction with its material and ideological offerings. In places where the idea of the state is experienced through the disproportionate power over employment and general opportunity, and where the vote to install one's party can mean the difference between starvation or plenitude, the ideological battleground becomes a style of electoral politics performed against the backdrop of the nation's dire economic and cultural "backwardness" and its needs for progress.

It is unclear whether these performances and performers discussed in this chapter constitute cultural "antagonizers," to use Chantal Mouffe's phrase, whether they want to demolish the Creole nation-state or whether they want to reform it. What they seem to seek is a different dispensation by and within it. They demand a more democratic celebration and practice of citizenship, taking into account the undesirable conditions usually silenced. What does it mean when these performers acknowledge that "not everyone is on the same page"? Certainly the performance of this "new" (to St. Lucia) culture of protest by these young urban middle-class youth is opposed by those who argue that such performances show the nation in a bad light and are "disrespectful of the national character." But these "irreverent" performances are not about generating a specific group identity, but rather, like the Creole state managers themselves, are concerned with the national identity which they depict as in collective crisis.

Two defining features of these contemporary cultural political forms above are the rejection of political party involvement and the attempt to broaden the democratic basis of political and cultural practice on the island. To examine these features forces one to assess one of the essential markers for creolization processes identified by analysts as a culture created in the context of oppression. In particular, although the colonial project was fragmented, in the sense that its mission of "native" submission was inconsistent and applied differently from one colony to another and within each colony itself,[37] a clear distinction needs to be drawn between the oppressiveness of power (a defining feature of colonialism) obtaining during slavery and colonialism and the postcolonial exercise of power. Which is to say, state power in the postcolonial period was and still is organized differently but also lived and performed differently. In the wake of Foucault's writings one may argue that the decolonization project promoted a reconfigured Creole cultural optic of governmentality and its promises of individual well-being and progress, signaling a very different kind of engagement than that with colonialism, welfarism notwithstanding.[38] Despite the existence of alternative visions of society, as palpably played out by Rastafarians and some pan-Africanists, Caribbeans generally looked to the state to offer and to receive guidance on how to be "good" nationals and, indeed, state-elites obliged.

In the early postcolonial era , however, failure to fulfill those promises by nationalist leaders within the institutions of governance was at once the source and outcome of the unraveling and rerouting of some foundational elements of the Creole project of decolonization.[39] It is not surprising then that this project spurred the rise of new Creole performances that selectively inscribed global forms of protest and satire, with attentiveness to local seasonings of discontent.

In chapter 5, " 'Gens Anglaises': Diasporic Movements Remixing the World with Post-Creole Imaginations," studies of transnationalism, diasporas, and deterritorialization provide the context for discussing the routes of rural Creole St. Lucians who migrated to England and then returned to St. Lucia. Such migration operates as a critical process that further disembeds ideas about the sociocultural separation of locality and globality and rearranges individual relationships to the state and national community and vice versa. The re-establishment of a locality leads to a tense renegotiation with the nation and state that ultimately involves a rerooting of the transnational in a significantly transformed historical moment. The chapter underscores the particular ways in which rural migrants re-search, redefine, and re-member the nation-state, and their places within it. Moreover, the chapter opens up an inquiry into the texture of the constitutive relationship between nationalisms and transnationalisms and their potential as processes that reconstitute and re-present the local within the global.

Chapter 6, "An eBay Imaginary in an Unequal World: Creolization on the Move,"[40] recomposes the argument for a historicized and relational approach to creolization that goes through and beyond the plantation in much the same way that Creole subjects have. Creolization within and across plantation societies occurred variously, as Michel-Rolph Trouillot pointed out. People supposedly tucked within its embrace lived multifaceted lives, engaging multiple temporalities and positions in the world economy, differentially participating in diaspora communities, and straddling places transnationally in *une poétique de Relation*. Membership in these communities has been contoured along a model of the local, unable to escape the exclusionary strategies employed by the state to differentiate between the national and the non-national, the *us* versus the *them*. But because agencies almost by definition exceed that which structures them, identities lived within codes are always strategic.

Can the idea of Creole cultures still hold in an era when there are no plantations, of the type that was central to the birthing of the Atlantic world economy and its differential systems of economic and cultural productions? Are we to commit the same error as New World theorists, who in post-plantation eras resorted to conceptualizing multinational corporations (MNCs) as new types of plantation, thereby obscuring the newness in the economy of the changing social relations and the changing directions of subjectivities?[41] Such an intellectual strategy is questionable. As noted, the technologies of the global and Creole culture continue to evolve outside of the structures and strictures of the plantation in a process of becoming like that of identity formation, as Stuart Hall would say.[42] Even as one recounts the horror stories of Haitians, particularly cane workers in the Dominican Republic, can one say that they function within reconstituted plantation complexes, knowing that those earlier plantations had a specific transnational, mercantile, connection that is absent today? Knowing that the sugar regimes of the past no longer exist? Likewise, are Haitians in the Dominican Republic "slaves," as were their foreparents?

No. To extrapolate from an earlier global condition, one which tied citizen and place to the global in more forceful and dominating ways, is to refuse to examine the historical situatedness, rationalities, and realities of the Dominican state and to deny the way in which the present moment is implicated in creating new elements that may seem dated. It would be a misrecognition of the complex particularities of racial imagining within Dominican history, particularities that set its history apart from other Caribbean places.

Achille Mbembe construes contemporary African realities as happening in a "time of entanglement,"[43] in time that is not a chronological continuity but a "range of disjointed moments, practices, and symbols that thread the historical relations between events and narrative."[44] This could likewise be said of contemporary Creole conditioning in the Caribbean. Indeed, the performance of various, often disparate forms of national identities along with the production of new sites on which such identities are transformed and reformed is a common occurrence in many Caribbean places, lending those places the tenor of an eBay site on which every ideology and expedient is up for auction and may be "bought" to suit the moment: government, antigovernment, church, antichurch, antidevelopment, proconsumerism, violence, cell phones, Japanese used cars, and so on.

Consider that the violence unleashed against Catholics attending high mass in St. Lucia was wrought by a duo of young unemployed men claiming to be Rastafarians, who smiled and joked all the way to their death sentencing.[45] Consider Obika Gray's account of a Jamaican political party gunman who remained an adherent of Pocomania, an Afro-Creole religion, even as he became chief underground executioner.[46] These cases suggest the manipulability of Creole identities in the face of state and party projects, but they hearken back to an older but certainly not archaic form of modernity when the future was shaped by supernatural beings: "boloms," "gens gajés," "devils," and Greek gods, an assortment of occult and bona fide African elements.[47] Of course, it was "Jah's" wish that the St. Lucian duo take matters into their own hands on that symbolic New Year's Day and destroy the evil Catholic Church by burning and slashing clergy and laity alike who were attending mass at the Castries Cathedral.[48] But their lamentations and rage against the state and politicians, against what they saw as political treachery and injustice, black victimhood, African redemption, has an uncanny modern ring.[49] Newspapers are rife with accounts of how Brazilians, black and nonblack, balance high-tech jobs with Candomblé religious obligations, appealing for Afro-godly intercession in the workplaces. These tendencies represent morphed moments in the creolization process in post-plantation spaces.[50] They constitute diverging memories of a plantation "past" reinterpreted, or re-presented, given the contextual needs and desires of the present, producing different relationships with power than that exercised through the gross dehumanization of human bodies, gods, and beings. This is a roundabout way of expressing the sentiment behind Trouillot's point that the past has meaning only in relation to the present.[51] Or, as Stephan Palmié might say, in relation to the way in which Afro religions are practiced, these imaginings constitute a different kind of historical interpretation, where the ghosts of a past actively intercede in present historical moments in a way that blurs the past and the present, the "modern" and the "traditional."[52]

The question is this: why in these contemporary global times, should particular Creole practices and expressions persist?[53] Is it still useful to imagine that creolization is a plantation-centered or Caribbean thing? In a post-plantation context, what happens to creolization processes? How Creole are rural Caribbeans for whom country and western music has become the staple of their localness? How might we conceptualize this absorption of "outer" forms expressing local desires and needs? How is power to be understood within that context? Is this not creolization redux (to be) continued under different circumstances?

In the epilogue, "Rethinking Creolization through Multiple *Présences*: Masks, Masquerades, and the Making of Modern Subjects," the problematic of local versus global identities and the formation of subjectivities in the context of creolization's universal deployment is highlighted. This epilogue reemphasizes arguments in favor of decentering creolization's specifically Caribbean and plantation focus but critiques creolization's deployment in contexts where power is erased. In particular, animated by Caryl Phillips's *The Atlantic Sound* and Paul Gilroy's *The Black Atlantic: Modernity and Double Consciousness*,[54] one sees a complex process of masking-masquerading involved in the "city-citizen" game, where exercises of power as "inseparable autonomies" between power and the subject are standard tropes of imagination of individuality, citizenship, sovereignty, place, and name.

Both Gilroy and Phillips provide useful entry points into these issues as they offer ideas about transnationalized community and identity. Phillips stresses the steadfastness of contemporary cultural parochialisms, which displace a political consciousness of blackness among Atlantic peoples, but in his capacity as a traveler, tourist, ship's passenger, visiting Atlantic ports implicated in eighteenth- and nineteenth-century mercantilism and colonially driven forms of globality. Gilroy stresses shared community and uses the ship as a metaphor to emphasize the routes in the roots of black identity and its politics of making place. In Phillips's *Atlantic Sound*, belonging is localized in Liverpool in a fashion that revises, or rather erases, particular aspects of its Atlantic connectedness. A place-based racism is bracketed from its black Atlantic connection despite the diasporic displacement that links people, blacks and others, along the contours of particular forms of modern social power, underscored by slave/plantation histories. In engaging with these discourses, the chapter (and the book generally) privileges a more complex view of creolization and the cultural practices that attend pluralistic Atlantic habituses, and it demonstrates how collective national histories are lived personally, as well as how transnational experiences critically reshape national lives, individual sensibilities, and collective spaces.[55] It problematizes the making of place(s) and calls for a perspective that embraces a larger global space for understanding Caribbean Creole consciousness, well beyond the black Atlantic, while being nonetheless mindful of the possible time-space and habitus limits to the chains of modern freedoms.

ONE

LOCATING THE GLOBAL
IN *CREOLIZATION*
Ships Sailing through Modern Space

From childhood, therefore, Creoleness made me aware of the complex labyrinth of the
family of human kind into which I was born in the twentieth century.[1]

The formation of the Atlantic as a zone of the world economy is not a question of
geographical determinism. Indeed, even to think of the adaptation of the social and
economic arrangements of the world economy to the physical and cultural environments of the Atlantic risks obscuring the complex historical processes through which
specific aspects of those environments and not others were selected and developed.[2]

A fragile reality (the experience of Caribbeanness, woven together from one side of the
Caribbean to the other) negatively twisted together in its urgency (Caribbeanness as a
dream, forever denied, often deferred, yet a strange stubborn presence in our responses). This reality is there in essence: dense (inscribed in fact) but threatened (not
inscribed in consciousness). This dream is vital, but not obvious.[3]

CREOLIZATION, SO APTLY described by Balutansky and
Sourieau as "that syncretic process of transverse dynamics
that endlessly reworks and transforms the cultural patterns
of varied social and historical experiences and identities,"[4]
has figured significantly in the Caribbean's complex histories of globalization, nationalization and regionalization.[5] It
has done so not only as process but, perhaps more importantly, as a problematic and politics that arguably has been
implicated in shaping pasts, presents, and possible futures.[6]
Indeed, as several scholars have highlighted, practices for
conceptualizing and strategizing development or spaces of
hope in the region have tended to deploy various models of

what may be called "Creole-isms" for articulating a cultural politics of Creole nationalistic and/or regionalistic, modernization projects.[7]

As Hintzen has recently argued, the Creole ideas of interdependency and literal mixture have been deployed in the forging of Caribbean spaces to support specific erasures of cleavages or a papering over plural-cultural, racial, and ethnic cracks for effecting the unstable paradox of "plural wholes" as represented by modern yet Creole nation-states.[8] Lloyd Best takes this critical stance further in his argument that these tactics of cultural adaptation or strategies of creolization that have been creatively expressed by diasporic populations to negotiate the structural effects of a hegemonic plantation cultural politics have nonetheless left the region in an unviable state.[9] Given these experiences in the region, for Best the essential problem of development was therefore not one of a cultural transition to the "modern" (albeit nuanced by Creole cultures, as emphasized by Arthur Lewis in the *Theory of Economic Growth*);[10] it was rather the radically deconstructive one of cultural transformation for "fleeing the plantation" and its racialized cultural and ethnic heritages of e/race/ing place, that is, the elision and (partial) loss of particularity and of presences.

However, while an understanding of the different kinds of cultural politics at work in the search for "catching up," "sustainable development," or "forging ahead" in the modern world system is important, the fundamental task of providing a more adequate theoretical and methodological framework for grasping the nature of the sociocultural change processes at work in modern times is still left as unfinished business.[11] In taking up this challenge we wish to shift the terms of thinking about modernity by arguing that the condition of "being-modern-in-the-world" is best grasped not through ideas of time per se but rather through expressions of place and, relatedly, space.[12] For though creolization studies have tended to focus on sociocultural practices—the outcome of distinct power relations—they have done so without a sufficient exploration of the connections linking the circuits of place, space, and "chains of power," which are conducting, producing, and disrupting such outcomes. Absent therefore from these accounts is a sufficient interrogation of the nature of the relationship between states and societies, or rather, between state spaces and subject places in the modern, and especially post-plantation era. This, we argue, would provide a window through which we can espy more fully practices invested with post-Creole imaginations and the cultural and ethnic or racialized struggles associated with creolization in the context of modern spaces, the apparent site of globalization processes. The post-Creole imagination as evoked in and routed through these processes is a central character in our stories of creolization here and speaks to stirred desires for making newness, that is, hopes for arriving in another future not present, and achieving a different space and place. It may be related to Derrida's idea that a structure of practical activity entails a *messianicity,* elucidated by Hoy as a concept that "drops the teleological story of progress, but retains the eschatological aspect whereby a *breakthrough* event can erupt at any moment" (our emphasis).[13]

Creolization/creolization studies (henceforth *creolization*) as elaborated in this text are thus also centrally concerned with sociocultural practices, including subject productions. But we address them through a method that, first, seeks to link these practices with their *emergent conditions of existence,*[14] or liminal *wombs of present space,*[15] and second, offers to treat the two as relationally constituted and transformed largely, but not exclusively, through modern conducts of power, namely, modern governmentality. It is our central argument therefore that an elision of one dimension or the other does untold damage to historical analysis and is least insightful in apprehending those cultural practices which one seeks to understand.

Our provocative rewriting or highlighting of the term is thus meant at the outset to disturb settled meanings and to allude to different kinds of "doubling" and "folding" processes that enter into the (un)making of Creole subjects, and into their worlds. In particular, doubling processes refer to modes of (un)making of identities or cultural forms of life. This is, of course, a central theme of poststructuralist perspectives that emphasize the double play associated with the articulation of Grand Narratives, as seen especially in Creole subjects' rootedness in masking projects of identity that are, however, routed through masquerades or limboing strategies of *différance,* complex countering conducts of life which, as Derrida emphasizes, produce the "movement in signification" and relatedly the "scenes of presence."[16] *Différance,* as doubling processes, is thus about the unsettling of, as Sylvia Wynter says, "the Coloniality of Being/Power/Truth/Freedom"[17] through (as Derrida emphasizes, and as we will later elaborate) the temporal and spatial processes of becoming something else. An understanding of doubling processes will, however, be inadequate without a related attention to the ontological dimensions shaping the character of these doubling processes; in brief, the dimensions of folding.

Deleuze used the idea of "the fold" and folding to stress the multiply seamed ontology of human being, the convoluted ontological conditions of existence, or complex wombs of "folding" space that enfold and pull differences together.[18] This supports a view of "the human subject as the outside folded in: an immanently political [and] social embedded subject."[19] We will draw upon this ontological premise but offer our own reading of the concrete nature of these complex wombs of space, as it relates to the *enfolding and dynamic folding* experiences of our Creole subjects. In treating *creolization* processes, then, our emphasis lies in *seeing* Creole subjects as "being" not only articulated through shadowy, masked, or ghostly identity relations but also in recognizing them as being located in, and moving through, ontologies of lived space. Accordingly, and in kindred spirit with Munasinghe's recent efforts to assess the explanatory potential of the concept of creolization,[20] we wish to also persist in examining something opaquely referred to as *creolization,* despite the hard-hitting critique by Stephan Palmié of the concept's historical contamination by the promiscuous flow of ideas across disciplinary boundaries.[21]

It is a banal observation, of course, that Caribbean or Atlantic creolization practices emerge in the context of power impositions of the colonial and later the national and developmentalist state, now the instrument of a neoliberal globalization project. However, in all these complexly translated phases of power, we argue that Caribbean sociocultural productions which *present* themselves through cultural and biopolitical strategies and seek to create difference *or* newness (that is, transformed or transmuted spaces *within* the context of the various contours of social power) are pivotally about assertions of self, affirmations,[22] or rather, *a will to place,* inducing a journeying from place to place. Place here is first to be read (in part) through Heidegger, who argued that place must be understood in an ontological sense. To do this Heidegger drew on the Aristotelian idea that place has a δύναμις (*dunamis,* an energy and potency) and is thus related to presence. For Heidegger, then, the standard translation of this Greek term as power or force was insufficient; rather, as he stated, to say of place that it has a δύναμις

> implies that the place [*Platz*] pertains to being itself, the place constitutes precisely the possibility of the proper presence [*eigentlichen Anwesendseins*] of the being in question . . . *Each being possesses in its being a*

prescription toward a determinate location or place [our emphasis]. The place is constitutive of the presence of the being [*Jedes Seiende hat in seinem die Vorzeichnung auf einen bestimmten Platz, Ort. Der Ort ist konstitutiv für die Anwesenheit des Seienden*] . . . The place is the ability a being has to be there.[23]

Thus, as Stuart Elden elaborates, "place is something belonging to beings as such, it is *their capacity to be present,* it is constitutive of their being" (our emphasis).[24] However, in our reading of "the will to place," as implied by the quote above, one ought to eschew any deterministic renderings of Heidegger's deployment of "prescription." This is necessary in order to better grasp the processes for "proper presence," as agitated by the will to place; processes such as the productions of space; translations of place; uprootings and re-homings of place; the movements from place to place; and its imbrications with the manipulations of the right and aesthetic of belonging as de facto or de jure "citizen" qua S/s/objects (henceforth subjects),[25] in certain places, times, and spaces.

Creolization processes, from this perspective of the will to place, are thus entangled with emancipatory projects tethered to geographies of making places, as well as ontologies of making place, processes which involve the imagining, making, transforming, transmuting, or transfiguring of subjects. Moreover, these practices of freedom are not just part of the undulating making/unmaking of complex subjectivities—as predicated upon post-Creole imaginations for making place in and through present time-spaces—but are also essentially linked to what may be referred to as the homing of modern freedoms for "proper presence," as we will elaborate, throughout the text, but especially in chapters 2, 3, and 5.

The making of place, interpreted here as the making of both place and places/spaces, as well as, the movements of self qua subject, involves pastiche tactics and strategies of bricolage;[26] the deployment of elements of the ready-made, drawing from and bridging the various fragmented histories and seas of larger contexts in which people have been placed.[27] This view seems to be also entailed in Marx's oft-quoted observation, "Men make their own history, but they do not make it as they please; they do not make it under self-selected circumstances, but under circumstances existing already, given and transmitted from the past."[28] If, that is, one seeks to read through these words an intimation of the coexistence of plural, as well as disjunctive and conjunctive, temporalities and the limitations implicit in the pursuit of the authentic or original in the context of modern social power, which, however, we highlight as modern governmentality—the conduct of conduct.

This chapter's focus is thus on the nature of Caribbean *creolization* in the context of modern spaces, and on its foldings of "the present"—the apparent time of globalization. In particular, in this project we try to provide a way of grappling with this difficult task of theorizing processes of cultural change and social history in a way that makes a critical intervention for the project of a "spatial history," which, as Elden argues, implies a need to "historicize space and spatialize history."[29] We hope to provide a reading of creolization that also appreciates yet complicates the interdependencies, the mixtures, and the cultural politics that are all part of the idea and experience of *creolization*. Through this chapter, then, and also as illustrated in the readings of performative histories in the text, we offer a perspective on creolization that seeks to "flee the plantation" while bringing on board a deeper understanding of the nature of the cultural and racialized politics and processes in which the region is not only embedded but contributes to. Certainly we believe that such an analytical framework is indispensable to any effective analysis of the politics of making newness and empowering social change in today's world.

CREOLIZATION AS SUBJECT AND PROBLEMATIC

Given the conflicting senses in which creolization has been seen to act in the shaping of Caribbean futures within what has been referred to as a world system, two focal questions have animated our empirical, analytical, and methodological foray into this subject. First, how are modern spaces and their foldings of the present—the apparent time and site of globalization processes—being constituted, located, and configured, and by what processes are they being reconstituted, relocated, and reconfigured? Second, with what effect for those who inhabit them? That is, how are the subjects of *creolization* processes experiencing and responding to the challenges and opportunities of making themselves and their worlds, or hi/stories (human-identity stories)?[30] These are some of the broader questions through which the globalization project and *creolization* processes can be explored. These questions are not only vital for grasping the new developments and disjunctures that underpin the modern globalization project but are also crucial for grasping the nature, texture, and effects of *creolization* in the present time, the epoch of globalization. Such a project is in turn underpinned by a concern to understand the nature and basis of strategies for negotiating and navigating the modern world, and one's place in and through it, by way of making place, in and through, the modern spaces of the present.

MAKING MODERN SUBJECTS:
THE PROJECT OF SPATIAL HI/STORIES, SHIPS
SAILING THROUGH MODERN SPACE

In engaging in this project of theorizing creolization as subject and problematic, our efforts are underpinned by Michel-Rolph Trouillot's very timely and important appeal to social scientists to treat "the miracle of creolization," which slaves in particular expressed in the ingenuity of survival, as a historicized process of "*selective creation and cultural struggle*."[31] This is interpreted here as a politics of making place, space, and relatedly presence, or at least "traces" of it. Thus, we offer to treat *creolization* as a *creative cultural evolutionary process* expressing modern projects of the selective making of modern subjects—and their correlated subjectivities or subject powers, as well as place and places/spaces—and not as a one-time event. We are seeking, however, to go beyond the plantation in demonstrating *creolization*'s present situation and global appeal, and to indeed argue for a "creolization-in-the-world,"[32] phenomenon that is engaging and perhaps moving the "history of the present" in its politics of making new worlds.[33]

This genealogical space of a "history of the present,"[34] brings attention to the social and political processes of "writing" on a "field of entangled and confused parchments, on documents that have been scratched over and recopied many times."[35] In the context of social histories, these texts are the cultural bodies or subjects, inscribed in social space, that become marked by the etchings of hegemonic and countering histories in the making and unmaking of modern subjects in the spaces of the present. The colonial (and postcolonial) body presents a particularly bloody example of those processes of etching in the entangled writing of "the history of the present," but as postcolonial studies have highlighted, such sites also record practices of both "mimesis and alterity" or a "liminal dialectics" of leaving and staying.[36] This is expressed, for example, in the politics of fracturing the "imagined communities" of the nation, by realizing that "to blaspheme is to dream"[37] or by "suffering for territory,"[38] in home staking presents, in the liminal spaces of "the modern," between here and there. Of course, we too will be seeking to disturb the lines of disjunctive thought in our discussions of emergent modern spaces, and their foldings, ranging from Afro-Creoles under colonial rule, to diasporic populations and post-Creole imaginaries surfing the virtual realities of the present.

Our sense of creolization-in-the-world, we believe, thus escapes simplistic readings of creolization as mere global melting pots of cultural hybridity and points toward its interpretation through a politics of "mapping the present," to adopt Elden's apt phrase. As Elden elaborates, a politics of mapping the present entails that

> Time, far from being calculated on a clock, is the moment future and past collide in the present, as the temporality of the moment. Second, the human in the point of this collision *is* its collision, as *Da-sein*, being-that-there, being the moment, *being as presence* [our emphasis]. The human in, *as*, the point of collision is simultaneously future and past in the present. But they are not solely temporal, *they are situated* [our emphasis]. Likewise, history too must orientate itself toward the future with reference to the past, by becoming . . . *a history of the present*. This history, of the present as presence, is also situated. This is what will be meant by the *mapping* of the present.[39]

This perspective, we believe, calls for a serious treatment of the role that persons qua subjects—that is, cultural bodies—play in historicizing space and thereby temporalizing time, *through and in*, space. Elden's concept of "mapping the present" also intimates the need for a model of process that can grapple with these situated dynamics in the making or morphing of history, which we argue a fuller specification of creolization processes can offer.[40] In making this vital step to generalize and dynamize creolization— the genealogical process of selective creation and cultural struggle—beyond the plantation, the pertinent questions that engage us here are as follows. What are the forces involved in the space and place making processes of "subjectifications"—subject makings and unmakings, enacted in the entangled mappings of the modern space of the present?[41] What exactly is changing through this entangled and historicized process-in-space; the genealogical space of a "history of the present"? And finally, as Bhabha has inquired, *how* is newness entering the world?[42] That is, how are subjects entering and moving its mappings in the modern spaces of the present—the apparent site, time, and epoch of globalization processes?

Whilst seeking to go beyond the plantation in showing *creolization*'s present situation and global appeal, given its apparent powers for transmuting the subject, our efforts are also sensitive to the spirit of Trouillot's concerns about the sorts of simple generalizations which have attended discussions of *creolization*. Any advance in the study of creolization will thus require inquiry into the *historical, spatial, and ethnographic contexts* anchoring these processes of "selective creation and cultural struggle," and an investigation of the complex interdependencies shaping them. Our argument therefore rests on the idea that one needs to complicate the processes involved in the formation of the Caribbean region within the Atlantic economy through analyses which emphasize *the relational spaces* of the strategic power relationships embedded in the making of places, as Tomich's epigraph above suggests.[43] For what Tomich ultimately argues for is a method grounded in a "spatial history," which interrogates how places like the Caribbean were being complexly constituted, indeed as part of a process of mutual constitution and entangled histories, to the extent that they were linked to seas and ports and other places via plantations, their labor, their bodies, especially the slaves', and their products, all of which were part and parcel of the making and unmaking of the Atlantic space. These complex historical realizations therefore involve paying close attention to the multiple streams of spatial influences that have disturbingly fed Caribbean people's "living memories"[44] and post-Creole imaginations as they negotiated and contested the spaces of modern power and its configurations and calibrations of their "degrees of freedoms" *and* their places.[45]

Such multiple streams in processes of creative adaptation and cultural struggle are caught up in but go well beyond the fixed diasporic routes that encounter the black Atlantic or some such similarly derived ethnic identities. And they more generally depend on particular historical, spatial, and ethnographic contexts and their endowments of necessities and contingencies, resources and constraints, conjunctures and disjunctures that shape and enable different transactional modes of "subject-being-in-the-world" at different places and moments in time. These emphases on the entanglements of, and multiplicity in, emergent historical processes, which creolization discourses have sought to interpret and unravel, have led us to argue, like Tomich, for a method of analysis that "presents a unified, multidimensional and relational approach" to the spatial history of creolization by exploring more deeply the relational spaces of the strategic power relationships embedded in the making of places and giving rise to the experiences of creolization as the *selective creation and cultural struggles for space and place.*[46]

However, while granting a need for systemic articulations of processes, as Trouillot and others have argued, one should strive to avoid reproducing Creole linguists and sociocultural theorists' inattention to the particularities of histories, which has resulted in the analysis of *creolization* experiences as a static totality. In contrast, we argue for a complexly historicized and open system of relationships and relations and suggest treating *creolization* as the morphogenetics of cultures of power; a process of selective creation and cultural struggle that expresses circuits of places in search of obscure futures and freedoms, as well as post-Creole "home spaces." We believe that Margaret Archer's term "morphogenetics," as deployed here, is useful to allude to two features in the dynamic of sociocultural systems.[47] First, that "culture systems,"[48] or cultures of power, as social power have no preset form or inherent natural state of equilibrium—the *morpho* element of the term—and also that changes are like a morphing, a transformation of one image, *or form,* into another. Second, that "culture systems" as social power take their shape from and are formed by persons qua subjects and thus originate from their activities, relationships, and all the intended and unintended consequences flowing from these; this is the second part of the term, the *genetics.* The whole term together implies a focus on the processes of change and transformation of cultures of social power, or state spaces and subject places in social life worlds, and, perhaps, societies.

In brief, then, the nature of modern *creolization* processes, *the politics of making place,* will be expressions of historically contingent, strategic, complexly entangled and situated politics of "selective creation and cultural struggle" to define or express places, and relatedly presence; to represent and reproduce spaces and its foldings of the present; as well as to engender newness (that is, post-Creole spaces) in the world. These thixotropic *creolization* processes have been largely articulated and translated through processes of modern governmentality: the conduct of conduct, emergent from liminal wombs of present space. It is thus from the open-ended exercise of situated and entangled modes of modern governmentality by Creole subjects that place, space, times, and newness are continually worked out, that is, as transformations of modern governable spaces and of the mappings of the present.[49] This recognition of a pregnancy of variety, multiple and counterfactual other presents, in the entangled present moment and spatial hi/stories of *creolization* is thus in keeping with Trouillot's legitimate concerns for historical sensitivity in creolization studies.

In logically developing and elaborating upon these perspectives on *creolization*'s selective creation and cultural struggles, we present our arguments in three steps: "creolization" historicized, "creolization" generalized, and "creolization" dynamized. In taking these three steps we hope to clarify the points in our argument by a critical navigation of literatures on creolization and hence through a critical engagement with certain theoretical and methodological approaches or paradigms. We will present the first two steps in this chapter and the final step in chapter 2, which outlines an extended sketch of our method for situating creolization as part of a project for spatial hi/stories.

CREOLIZATION HISTORICIZED

Trouillot calls for studies that transcend simplistic and naturalized invocations of history, and for history to be interwoven into the analysis of creolization, as it affected various territories and plantations. He proposes four contexts which may illuminate the strategy, style, and substance of creolization processes. He states, "Using time, space and power relations as my main markers, I suggest four such contexts for the study of creolization: 1) a frontier context; 2) a plantation context; 3) an enclave context; 4) and a modernist context."[50] Trouillot defines as frontier context a pre-plantation situation characterized by significant contact between Europeans and African slaves. The duration of such contact may have affected the emergence of Creole languages. In the plantation context, the plantation is the primary determiner of life "during and immediately after the centuries of legal enslavement."[51] The enclave context refers to the relative isolation provided, for instance, in Maroon communities. The modernist context refers to processes of creolization following the decline of the plantation, slavery, and colonialism, which involved, according to Trouillot, "a different kind of technical and institutional support to creolization." As he puts it, it implies also a sense of global history and the awareness of progress—or backwardness—which are part of modernity and which spread quite unevenly among Caribbean populations from early conquest until the second third of the twentieth century. The degree to which the awareness of both "target cultures" and facts of power become explicit and voiced, and the degree to which organic intellectuals harness institutional and technical support for cultural practices, help to define a modernist context.[52]

Trouillot cautions against overemphasizing the plantation, preferring instead to treat the plantation as a conceptual handle for a type, an ideal, nowhere, ever extant. Rather:

> Thousands of plantations that tried to conform to the ideal type, but always within the limitations imposed by specific circumstances. [It] implies that in every instance, there were limitations to economic efficiency, to the organization of settlement, to planters' political power, to the cultural apartheid premised in the organization of labor. The very actualization of the institution, whether or not premised on the planter's pursuit of the ideal type, allowed the slaves much more room to maneuver than implied by the type itself.[53]

To consider the plantation as a single, uniform entity, with one type of labor regime defining master-slave relations, becomes even more problematic when one considers that the main crop of plantations varied. There were plantations producing indigo in Saint Domingue, timber in Belize, cotton along with woodcutting in the Bahamas, and slaves servicing animal pens in Jamaica. Moreover, slaves not only worked on plantations but they also worked as domestic workers in places like Puerto Rico.[54] Felix V. Matos Rodríguez confirms that in the city of San Juan in 1872, slaves were mostly women between the ages of ten and forty.[55] Anne Pérotin-Dumon's work in Guadeloupe shows a far more dynamic population living in the cities and goes a long way in adding complexity and texture to our understanding of creolization.[56] She demonstrates the gendered effects of economic manumission on women and military manumission on men, resulting in the sociocultural differentiation of the population of Basse-Terre and Pointe-à-Pitre. The sole creators of the family, like the Indian mothers of "Zambos" in sixteenth-century New Spain, founding mothers, transmitted French cultural values to their families.[57] They were joined by escaped slaves seeking to belong to the stratum of free coloreds. When one takes into account such research it quickly becomes clear that the processes of creolization were various, restricted by neither crop, nor occupation, nor even space.

Even before African slaves set foot on plantations, African continental developments shaped their emergent processes of *creolization,* that is to say, adaptation and creative cultural exchanges were also ongoing from the barracks to the transport ships to the slaves' final destination. John Thornton, in disputing the randomization arguments popularized by Sidney Mintz and Richard Price,[58] argued that "slave ships drew their entire cargo from only one or perhaps two ports in Africa and unloaded them in large lots of as many as 200–1,000 in their new Atlantic homes,"[59] concluding that "the slave trade itself did little to break up cultural groupings."[60] In all likelihood, however, slave sales separated slaves from common areas. Even so, a number of planters actually built self-sustaining communities composed of slaves from common areas.[61] Expectations of what to expect in the New World may also have played a role in how the enslaved positioned themselves within plantation societies, thus influencing the texture of creolization, leading Paul Lovejoy and David Trotman to conclude that "Creole society is not created from the adaptation of a generalized African background but from the specificity of the expectations and actions of identifiable individuals and communities."[62]

In tracing the experiences of creolization historicized, Trouillot also calls for one to recognize, articulate, and unsilence the (in)differences of global history that have bound Creoles, creating the conditions for linked differences within and among complex creolization processes. The focus on locales therefore ought to be considered within the supraregister of global history's connectedness and its effects upon the production of (in)differences, and related in/formalizations.[63] Attention to these world systemic, structural dynamics of deepening and complex interdependency is vital for understanding the time-space-power dimensions of emergent modernist and contemporary neoliberal globalization, as well as the modernist Creole transformations of Atlantic social and historical space and beyond.

Creolization historicized has thus to take into account the particular challenges to forms of older creolization processes in the light of the global modern contexts. The current neoliberal phase of globalization presents neither an entirely internal nor external force but rather re-presents the latest entangled context, in which creolization undergoes challenges of a different sort as particular interpretations and symbolic forms are contested and undermined, displaced or reformed through negotiations with those considered legitimate bearers of Creole traditions. Accordingly, Caribbean creolization, in its origins and evolution, has always been shaped by global processes of transnationalism, nationalism, and citizenship, "selective processes" which it also influenced. The study of creolization can thus continue to make important contributions to debates about "the global" and "local," as well as "the informal," given that it embodies the temporalities of the national, transnational, and transcultural, though in the modern period defined and tied to the rituals of state and global governance, nationalism, and people's responses to such since at least the colonial period.

In brief, Caribbean creolization's local manifestations relate to, or are articulated with, other Creole manifestations elsewhere so that "its" Creole practices are constantly refreshed and transformed by various cultural transactions produced under varying conditions within the wider world. This book's chapters, however, move beyond the issues of origin of African American culture writ large, which more often than not obscure productive insights into the contemporary substantive and contextual transformations within which processes of creolization are created and altered within the current palate of social choices.

CREOLIZATION GENERALIZED:
BEYOND THE PLANTATION ENCLAVE
OF CREOLIZATION STUDIES

This section is animated by the current attempt to universalize the concept of creolization, extending its application well beyond Caribbean and former plantation societies, and the responses to that attempt. We argue that *creolization* can indeed be read into the world, but its imbrication should be treated as "stitches on time," to borrow a valuable phrase from Dube,[64] intricated through global—that is, here and elsewhere—spaces. This marks what we have called a "creolization-in-the-world" process, which is entangled in the "mapping of the present" and has been articulated within diasporic traditions but has gone beyond them as well. "The unity is submarine,"[65] indeed, but we may wish to add here that the process is also deeply entangled, if not extraordinarily convoluted.

Thus, as emphasized in early creolization studies, the outcome of efforts to adapt, resist, and accommodate the slave regime and to forge cultural communities and selves constituted a set of practices that sheltered slaves from the generally oppressive conditions of slavery and created the conditions for the existence of even thriving alternatives in many short-lived communities. Never constituted by practices rooted in an unchanging past, the process afforded its practitioners the mechanisms to stake claim to their present locality and humanity, while still being thoroughly invested in futures. They involved practices and beliefs, all of which contributed to coming to terms with their lives and their making in the Americas. These were manifested in a range of areas, from labor bargaining strategies to work to land tenure practices, for example, customary (family) land tenure, from religious orientations to musical (lyrical or rhythmical) improvisations, from attitudes to death to those of birth, and generally in all else associated with a process of deterritorialized and reterritorialization.

These polycultural practices were never geographically bounded, nor ever solely plantation derived, but they were always porous, contingent on the power of slaveholders, colonials, and others within the slave community and outside it. Charles Carnegie and others compellingly demonstrate the richly textured transnational lives of Caribbean traders and runaways before and after the formation of politically sovereign nation-states as they crossed borders at will.[66] Hardly contained by situational knowledge, subjects across the Atlantic parlayed their knowledge of the importance of citizenship or subjecthood in ways which thwarted or denied their enslavement. D. Barry Gaspar's account of Cape Verdeans captured illegally by a British captain and taken to the West Indies, who used their Portuguese to draw attention to the illegality of their capture, demonstrates the awareness of the Atlantic colonial crosscurrents. As Gaspar put it, "They certainly understood what they should do to recover their freedom and drew attention to their Portuguese identity as "Subjects to the King of Portugal," although they obviously carried multiple identities."[67] In that sense, insofar as these forms of struggle and new cultural practices appeared elsewhere, the wider Atlantic world was shaped by these sited practices, and local places were globalized. In short, globalisms of various sorts were localized, and localized forms fed back into global processes, further elaborating the Atlantic region but going beyond it as well.

Insofar as creolization's explicit plantation manifestations appeared only in the Americas, the Americas are set apart but are nevertheless set within "global spaces"—here *and* elsewhere linked in locales—providing and incorporating the effects of this particular globalizing system. Linda Heywood's work on the impact of Africans in Portugal partially highlights this phenomenon. According to Heywood, the first blacks who went to Brazil, to areas such as Sao Paulo, came from Portugal, not from Africa, where in 1505 they numbered between 136,000 and 151,000. This means "that many of the cultural adaptations that had already taken place in Portugal, Kongo and Angola had been carried with the slaves to Brazil."[68] For example, in Portugal many were involved in the Catholic brotherhood.[69] It cannot be overemphasized that local manifestations of creolization processes in the Caribbean have always been multispaced, multitemporal, and, importantly, transcultural and multitraditional. In this regard, the plantation should thus be analyzed as a local manifestation of labor and social organization linked to other time-spaces, marking it off as a single element within a plurality of temporalities and labor organizations that exist across different spaces, within and beyond the Atlantic world economy. Further, given the slave's development of their social powers under conditions of violence, the plantation can also be seen metaphorically as a disciplinary border, as life within its borders involved temporal and physical crossing into new subjectivities requiring the exercise of modern biopowers and biopolitics.[70]

Although advanced as a research project, intimations of this complex approach to creolization appeared in the work of Kamau Brathwaite.[71] Writing in the context of the pluralist versus the plantation models of Caribbean society, Brathwaite seemed quite prescient when he argued, "This social reality may be as much figment as fragment: a result of our apprehension of reality; [and] that the pessimistic/plantation view of Caribbean society, to put it another way, may very well not be the last word on Caribbean society."[72]

Moreover, still positioned within the pluralist and plantation society paradigms and restricted by the vocabulary and issues of the time, he offered a more profound assessment of what was needed to advance the research but also the society's political agenda: "In the seventies our research will have to equip us to more precisely observe, account for, and assess agents of change: the changes (material, spiritual and electronic) in the inner and outer metropoles; and the processes of change *within and between inner and outer* plantation. And we shall have to try to describe those *specifically/totally:* as socio-national phenomena, as regional phenomena, and as hemispheric occurrences"[73] (our emphasis).

In concluding, he reemphasized that "the unity is submarine,"[74] again using the phrase to conjure the complexity and vastness but still untapped properties of the Caribbean region's cultures. Edouard Glissant aligns his idea of "subterranean convergence" with Brathwaite's submarine construct, when he likens it to the exploration of Caribbean histories, as opposed to the single linear tightly scripted History in which the Caribbean has been inscribed. It is these divergent histories that have "roared around the edge of the Caribbean."[75] Glissant thus explains "submarine roots" as "free-floating free, not fixed in one position in the same primordial spot, but extending in all directions in *our* world, through its network of branches." He concludes that "we, thereby, live, we have the good fortune of living, this shared process of cultural mutation, this convergence that frees us from uniformity."[76]

Though Brathwaite's method seems to suggest a layered, rather than an interwoven, mutually constituted history, it does open up spaces closed down by plantation and plural-society analyses and tentatively moves away from the idea of an autochthonous localness, considering his use of the term "hemispheric" to denote its reach. In this sense, at least in this particular essay, Brathwaite's schema for the location of Caribbean cultures goes beyond Caribbean places and their peoples. However, this larger "hemispheric" setting often serves as a backdrop, rather than a constitutive space for the production, reflection, and reconstitution of *creolization* processes in the region.

In teasing out the social movements forming these constitutive hemispheric spaces, the notion of a transcultural, multitemporal, or "diasporic habitus" is useful here to suggest a broader Atlantic space/world connection that involves the borrowing and morphing of traditions.[77] Also, the concept suggests that the practices (or articulating conducts) embedded in this habitus are effecting paradoxical "double movements" of staying and leaving or liminal performances of moving and returning, movements from which Caribbeans ultimately drew to forge strategies for the salvaging of humanity and the building of spaces and communities of hope.[78] The concept "diasporic," as a qualifying term, is meant to signal not just the existence of diasporic populations and transcultural encounters, but also to bring into play the strategic temporality and politics of re-presenting as guided by diverse imaginations of home, tradition, or place, a point empha-sized, of course, in critical discourses on diaspora.[79] Habitus, however, re-mains as a conditioning force forming agency, or as a "womb of space" productive of boundaries, ontologically shaping yet also enabling the emer-gence of these conditional and strategic politics articulated in movements of people seeking translations of place.

In theorizing habitus, Bourdieu posits that "the states or social contexts associated with a particular class of conditions of existence produce *habitus,* systems of durable, transposable dispositions, *structured structures predis-posed to function as structuring structures,* that is as principles which generate and organize practices and representations that can be objectively adapted to their outcomes without presupposing a conscious aiming at ends or an express mastery of the operations necessary in order to attain them. The habitus, a product of history, produces individual and collective practices— more history—in accordance with the schemes generated by history. It ensures the active presence of past experiences, which, deposited in each organism in the form of schemes of perception, thought and action, tend to guarantee the 'correctness' of practices and their constancy over time, more reliably than all formal rules and explicit norms . . . the habitus, embodied history, internalized as a second nature and so forgotten as history . . . is the active presence of the whole past of which it is the product and so ensures the permanence in change that makes the individual agent a world within the world."[80] This notion of habitus thus helps to clarify the complex traditions of Afro-Caribbeans dislocated within the Atlantic world. To this end, habitus operates within and beyond the sensibilities of the black Atlantic, which emphasizes black consciousness.

Accordingly, in building on a notion of a diasporic habitus, we are inter-ested in expanding it beyond notions of blackness and ethnicity, though cognizant of, and indeed sympathetic to, black diaspora literature's focus on race as the structure of identity and the way in which blacks inhabit a temporality more or less based on deprivation and "waiting in line" gener-ally.[81] Though much of this literature originates from the United States and generalizes from the specific racialized sensibility there, the use of diasporic habitus here conjures up the idea that we cannot escape our pasts (or rather the conditions of our existence in "being in the world," which is differentially structured, experienced, and imagined) even as we engage in articulating the experience of movements given diverse post-Creole imaginations. As deployed here, the notion also foregrounds the experiences of ordinary peo-ple,[82] in an attempt, as Bourdieu intended, to make sense of, or to account for, people's common sense, their traditions.

However, while the notion of habitus accounts for the integrative condi-tioning of individuals, classes, or groups generally within a certain set of conditions, or, as Bourdieu put it, a set of "objective regularities" which inhibit the production of "extravagances," and despite the notion's inven-tiveness, it limits a proper grasp of the emergence of diversity, difference, alterity. This is so even though Bourdieu stresses that habitus contains within itself tendencies of transformation, hinting at a never closed system. That is to say, the conditions which produce regularities also produce irreg-ularities, sanctioned though they may be. Values, meaning, interpretations, and practices, in other words practical senses, may be produced in excess of the conditioning elements of the habitus, "not as pure alternatives, but from within those very structures."[83] But, and this is the critical point, even apparent regularities are always partial, systems are always incomplete in virtue of the possibility if not the actuality of resistance, exercises of agency, cultural struggle and selective creation, as well as *différance*. How these dynamics or movements in practical senses are being accomplished, and the nature of the forces involved in the context of creolization processes form the subject of this text.[84] In this regard, the book highlights diverse aspects of contemporary cultural transformations at the level of both the state and the people, some of which appear somewhat like Margaret Thompson Drewal's Yoruba practitioners who operate not from structurally grounded or "fixed" habitus positions but from "heterogeneous ensembles of ac-quired, embodied knowledges that, when performed in combination, rec-onstitute and transform themselves and social situations."[85] These are im-provisations that embody the new and old in new situations, exercises in liminal performance.[86]

Caribbean sociocultural strategies are folded in time, space, and power relations and thus are necessarily exercised through the context of the vari-ous contours of modern social power and through the struggle for "proper presence": that is, desires for place, which have implicated manipulations of the right and aesthetic of belonging as de facto or de jure "citizen." In its double articulations of place and space, then, *creolization* processes were, and are, emancipatory projects tied to the imagining and making of mod-ern subjects and the homing of modern freedoms.

FLEEING THE PLANTATION:
THE POST-PLANTATION ERA

What is the post-plantation era, and the post-plantation Creole condition in the Caribbean? And what are the claims that we make about this particular neoliberal and globalized era that reconditions and reconstructs the earlier positioning of Caribbean Creoles, destabilizing the very conditions and practices that regularize the social structures and processes? In a conversation about the Institute of Global Studies that he directed, Michel-Rolph Trouillot stated, "The global village is now a cliché. But those who work on the Caribbean know that the world was global since at least 1492. Europe became Europe, in part through severing itself from what lay south of the Mediterranean, but in part also through a Westward move that made the Atlantic the center of the first truly global empires."[87] We concur with this perspective, and this point is missed in much of the work on globalization, but Trouillot would agree that the current neoliberal project visited on disparate places and people has witnessed the emergence of new sets of social relationships dislocating the moral economies of those "peasants working for capital" (33 percent or much less now of the Dominican whose lives he so rigorously detailed),[88] and no doubt disrupting older forms of creolized performances.

Those Dominican "peasants" of whom he wrote now operate under a different banana regime, which requires them to compete with wage workers on large banana neoplantations, producing "dollar bananas" in the Latin part of the Americas, Honduras, Ecuador, Guatemala, and Mexico. It is possible even that these "peasants" no longer work for agricultural capital but are now fully immersed in Dominica's growing transport or tourist industry or that for the most part they rely on remittances sent from relatives abroad. Perhaps, more importantly, those family relationships and forms of sociality that gave moral meaning to neighborliness, which once bolstered households for whom family consumption was more central than the production of saleable surpluses, may have disintegrated entirely. They, and the matrix of institutions of governance implicated in these developments, have reconstituted their earlier relationship in the light of state divestment and structural adjustments limiting their earlier developmental commitments. As has been acknowledged, under pressure to facilitate these processes of globalization from within, nation-states have undertaken a massive project of redefining citizens, privileging those who can take advantage of this new hypercompetitive environment and who more or less abet its various ideological tenets.[89] All of this leads to the restructuring of definitions, practices, and expectations associated with older (modern) forms of Creole traditions.

ENCOUNTERING GLOBALIZATION: THE CURRENT NEOLIBERAL CONDITIONING OF THE POST-CREOLE IMAGINATION

Discourses on growing "deterritorialization" occasioned by migrations, forced or voluntary, the pervasiveness of spatial and political diasporas,[90] the ungluing of patriarchal pacts of a particular order, the resultant familial tensions that these incur, the continued racialization of work, the growing levels of informality, and the redefinition of states—all these are some of the more potent concerns of globalization studies. Although many theorists underplay the conditions under which they are produced, such developments can be linked to the recurrence and regulation of the recent phase of economic and cultural globality. A pervasive quandary within globalization studies is a question of the emergence of sameness or convergence in historically different locations. For example, one finds in several writings the idea that globalization entails (1) "processes of economic systematization, international relations between states, and an emerging global culture of consciousness";[91] (2) the more visible shrinking of space and the disappearance of localizations; (3) the collapse of universalism and particularism; (4) the extension of risk and trust globally; and (5) "the progressive culturalization of social life."[92] The argument that capital in this late modern era, unlike its previous pattern, redounds to everyone's benefit as it undermines unproductive states, making geographies irrelevant, needs to be seriously qualified and even exploded.[93] Fortunately, this exercise is currently underway. For example, Arrighi, Silver, and Brewer, focusing on the North-South divide, argue that while the gap between the First and Third Worlds has been significantly reduced in terms of industrialization, this has not led to a convergence of income earning levels in these regions. In other words, the divide between formerly First and Third World nations remains an enduring dimension of contemporary global dynamics. And they conclude that "the virtual absence of any positive correlation between income and industrialization performance suggests that, for most countries, industrialization turned out to be an ineffectual means of economic advancement."[94] Thus, there is little evidence to suggest that new developments associated with this new phase of capitalism have significantly erased the contours of the old international division of labor, where the majority of the inhabitants of the Caribbean, and many places elsewhere, can still be assumed to get less of the benefits that flow from the cumulative concentration effects of market liberalism, cultural creolizations notwithstanding.[95] They have fewer choices as poor people, women, children, the aged, and as nonwhites, persons of color. That is to say, with particular reference to the peripheries, inhabitants there cannot simply choose at will from a buffet of goods, services, and locations now made more available and accessible by transnational corporations (TNCS) and mass media. For it is still a legitimate argument that more people who live in those Third World places bear a heavier share of the burden of life that globalization generates than those who live elsewhere; or, put another way, fewer people who live in the periphery enjoy the benefits of globalization and the neoliberalized market that accrue to those living elsewhere in industrialized countries.[96] This is not to ignore the racialized, class, and gendered marginality that occurs in the core and that disallows large numbers of people from partaking of the fruits of late modern capitalism, displacing the working poor and the unemployed in overly industrialized places and making their situation comparable to that of their counterparts in less industrialized places around the world.[97] Although globalization studies point to the need to go beyond conceptualizations of local and the global, they often do so from the perspective that these reputedly distinct areas constitute separate arenas that overlap or intersect. In short, the unit of analysis operates on the same terrain of the nation-state, the space that they seek to decenter or dislocate, making their critiques problematic.

Seeking to downplay the analytic divisions between the global and the national, Saskia Sassen argues that one of the more vital elements of globalization is the formation of new spatialities and temporalities, that globalization is a partial though strategic project. For Sassen this does not mean that the global and the national inhabit two different arenas. For the most part, they overlap. Sassen argues that "one way to conceptualize these insertions of the global into the fabric of the national is as a partial and incipient denationalization of that which historically has been constructed as the national, or, rather, of certain properties of the national." Referring to "frontier zones" or borderlands within the nation, where the global and the national overlap, she uses the concept of "regulatory fractures" to describe "a series of economic activities brought on by globalization which take place in national contexts but that are sufficiently novel in some of their features (organizational or locational) that while they do not appear to violate existing regulatory frameworks, (they) cannot be said to comply with them either . . . Global cities include dense and complex borderlands marked by the intersection of multiple spatio-temporal (dis)orders."[98] A similar idea was broached earlier in dependency theories, in the notion of "enclaves" (appearing in Third World spaces)—industrial spaces within the national whose tempo was engineered by outside firms, thus leading to social and economic relationships, neither national nor international,[99] as in the mining or the oil sectors and as opposed to agriculture. For the dependency theorists, multinational corporations (MNCs) with nation-state or state compliance and encouragement were largely responsible for these distinct highly capitalized sublocales within the borders of the nation-states. Within these special locations and enterprises, elite workers had more in common culturally and materially with those living elsewhere in the industrialized North—the location of global cities—than with their fellow nationals working, say, in the subsistence agricultural sectors or low-level manufacturing or mineral concerns. In other words, both paradigms, dependency and globalization, partake in the notion of the hybridization of time-space under different modern industrial rationalities and technologies, namely, modernization and neoliberalism, except that the former is binary and vertical, comprising of a relationship between core and periphery, and the latter connotes an all-encompassing relationship.

Considering these "regulatory fractures," to use Sassen's formulation, it would seem that capital operates by rearranging and adapting to the socioeconomic and cultural spaces of nation-states, at the same time that it creates novel configurations operating within different time-spaces and zones. The sociocultural tendencies within local/national spaces condition these spatiotemporal ruptures, imparting differences to them. These developments are hardly limited to nonindustrialized countries. The high technological worlds of global cities themselves call forth these networked spaces and occupations filled by low-paid, low-skilled migrant workers, women, and people of color.[100] How these linked processes operate with and without the state is a historical problematic. MNCs always relied on concessions from nation-states to set up shop. Thus a different kind of political balance facilitated their brand of production, one hardly required now, given the enormous imbalances that tip the scales of power in favor of the investor over the nation-state. These asymmetries of power were still, furthermore, being actively promoted. Consider, for example, the proposed Multilateral Agreement on Investment (MAI) (later dismissed) whose performance requirements would leave no doubt as to who called the tune. The MAI had set out strict guidelines that prohibit governments from interfering with the "natural" order of the market, in short, from attempting to regulate the production of goods and services within their territories. Thus, "the full freedom of the investor [takes] precedence over any other social, cultural, political, or economic interest, goal, or value of the countries, regions, and communities toward which the investment is directed." And "any effort to redirect, change, regulate, promote, limit, or ban any of the investor's activities constitutes *discrimination* or *distortion.*"[101] Certainly, these sorts of developments call for a sustained analysis that interrogates the relationships that constitute global and local.

In dealing with this problem of the nature of the interconnectedness of the global and the local, the world systems school was very prominent in suggesting how one should conceive of the interdependencies within the world. However, as an idea it has been heavily criticized in the debates that emerged against world systems theory. For example, analysts including William Roseberry, Roland Robertson, and Ulf Hannerz denounced it for its inattention to the periphery considering its core-centeredness,[102] which characterized peripheries as highly dependent, obfuscating the "relative autonomy" of peripheries and "the interplay between the global and the local which may result from this."[103] Robertson's critique of the system's theory is more nuanced than one might expect of a denunciation, however. What he questioned was "the ability and even desirability to grasp the world as an analytical whole," preferring instead an analysis that centers on "relations between cultures."[104] Anthropologists who believe that "culture" or the periphery should be studied in all its diversity, like Eric Wolf, also pointed to the limitations of world systems for those who study "micropopulations." As Wolf pointed out, world systems theorists, such as Immanuel Wallerstein, "omit considerations of the range and variety of such populations." Moreover Wolf suspected that "periphery" was a substitute for "traditional society."[105] And so the "anthropological quest for cultural diversity" has to be pursued outside the predictable, even debilitating (for the people of the periphery) designates of world systems thought.[106] Undoubtedly, world-systems theory refocused the wider picture, or as Sidney Mintz put it, "world-systems forces us frequently to lift our eyes from the particulars of local history."[107] At the same time, however, the events "on the ground" are critical to analyzing the ways in which locales are implicated in undermining and refurbishing the architecture of the world economy.[108]

Recognizing that diversity within local places may be globally constituted offers a partial reprieve of sorts but reproduces the sense of separate, though networked or linked, places. Moreover, the economy is unwittingly calculated as a distinct sphere. Hence, Arjun Appadurai's conceptualizations, ethnoscapes, financescapes, technoscapes, and so on, selective representations of the muddled social life to be sure, principally serve to orient one to globalization's multiple facets and act as one way of focusing on national disjunctures and the disjuncture of the nation.[109]

As such a conceptual and methodological reworking and transformation of a "systems approach," or methodological orientation, may still be warranted in order to focus on globalizing or integrating tendencies, as well as reexamining processes of continuity and rupture as they define sociocultural changes since the late twentieth century. This orientation would allow, for example, taking into account global historical patterns that delink developments along national lines, that is to say, that methodologically and analytically question nation spaces and highlight transnational spaces, although serving, strangely enough, to generate discourses that reinforce specific types of nationalism. With a "systems orientation," one is therefore afforded the opportunity to raise certain kinds of questions. For example, how is it possible to produce understandings about the highly differentiated ways in which globalization is lived without "falling back into an anthropological nativism that postulates supposedly isolated societies and uncontaminated cultures, past or present? Nothing is to be gained from the dated assumption that 'real people doing real things' inhabit self-enclosed and self-sufficient universes."[110] Of course, this is less the thinking now than at the time when Wolf penned those thoughts. Do theoretical paradigms conceived methodologically in terms of "national society and nation-state" usefully analyze the cultural changes now underway? And if not, what new paradigms and new concepts can accommodate the dynamic movement of culture, whether lived in diasporas or commuting migrant communities, as witnessed among Puerto Ricans, Kuwaitis, Filipinos, and others?

How can cultural practices be reassessed through a global analytic, in a way which does not neglect the myriad ways that incorporate the imaginary attachments to national maps and the spaces that they conjure? How can a concept like *creolization,* whose deployment now connotes universal availability, even accessibility via transnational transfers, be used productively to generate new theoretical paradigms highlighting sociocultural echoes and similarities across territories, while foregrounding the ways in which power shapes what is received, and how it is consumed by the world's diverse populations who, more or less, inhabit different but related modern temporalities and spatialities in a neoliberal economic, globalized era? These questions have served to animate an extended sketch of a method for analyzing the *creolization* phenomenon presented in the next chapter.

TWO

CREOLE TIME ON THE MOVE

What is at issue is the way we analyze and understand the production of specificity and uniqueness.[1]

Maybe the target nowadays is not to discover what we are, but to refuse what we are. We have to imagine and to build up what we could be to get rid of this kind of political "double bind," which is the simultaneous individualization and totalization of modern power structures. . . . We have to promote new kinds of subjectivity through the refusal of this kind of individuality which has been imposed on us for centuries.[2]

Clearly time cannot achieve emancipation at one stroke, or en bloc. It is not so obvious, however, that such a liberation calls necessarily for morphological inventions or for a production of space.[3]

Time on the move.[4]

CREOLIZATION DYNAMIZED

IN CONSIDERING *creolization* as a dynamized process, Dale Tomich's perspective on the unity of the world economy offers a crucial entry point.[5] Critical of the world system perspective and that of the nation-state–based modes of production, Tomich argues that both operate in similar discursive terrains.[6] He writes, "Attention to the specificity of forms of social production allows us to comprehend the world economy not simply as the sum of its parts or as an abstraction over and above them, but as *distinct relations among particular social forms and material processes of production, integrated with one another through definite modes of exchange and political power-as a structured and differentiated whole changing over time*" (our emphasis).[7]

Thus, neither class nor the national are either internally stable or bounded but are rather brought forth as products "of multiple and diverse yet interrelated relations and processes of varying intensity, extent, and duration."[8] Hence, while local socioeconomic and sociocultural relationships are also engendered and constituted beyond their specific locales, their modes of expression are embodiments of "plural, heterogeneous, and unstable relations generated by the multiple relations and processes, operating simultaneously across varying spatial and temporal scales."[9] This perspective permits the "disclosure of the complex, uneven and contingent processes within the totality of interdependent relations that form particular class relations as an historical outcome."[10]

Tomich's conceptualization offers an alternative to both Marxian modes of production and market-determined world systems approaches, one that recognizes intersecting and interrelated processes of space and place making in the formation of locales. Each particular configuration within such locales, whether of economy, class, ethnicity, or identity, is constituted and reconstituted across time and space, as a fundamentally unstable linked phenomenon. Tomich's approach at once recognizes the inner and outer localities of the global, and grasps these time-spaces as relational processes. And it is their complex interdependent workings that constitute the modern world economy. To speak to the development, as in formative constitution, of the world economy privileges these diverse elements which compose it and deemphasizes an abstract world market that subjugates and determines locales and the experiences of locals, as top-down world system analysts would have it. The approach thus rejects the idea of autonomy and internality of transformation or of social divisions such as ethnicity, or class, or even "consciousness of the world as a whole."[11]

Applying this method to the study of the plantation and slavery organization in Martinique and Cuba, in *Small Islands and Huge Comparisons* Tomich compares the Martiniquan plantation sugar production in the nineteenth century with that of Cuba, tracing the two countries' divergent developments: Martinique's decline and Cuba's ascendancy in the context of world economic developments. He examines the ways in which these created the conditions for the peculiar sugar economies and slave histories of these two Caribbean islands and for those of the entire Atlantic world. What hitherto appeared as autonomous, internally generated transformations, even isolated through formally comparative "cases," turn out to be far more complex instances of moments of the development of the world economy in specific locations. Thus are local Caribbean histories articulated in contexts larger than their specific locales, making it possible to argue for the region's transnational sociocultural and economic histories, its Atlantic associations within and without.[12]

Furthermore, with this "unified, multidimensional and relational approach" to the formation of the Caribbean within Atlantic space, colonial and postcolonial formations appear less as succeeding linear histories than as complex, dependent, relational, material, and discursive formations. This allows the postcolonial to be treated as a global condition affecting the relationship of, and between, colonial, imperial, and the former colonial differently. Given the nature of relational histories, cultural practices within the postcolonial draw upon colonial practices, making identity within those histories' loci highly complex and ambivalent, "unavoidably inclusive of the colonial."[13] Against this backdrop, binarisms assume only generalized analytical statuses as expressions that appear to constitute the particularities of their places. Having performed this work, they need to be returned to the textured constituents representing the larger unity of world space. Thus, as Juan Flores advised, "Rather than going from the larger panconglomerate concept to the particular; start from the particular, have an *optic* to define the relationship between the particular and the universal when considering contemporary cultural relations" (our emphasis).[14] But, we add, do so acknowledging the symbiotic relationship between them.

In this spirit, focusing primarily on the Anglophone Caribbean, mainly from the sites of St. Lucia and Jamaica but incorporating other Caribbean places, we aim to demonstrate how the new time-spaces emergent within the context of the neoliberal globalization economic project destabilize citizens' former relationships with state institutions and their ideologies, setting in motion new dispensations influencing the cast and orientation of cultural forms. Not quite a postdevelopment era, as others proclaim,[15] under this new dispensation, "development" in the Caribbean, at least of a certain type, has been dismantled or restructured, even aborted.[16] A new relationship with citizens looms in which they are urged to become "world class or no class."[17] No longer is the world interested in its more vulnerable citizens, those occupying such economically inconsequential places as the Caribbean, despite the fact that in the eighteenth and nineteenth centuries the region's free and unfree peoples fueled the Atlantic world economy and that, from the twentieth century to the present, large numbers of free Caribbeans have migrated to rebuild Europe's shattered infrastructure and to take part in U.S. imperial, private, and corporate ventures in Cuba, Costa Rica, Panama, and the United States itself.[18]

Clearly, then, since Tomich's principal problematic was undermining the extreme arguments of world systems and modes of production analysts, in order to produce a method to grasp the intertwined histories of the world, his approach is a useful corrective from which to deepen the grasp on the Caribbean's sociocultural histories in their entanglements with global phenomena. However, in order to further elaborate on the nature of *creolization processes* that are being articulated in the world, we argue that one needs to introduce two further conceptual breaks from the world systems framework. First, one needs to shift from a singular focus on "the power of economy"—that is, the capitalist world economy, which remains the principal theorized social power constraint even within sophisticated approaches to world systems analysis such as that offered by Tomich and McMichael— to that of the "economy of power" or modern governmentality. This shift, we believe, allows for coming to terms more adequately with the conditions driving the experiences of both lived and systemic crises within "modernity," as emphasized by Gilroy in *The Black Atlantic* and as especially manifest in the (former) slaves' experiences of the modern world in relation to the processes and politics of making place and presence.[19] Second, one needs also to make a shift from a Cartesian conception of space as extension and potential possession, a conception that pervades world systems analysis and reinforces its tendency to universalize history.

Accordingly, in unsettling discourses on *creolization* from the plantation enclave, we argue that while *rooted* in geographies of Atlantic space as such, *creolization* might well be better understood as a specific kind of ontological conditioning process which has attended the formation and mapping of "cultures of power," or "culture systems,"[20] and their complex ensembles of space. A concern with space is certainly a core theme in discourses on *creolization,* and not simply at the level of physical geographies but more so in terms of the imaginations of geographies that pervade the political and cultural struggles for space in the world, as is particularly evident in the work of Glissant and Brathwaite, as well as in the poetics of Wilson Harris, among others.[21] These authors have explored the possibilities for "making space," through the inner space of the imagination, expressed in genres of literature, which as Ato Quayson demonstrates offers a critical medium through which one may "read for the social," a method which involves an oscillation between the domains of "the literary-aesthetic, the social, the cultural and the political."[22] In what follows we wish to add to this probing work on (social) space by examining the links between space and place in order to make clearer the signal importance of what we have termed the "will to place." For this next step we draw on the work of Henri Lefebvre, who teases out the nuances of the production of space as simultaneously spatial and social space, utilizing yet extrapolating beyond the Marxian analysis of the production of social being.

THE PRODUCTION OF SPACE

In treating space, we make the break from a Cartesian conception of space as extension and potential possession (space as an empty container, a matrix) to a Lefebvrian conception of (social) space as "product" (and rhythm). The first conception implies viewing space as a binary configuration defined through location and boundaries for containing and relating objects, while the other presents space as a triad which is configured through representations of space, representational spaces, and spatial practices.

In brief, representations of space point to the conceptual ordering and calibration of the *forms* of space, as evident, for example, in the naming of social formations as "traditional" or "modern." Or as Simonson explains, it is "connected to the dominant 'order' of any society and hence with its codes, signs and knowledge about space."[23] Representational spaces identify "space as directly lived through its associated images and symbols,"[24] thus marking the articulation nodes of (contested) representations, positions, or places in social systems. The articulations of society's symbolic ordering are, of course, exercised through the "spatial practice of society" which "secretes that society's space; it propounds and presupposes it, in a dialectical interaction; it produces it [as] slowly and surely as it masters and appropriates it."[25] Spatial practices thus allude to both the production of social space and the imaginations of spatial forms characteristic of them; that is, the *spatial designs* of places.[26] For example, this is seen in the production of urban space (motorways, built urban environments, cities),[27] as well as rural space (plantation systems, countrysides)[28] and subject space (racialized phenotypes of subjects; racialized sites, for example, "the Dark Continent," "geographies of blackness," nationalities).[29] Accordingly, an understanding of spatial practices, as Donald Moore et al. have argued, requires recognition of the "simultaneity of symbolic and material struggles, refusing an assumed distinction between 'merely' symbolic recognition and material resource distribution. The cultural politics of representation . . . enables us to conceive of how race, nature, and differences simultaneously shape both the very terrain that produces political subjects and the claims that these subjects make to rights, resources, and their redistribution."[30]

In order to grasp the nuances in these complex dynamics for the production of space as conducted by spatial practices, we wish to pause here to consider carefully several critical emphases that Lefebvre flagged, as we believe these dimensions of his analysis of (social) space have not been adequately brought out in the discussions on space. Yet we consider these nuances as key to enhancing the interpretation of creolization processes. First of all, as Lefebvre states, in analyzing space, one is "no longer [addressing] a matter of this space or that; rather it is *space in its totality* or global aspect that needs to be subjected not only to analytical scrutiny (a procedure that is liable to furnish merely an infinite series of fragments and cross sections subordinate to the analytical project), but also to be *engendered* by and within theoretical understanding" (first emphasis ours).[31] Second, and of essence in grasping the peculiarity of space, "this space is now and formerly a *present* space, given as an immediate whole, complete with its associations and connections in their actuality. Thus production process and product present themselves as two inseparable aspects, not as two separable ideas."[32] At least two powerful implications flow from these guidelines for a conception of space.

First, space as "product," means that space is conducted (*and* counterconducted) through complex processes of production as made through spatial practices. This feature of space as product *and* rhythm can be seen in Gilroy's analysis of the experiences of black people, their pattern of movement transformation and relocation in the Black Atlantic.[33] Sibylle Fischer takes Gilroy to task, however, for allowing little room for thinking modernity through slaves' active and critical production of its spaces, thus leaving them merely as "conscripts of modernity," as David Scott dramatized,[34] and thus in a situation where, as Fischer states, the "slave's relation to history is that of insertion, not that of construction."[35] This is a critical point as it speaks to a view of social history as being predicated upon, as well as fractured by, multiple processes of production intricately wombing and weaving re-pre-sentations of space. Accordingly, and in general, the flow of these spatial processes of production will be subject not only to antiphonal rhythms of reproduction and transformation—as expressed through the performance of creative movements, sounds, vibrations, and spacing temporalities (lag-ging, syncopation, meters, and so on)—but also to arrhythmic flows. In the context of the present discussion, the latter points to the very moment where modernity is rendered open by the poetic stillness of the unspeakable pres-ent, the Derridian "trace."[36] Bhabha, through his reflections on Aila, the loyal wife of Sonny, the political activist in Nadine Gordimer's novel *My Son's Story*, speaks to this "strange stillness" that expresses itself in the performa-tive of life itself. He intimates its political significance, through a poignantly captured moment of encounter between Sonny and Aila that discloses some-thing more than the "familiar"—"a hidden face," a "vivid strangeness" that cannot be seen but "had to be recognized." This strange stillness, as Bhabha notes, alerts us to the "gaps in the story," "moments where the private and the public touch in contingency."[37] And despite Fischer's pointed intervention on the tendency to erase the opaque yet "constitutive presence" of the slave in "modernity," we suggest here that Gilroy also tackles this issue through his introduction of the idea of syncopated temporality—a different rhythm of living and being in which "the night time is the right time," underscoring the importance of "invisibility." This "invisibility" is explained by Ralph Ellison as giving "one a slightly different sense of time, you're never quite on the beat. Sometimes you're ahead and sometimes you're behind. Instead of the swift and imperceptible flow of time, you are aware of its nodes, those points where time stands still or from which it leaps ahead. And you slip into the breaks and look around."[38] Accordingly, being sensitive to space as product and (ar)rhythm reinforces not just a sense of incompleteness in presenta-tions of space as product but also a sense of undecidability in fixing the nature of space, or its deemed regularities for lending weight to the treatment of space as end product.

This element of undecidability and incompleteness associated with space as product and (ar)rhythm is captured by Derrida's concept of *différance*, which lays the stress on the mo(ve)ment of meaning. He therefore elabo-rates *différance* through the dual terms of difference/separation/spacing and detour/relay/temporization.[39] This concept of *différance* has become critical to investigations of not just texts but also the analysis of social and cultural histories. For example, it pivotally underlies Homi Bhabha's critical interventions on the postcolonial condition that addressed the problem of articulating a theory of the *liminal politics* conducted for making newness in the spaces of "the present." That is, he theorized how the subject engages in a politics of becoming-out-of-time-in-space, by fracturing time (Derrida's spacing, "the becoming-space of time") and thereby historicizing space (Derrida's temporization, "the becoming-time of space").[40] Accordingly, in his reading of the cultural politics of "postcoloniality," Bhabha argues that what is "politically crucial is the need to think beyond the narratives of originary and initial subjectivities and to focus on those moments or processes that are produced in the articulation of cultural differences. These 'in between' spaces provide the terrain for elaborating strategies of selfhood— singular or communal—that initiate new signs of identity, and innovative sites of collaboration, and contestation, in the act of defining the idea of society itself."[41] Moreover, in the practices expressing a liminal politics for the nation, the vector that unsettles the spaces of the nation is the "distracting presence of another temporality that disturbs the contemporaneity of the national present . . . the repetitious recursive strategy of the performative."[42] The stress in this analytics of cultural "power, process and practice" is thus on a conception of social space as product and (ar)rhythm.[43]

Space as (ar)/rhythmic productions is thus central in grasping the ontological and real interdependencies of space and time as complexly conducted through the lived space-time of spatial practices. In particular, it affords an understanding of the critical significance of the deployment of strategic temporalities in the liminal performance of space, as flagged, for example, by Gilroy's "syncopated" and "diaspora temporality,"[44] as well as in Bhabha's insistence that the "time-lag keeps alive the making of the past" and his emphasis on appreciating the political significance of the "rhythm of the swift and slow of human doing."[45] Space is thus always lived as liminal space—the present, always a "prisoner of the passage"[46]—even as it is strategically lived as *différance* (becoming-out-of-time-in-space). Consequently, spatial practices are everywhere situated as liminal practices excited by, as Bhabha has stressed, the vital dreams of "post-present" space-times.[47]

This takes us to our second observation on Lefebvre's analysis, which is that "theory" is, from within and without, integral to these spatial practices that "secrete society's space." Thus, representations of space, the symbolic codes ordering social space and conducted by spatial practices, are "shot through with a knowledge (*savoir*)—i.e., a mixture of understanding (*connaissance*) and ideology—which is always relative and in the process of change."[48] It is thus impossible, as the literature on space has emphasized, to analyze space outside of knowledge-power matrices: space is *always particularized* by power, or rather *by mappings of power,* to be provisionally understood here as a field of "forces, attractions and coexistences."[49] But what is vital to recognize here is that such mappings of a "space of power" *always work to produce space totally.* In particular they work by abstracting differences in the history of space in order to establish a *spatialization of time* (Cartesian time) and a calibration of a "place in time." Indeed, in making a similar point, Lefebvre emphasized that "theory reproduces the generative process [of space]—by means of a concatenation of concepts, to be sure, but in a very strong sense of the word: from within, not just from without (descriptively), *and globally*—that is, moving continually back between past and present [space]" (our emphasis).[50]

Accordingly, in all these productions of space, what is at stake is always a "present space" that is being systemically constituted as a "Present/present space"; that is, one that is constituted through doubling and folding processes. In other words, we believe Lefebvre's stress on "*present* space" is not only an emphasis on the dynamic process of space as liminal performance, space doubled as product and (ar)rhythm, but also an emphasis that representations (representations of space and representational spaces) seek to fix the "form of life" possible for the present, by an ontological folding of subjects in *the* present. This, we argue, is done by specifically "spacing place," or rather, "mapping the present." We will now use this framework to illustrate how one's place and presence are situated, or how they may be folded into (social) space. That is, we now wish to turn attention to practices and forces involved in mapping the present, especially in the contexts of the time-space of the modern.

THE WILL TO PLACE IN THE MAPPING OF THE PRESENT

In his reflections on the debates on creolization, Richard Price emphasized the need to pay close attention to the specificities of history and place in the stories that could be legitimately told about it.[51] These lived contexts of experiences are certainly of vital importance in reading the history of *creolization* as selective creation and cultural struggles for space by the slaves, and others, forcibly and otherwise entangled in the relational geographies and histories of Atlantic space (and beyond). But the contexts in question were not just geographies of space but also triads of space that sought to define and fix "place," or the capacity to be present, in certain social spaces albeit contingent on complex productions of space. Indeed, if one is to grasp the complexity of cultural development *as social process* and not just cultural end products as Mintz and Price have argued, and if one is to pay attention to the full implications of Ira Berlin's stipulation that "understanding that a person was a slave is not the end of the story but the beginning, for the slaves' history was derived from experiences that differed from place to place and from time to time and not from some unchanging transhistorical verity,"[52] then, in considering "place," elements to be included not only are the relations of physical geography, temporal histories, and cultural imports but also the ontologies of (social) spaces that articulate bodies into hetero-geneously constituted (subject) places.

This multiple (ontological) grounding of "place" resonates well with the phenomenon of "flexible ethnicities," addressed by Berlin, "whereby new identities [in the Americas] took a variety of forms . . . giving nationality or ethnicity an ever changing reality and with it new meanings . . . Identity was a garment which could be worn or discarded.[53] Ethnicity is, of course, not the only social garment that one may be disposed, or constrained, to wear in fashioning one's place in the world, through the selective and creative pro-cesses of *creolization*. The postulation then of a relationship between (so-cial) space and (subject) place brings into relief these issues of situated rationalities, agencies, and structural or more broadly (social) spatial re-sources (as well as constraints). It also points to a need for an even closer empirical examination of the processes by which "place" is being appropri-ated and moved, and also for a further inquiry into the nature of these place articulations with space. That is, one needs to continue to ask the question: How and through what kind of articulations with (social) space are these politics of place, being expressed? Indeed, this question may be seen as lying at the heart of Achille Mbembe's deeply provocative inquiries on the African postcolony. There he emphasized the ways in which the space denoted as "Africa" has its being-in-the-world shaped and fundamentally constrained by the efforts of the West to constitute its own identity or space dialectically through e/racing the place of "Africa."

In relation to this question, the point we wish to press here is simply that when discussing processes of *creolization,* not only sites, relations of juxtaposition, but also predicates for a state of presence must be considered. It is from these "wombs of (social) space" or those emergent conditions that constrain and tendentiously calibrate capacities of "being-in-the-world" (with different degrees of power—ranging from naked violence to more subtly and complex force relations) that the "will to place" is forged. In other words, these complexly conditioned agentive causal powers and desires represent the font for the will to place. In examining *creolization* processes, we argue that this will to place acts pivotally, as an expression of social life, or, as Tim Ingold so insightfully states, as an expression of "the temporal [and strategic] unfolding[s] of consciousness through the *instrumentality* of cultural forms."[54] These expressions of social life embodying the will to place are rooted and routed through the existential and political constraints of represented space that are mapping the present. The will to place thus acts to guide struggles against the "unhomeliness" of the present space, or its erasures of place, and motivates the quest for imaginations of "proper presence." It operates accordingly as the force reflexively orienting self-conduct and giving directionality to the practices of negotiating and navigating spatial hi/stories in personal, as well as social and collective projects of making place.

The postulate of the "will to place" is thus unhinged from any attempt to invoke a transcendental consciousness or overarching teleological script on history, or even a resolute being-toward-death, which is viewed by Heidegger as an essential expression of singularity, or separable autonomy. In our deployment of the concept of place we wish to deconstruct Heidegger's central term, "prescription," to allow for the play of *différance,* multiple meanings or ambiguities in its interpretation, in order to eschew any seemingly deterministic traps set by this concept as deployed by Heidegger. In our framework of *creolization* as selective creation and cultural struggle, the will to place, the stimulus for journeying from place to place, may thus be detected in the quotidian exercises for expression of place, as ontologically represented in the Heideggerian (social/spatial) state of *Da-sein,* "there-being," in the world, as well as in those anticipatory exercises for place that (a) exceed and criticize the constituted boundaries, or limits, of represented space, and (b) are routed through post-Creole imaginations.

In order to address the second issue of the kind of articulation between space and place that was raised in the question previously posed, we now wish to envisage the triad of space—*through* which agents' agential capacities are shaped, but not determined, and *from* which a will to place is elicited—using Lefebvre's ideas of function, form, and structure as the basic categories constituting any state of space and, relatedly, representing any mapping of the present.

To briefly elaborate, form establishes boundaries, largely through a calibration of one's *place in time*. In other words, it locates and relativizes one's place in lived time; it spatializes time and so identifies and founds "the world" one inhabits; it acts to virtually stipulate, in effect, a sign: "you are here now," which includes defining the boundaries of inside and outside, beginnings and endings of inner and outer (social) space. In general terms, form sets up the conditions of possible being and becoming-in-the-world, the terrain of the knowable (and the unknowable), the livable (and the taboo), or possible scenes of presence and power which thereby demarcate and segregate possible practices for exercising the capacity to be present. In short, form orders the representations of (social) space for a possible place-in-time. In order to grasp the powerful forces at work in constituting form, one may consider here two phenomena operating as critical modes of producing "form," namely, "the nation" and "the home." Both are quintessentially concerned with boundary work, or as Edensor argues, with providing a "common-sense spatial matrix which draws people and places together in spectacular and banal ways."[55] In speaking concretely to modernity, Trouillot also highlights this fundamental boundary work when he states that "modernity has to do not only with the relationship between spaces and place, but also with the relationship between place and time. For in order to prefigure the theoretically unlimited space [of modernity] . . . one needs to relate place to time, or, better said, to address a unique temporality, that is the position of the subject located in that place."[56]

Structure expresses the virtual necessities of practical life, the structural conditions of possibility for agency, for *Dasein*, that are constraining and enabling of a certain ethos, a certain conduct, a certain place, and exciting practices of freedom. Structure, of course, corresponds with representational spaces, or the sociocultural position-practices that one occupies in social life, for example, teacher-student, employer-employee, man-woman, black-white, or Afro-Creole, African, Indian, Asian, citizen-alien, and so on. However, as Lefebvre explained, "This [i.e., structure] is the dominated —and hence passively experienced—space which the imagination seeks to change and appropriate."[57] One should be clear here that Lefebvre's reference to "passive experience" is not a synonym for an absence of agency, or a latent contradiction in analysis, but rather identifies the stratified form of practical life, where actions take place with varying levels of consciousness and timely moments of strategy. Bourdieu's concept of habitus can be usefully recalled here to help underscore the point that practical life is *not* a continuous exercise of conscious (or even discursive or strategic) agency, even though social being or doing in the world presupposes a continuous presence of agency, that is, the condition of being in action and the causal power to have done otherwise. But as argued in chapter 1, habitus cannot be held to be all encompassing of social life movements and indeed can be deployed strategically, as is the case of the diasporic habitus.

Function defines the expected hopes from the articulation of form and structure; it designates the virtual promise of a future "proper presence," not yet present but expected to be possessed. It therefore points to a place-in-future-time, inspiring post-Creole imaginations of "proper presence" and desires for becoming *beyond* one's current place, that is, for making circuits of place. Function in articulation with form "informs" structure and thereby simulates a virtual matrix that guides conduct and seeks to elicit consent (if not consensus) for one's placement in the present, by inciting dreams of a place-in-future-time, or of post-Creole home spaces, that is, "proper dwelling places." This matrix of space operates to historically situate and map each person's place-in-time and thus establishes the boundaries of one's place in the *present*, by a process of triangulating form, structure, and function. Figure 1 shows this Lefebvrian panoptican for mapping one's place-in-time or for *mapping the present*. The individual's attempt to dynamize his or her "place-in-time" is linked to the articulation of these forces in experience brought to bear through this mapping.

Despite the force of this triangulation of space and its real and inescapable presence the matrix of space attains the status of only a virtual causal force. In other words, its formal pressures and attractions do not determine human experiences, that is, they do not establish a closed "system of space" that is independent of, or irrespective of, human agency. Accordingly, while

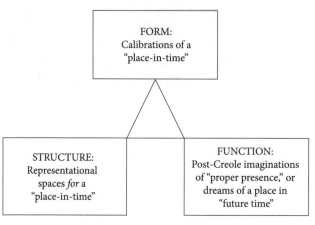

1 Mapping the present

the triangulation of space may tend to virtually fix place, it cannot actually do so, in-so-far as these relations of forces, or spatial pressures and attractions, are always conducted by human agency and secreted by spatial practices. Overall, then, while the triangulation of space remains the predicate for agents to exercise the capacity to be present, the dependence of space on human conduct fixes the essential duality of space, as both condition and outcome of agency. Or as Lefebvre states, "Social space can never escape its basic duality, even though triadic determining factors may sometimes override and incorporate its binary or dual nature, for the way in which it presents itself and the way in which it is represented are different. Is not social space always, and simultaneously, both a *field of action* (offering its extension to the deployment of projects and practical intentions) and a *basis of action* (a set of places whence energies derive and whither energies are directed)?"[58]

POWER, SPACE, AND PLACE

In grasping the relations between space and place, it is necessary to turn to relations of power. In fact, as Lefebvre makes clear, power is essential in determining the way in which we experience space, hence his distinctions between absolute, abstract, and appropriated space. All three reflect a politics of space, which in turn shapes and provokes a politics of making place. Briefly, absolute space refers to the historical introduction of structural distinctions of status, segregating social life and (physical) sites into the sacred and profane. Abstract space is related to absolute space, but Lefebvre uses the former concept to define a specific space of domination. In particular, abstract space identifies a space of violence in the social production of space that seeks to suppress difference or the expression of alternative forms of social life/labor; a process (for Lefebvre) that presupposes or requires the introduction of capitalist social relations.

Appropriated space is meant to identify the processes which disrupt "formal space," that is, representations of space, in order to introduce one's own sense of space or to particularize space through spatial practices. Thus, for example, in first introducing this concept, Lefebvre drew a distinction between acquiring an appreciation of the cities of the ancient world through their artifacts and texts and having knowledge of the ancient cities in terms of their "own spatial practice: [which] forged its own—*appropriated*— space."[59] However, the appropriation of space implies not just the existence of nuances in, or concrete styles and rhythms of, the reproduction and conduct of spatial practice; it also refers to the counterconducts of space for the production of new space, namely, Lefebvre's "differential space." This meaning is strongly emphasized by Lefebvre. He does this by contrasting dominated space with appropriated space, and also by his comment that "property in the sense of possession is at best a necessary precondition, and most often merely an epiphenomenon, of 'appropriative' activity. An appropriated space resembles a work of art, which is not to say that it is in any sense an imitation work of art."[60] This concept of appropriated space may thus be related to our ontological concept of "place," as "the capacity to be present," by subjects, given that an "appropriation" of space is an index of creative capacities exercised through space.

Overall, Lefebvrian space, like Foucauldian "chains of power," is perhaps best "analyzed as something that circulates, or rather something that functions only when it is part of a chain . . . it is never localized here or there, it is never in the hands of some, and it is never appropriated in the way that wealth or a commodity can be appropriated."[61] It is against this interpretive background that we now examine the ways in which *creolization* is implicated in the making and unmaking of modern space, power, and time, and thus in spatial hi/stories.

For us, given the above, the vital ontological or spatial condition of *creolization* was the presence of an incipient mapping of the present that opened the potential for producing, occupying, and configuring space differently. This emerging, or rather liminal, "womb of *present* space" has become increasingly defined as "modern" through a complex knowledge-power episteme emergent in the entangled site of Atlantic space, an episteme identified by Foucault as "modern governmentality." Accordingly, the political process of making modern space has partially realized, though not without contest, a particular state of "coloniality of power" engendering related "geographies of imagination," as Quijano, among others, has highlighted.[62] The corollary of this political process has thus been, of course, the difficult problem of establishing *actual places* for the location of cultures of modernity that bear this incipient mapping of the present, a mapping distinguished by an attitude—"a mode of relating to contemporary reality" and an ethos—a particular "way of thinking and feeling; a way, too, of acting and behaving that at one and the same time marks a relation of belonging and presents itself as a task."[63] But in the context of "racialized" domination, even this process of spatialization has raised questions regarding the proper identification of those places locating the cultures of modernity, a questioning that has provoked a sustained interrogation of the Caribbean's modernity in historical time, by, most notably, C. L. R. James, Sidney Mintz, and more recently David Scott and Sibylle Fischer.[64]

In practice, the contingent emergence of modern space (with its hegemonic foldings of the present) has lent itself not just to racialized wars of occupation and settlement but also to ambiguity and contradictions, as well as paradoxes, in the struggle to create, and in particular, rather home-stake present histories and modern freedoms.[65] These *creolization* processes of selective creation are thus not determined by singular ambitions to map the present. Moreover, as emphasized in Wilson Harris's politics of poesis, they may also involve imaginations "to void" present spaces, for an "otherwise homing" of space and place.[66] Creolization processes for making place/s are thus intimately at work in the strategies for settling, unsettling, and voiding "present spaces." They are not only manifestations of the spirit and "double consciousness" of the critically modern, as Gilroy emphasizes, but in a vital sense we argue that they are also expressions of the spirit and "place consciousness" of the critically present.

Indeed, as Saurabh Dube has emphasized, "to register the contingency and plurality of modernity is not merely to harp on alternative modernities but to stay with such modalities of power, formations of difference, and their restless interplay."[67] "Modern space" is thus situated as an unfinished genealogy of the *present* in ongoing and open political processes of transformation, transmutation, and transfiguration.

In stressing *creolization*'s entanglement in this politics of mapping the present, one continues the movement away from hierarchical and binaristic treatments of global and local spaces and instead considers both as composed by relational histories being articulated in, as Glissant has argued, "une poétique de la Relation" (a poetics of Relation).[68] This perspective on *creolization* also develops upon, though not uncritically, a crucial and later theme in Heideggerian philosophy, that of "placing and journeying" in which time and space are being produced simultaneously rather than, or in addition to, being produced hierarchically.[69] Our perspective is also reminiscent of "the Althusserian view of the need to observe the many variations to the structure of the whole that themselves disclose the contestatory temporalities inherent within such wholes."[70] For Althusser: "This time, as a complex 'interaction' of the different times, rhythms, turnovers etc., that we have just discussed, is only accessible in *its concept*, which, like every other concept is never immediately 'given,' never legible in visible reality: like every concept this concept must be produced, constructed."[71] Overall, our perspective wishes to reinforce a sense of a densely entangled and complex fluidity in the lived space-times of life within *creolization* processes, wombing, conducting as well as fracturing and voiding, the time-space continuums in cultures of modernity that flow from its ostensively political mapping of the present.

Of course, David Harvey's *Condition of Postmodernity*, which mainly draws upon the ideas of Heidegger, Marx, and Lefebvre, also offers a serious engagement with the production and experience of the spatialization of time and space in the present.[72] However, we are more interested in the temporalization of present space, rather than in the processes of the production of abstract time-space, the latter being the technique for spatializing time, or seeking to fix "forms of life," or being-in-the-world. Our attention is on, so to speak, "Creole time on the move," a shift of emphasis, however, that does not seek to dismiss or downgrade the strategies of domination that work through the superimposition of a Cartesian concept of space, as location and boundaries, on time. These hegemonies, as noted before, work to evacuate critical differences in the experience of space by prioritizing the spatialization of time (engendering the archway of homogenous empty time) over the temporalizing of space, that is, spatial history. But unlike David Harvey, for example, we are less concerned to emphasize the ultimate or apparently ineluctable mapping of time-space through the axes of global capitalism, and more concerned to point to the ways in which the activities of subjects, engaged in *creolization* processes of making places, are entangled in the mapping of an emergent but liminal moment for reconfiguring *the present.* This liminal space renders the present moment sensitive to various critical resistances, or "limit point experiences," as well as practices of "desistance."[73] *Creolization* processes express not just a miracle of genesis, as recognized by Trouillot, but continue as the processes of an unfinished and open liminal genesis—an "unfinished genesis of the imagination."[74]

To consider more carefully these *creolization* processes in states of liminal genesis, we wish to return to the "modalities of power, formations of difference, and their restless interplay" as Dube advises. Thus in the next section we enquire into what exactly is the nature of this present governmentality and its modern governable spaces? What are the (ontological/spatial) elements in the constitution of modern governmentality ensembles conducting (and counterconducting) modern power? And how generally does the politics of conducting modern governmentality contextualize and temporalize the spatial hi/stories of *creolization* and its entangled expressions of selective creation and cultural struggle? In what follows, we will provide some perspectives on these questions, but these interrogations also inform the raison d'être of this text, so our effort to tease out perspectives on these issues here will also be complementarily expressed through the examination of the performative histories of *creolization* that form the flesh and blood of the text.

MAKING MODERN SUBJECTS:
THE POLITICS OF MODERN GOVERNMENTALITY

The theme of governmentality emerges in Foucault's work after *Discipline and Punish* (1975), in a series of lectures between 1978 and 1979, and is used by him to link his interests on the "genealogy of the modern state," or rather the modern "state as a whole" and the "genealogy of the subject," the theme of his *History of Sexuality*.[75] In particular, governmentality, as conduct of conduct, is used to show the mutual constitution of the making of the subject (the ways that people conduct themselves, e.g., responsibility, ethics) and the formation of the state (forms of power and domination, e.g., sovereignty, disciplinary society), as married by the "technologies of the self" and "technologies of dominance."[76] Accordingly, as Lemke has stated: "All in all, in his history of governmentality Foucault endeavours to show how the modern sovereign state and the modern autonomous individual co-determine each other's emergence."[77]

Generally speaking, governmentality—as conduct of conduct—refers simply to broad issues of guidance and does not represent any particularly distinctive phenomenon as such. It is undertaken by individuals, households, groups, or institutions and involves a reflexive monitoring and rational structuring of control over a series of events or objects that enables a course of action to be realized or executed or makes a set of actions possible. It thus extends from exercises of self-control, management of households, and administration of states, to the spiritual directing of the soul. Modern governmentality, however, points historically to a "specific form of representation; [and] defines a discursive field in which exercising power is rationalized. This occurs, among other things, by the delineation of concepts, the specification of objects or borders, the provision of arguments and justifications, etc."[78] Discursive fields should, of course, not be conflated here with "thought, mind or the Subject" but be related to "limited practical domains that have their boundaries, their rules of formation, their conditions of existence."[79] Modern governmentality represents then a specific way of acting and is thus a generative mechanism—a law of tendency— for the ontological expression of a specific "form of social life" through new configurations of cultures of power.[80]

In elucidating the specific character of this *modern* political rationality, Foucault emphasizes that it entails a transformational discontinuity with a conception of the art of government centered around the "*sole interest of the prince* (sovereign) *as its object* and principle of rationality" (our emphasis). As Foucault explains, in this model of power's exercise of rule, or rather, how it might be carried on, the sovereign/prince stands in a "relation of singularity and externality, and thus of transcendence, to his principality . . . [the latter] understood as the prince's relation to what he owns . . . his territory and his subjects."[81] In this construal of sovereign power, the goal is thus to establish a radical line of discontinuity, an essential divorce between the exercise of power of the sovereign/head and any other kind of power exercised in the society/body. In contrast, the art of modern governmentality centers on a continuum of "objects," "in both an upwards and downwards direction," which are all married to a single rationality of government. This causes a shift of focus from the sovereign/head as the essential locus of power, and from the conception of power as one of "singularity and externality" in the exercise of rule, to the modern art of government focused on *each and all*—that is, the society/body as a family of individuals and citizens. This latter focus thus represented the introduction of "economy" into the space of power and with this shift came correlated "techniques of rationality" relating to the "government of the self" (technologies of the self) and "government of the other" (technologies of domination). Modern governmentality is therefore not just that which is identifiable through discursive texts but as a specific mechanism of power, *as guidance,* it is indissolubly implicated in nondiscursive practical activity.[82] In brief, as Aihwa Ong has recently summarized, modern governmentality "refers to the array of knowledges and techniques that are concerned with the systematic and pragmatic guidance and regulation of everyday conduct."[83]

This reconfiguration of knowledge-power involved in the emergence of possible forms of "the present," and related capacities to exercise place, clears the ground for different regimes of power to take hold, masked with their truth-effects or new categories of appropriate subject-being-in-the-world. Of course, the shift in political concern for the making of modern subjectivities relates ostensibly to the fostering of life, in its new forms, through biopolitical techniques targeting both the human species (as elaborated in its scientific and political categories) and its populations, as placed in modern spaces, as well as the body, and its individuals, as similarly placed. Or, as Foucault states, "modern man [becomes] an animal whose politics places his existence as a living being into question."[84] This regime of power furthermore sets off the modern dilemma, or double bind, of seeking to execute a form of institutionalized state power that is both individualizing and totalizing in its political effects. It should be noted here, though, that while these themes of "the political" have become prominent in contemporary political discourse, this "present politics" has already stimulated countering waves of post-political questioning.[85] It is vital to emphasize here, moreover, as Mitchell Dean does, that modern governmentality "*does not exhaust* the terrain of politics, but makes intelligible certain of its practical, technical and epistemic conditions of existence" (our emphasis).[86] This point is particularly well brought out by Donald Moore in his examination of the spatial struggles for place by the villagers in Kaerezi, but it is a point which also underlines much of the recent analysis of power in the postcolony, and of course this text's examination of the selective, and often critical, historical mo(ve)ments of *creolization* to the "changing same" spaces of modern times.[87] We highlight a few points of our approach to this complex process of "modern" translations of power/space/place and time below.

POWER AND ITS SUBJECTS:
THE MIMETIC PROCESSES OF
MASKING AND MASQUERADE

In this text, as well as in others concerned with the politics and processes of cultural change and social history, examinations of the selective historical engagements with modern cultures of power point to varied and complex processes of masking and masquerading at play.[88] Indeed, more generally, they point to dynamic processes of critical mimesis which involve "the act of producing a symbolic world, which encompasses both theoretical and practical elements."[89] Mimetic practices are thus more than imitation; as Quayson suggests, they reflect the imaginative and critical journeying for forms; a search moreover, as we have argued, that is concerned with the enablement of "proper presence."[90] In a similar vein, Aching has also emphasized the visual politics (shaping visibility and invisibility) that are at stake in the modes and strategies of representing through masking, pointing to how "masking practices negotiate degrees of recognition, misrecognition, and non-recognition between *masked subjects* and *viewing subjects*."[91] Accordingly, as Aching asserts, "Real, figurative, and rhetorical masks and masking devices maintain forms of (self) knowledge in abeyance. And because knowledge and ignorance do not exist in social isolation but in competing conditions . . . ways of seeing and masking are fundamentally socioeconomic and ethical concerns."[92]

These complex mimetic processes of masking and masquerading under the conditions of modern governmentality may be also seen as sustaining a home making (staking) liminal dialectic called forth through the "city–citizen" game. The concept of "home making" here operates in a parallel fashion to nation making, as it relates to, in Edensor's words, "the ways in which 'we makes ourselves at home' in the world according to social and aesthetic conventions about conviviality, domesticity and furnishing and decorating space."[93] A critical and deeply problematic element to this home-making practice, however, "includes the domestication of things and experiences from the external world, of otherness, so that a kind of vernacular curation takes place whereby items are assigned to places in the home. The distribution of 'foreign-ness' within domesticity is usually contained, rarely takes over the home, and is contextualized as *style*. The importation of exotic and unfamiliar objects and aesthetics is thereby incorporated to mark out difference, and operates as a form of distinction."[94] These aspects of homing bear significantly upon Creole practices under the "coloniality of power," as we highlight in chapter 3. Finally, we wish to highlight that in this "game" of homing modern powers, the exercises of power as "inseparable autonomies" between power and the subject provides the central masking trope for imaginations of, and desires for, individuality, "citizenness," and sovereignty.

The perspective of masking-masquerading thus forms a key emphasis for this book, with specific attention being placed on the state—qua institution as strategically caught up in these identity (or nonidentity) struggles for navigating and negotiating Creole subjectivities through the present, given that it seeks to combine "those two games, the city-citizen game and the shepherd-flock game"—in strategically sustaining itself in modernity.[95] This tendency in the modern state's practices reflects the ontological interpenetration of the state by both power and its subjects, even as it strategically acts as a mediator of their interplay. Accordingly, imagined modern states remain as "powerful sites of symbolic and cultural production that are themselves always culturally represented and understood in particular ways."[96] Or as Migdal would say, modern states express "state in society" relationships which are governed by the interaction of image and practice.[97]

This is readily seen in chapter 4, for example, where "Lucians" perform the state's representations of power and its subjects, even as they subvert its presentations in their critical mimesis of state space and subject place.

However, by virtue of experiencing social power within—as a representative and governor of "biopolitics" in the city-citizen game—and without—as the agent of modern social power in the shepherd-flock game—the modern state holds a strategic role not just in the mediation of the relationship between modern power and its subjects, given these two games, but also in the transformation of that relationship.[98] In particular, the strategies of the state in terms of "its survival and its limits on the basis of the general tactics of governmentality" will set in motion changes in states of consciousness and experiences,[99] which will disturb the nature of the "governmentalization of the state" and create tendencies for the reconfiguration of social power *in* the very processes of the state's governmentality tactics.[100] St. Lucia's transnational citizens, as discussed in chapter 5, provide an example of these processes of disturbance as these flexible citizens mediate the tactics of nation building, by processes of leaving and returning, staying and leaving. These "state in society" relationships are thus critical elements to grasping the tributaries of *creolization,* as situated processes of selective creation and cultural struggle for places and hence spaces.

Indeed, in generally interpreting these *creolization* processes, we wish to suggest here that agents, in general, are led to form their bodies, selves, and their state spaces, in their (un)making of modern subjects, through what may be called "mo(ve)ments of mimesis."[101] That is, through mimetic social mo(ve)ments, subjects are engaged in processes of negotiation, deploying representational and knowledge strategies of "masking and masquerading" in order to move (morph) their "state spaces," and related "subject places," for a sustainability of place, or for a proper "homing" of places.[102] But in this process they articulate both a *movement* of space and a *moment* of becoming (or not) out of time, in their search for form, or re/mappings of "the present," that promise "proper presence." The mimetic mo(ve)ments in such strategic exercises of making places—particularized by spaces, times, bodies, rhythms and places—thus constitute the basis for the journeying from place to place for homing modern freedoms.

THE ONTOLOGY OF GOVERNABLE SPACE
IN MAPPING THE PRESENT

In seeking to elucidate the "conditions of existence" informing modern *creolization* practices and experiences, we wish to now highlight the several ontological layers of this modern space of power. To this end, we find Nikolas Rose's specification of "governable spaces" useful as it allows one to elaborate certain further distinctions on the relation between space and place. As he points out, "The process of governing . . . does not just act on a pre-existing thought world with its natural divisions. To govern is to cut experience in certain ways, to distribute attractions and repulsions, passions and fears across it, to bring new facets and forces, new intensities and relations into being. This is partly a matter of time. . . . It is also a matter of space, of the making up of governable spaces: populations, nations, societies, economies, classes, families, schools, factories, individuals."[103] Governable spaces, he continues, are "modalities in which a real and material governable world is composed, terraformed and populated."[104]

In short, one may consider that productions of governable spaces are practical and political exercises engaged in making a topology of space, more or less consistent with the desired triangulations of (social) space. This topology of governable space thus speaks to a literal mapping and ostensive folding of the present, and is thus at the heart of projects to institutionalize virtual state systems, or state spaces, or rather mappings of the present. Of course, this is not simply an imposition of "spaces of power" on people; rather, any topology of space sought presupposes a duality of space for its very possibility of spatial expression. As Rose again emphasizes, "Governable spaces are not fabricated counter to experience; they make new kinds of experience possible, produce new modes of perception, invest percepts with affects, with dangers and opportunities, with saliencies and attractions."[105] Government thus only becomes operable through "component parts [that] are linked together in some more or less systematic manner by forces, attractions and coexistences."[106]

The duality of space provides the disjunctive space needed for the "writing" of present histories and the negotiated mapping of the present. These lived spaces of *creolization* processes produce what we refer to here as the typographies of place(s). These are expressive of the circuits of place (that is, appropriated space) that are achieved through translations of, and counter-

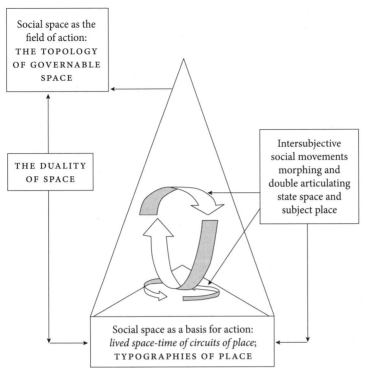

```
Social space as the
field of action:
THE TOPOLOGY
OF GOVERNABLE
SPACE
```

```
THE DUALITY
OF SPACE
```

```
Intersubjective
social movements
morphing and
double articulating
state space and
subject place
```

```
Social space as a basis for action:
lived space-time of circuits of place;
TYPOGRAPHIES OF PLACE
```

2   Governing space:
The dynamics of modern power given the Lefebvrian duality of social space

conducts to, topologies of governable space. Overall, this relation of forces entrenched in the duality of space produces a dynamic state system of cultural power that may be represented as a pyramid of social power / space. This pyramid is composed through structural, institutional, and intersubjective social powers (indicative of a stratified ontology of social space / power), and it is being continuously translated and morphed given the duality of space, as illustrated in figure 2.

The process of governing space may thus be represented as a "versatile power equilibrium" of strategical relationships, with the sociocultural practices of *creolization* being the means thereby for both sustaining and violating such contingent equilibria.[107] In other words, *creolization* processes enact and produce *historically contingent*, strategic, and complex modes of governmentality which tentatively establish strategic balances of power that redirect the morphogenesis of cultures of power, as well as remapping the present and its topologies of governable space. In the next section we present a model for exploring creole time on the move in order to highlight the temporalities that are being stitched together to engender these complex mo(ve)ments in *creolization* processes by developing a realist framework for social theory.

THE MORPHOGENESIS OF CULTURES OF POWER: MOVING PLACE THROUGH THE TIMES OF *CREOLIZATION*

In order to explore the analytics of this morphogenetics of cultures of power, we draw upon Margaret Archer's *Realist Social Theory,* where she has argued, deriving from the philosophical orientation of critical realism,[108] that in order to address the question of articulation between *the people* (persons qua subjects) and *the parts* (the conditions of social power for agents' social formation), it is necessary to maintain the notion of emergent properties at the level of agency and structure and hence subscribe to a model of complex ontological stratification of social life worlds. This allows, she argues, for a study of their dynamics of transformation and avoids collapsing into either models of individualism or holism for explaining social processes. In contrast, according to Archer, "the morphogenetic task is to supply an account of how the powers of the 'parts' condition the projects of the 'people'—involuntaristically but also nondeterministically, yet nonetheless with directionality."[109]

Her elaboration of several models on the morphogenetics of structure, culture, and agency develops upon the critical realist's Transformational Model of Social Activity (TMSA), introduced by Roy Bhaskar,[110] by deploying time to link structure and agency. In particular, her model of the process of morphogenetics is held to allow for the complexly time-structured and mediated ontological interplay between the parts (which she analytically separates into the Structural Emergent Powers (SEPS) of cultural and structural systems) and the people.[111] This culture-structure dualism in the model is treated as an analytical one. That is, Archer is only seeking to *analytically* separate a culture system as a source of representations or ideas, norms, or ethics from what is identified as the structural conditioning of material interests. This could be a useful strategy to detect the nuances of transformational dynamics (morphogenetics) in societies or social formations, but one should be vigilant in recognizing the ontological interdependencies present among structuring powers. In concrete analysis one is always dealing with processes of sociocultural interaction, her middle term in the morph relation, which addresses actual processes of change, or the exercise of social power through specific social relationships or transactions. To keep structure systems and culture systems analytically separate may, however, allow for a better conceptual grasp of the uneven, nonlinear, and entangled ways in which social changes are experienced. In the morphogenetic model, the analytical exercise involves moving from Phase 1 (structural emergent powers—conditioning) to Phase 2 (sociocultural interaction) to Phase 3 (structural elaboration–morphogenesis; and structural reproduction—morphostasis).

While one may still wish to engage Archer on her substantive arguments about the theories of the world and the nodes and modes of articulation taking place between persons, agents, collectivities, and structurally emergent properties that she has developed, her contributions, we believe, are critical for thinking through the relations between power and the subject. In particular, Archer's social models allow for an engagement with vital questions regarding how the relationship between Creole subjects and their social spaces is moved, reproduced, transformed, or morphed.

Grasping *creolization* processes through a cycle of morphogenesis involves an analytical breakdown of this multitemporal process into its three articulating and dynamic components. Figure 3 illustrates the temporalities effected in *creolization* practices. In emergent spatiotemporality, $T1$, there is the structural conditioning of emergent topologies of space entangling histories being fractured and weaved through incipient *creolization practices*. This liminal womb of time-space—paralleling Mbembe's "time of entanglement"[112]—represented through $T1$ expresses both an ontology of space being given for mapping the present, or situating cultural bodies and their places-in-time, as well as processes of emergent subjectifications. Yet even as these conditions secrete the orderings that are lived as constraints that enjoin, frame, shape, and fold into agents' complex and creative engagements with power, they do not determine the expressive capacities at play. This entanglement in, and partial conditioning by, emergent spatiotemporality stimulates a wrestling with the conditions for expressing place and moving one's place-in-time. Conceptually, this dynamic process is mapped through $T2$-$T3$ temporalities, which represents the double articulating liminal practices of *creolization* that are both disruptive and re/productive of ordering constraints in topologies of space. In particular, this liminal temporality speaks to the contesting wills to place embodied in the *creolization* projects of making (and unmaking) subjects and their historically specific mappings of the present. Accordingly, this spatiotemporal dimension of the process of creolization calls forth the limboing strategy of "making place" which is the basis for subjects negotiating their differences across the spaces of hegemony and its silences of nonidentity.[113] Limbo symbolizes here then the liminal processes of transformation by negotiating space through chains of power; of making space where there is little or none, and transforming constraint into degrees of freedom.[114]

The temporalities being effected in the $T1$-$T2/3$ cycle of social movement, or critical mimetic mo(ve)ments, are thus focused upon determinate exercises of power. These "time"-linked components in the morphogenesis process allows for understanding the differential temporalities inherent in the force relations through which agents are negotiating and navigating their "subjectifications" and "subjectivities." They also ensure against the reification of ontology while maintaining the emphasis on the complex ontological forces at play for shaping and expressing one's place in and through time.

Finally, the spatiotemporal tendencies being engendered through such complex processes of negotiating and navigating spaces of power press outward into the social world to find at least partial expression within the last spatiotemporal component of the process of morphogenesis, $T4$. This component represents the expressed processes of structural re/production and elaboration and transformation and accordingly secretes the effects of the ongoing re/formation and trans/formation of Creole subjectivities and subject powers. In this respect then, $T4$ embodies what may be termed "creolization effects" paralleling Foucault's "governmental effects," as it provides (partial) revelation or disclosure of the effects (and affects) being induced by the transformational activities of social agents given their post-Creole imaginations of freedom in search of "proper" place or presence. This "phase" thus analytically completes the morphogenetic cycle of *creolization* as the critical mimetic mo(ve)ments of modern cultures of power and relatedly creolized social powers and subjectivities. Modern *creolization* processes thus conceptualized may be roughly likened to the production of circuits of value, or Marxian M-C-M′ surplus value chains, but with a twist, as the social transfor-

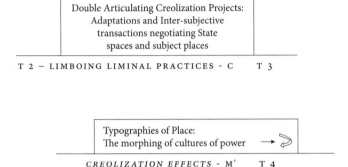

Topologies of Space:
The structural conditioning of
modern governmentality,
or the governmentality effect

T 1 – LEMBE - M

Double Articulating Creolization Projects:
Adaptations and Inter-subjective
transactions negotiating State
spaces and subject places

T 2 – LIMBOING LIMINAL PRACTICES - C   T 3

Typographies of Place:
The morphing of cultures of power

CREOLIZATION EFFECTS - M'   T 4

Source: This diagram represents a critical adaptation of Margaret Archer's model of the morphogensis of culture. The three overlapping phases in her model are T1: cultural conditioning; T2–T3: social-cultural interaction; and T4: cultural elaboration. See M. Archer, *Realist Social Theory: The Morphogenetic Approach* (Cambridge: Cambridge University Press, 1995), 193.

3   Temporalities in the morphogenesis of cultures of power

mations taking place are not exhaustively given through commodity chains per se but rather are being effected more generally and strategically through (and against) "modern" chains of spatial power, the catalysts for circuits of place.

In brief, then, as illustrated in figure 3, topologies of space, which are ordered in a complex situation of modern governmentality (M: metaphorically entailing a "Lembe" or ritual of marriage with power),[115] are morphed through multitemporal and double articulating liminal practices, or limboing strategical conducts (C) engaging concrete processes of selective creation and cultural struggle. This determines the morphing effect (M') on complex modern cultures, as produced by typographies of place. These time, space, place, and (cultural) body structuring dynamics entangled in, and being engendered through, the morph cycles of *creolization* processes exist as the constitutive elements that are being staked in our morphogenetic model of *creolization,* and hence are the elements at stake in the politics of *creolization* and its critical mimetic mo(ve)ments.

THE POLITICS OF THE CROSS:
MAKING PLACE IN THE ATLANTIC AND BEYOND

By way of summarizing our perspectives as laid out earlier, we believe that it may be useful to think of the *creolization* processes of "selective creation and cultural struggle" as articulating, so to speak, a "politics of the cross." In our model of *creolization*, the politics of making place, and relatedly space, in the world is thus pivotally engendered by the interaction between vertical demands on the subject-being-in-the-world that "exercise existence," as Mbembe would say, and the self's horizontal necessities for circuits of place, as expressed by the subject's double articulating double movements through and against imposing mappings of the present. This intersecting dynamic of vertical demands (the interpellation of subjects by state spaces-subject places) with horizontal necessities (the struggle for moving one's place-in-time by morphing cultures of power) combines then to re/constitute and re/produce the spatially and temporally complex politics of the cross. In this condition of entanglement, the cross symbolically expresses an ironic and paradoxical politics of differencing and *différance*, of staying and moving, of leaving and returning, in the sacred and profane politics of space and place. Accordingly, the relation of forces embedded in, and symbolically expressed through, the "politics of the cross" establishes an open-ended dynamic for morphing spaces (or cultures of power), for engendering circuits of place, and for sustaining hopes of "future times," as well as homely dwelling places given post-Creole imaginations of "proper presence."

Given the context of such complex and open systems, when empirically examining the interdependent and dynamic relationships implicated in *creolization*'s politics of place, one is forced to move beyond the confines of the Caribbean nation-states, if only (as a start) for the simple reason that reticulated Creole identities are produced and refurbished in and beyond Caribbean spaces. In this regard, though addressing particularly the production of British black identities, Barnor Hesse's analysis provides us with a useful ethnographic framework for formulating theoretical propositions regarding *creolization*'s mediations of transnationalisms and vice versa, by seeing these mediations as diverse trajectories of recursive movements of people, antiphonal cultural forms, and bonds (forced and free). To elaborate, Hesse cites three spheres through which black British identity is refurbished, beyond the parochial British templates. First, through the "migratory orbit of familial ethnicities," as "migratory subjectivities are regularly animated and ethnicized by communication or involvement with the diasporic locations of economic investments, cultural belongings and political loyalties."[116] Second, "as antiphonal forms of commodification in popular culture, through music, film, literature, sport, fashion or the vernacular," and third, through forms "of political, cultural and intellectual relations of elective affinities."[117] In following through on this, and as a way of grounding *creolization* studies, these three spheres, we believe, may be used to investigate the sites of *creolization*'s global articulations. At stake in these articulations are our Creole subjects, routing through modern space, yet with cultural bodies rooting in the multiplicity of diasporic habitus that they compose, recompose, and transpose for the making and unmaking of their times, spaces, places, and (cultural) bodies. We turn now to the ethnographic and historical explorations of these subjects in their liminal and critical mimetic mo(ve)ments negotiating and navigating space and place, as they move through the seas of present hi/stories.

THREE

DECENTERING THE "DIALECTICS OF RESISTANCE" IN THE CONTEXT OF A GLOBALIZING MODERN

Afro-Creoles under Colonial Rule

If the global really is, part of the constitution of, and therefore inside, the local, then the definition of the specificity of the local place cannot be made through counterposition against what lies outside; rather it must be made precisely through the particularity of the interrelations with the outside. It is, if you like, an extroverted notion of the identity of place, an internationalist constitution of the local place and its particularity.[1]

The Work of a Slave: But how does one get from the colony to "what comes after"?[2]

MUCH RESISTANCE-CENTERED research about Caribbean peoples, ensconced within cultural traditions not easily described by notions of Western and non-Western, overlooks or critically downplays the practices of accommodation, "dwelling," or homing and its powers for freedom(s).[3] Yet this position seems hardly justified given the "double articulations" through which the histories of "the local" and "the global" have been made. At a minimum, then, as argued in the first two chapters, in order to more adequately elucidate the processes by which Caribbean peoples substantively transform their contexts of being-in-the-world, one needs to more closely examine these political dynamics through an optic that can better link place, space, and the morphogenesis of modern cultures of power. Indeed, many valuable insights into the processes and politics of making modern freedom will be overshadowed unless one deploys, so to speak, a "double vision" of lived experiences, one that can be sensitive to the duality of space, and perforce its double movements, in the making(s) of both (subject) place and (state) space.

Both C. L. R. James's notion that the slave plantation was a prototype of the modern factory as well as Sidney Mintz's idea of Caribbeans as Westernized subjects not only underscore how troubling are the distinctions Western and non-Western for treating Creole subjects but also highlight the entanglement of the identity and power of "the global" in the practices of "the local." Accordingly, the politics of accommodation, or, as Sheller comments, Afro-Creoles' struggles for "homes-in-migration in ongoing processes of 're-homing' place" and their *home staking* struggles for "generating new modes of dwelling with difference" are therefore ineluctably and critically engaged with a global politics of space.[4]

In particular, the practices and politics of accommodation, dwelling, or homing may be seen as the processes of a critical mimesis articulating a liminal politics of disarticulating and rearticulating given places, given spaces, and their cultures of power. It is through such limboing practices that Afro-Creoles under colonial rule (in its various guises) work to effect, to borrow an apt phrase from Boisseron, a "Creole line of escape" from existing states of "unhomeliness."[5] These particular ideas, however, have scarcely been explored and integrated into the investigations of the lived practices of Caribbeans as conducted through their moments of fractured modernity and their double movements of identity, space and place.

In contrast to my argument that one needs to more deeply examine the politics and practices of accommodation, and thus to ferret out the nuances and political effects of Afro-Creoles' limboing struggles for place, dwelling, or a homing of freedom, there has been a marked shift within the critical debates on the process of creolization toward emphasizing the fundamental primacy of a dialectics of resistance. In particular, what tends to be stressed here is that a politics of ostensive opposition and conflict (as reflected, for instance, in Puri's recent arguments in the *Caribbean Postcolonial*), or indeed a high politics of resistance for (ultimately) realizing some kind or level of absolute transcendence from the system, has been and must always be central to, and privileged for, the forging of Caribbean places and freedoms. Accordingly, Caribbean places have been considered sites of ideological, economic, and sociocultural formations, where identities are forged essentially in contestation.[6] Richard Burton, for example, though drawing upon the framework of Michel de Certeau, still opts to define "resistance" as sets of oppositional practices which rely on sources *outside* of the hegemonic culture. This is contrasted with oppositional practices which rely on the system and hence are seen as ultimately reinforcing the dominant culture. These latter practices are described by Burton as simply "opposition," in contrast to de Certeau's own treatment of them as "resistance." He then concludes that Caribbean culture is simply *oppositional*, since Caribbeans have so "internalized" the colonial-derived culture that they draw upon it even when they appear rebellious. Burton, however, also calls attention to the "continuum of overlapping and competing cultural forms, all of them creole or creolized, 'Euro-Creole,' 'Meso-Creole' (the 'middle culture,' corresponding to the mesolect of 'middle language,' of the free colored classes and certain sections of the slave elite), and 'Afro-Creole.'" He emphasizes that "these indicate no more than 'zones' on the cultural continuum, each differentiated from its neighbors and competitors rather than totally different, and each further subject to a range of important internal variations,"[7] highlighting the range of spaces and cultural repertoires within which Caribbeans maneuver.

Given this ontological appreciation of the pervasiveness of blurred lines and boundaries in sociocultural spaces, however, one wonders whether it is still useful to continue to conceptualize the political spaces for these relatively flexible traditions through a Cartesian logic that stresses transcendence and separateness, total insideness and outsideness. Indeed, Burton's distinction between resistance and opposition seems to be justifiable only in the context of a tacit ontology of social history that works itself out through an inexorable, teleological, and binaristic logic of dialectical resistance. This social model of freedom expects that practices of freedom, if they are to be truly and ultimately effective, must engage in a high politics of resistance, or a Gramscian "war of position" for arriving at the ideal of absolute transcendence, *the end* of history. Unfortunately, this model, when adopted as a critical lens for understanding historical practices and processes, obscures or misses out on the paradoxes and ironies of actual processes of constructing hi/stories and freedoms. Moreover, its fundamentalist political plot transforms the open-ended performative practices of freedom for opaque futures into mere media for the inexorable unfolding of a logic of structural and cultural conflict.

Perhaps, instead, it might be far more useful to stay with the insight, as

Karen Fog Olwig does, of addressing a somewhat fluid, entangled, and border-crossing cultural politics that draws upon multiple cultural traditions, or rather, as Gilroy suggests, "living memories," when interrogating the lived practices of freedom of Caribbean people.[8] Thus, even as Caribbeans struggled ostensibly against colonialism's and postcolonialism's authoritarian, racist, classist, and sexist expressions, these masks of hegemonic power are critically engaged and transformed not so much from *outside* contexts of power but rather *through* its critical appropriation, in the place-making exercises of *différance*. In other words, a politics of resistance is ineluctably expressed through Caribbean people's practices of accommodation which entail temporal and spatial double articulations of power in a liminal politics of critical mimesis. From this perspective, Afro-Creole practices of freedom are interpreted not as an autonomous *will to transcend* but rather as a *will to place* in homing modern freedoms.

An important segue into this research on the politics of accommodation is the argument by Aníbal Quijano and Immanuel Wallerstein that the resistance of the Americas against the globalizing tendencies of capital and of the interstate system is not necessarily framed by the sociocultural reservoir of a traditionally grounded historicity but by the "flight to modernity." This is an important perspective, yet this "flight," seems to be too narrowly interpreted as a sheer pragmatic or reactive historical necessity. This narrow reading is evident from their view that "the flight to modernity" came about largely because the Americas were unlike the peripheral zones of Europe, where "the strength of the existing agricultural communities and of their indigenous nobilities was considerable," allowing them to frame or structure their cultural resistance in terms of a certain historicity.[9]

For Wallerstein and others, the widespread destruction of the indigenous populations of the Americas, and with them their fabled historicities, *forced* a mass recourse to (a sanitized Euro-) modernity. All subjects of the Americas therefore were incorporated into a system of ideological cultural and economic production that ethnicized populations hierarchically and promised abundance via material consumption and, though reinforcing various social and political inequalities, touted liberal democracy and equality.[10] Later, in the postwar period, when the United States assumed the mantle of a global hegemonic power, its ideological, cultural, and political fundamentals became integral to the modern world economy. Despite advances in material production, the tenets of coloniality continued to hold sway in this reorganized social order. It thus seemed as if "Americanity was the erection of a gigantic ideological overlay to the modern world. It established a series of institutions and worldviews that sustained the system, and it invented all this out of the American crucible."[11]

While this analysis carries with it a certain erasure of the degrees of freedom, or difference, at play in the hegemonic "mapping of the present," it highlights nonetheless the violence and disruptiveness of the world in which people were caught up and through which they would seek to chart their place, their subjectivities, and their imaginations of post-Creole spaces. Our interpretations of the processes of *creolization* offered earlier indeed limit the sense in which one may proffer an (absolute) "outside" to those entangled in this incipient modernity after being caught up in the violent vortex of its formation. Nonetheless, histories were disrupted, as well as prior dwelling places, in the formation of the Americas which induced the stitching together of heterogeneous times, spaces, and bodies in the complex articulations of modern "insides" and imagined other sides, marking or mapping the spaces and times of entanglement. Moreover, the diverse, often promiscuous spaces and sociocultural practices that were being produced through the processes of uprootings and rehomings in the context of modern space represented contesting possibilities (however partially exercised) that challenge the future of these Atlantic spaces and places. Accordingly, as John Thornton points out, countercultural modernities have come from within an Atlantic world space whose seams folded back into Africa but yet go well beyond that continent.[12] Therefore, one can neither entertain notions of peasants and plantations, colonial and anticolonial, nor explore African versus European constructions nor, for that matter, Caribbean–East Indian, Chinese, or other Creole constructions without referring to the constructedness of their dialogical vertical and horizontal connections that have induced the diverse "flights" to particular modernities.[13]

These observations on the bricolage that is modernity's space serve here as the constitutive backdrop for this chapter's exploration of "rural," or rather land-based, working peoples' practices of freedom under colonialism. These practices of freedom and their politics of accommodation or dwelling are specifically discussed through the notion of "citizenness."[14] "Citizenness" refers to the struggle for humanity, dignity, economic survival, a place in and through the world economy, in short, all the interrelated processes that implicate "the flight to modernity," a rehoming of place, and the development of a creolized identity. I apply this construct of citizenness by treating it as a limboing counterconduct of modern power and for liminal movements within and across power relations. Thus, through limboing strategies land-based working peoples aimed at moving themselves through colonial and other spaces, transversally challenging the cultures of power even as they secreted familiar Atlantic symbols of respectability. The limboing required in founding practices of resistance is always open, that is, open to leading to unexpected elsewheres and even unforeseeably to their own forms of subversions. In what follows, I examine these critical mimetic mo(ve)ments that Caribbeans were engaged in, through their politics of accommodation with modern power, in order to go beyond the strictly legal and political struggles over space that were (and still are) integral to smallholder life under colonialism in a dynamic global context.

Situated by their forced exile from the soils of prior dwelling and displaced from the West's institutional and formal Old World historicity, Caribbean smallholders and working peoples generally used transitional mimetic props, sometimes linked to colonial practices and identities. And in this way they refashioned hi/stories and futures, in an ongoing process of rehoming present places. Such strategies of dwelling express a paradoxical politics of both placement and mobility, staying and leaving, attachment and detachment, of remembering and dreaming, all with a critical consciousness that reconstructed selves through the present spaces of Atlantic modernity. The histories of the Afro-Creoles did not therefore provide a clear track of Creole escape that they could turn back to, as that history had had its course irreversibly drawn into the circuits of the dense and turbulent seas of present hi/stories-in-the-world. Theirs was thus a "past" that was thorny, reminisced, imagined, constantly recast discursively, dependent on the nature and quality of Caribbeans' present encounters. It was not a past immediately or directly recoverable for mounting a transcendent flight from modernity, even though it served as a past re-membering for struggles against modernity's offensive political projects for homing place in violent mappings of the present that (dis)located Afro-Creoles' place-in-time. In citing Caribbean working peoples' various socioeconomic and sociocultural strategies, we can therefore expect to find evidences of conflicted yet accommodating and re-membering colonial selves.[15]

Colonial plantation practices as well as the practices of the colonized in the Caribbean drawing particularly on developments in St. Lucia and Jamaica reflect the complexity of this struggle for citizenness, which is part of, though often antithetical to, global Western developments. Take Jamaica, for instance; incorporated into the world economy since the mid-seventeenth century, it has had an uninterrupted history as a sugar-producing colony of England. Its evolution closely followed Lloyd Best's model of a pure plantation economy, with its rise and decline of sugar production.[16] St. Lucia, on the other hand, caught in the rivalry between England and France, became an English colony after 1830.[17] Although the British slave trade was abolished in 1807, slavery persisted in the British territories until 1834, thus the rise of St. Lucia coincided with the maturation and decline of Jamaica as a sugar producer. Constrained by the abolition of the slave trade and bankrupted as a result of the economic crossfire between rival colonial powers, the sugar industry in postemancipation St. Lucia grew in spurts according to a sharecropping system known as *metayage*, which revitalized exports. These developments contradict the argument that "the fabric of St. Lucian society has not been patterned by a close relationship with the outer world"; at best such an argument is misleading.[18] St. Lucian society was indeed defined and reconstructed by its relation to the international world, which underscores Tomich's point, though it was made in the context of the French West Indian colony of Martinique, that "instead of approaching world, national, and local dimensions as discrete empirical entities, it [is better to treat] them as mutually formative parts of a larger whole."[19]

Living in the spaces and "times of entanglement," colonial working peoples led complex lives that cannot be understood solely in terms of (usually plantation) resistance, as the conditions for any possible resistance rested in their "modes of dwelling." Indeed, while they resisted some encirclement by plantations, their lack of, and desire for, economic options drew them into larger systems of domination and promise and led them to adopt and adapt various strategies in their quest for citizenness. Moreover, as noted in chapter 1, the plantation was not the only locale of their experiences. In all their locales, however, they maneuvered variously through given structures of existence, in ways that reinforced or altered given representations of being, given their pursuits after post-Creole imaginations of home spaces or "proper presence" that were rooted/routed through their ideas of a better life. These imaginations were at play even as, or rather especially as, they engaged in a politics of accommodation with the given notions of "the good life" circulating in the colonial world economy and space. Undoubtedly, working peoples resented colonial strictures that diminished their economic, political, and cultural options, but they also engaged with elite definitions of respectability, and many even craved it. At times they used such standards as a polyvalent measure of self-worth. This partially explains why St. Lucians reproduced and satirized representations of the monarchy and state institutions in their festivals, reinvesting them with new, ambivalent meanings but alerting the populace to their existence and power, and thus assisting in reproducing their rules. The establishment of friendly societies, veritable cooperative insurances against misfortunes, also was instrumental in the forging of their humanity through a palpable circumvention of those institutions which excluded them.

Opposition to these institutions of discrimination as well as to the states' policies of exclusion during the colonial period organized rural working peoples of the Caribbean in ways that produced an overlapping of economic strata. Thus, incipient smallholders, members of the black intelligentsia, professionals, artisans, and wage laborers all protested against colonial rule, protests that were shaped by colonialism's forces to distance, marginalize, trivialize, racialize, and decertify them as citizens. Working peoples struggled against the authoritarian tendencies of the colonial institutions in order to protect or secure their socioeconomic, political, economic, and cultural practices. And whether as remnants of African culture, adaptations, or syncretisms, though often inexact and ambiguous, Afro-Creole working peoples' rehoming movements were practices of freedom that often forged cultural identity, as distinctive cultural styles based on a critical mimesis of the practices of the elite. Sometimes a mimicry of "elite" culture, sometimes a parody, sometimes a contestation, such practices were also part of a globally constituted local context. But even though their practitioners were systematically denied an equality of humanity, as well as the more humane material benefits of modernity, they nevertheless desired and pursued the benefits of place in their quest for belonging, and in their quest for homely places and spaces. Faced with these practices and politics of accommodation, especially when such groups became politicized or rejected certain policies, the colonial authorities had to respond despite their undisguised disregard for these rural working peoples.

That these complex cultural and economic forms often expressed overt resistance is only part of the more complex story of Afro-Creoles' liminal politics across spaces "here and there." As emerging "world citizens," navigating and negotiating their place in modern space, Caribbeans strategized using available means, creolized techniques of freedom fashioned by custom and immediate necessity but not always "locally" generated.[20] The construction and shaping of citizenness was never a secure shelter for working peoples, however, as they had to "suffer for territory" in the processes of rehoming place and thus had to deal with the vagaries and vagueness of their place in modern space. This included responding to the intensely erratic and uncertain quality of global capitalist relations, particularly as regards agriculture via plantations. But the desire for citizenness, which was attached to both their stakes in homing place as well as their imaginations of post-Creole home spaces, not only drew many smallholders away from the plantation but also shaped their future participation in global commerce, trade, and culture, formally and informally.

Finally, because the colonial state exercised its powers to shape various economic and cultural options, how Caribbeans reacted to these options or themselves sought in proactive ways to refashion their modes of dwelling in the context of global capital accumulation and processes of cultural re/production bespeaks the changing shape of citizenness (state spaces, subject places) and processes of *creolization*. To use Gilroy's deft phrase, the "antagonistic indebtedness" of the Caribbean to the West,[21] and, I should add, of the West to the Caribbean (though this is not a point I wish to pursue here), leads Caribbeans to ambivalently embrace a style of Westernness, in a space which paradoxically inscribes Caribbean Creole subjects as being at once "inside" and "outside" of the spaces of the modern. This is a situation which has increasingly led to an acknowledgment of the plurality and nonlinearity of spatial and temporal processes in social life worlds, as researchers confront the limitations of the constructs of "society," "globalization's globality," and "culture."[22] Framed by these concerns, using oral, historical, archival, and secondary accounts of these pluralities, I examine the economic paths smallholders followed: the tradition of family or customary land tenure and the substance of select cultural performances in public festivals, in which cultural and economic components mix indistinguishably.

THE SCHOLARLY LURE OF RESISTANCE:
ROMANCING THE PEASANT

Researchers are fascinated with Caribbean smallholders, also called peasants, who for them embody the authentic spirit of Caribbean society. Whether in Jamaica, St. Lucia, Guyana, or Carriacou, oppositional chronicles of so-called peasants under colonial regimes abound.[23] These smallholders receive loud praise for the near-revolutionary roles they played during the colonial period, but thereafter there is silence. In the colonial period they are viewed as vibrant and resistant, makers of alternative economic and cultural systems. In the postcolonial period, their militancy is often questioned, attributed in part to the migration of leadership to urban areas and to contemporary efforts to resist peasantization.[24]

Although the expansion of European capitalism created the Caribbean, Caribbean "peasantry" is quite unlike its Western European namesake.[25] Caribbean "peasants" reputedly originated through a slave labor process, not through a free proprietorship system, as in most Western European societies. During the postemancipation period, peasants were "villagers" living on the outskirts of the plantations, and their decline was attributed to the restoration of plantation production and the restrictive role of government policies. They were reconstituted, "becoming peasants in some kind of resistant response to an externally imposed regimen," and their emergence was "simultaneously an act of Westernization and an act of resistance."[26]

Because the so-called peasantry emerged from the plantation labor process, we are persuaded to track its emergent identity along this trajectory, which, to its credit, highlights the former slaves' agency in shaping their own present and future. An unfortunate outcome of this trajectory is the transhistoricizing and essentializing of the smallholder's emergence so pervasive in the work of plantation economy theorists, even as other analysts highlight the internal differences that distinguish members of the post-emancipation smallholding stratum.[27] Often disregarded also is the influence of the world economy, in which the state, through its institutional appearances, shapes and reshapes the conditions under which rural Caribbeans and their diverse cultural practices are constituted. Neither peasant, capital, nor colonial powers respected the geographical edges constituting the colonial spaces of authority, and, in their own way, they manipulated their meaning. Nevertheless, these issues remain insufficiently explored in

Caribbean studies, in relation to identities, notions of resistance, and Afro-Caribbean culture.

Specific pronouncements on culture in the Caribbean evince a similar shortsightedness. They isolate "peasant" practices, highlighting either the African dimensions or the creolized forms and read these solely as expressions of resistance to dominant Eurocentric ideologies or practices.[28] They speak of "peasant cultures" that resist and adapt but they fail to explore the mechanisms and dynamics, or rather entanglement, inherent in new and reconstituted practices, a tendency of resistance studies generally. As Abu Lughod argues,

> Despite the considerable theoretical sophistication of many studies of resistance and their contribution to the widening of our definition of the political, it seems to me that because they are ultimately more concerned with finding resistors and explaining resistance than with examining power, they do not explore as fully as they might the implications of the forms of resistance they locate.[29]

In addition to bolstering an analysis of resistance by considering the relations of power itself, one might also examine in detail the resistors' lives. A careful analysis of resistant cultural expressions must ask, furthermore, resistance in relation to what and whom? To which aspects of power and with what liminal effects on the smallholders' identity vis-à-vis "others," each other, other groups, other places, spaces, given the specific configurations of symbolic, structural, and institutional resources, at play in these relations?

Though these economic and culturally resistant expressions are weighted with political intent, to borrow Bhabha's words, they are "an ambivalence produced within the rules of recognition of dominating discourses as they articulate the signs of cultural difference and reimplicate them within the deferential relations of colonial power-hierarchy, normalization, marginalization, and so forth."[30] As an example of this phenomenon, Bhabha recounts how the Bible is selectively incorporated into the Indians' world. As did slaves, Homi Bhabha's Indians sift, select, and reject on the basis of their own cultural proscriptions, thus destabilizing the "God-Englishman equivalence."[31] However negating the colonial project was, Indians (like the slaves) become, wittingly or unwittingly, partial to the missionaries' point of view. They must accept the Bible before they can select what they want out of it, and because the Bible does not entirely conflict with the Indians' own particularities, they are free to absorb it. In a very different anecdote, Mintz points out similarly how monolithic notions of resistance are challenged: "The cook of the master's family, that faithful lady who prepared the meals three times a day, sometimes put ground glass in the food of her diners. But she had to become the cook before this option became available. What I mean to say, of course, is that the idea of resistance is really very complicated, ideological considerations aside."[32]

The inherent complexity of resistance is therefore embedded within processes of citizenness, or making place, which in the Caribbean emerged within a context of several presences, not least a *présence neo-Europeene*, which accommodated, made use of, even as it ultimately derided other presences such as the *présence neo-Africaine* in the context of Americanity.[33] The *présence neo-Europeene* is self-evident. The *presénce Africaine* requires the Caribbean to be seen as part of the Americas, a site of capitalist, non-capitalist, and ideological production in a hierarchical coloniality.[34] This coloniality assumed a particularly violent form in the Americas due to the widespread destruction of indigenous communities and the forced displacement of Africans to the region, thereby dramatically limiting the possibilities for basing a resistance on local historical communities. Thus, as Quijano and Wallerstein argue, resistance was less likely to be framed in the claims of historicity than in the flight forward toward a certain kind of "modernity."[35] For example, various sorts of racial categorizations that came into being in the Americas did not exist prior to the modern world: "They are part of what make up Americanity and have become the cultural staple of the entire world-system."[36] Yet one should add that parochial Western values related to citizenship and gendered citizenness (intersecting processes), with their derivative notions and practices of class and respectability, were likewise in a process of morphogenesis when conveyed and practiced locally, or when mimetically recycled within and against their original pretexts. What I am emphasizing here is the view that the peoples of the Caribbean, even in their flights to modernity, were productive of ongoing cultural difference, and indeed of an unmanageable presencing of subject bodies and identities, through their everyday yet extraordinary practices of making place in the hope of recalibrating and transfiguring mappings of the present.

Or, as alternatively expressed by Gupta and Ferguson, one should assume "that the identity of a place emerges by the intersection of its specific involvement in a system of hierarchically organized spaces with its cultural construction as a community or locality."[37] So, too, the identities of its citizens, albeit more expressive of "cultural styles," namely, mimetic signifying practices and processes transversing boundaries of place and space. To see otherwise is to fall prey to constructions that sharply distinguish the global from the local, treating the latter as a pristine site distinct from globalized influences and, in the case of the Caribbean, falsely viewing the local as overwhelmingly dominated by practices occurring on plantations, the wall against which all resistance seems to echo.

DOMINATION, COLONIAL PREROGATIVES, AND THE CONDITIONS OF FLIGHT WITHIN MODERNITY

Much has been written about planters' and freed persons' competing claims over the terms and conditions of the latter's labor and about the biases of the colonial state toward their economic and cultural practices. Here, I summarize the more salient points in order to demonstrate that local resistance against coloniality, which in itself constituted a face of modernity, consisted of a flight to modernity that engaged the market at a global level.

Though early colonialists were openly resistant to the Caribbeans' economic and cultural politics of liminal and mimetic mo(ve)ments, they accommodated many of them. Central to colonial ideology was the maintenance of plantation agriculture over smallholder farming. In Jamaica, for example, the crown colony government of 1865 claimed that it would arbitrate relations between antagonistic racial groups, protecting them from each other.

The impartiality of rule claimed by the colonial authorities was never realized. Land and taxation policies under crown colony rule were a continuation of those which prevailed under the planter-dominated government. The colonial regime effectively crushed the smallholders, while strongly supporting the planters and their plantations. According to Roy Augier, "The money spent on the crops of the small cultivator, the time and energy spent on his problems were as nothing compared with what was lavished on plantation agriculture,"[38] true for much of the Caribbean. As a result, whenever possible, freed persons acquired plots of land and used them to restructure their relations with the planters and plantation production. One way was to partially or completely withhold their labor power; another was to select the plantations they would or would not serve.[39] Because plantations were labor-intensive enterprises linked to the global circuit of capital accumulation, these acts were a threat, or at least were perceived as such by planters and colonials. To retaliate, "[they] turned to legislation to compel the labour that they failed to exact on the estates. Through a variety of laws dealing with vagrancy, tenancy, the recovery of small debts, fishing, and peddling, the Assembly tried to strengthen the hands of the employers and at the same time to restrict the opportunities of alternative employment."[40] By becoming smallholders, the freed persons circumscribed the power of the colonial authorities and planters, who required a class of proletarians, ready for work on plantations. But how far did the status as smallholders remove freed people from practices of domination? What kind of communities did they set up? What economic and cultural practices did they follow? How and in what ways did these practices sustain, reproduce, or disturb elements of coloniality?

STRUGGLING TO PARTICIPATE DIRECTLY IN WORLD ACCUMULATION PROCESSES

In his *Notebook III*, Marx joined the debates regarding postslavery developments, highlighting the labor situation in the West Indies. He wrote that former slaves were interested in their own welfare, observing that they greet,

> the planters' impending bankruptcy with an ironic grin of malicious pleasure, and even exploit their acquired Christianity as an embellishment for this mood of malicious glee and indolence. They have ceased to be slaves, but not in order to become wage labourers, but instead, self sustaining peasants working for their own consumption, because autonomous wealth as such can exist only either on the basis of direct forced labour, slavery, or indirect forced labour, wage labour.[41]

The former slaves' reluctance to function as poorly paid wage labor for any plantation, the existence of significant amounts of abandoned land, the mobility that migration offered, and the repressive measures adopted by the planter class to create proletarian labor with minimal access to the means of production led to new overlapping interrelated forms of production and to new social relationships. Because smallholders emerged when the planter class and colonial representatives sought to preserve the plantation as the preferred mode of agricultural production, they faced tremendous pressure in their quests to be independent of the plantation or to engage it in new ways. Examining varied forms of labor and production helps therefore to explain the socioeconomic or material ways in which citizenness was pursued, and to see how smallholders attempted to reorganize their households and their agricultural production in relation to the existing order.

Smallholders in Jamaica, for the most part, entered multiple arrangements to strategize their relations with the plantation. In the period following emancipation, three overlapping strata were created: "those who owned and worked freeholds, and were employers themselves, small freeholders who as well as cultivating subsistence depended on the plantations for employment and those who continued to labour on estates while renting cottages and provision grounds from estate owners."[42] It is the first two tendencies identified by Hall and others that have been the focus of several works documenting the rise of an "independent" smallholder class.[43] These smallholders emerged through their own efforts, purchasing land despite the planters' attempts to block sales. Others squatted on available unoccupied lands. Sometimes churches, which wanted to create fully independent smallholders so that each could "go to any estate he pleases to work and to return to his home and family when he has fulfilled as a hireling his day's employ," purchased land for resale to its members, Baptists, for instance.[44] Nevertheless, full independence and control over economic options were exceptionally difficult, if not impossible, to attain. The great majority of the former slaves who fled the plantation continued to depend on it in various ways and degrees for their livelihood,[45] leading to an existence that has been referred to as a hybrid, "neither peasant nor proletariat," and which Rodney, probing Guyana's history, referred to more broadly as "working people."[46]

Despite such difficulties, and under its stimulus, there emerged throughout the Caribbean, a substantial body of diverse subsistence cultivators, producing for the domestic market. In 1890 in Jamaica 55 percent of all agricultural output was attributed to smallholder production.[47] Smallholders were the primary cultivators of ground provisions produced for the domestic market.[48] Smallholders were also involved in manufacturing crude sugar for the domestic market. In 1870, for example, the consumption of sugar in the local market reached 6,000 tons.

On both islands, smallholders were known for mixed cultivation practices. In Jamaica they grew arrowroot, logwood, and coffee, and the cultivation of these crops increased throughout the 1850s. Much like today's informal-sector traders, smallholders manipulated production in order to exploit market fluctuations. Thus "the years which brought a decline of arrowroot also brought an increase in the production of lime juice and a new development in the growth of bananas."[49] Despite political marginalization and legal landlessness, smallholders were able to survive by becoming wage laborers, producing for the domestic and export market and pursuing whatever else was available through migration.[50]

EMBRACING THE WORLD STAGE:
FROM SMALLHOLDERS TO CONTRACT FARMERS

The late nineteenth century witnessed the decline of the planter class and Britain's diminishing worldwide hegemony, a transformation in the condition of colonial modernity. The rise of the United States as a dominant economic and political power created a new environment in which new or reconstituted forms of agricultural production flourished. In Jamaica, barely twenty years after emancipation, smallholders became contract farmers of bananas.[51] They resisted ties to many plantations. By setting up modes of existence independent of the plantation, they worked themselves into the networks of wider market systems which not only fostered newer forms of socioeconomic and cultural dependence but also made possible the realization of a particular grasp of citizenness.[52] A different smallholder stratum emerged among newer forms of agency. Its members became New World subjects more directly engaged in world economic processes, from which only a few would significantly benefit.

The emergence of the banana trade in Jamaica signaled smallholders' maturation as producers of export crops. By 1900, bananas were a major export crop, thanks to the persistence of smallholders and the financial backing of new entrepreneurs.[53] Members of smallholder households cultivated 80 percent of the crops intended for the United States on plots of land covering less than ten acres, and those households were prosperous.[54] According to Thomas Holt, "The number of bank depositors and their total savings increased from 238 with £5,000 in 1880 to 778 with £10,155 in 1889, representing a 100 percent increase in the value of the deposits and better than 200 percent in depositors. Much of that growth came from small depositors, which suggests a more prosperous peasant class."[55] Though most smallholders cultivated freeholds, this group also included tenant farmers. The classes overlapped considerably, and production locations were inconstant. To be sure, there was transformation, but for many, the transition from smallholder production for the domestic market to production for the export market was short-lived. According to Holt, "One result of the increased demand by estates for property suitable for bananas was that buying or renting their own plots became more difficult for peasant growers. By the 1890s land rental rates in Portland soared to twenty to twenty-four shillings per acre per year, driving many peasant producers to become tenants to Baker or some other estate owner."[56]

Large-scale planters, competing for land, squeezed smallholders out, forcing them to become wage workers on banana properties or to turn to other types of work in the colony or elsewhere. Internal and external migratory movements took peasants to distant rural areas, towns, and other Caribbean locations like Cuba, Costa Rica, Panama, and, later, to the United States and the United Kingdom. The quest for livelihood and citizenness took Jamaican smallholders beyond the geographical confines of the rural and urban Caribbean to other parts of the expanding world economy which benefited from variegated labor and entrepreneurship.

CREATING A SPACE FOR GETTING TO ANOTHER PLACE WITH *METAYAGE*

In the transition to free labor, St. Lucia, a sugar-producing colony since 1807, experienced labor shortages. Indeed in the immediate postemancipation period, the island's economic collapse appeared even more imminent than Jamaica's. Although the sugar industry grew significantly from 1842 to 1883, severe indebtedness and land scarcity on the island forced planters to establish the *metairie* or *metayage* production system (a form of sharecropping) in the 1840s and 1850s. The decline of the sugar industry in St. Lucia, unlike other Caribbean islands, gave rise to such new social relations between sugar planters and freed peoples.[57] *Metayage* created the illusion of an equality of mutual dependence, though in reality it favored those who owned the land on which crops were grown.[58] Despite this unequal situation, some small-holders were able to exploit the system and became small farmers producing for export and the domestic market. According to Marshall,

> [The] small peasant sector continuously displayed resourcefulness and some innovation as it tried to develop a survival economy or a "counter-plantation" system. It expanded small manufactures (charcoal, hoe sticks, farine manioc); it consolidated the logwood industry; it kept up the cultivation of cocoa before its potential as a second cash crop was recognized by planters after the 1850s; it captured a share of the local market for cane syrup by developing "lilliputian" cane mills; it expanded the domestic food supply. But its full potential could never be realized because the restriction on land settlement and discriminatory taxation of peasants' land and produce severely constrained its growth and activity.[59]

In this account, Marshall fails to dwell on the class differentiation taking place among smallholders, a process similar to that in Jamaica, which re-shaped the modern conditions under which the smallholders and working people operated and coloniality performed. Many, including the better-off smallholders, shed their dependence on the plantation in favor of the hier-archical world economy only to inherit its cultural baggage of individualism and material success.[60]

STRATEGIZING: SUBVERSION AND ABSORPTION

This abridged economic history of working peoples complicates more pop-ular accounts focusing solely on resistance strategies of creole "peasants." Newly freed persons pursued independent subsistence production, more often than not, encircled by plantation production. Though both planters and smallholders struggled to expand their territory, some banana farmers becoming tenants or wage earners or both, others becoming middle farm-ers producing primarily for the export market, most were not so fortunate.

St. Lucia plantations' demise spawned *metayage*. *Metayage* served to accommodate coloniality and, because it led to the formation of a new class of persons, to shape a new kind of citizenness. Some metayers took advan-tage of contract loopholes, exploiting the vulnerabilities of bankrupt plant-ers; others became upwardly mobile smallholders (through their own inge-nuity).[61] Though dubious about the benefits of colonialism, smallholders and working peoples alike framed their resistance in terms of a flight to modernity, which entailed engaging colonial elite assumptions about hierarchy and material progress or, more radically, wanting what elites denied them, that is, making the notion of citizenness more demographically inclusive and materially meaningful, though subverting their proprietary locations as well.

The transition from subsistence production to smallholder and commercial small farming to wage labor involved struggles against and within the colonial system. Like the Americans of the eighteenth century, who at first wanted only partial independence from Britain, smallholders' demands were modest, though far-reaching. They wanted to participate in the political and economic governance of the islands. Moreover, they wanted an end to policies that favored plantation production at their expense. Though it was not consistently articulated, they were concerned about their blocked economic or class mobility.[62]

In a petition to the governor submitted before the outbreak of the Morant Bay Rebellion in Jamaica in 1865, rural Caribbeans declared their support for a reformed colonial system. They complained, however, about the inadequacies of colonial rule in protecting their properties.[63] The list of grievances does not call attention exclusively to the planters' particular oversights because some of the mentioned misdeeds were committed by fellow smallholders. A dissatisfaction with life in the colony is clear, however, centering on disturbing agricultural conditions and framed in terms acceptable to colonial definitions of respectability and socioeconomic advancement, from which smallholders had been excluded.

Similar sentiments were expressed about colonial policy in St. Lucia during the 1840s. St. Lucians objected to a road ordinance forcing them either to provide an annual corvée of eight days' service on the roads or to pay a monetary fee to the government. They challenged the policy in class-specific terms:

> While we poor labourers are compelled to perform our allotted tasks, or pay a fine or go to jail the rich Proprietor allows his hedges to remain untrimmed and forests to throw their shadows in our path, in spite of the enactments of that law, in defiance of its penalties, which he laughs to scorn. Is this justice—even-handed justice?[64]

When these demands were not met, the island saw in 1849 a major rebellion, in which St. Lucian smallholders, like others elsewhere in the region and the

Americas, aligned with other propertied individuals and non-smallholders. They selected leaders, many of whom lived in the material world of the propertied classes but moved comfortably among the peasantry, Henry Boy, for example. Thought of as a respectable-looking laborer, he spoke the languages of both the colonials and rural Caribbeans. Boy was a pious churchgoer but was so incensed by the taxes that he exhorted people not to pay and allegedly threatened colonial officials. As a result of the ensuing unrest, he was imprisoned. According to one colonial report, "on the very day the priest exhorted his flock to pay the tax, this pious prisoner, placing himself at the church door, enjoined the people as they came out not to pay, and actually collected money for the petition."[65] Perhaps worst of all, however, Boy threatened that, if the governor did not yield on the matter of the taxes, there would be "*mauvais desordres.*" The state prosecutor observed with belated wisdom that there were indeed "*mauvais desordres*" on the March 5.[66]

In Jamaica, the leaders of the 1865 Morant Bay Rebellion were likewise a multiclass group. They belonged to a stratum that had much to lose in the event of widespread destruction. Clinton Hutton describes them:

> Among them was Richard Harris, formerly a labourer and resident of Cross Paths. He had seven acres of land in sugar, coffee and provision cultivation. Harris had 100 acres of land which he bought at £2.10s per acre. With a sense of pride and achievement Harris said "I hired labourers and worked myself." There was Richard Davidson, a shopkeeper who also reared pigs, fowls and cultivated coffee and ground provisions. Then there was George Hamilton who had his own land and shop from which he sold salt provisions. When his shop was burnt he lost £82. There was Stephen Telford, a rural constable. He was self-employed, working his own land. He owned 50 acres of land, four houses and a shop. In the suppression that followed the October 11, 1865 armed confrontation it was this section of the Black population that lost the most.[67]

Smallholders sometimes cast their discontent in a language capturing the lived intertwinement of class and race. The source of both their problems and their hopes, the sugar industry's declining plantations concerned them foremost. Paul Bogle, a leader of the Morant Bay Rebellion, was a baker and smallholder who had horses and a bank account (then a rarity). In mobilizing his fellow dissenters, Bogle declared that it was "now time for us to help ourselves—skin for skin. The iron bar is now broken in this parish."[68] As Holt argued, Bogle had his men construct a "rude field-work, by felling large trees, which were used to erect barricades across the roads. Bogle reportedly told his men—after drilling them on the twelfth—that the country belonged to them and they would take possession of it. They were ordered, as their ancestors in 1831 had been, not to destroy the sugar works, because they wanted sugar to make for ourselves."[69] "Rural" Caribbeans sought to rid themselves of the inequities of colonialism.[70] They resented their second- and third-class status under colonialism, though they continued working in areas which allowed them some degree of control over their own lives. They wanted an end to the colonial racialisms that cast them, at best, as happy-go-lucky children, at worst, as lazy Quashee (a derogatory name used for poor rural, sometimes urban, black people), and latent barbarians who at the slightest provocation could slip back into "savage," anarchic, "African" ways. Large numbers of them were prepared to challenge the system's injustices to engage in democratic struggles. They wanted "taxation with representation" and an end to colonial excesses. They wanted the means to earn a decent living. In a society where land was inaccessible but where economic opportunity revolved around its possession and use, smallholders wanted land. They wanted an inclusive political system. They wanted what other colonial subjects had been grudgingly granted.[71]

The mid-nineteenth-century vestry politics of a stratum of black Jamaicans and the rationale of friendly societies in the Leewards discloses the content of these strategies of belonging. Swithin Wilmot's account of black political strategies demonstrates the close intertwinement of resistance against exclusion and the incorporation within elite institutions of governance. In his analysis of vestry politics of Kingston and St. David and in Portland and Metcalfe, Wilmot shows compellingly the ways in which race was manipulated and superseded in the complex political strategies deployed by blacks. For the former places, he concludes that "blacks in urban and rural Jamaica constructed important political linkages with elements of the coloured and Jewish groups enabling the blacks to infiltrate institutions and to manipulate them for their own advantage."[72]

Strategies of uplift undertaken by middle-class blacks throughout the Americas coincided with their incorporation within bourgeois mores, elements of which they opposed as well as adopted. Kevin Gaines's account of the U.S. black uplift ideology considers its tragic effects upon working class people and women, both of whom were particularly marginalized by "race men and women" who in their neuroses to belong to bourgeois white U.S. society, which in any case was defined by their peripheralization, demeaned their less fortunate kin.[73] The Caribbean was not without its own uplift strategies, which involved the implicit silencing of alternative ways of seeing and experiencing transformation. Organizations like friendly societies instrumental in the rise of the black middle classes were also avenues that facilitated the clustering and eventual prominence of that class, but they also furthered the upliftment of lower income working peoples. It is conceivable that working peoples also considered these organizations as pivotal to their socioeconomic and cultural advancement. According to Glen Richards, friendly societies, which expanded rapidly in the postemancipation period, have been "traditionally associated with working-class aspirations for social betterment and upward mobility."[74] Through membership in friendly societies, working peoples channeled their discontent with working conditions and forged alliances with members of the incipient middle classes. Commenting on their class composition, Richards avers,

> The wide diversity in social backgrounds of the members of these friendly societies, ranging from the independently wealthy to the poor agricultural labourer, made racial identification a more potent source of organizational unity than appeals to class solidarity. Although friendly societies were predominantly working class in membership and character, their leaders were usually upwardly mobile, self-made men, who were moving away from their working-class background towards the comfort of middle-class status and sensibility. A major role of the friendly society was the inculcation of middle-class values of consensus, thrift and respect for property rights in the ranks of the working class. They aimed to teach middle-class social mores and morals to ordinary workers through bringing them into beneficial contact with their social and intellectual betters.[75]

By Richards's account, membership in friendly societies was a variant of uplift strategies underway throughout the Americas as subaltern people scrambled to find ways to make themselves acceptable within the ruling stratum's cultures of power, and in the process to press for upward social mobility. Ultimately these accommodative strategies were aimed at declaring their humanity, their presence, and their place in time.

These diverse struggles of working peoples reflect, then, various complex strategies spanning trajectories that were ideologically and temporally multidimensional. Working peoples in their practices and politics of accommodation moved along several different, even self-contradictory paths, suggesting indeed the Fanonian idea of the oppressed wanting what colonials had yet also wanting to disrupt the whole order, or some part of it, or at least to effect a change of regime. Moreover, in each of these, complex desires were brought to bear in a struggle for self-expression, for presence, for place and space at different times or moments in the present. Overall, these complexly articulated attachments to modernity caution against any reading or writing of hi/stories predominantly in terms of a monolithic dialectic of resistance seeking recourse to a being "without" or being fully "outside" the system.

AMBIVALENCIES: OF AND BEYOND "WINKS AND STRUTS"

Analysts often highlight disparities between the "folk" and "elite" cultural practices, frequently conceptualizing the former in terms of an African, "counter-plantation" system, and the latter in terms of a European approach, engaging in a romanticism of working peoples.[76] This approach reinforces a deceptive dichotomy in the quest for an understanding of Caribbean citizenness. A prime example of this binarism is the juxtaposition of a more or less gendered reputation and respectability as diametrically separate tendencies of Caribbeans, advanced by Wilson.[77] Reputedly the business of menfolk, "reputation counts for more in the public sphere among their own kind" and is seen as distinct from the respectability of the elites' hegemonic culture. Moreover it is as if reputation is only a gendered concern, with no claim to a classist or even sexist dimension as well, considering men's overall domination of the Caribbean public sphere. Shalini Puri takes analysts to task for their privileging of reputation and the concomitant "shrinkage of the field of contestation." My critique focuses more on the issue of entanglement rather than on the identification of or the need to focus on the particular political, which is Puri's quarrel.[78] Though analysts are aware of the overlaps and ambivalencies interwoven into the Caribbeans' practices, they hesitate to produce textured accounts which more fully represent Caribbeans' entangled cultural practices. Thus, institutional and cultural differences observed in Caribbean social structure reflect M. G. Smith's description of West Indian society as plural, characterized by institutional cleavages and discontinuities. Very briefly, Smith argued that because the community of values or social relations between and among groups was correspondingly low, sections of the populations, browns, whites, and blacks, constitute autonomous bearers of ideational and institutional differences.[79] By framing cultural practices in such an oppositional matrix he omits the flight to modernity which everyone made and continues to make, variously and vicariously.[80] Such plural and neoplural society accounts, to their credit, highlight the formation and reconstitution of citizenness, the attenuation or dispensability of its specific forms, and the overlapping and shared assumptions affecting different raced and classed populations. They suggest the possibilities of alternative cultural forms, if not of actual cohesive systems, and highlight the existence of complex, countercultural practices. Yet were there in fact these autonomous communities of rural Caribbeans who followed a system of rules and rituals distinctly separate from and subversive to those of the elite?[81] Or were there simply cultural tendencies constructed within and against particular domains of power that were constantly improvised, given the demands of particular maneuvers for making place given post-Creole imaginations?

Olwig identifies "almost closed communities on St. John in the Virgin Islands that existed during and after slavery." She argues that "because these communities were based on a shared system of cultural values and economic activities rather than on shared physical locations, they have been able to survive the demise of rural village life to become the basis of St. John's culture."[82] Maroon communities and others similar in nature existed throughout slavery and they more or less withstood the fragmentation and reorganization of space attending emancipation. Yet even among these there was considerable mobility, and because some Maroons had extensive links with plantations and their personnel, their cultural expressions may have been learned there.[83] Writing about St. Lucia, Louis relates how some villages on the island had enduring communal ties. The village of Gros Islet, in the north of the island, included estate laborers who had lived together since slavery. In the words of a stipendiary magistrate, "It is not seldom that in different parts of the district are to be seen five or six huts, placed near to each other, forming a kind of 'hamlet.' Generally these houses belong to different members of the same family, who jointly rent or purchase a certain quantity of land, which they then cultivate in separate portions."[84]

Whether composed of old former slaves or African immigrants of a later period,[85] such villages invariably contained some living or residual alternative cultural practices.[86] One reason for the survival of these practices may have been less the usual degree of harassment by elites, whether planters, church officials, or the colonial state, than the relatively isolated location. No compelling evidence exists, however, to suggest that such villages shared distinct counterhegemonic systems, nor could it be said that the provenances of their reinvented historicities were nonmodern. All thrived more or less on ambivalent, ambiguous, and improvisational cultural practices during and after slavery, as a few of the following examples suggest.[87]

CREOLE SOCIAL CLASS DRESSING: OF FASHION AND POLITICS

Ideas of respectability, class, and ethnicity intrinsic to the modern world existed in the interstices of island life and affected the cultural lifestyle of local peoples. This is not to argue that everywhere these manifestations of inequality registered in the same way. Nor is the argument here about sameness throughout a seamless colonial project. In the Americas British coloniality was different from its Iberian and French counterparts. In St. Lucia, style of dress during the colonial period was very class conscious. Oral accounts by a local luminary, the late Euralis Bouty, who grew up at the turn of the last century, attest to the fact that the current national dress, the *madras* and *dwette*, "were worn by the middle and lower class of the society like the dahs (helpers and servants or maids) . . . the aristocratic formal dress was of Victorian style. The gentlemen wore frock coats and bowler hats while the ladies wore the decollete (day-col-tay) tight fitting bodice with frills, with crinoline petticoats and very large skirts. Such costumes must have originated from England. The Madras, Dwette and Victoria Style costumes all had their origin in Europe."[88] Class considerations therefore crisscrossed the Caribbeans' cultural expressions, reflecting global and local accommodations to elite and/or colonial modes of being or, at least, of dressing. Many of these cultural practices may have been parodies, to be sure, but many also were imbricated into the daily lives of Caribbeans. It is therefore important to see these styles not simply as mindless mimicking or rejections but as complex signifying practices which generate various rewards from key elements within the establishment or within one's own set. They are composed of many level winks as well as struts.[89] As James Ferguson stated in a different context, "styles are motivated, intentional, and performative but not simply chosen or lightly slipped into. They are like gender, strategies of survival under compulsory systems."[90] Here, they take place in a context where, say, appearing to be respectable has its distinct rewards.

THE FLOWER FESTIVALS:
VIVE LA ROSE! VIVE LA MARGUERITE!

The flower festivals of St. Lucia, considered a locally forged "folk" expression, were marked by class divisions present but not restricted to that island.[91] This aspect is hardly explored in the literature analyzing Caribbean cultural practices, in part because of the general scarcity of primary information on the "societies," as the flower festivals were called. Yet the association of loudness with vulgarity and of subtlety with gentry clearly suggests a Victorian sort of class division between and integral to the structural organization of "folk" groups like the Roses and the Marguerites.

Very little is known about the origins of the flower festivals, though they are known to have existed during slavery. Henry Breen, a colonial administrator, suspects that their origins paralleled the political rivalries of an earlier period:

> It appears that at one period they were invested with a political character; and their occasional allusions to English and French, Republicans and Bonapartists would seem to confirm this impression. Their connexion with politics must have ceased at the termination of the struggle between England and France from which period their rivalry has been confined to dancing and other diversions.[92]

Other observers stress an African derivation, as in this account:

> In 1844, Africans came to St. Lucia to work . . . captured off ships by the English. They settled in Piaye, Canaries, Ravine Poisson and Vieux Fort. Two strong African traditions were the Kele and the Flower Festivals. The flower

groups came under the protection of the church because of the threat of suppression and accusations of licentious dancing and behaviour.[93]

But this African dimension cannot be verified. Flower societies catered to most of the laborers on the island.[94] Members of the upper classes patronized them, albeit with minimal involvement. Louis speculates that these societies may have reemerged in the 1840s as instruments for forging collective identity or maintaining an identity already formed, for they brought together the residents of scattered communities, hamlets, and villages.[95] Louis fails to note, however, that these societies, by virtue of their reproductions of the social class and occupational divisions within the society, accommodated power inequalities or saw them as ineluctable. This of course differs from African cultural forms like Myal, which both established churches and governing colonials opposed. Flower festivals may be said to have mimicked the status quo, that is to say, presenting familiar forms to colonials and the establishment generally. This point has been observed for other parts of the Caribbean in the postcolonial period, suggesting the persistence of coloniality after its political demise. Writing on the issue of hierarchy in the Guyanese community of Cockalorum, Brackette Williams states,

> Community members have traditionally operated (and still do, in large measure) in an ideological field formed of a simultaneous recognition and commitment to both egalitarian and hierarchical principles of social organization. Not only do they recognize the fact of material inequality, but they also view the quest for inequality as legitimate. While material differentiation is in part, a simple consequence of individual efforts to improve their material existence, there is also a conscious effort to acquire particular goods, services, and relationships, because these are considered indicators of social and moral superiority.[96]

It is the support for hierarchy which is the issue here, and therefore a rationale for the fact of inequality. The St. Lucian flower festivals were celebratory and competitive with a distinctly religious orientation, and their societies proved susceptible to the influences of the dominant Catholic Church. They secured their participation in that elitist institution by donating sums of money and assisting in the repair of church buildings. Commenting on this situation, Breen wrote that the societies had been very beneficial to communities and the clergy:

There is scarcely a parish in the Island that does not owe the erection of its Church to the subscriptions raised by one or the other of them, and where they have not built the Church they have enlarged it or furnished it with a marble altar and other suitable ornaments. The most recent instance is the Church of Micoud, a substantial stone edifice erected by the Marguerites of that quarter. At the opening of the Church in August last, the Curé of Micoud, assisted by the Curé of Dennery, said High Mass for the Marguerites, and in the evening took his seat at their "Belair."[97]

A harmonious state of affairs did not last, however. Despite contact with the church, members of the societies took umbrage at any criticism of their practices. They cherished their groups. Noting transformation among the groups, Breen cites a new (ca. late nineteenth century) tendency to spend more money on their children's education and on land purchases than on the church.[98] If working people engaged in these festivals they surely sought to influence the church; but by doing so, they were also subject to it. The Catholic Church still draws its strongest support from rural society, a relationship which raises questions about the autonomy of the "peasants' institutions" and demands a particularly sophisticated interpretation of such a relationship. Aspects of the organization and performances of these societies illuminate the culturally ambivalent relationships that blurred the boundaries between working peoples and elites and reveal the socially textured pursuit of citizenness on the island. If the ritualized acceptance of monarchical relationships was African derived, it was certainly one which remained resilient despite colonial strictures or was a practice encouraged or overlooked by colonial elites.

Hierarchical in structure, both La Rose and La Marguerite appropriated royal and aristocratic symbols and ritualized the accompanying roles. They had (and still have) kings and queens, princes and princesses, and "a number of other pseudo-legal, military and professional personnel including judges, policemen, soldiers and nurses."[99] Yet these were not merely carnivalesque roles but lived ones that were performed in the role players' communities. According to Patrick Anthony,

The element of role performance or masquerading is evident from this internal structure of the groups. For, all of the roles performed during the festival, kings, queens, doctors, lawyers, etc. are roles far beyond the real aspirations of the "folk population" in ordinary life. Herein lies the carnival ethos that is so much part of Caribbean society. At carnival time whole sections of the population will put on "masks" and assume for two days roles they will never be able to assume in real life. Although the role performance in the flower society becomes most evident during the festival period, they are more permanent than the "mas" someone plays at carnival time. If one plays a king or a queen in a band for carnival, then one assumes these roles only during the days of revelry. Not so with La Rose and La Marguerite. One can be a king or a queen for several years, with influence from these roles extending beyond the contours of the festivals into real life.[100]

Here we see porous role performances displayed at public festivals. These roles are not only wishes or aspirations, as Anthony asserts or the local newspaper cartoons suggested, nor are they simply carnivalesque parodies. Rather they are normativized sociocultural expressions of rural communities, perhaps a tribute to, and a mockery of, monarchy as performed in the colony, considering that such parades were a critical part of the exhibition and display of colonial power.[101] The longevity of roles in regular community life may be related to the leaders' standing in their communities. It may be that those elected to perform royalty were already community leaders of sorts. Daniel Crowley observes that although choosing leaders is a democratic process, it is popularly accepted that those who are chosen can afford the cost of the required costumes.[102] Poor St. Lucians cannot be royalty because they have neither money nor influence in their own communities. Though respectability is seldom associated with the poor, they desire a form of it, perhaps not exactly the forms practiced by elites but, as many studies have shown, crafted around their own circumstances but incorporating elite forms. As Crowley observes, "Ideally, the king and queen found the society, and because of private wealth, position, or connections, they are expected to protect and defend their followers in lawsuits, lending money, giving advice, and obtaining jobs."[103] Crowley relates how democracy is mediated by practical considerations:

In one case neither of the founders felt he could afford the costly robes of office, so they chose a prosperous female member as queen. The rest of the members objected to this appointment, and there was a deadlock until a popular female relative of the male founder allowed it to be known that she would accept the throne if it were offered. She led her group successfully for over sixteen years. This queen chose her own king because of his qualification of having the necessary money for costumes.[104]

Though choosing leaders may appear to be a democratic process, it is a procedure with political implications, measured in public display. Crowley's argument that democracy is mediated by "practical considerations" hints loudly that these considerations coincided with mainstream (read dominant) ideas of respectability.

To be respectable is to be absolved from "savage" proclivities. In colonial, postemancipation St. Lucia, respectability was the highest step on the ladder of social distinction. One could be called "insolent," a most degrading epithet, in the absence of evidence of respectability.[105] Respectability made all human beings seemingly equal. In spite of difference, they were party to a cultural contract.[106] Consider here the story of the fighting women from the societies of La Rose and La Marguerite. Brought into court to answer charges of reckless behavior and accompanied by throngs of their supporters, each group hoped for legal vindication. The women were taken aback when the judge reprimanded them, calling them "respectable" ladies engaging in vulgar behavior. Thereupon, according to reports, the two women were embarrassed. Their supporters were silenced by a formal acknowledgment of their respectability by a judge! Achieving citizenness was a responsibility both self-fulfilling and collective. It was as much a public venture as it was a private one.

The now extinct A-bwé, a songfest obscure in origin and confined to the northeastern section of the island, Gros Islet, the Marquis Valley, and Dennery, likewise highlights ambivalences about resistance and shows how the deeds of others are filtered into the cultural production of rural peoples. A-bwé took place in November and December, being calendrical.[107] Participants gathered around a long row of tables, on which were set saucers of fine salt, peppermint lozenges (called "extra-strong") or rock-mint (*le mênthe*), bottles of rum, and tumblers. The fète began with the host welcoming guests, asking for good behavior, and urging members to contribute a fee to cover the cost of refreshments. According to Simmons,

> The speeches and songs are a very Frenchified French Creole, a macaroni language, using many French words and idioms. For instance *la foret* is used instead of *grand bois* for "forest" or high woods. These songs appear to be 17th or 18th century origin, ballads introduced by the French army.

These ballads, over 100 of them, deal with kings and queens and knights, voyages, deeds of valour, seductions, "evenings at the inn" and wars. Although in French Creole, these tales are fragmentary and difficult to interpret, the tellers themselves are vague regarding the meanings. The story-teller or Chantwell sings the verse, the audience joining in the chorus. There is no musical accompaniment, but there are liberal sucking of peppermints and salt (to minimize huskiness in the vocal chords) and sipping of white rum, which act is termed in the local creole as, "wuze gorge" or "sprinkling the throat."[108]

This preference for the French language and the formality associated with "elite" culture reflected a mimetic appropriation of "proper presence." This was achieved paradoxically, however, through a mimicry of status relations that re/produced colonial imaginations of the sacred and the profane, and where, at least on stage, French Creole's inferiority had to be symbolically affected. Parallels of seemingly self-contradictory selves exist elsewhere in the Caribbean. On St. Lucia, French Creole was considered the language of the *malawe* (the suffering poor), those deemed less than respectable. Similarly, Gordon Rohlehr states that in Trinidad, French patois or French Creole gave way to English because of the sustained colonial attack by the English dating from the 1880s. Rohlehr observed, "It became prestigious among calypsonians to be able to speak English and to be able to sing in English." They even chided those among them who could not master "the prosodic or the metrical elements of the new imperial language."[109]

A-bwé participants considered themselves French enough to sing ballads celebrating conquests by the French, army songs that they perhaps only vaguely understood but which were etched into their memories.[110] Nevertheless, in reminiscing about the past, the master drummer of Piaye recalls songs notably sung *only* about "black man's culture." In this sense, he makes St. Lucian culture into a thing distinct, identifiable, pristine, localized, and incontestable: "We made up songs reflecting the culture of St. Lucia. We made them up except the African dances which came from Africa to us . . . I have never heard any songs associated with cocoa . . . That's the white man's work, there was no music attached to it. Music such as what we are talking about was black man's culture."[111] Apparently the narrator of these memories is oblivious to the ambivalence of this past. He remaps his present place and presence by submerging cultural and social constructions drawn from the experiences of and with other groups, even from those world spaces that have intersected with St. Lucia and fashioned the narratives of its complicated past. This interpretation of St. Lucian culture is not surprising, however, nor does it merely reflect individual sentiment; rather it points to a certain politics of place in St. Lucia at the time this interview was conducted. In particular it reflects a period of heightened sensibility toward the purely African contribution to St. Lucian culture and its power for refashioning place that occurred between the late 1970s and early 1980s.

CONCLUSIONS

The approach adopted in this chapter differs from fundamentally oppositional accounts that chronicle individual aspects of the Caribbeans' social-cultural landscape, in that I emphasize the mimetic manipulation of cultural space—the use of strategies of various kinds of accommodation, connivances, and witting and unwitting subversions above, beneath, and parallel to the symbolic world deemed respectable by colonials. Such a process of citizenness called for multilayered maneuvers to aid, say, the acquisition of land as a critical positioning in the economic and cultural politics of belonging. Land ownership was key, but even so, the independence of the plot was more illusory than real. As Brodber reminds us,

> The development of the plot (in Jamaica, the main but scarce economic option of the colonial period) with its interdependence between farming, trades and commerce, continued through the 20th century to 1923 to be a distinctly discernible form. But neither as a set of relationships nor as lands owned by black peasants was the plot a discrete system. In both senses the plantations, the colonial elite, and colonial ideology surrounded it and crossed its arc at key points. The administration of the island still lay in the hands of the larger plantation interests: such matters as the percentage of its income to be paid to the general upkeep of the island was not decided in the plot. In addition, most of the land in the island was owned by the planting interests so that the plot's expansion to include a new generation depended on the willingness of the large landowners to sell. How to engineer this increased space was a constant question for young blacks, who saw making a living from own account farming as the way to independence from the plantations.[112]

The process of citizenness in the Caribbean during the colonial period represented traditions of both local resistances, not necessarily political, and varied other maneuvers, accommodations, and adaptations to coloniality and global developments. Resistance, then, is a layered process, and outcome, and it is the nature of the process that should fundamentally and equally concern us. Certainly, resistance as practiced through a politics of accommodation is experienced as a multifaceted conductor of tendencies, some of which remain unacknowledged by social actors, even as they are implicated in liminal mo(ve)ments leading to indefinite elsewheres, opaque futures. The more political forms of resistance represent a translation and augmentation of these tendencies (and their challenges to given states) into reflexive strategies ostensively aimed at the transformation of relations of power and hegemonic relations of place. Rural Caribbeans who participated in the St. Lucian flower festivals, for example, were pro-royalty and sought, after a fashion, to bring it within their reach. In doing so, royalty was at once subverted and "vulgarized," considering that those who institutionalized it regarded Others like St. Lucians as outside its embrace. But Caribbeans, in reaching for it, become accommodated and thereby are able to appropriate their place, paradoxically through its elitism; yet, it is one rendered banal by bringing it into their communities, making it accessible to everyone, even as they maintained a colonially derived hierarchy, shared with other Caribbean communities in an expanding system of global inequality. It was, as Williams noted of Guyanese racial relations, at once egalitarian and hierarchical.

The tensions associated with power maneuvers must thus be examined carefully through the Caribbeans' experiences of an open and widely traversed world. Participation in local projects of colonial empire building was also part of the wider dynamic of a capitalistic modernity carrying ideological and cultural implications. Working people's involvement in the evolving global system and in the middle-class, bourgeois-derived value system deepened over time. The formation of working people and the places they inhabited abetted the expansion of this globality. And it was carried out within the local interstices of their Creole diasporic habituses.

Beyond the limited opportunities presented by the plantation/peasant/ conflict model lie the spaces engendered by a politics of making place. Its liminal mo(ve)ments seek a Creole line of escape through a zigzagging and recursive politics of accommodation, staking homes and re/homing places among the interwoven braids of various *présences*. Some central *présences* that remain underrepresented generally require exploration, for instance, the neo-Indian and neo-Chinese cultures, more present in Cuba (the latter), Guyana, and Trinidad and Tobago. Identities being mapped by such presences are, however, constantly being reworked into strategies for confronting and refashioning a "coloniality of power" (as Quijano would say), expressed locally and elsewhere. In speaking to the complex processes of *creolization*, this book's perspective of seeing this as a politics of making place(s) and space(s) seems of particular urgency now, especially in light of the ongoing tensions between the various nationally lived constructs of Indianness and Africanness in Trinidad and Tobago and Guyana, for example; but its arguments reach out to address other conflicted elsewheres in Atlantic space and beyond.

FOUR

POWER AND ITS SUBJECTS IN POSTCOLONIAL PERFORMANCE

What Africa as a concept calls fundamentally into question is the manner in which social theory has hitherto reflected on the problem (observable also elsewhere) of the collapse of worlds, their fluctuations and tremblings, their about-turns and disguises, their silences and murmurings. Social theory has failed to account for time as lived, not synchronically or diachronically, but in its multiplicity and simultaneities, its presence and absences, beyond the lazy categories of permanence and change beloved of so many historians.[1]

RECENT POSTCOLONIAL and globalization studies direct attention to the strategies of maneuver and the multiple, even contradictory, responses that people engage to cope with the rapidity and intensity of transformations to social and cultural spaces in the context of structurally adjusted economies and the currently unfolding neoliberal global order. As Achille Mbembe and other African analysts note, these responses challenge the social sciences' dualistic methodologies for grasping the social dynamic, and they question the facility with which writers pronounce on issues of resistance and hegemony. In his own coming to terms with these issues, through his writings on Africa, Mbembe offers a different take on those postcolonies, one which aims to transcend (primarily) Western-produced social scientific interpretations that utilize binary notions of Africa and Africans and their sociocultural interactions with the elite, particularly the political elite, or their interactions with the institutions of juridical power. In particular, he engages in an analysis of the politics of connivance, the idea of how people toy with power. According to Mbembe, "Precisely because the post-colonial mode of domination is as much a regime of constraints as *a practice of conviviality and a stylistic of connivance* . . . the analyst must be attentive to the myriad ways in which ordinary people bridle, trick, and actually *toy* with power instead of confronting it directly."[2]

Mbembe dubs sub-Saharan Africa, in particular Cameroon, a postcolony, which he defines as a "timespace characterized by proliferation and multi-plicity: an era of dispersed entanglements, the unity of which is produced out of differences . . . an overlapping of different, intersected and entwined threads in tension with another."[3] Within this time-space, Mbembe seeks to apprehend what has been construed as Africa's negative excesses of power, namely, "coercive and vapid ceremonialism, political sycophancy, corrup-tion, sensational and flamboyant violence which leads to death not as a form of punishment, but as a practice in and of itself, and presidential grandiosity and pomposity." These for him constitute veritable elements of an "aesthetics and stylistics of power."[4]

Drawing upon Bakhtin's notion of Rabelaisian "grotesque realism" and the carnivalesque elements of medieval and Renaissance European folk humor, Mbembe dispels Bakhtin's argument that corporeal idioms subvert official culture, instead claiming that the carnivalesque and the grotesque are state crafted and state perpetrated, and that no subject can escape them. Indeed, African subjectivity is trapped within this state-commandeered register of banal power.[5] This particular aesthetic is not contoured along linear time, nor is it fractured along dualisms of power and its resistance, oppressed or oppressor. Instead what it discloses is the tacit complicity and mimicry, the conviviality of the African subject with the state. For Mbembe the postcolonial condition encompasses the potentate, with his statecraft monopolizing the society, along with "his" subjects, so much so that society internalizes the "banality of power." Such a configuration of power leads to the "zombification" of leadership and followership, a mutual process of disempowerment. "Resistance" therefore is not an issue because of the conditions of "exercising existence" within this "intimate tyranny." The sharing of the time-spaces of the "grotesque and the obscene" creates a mutual and reciprocal habitus, which constitutes the postcolony. In this habitus, connivance, trickery, and toying with power become the order of the day, as Africans connive with the postcolonial potentate and the states' carnivalesque extravagances and excesses of power. Thus, play, ribaldry, humor, and derision cannot be equated to Bakhtin's sense of unofficial folk culture and tactical subversions, because "to a large extent, the outbursts of ribaldry and derision are actually taking the official world seriously, at face value or the value, at least, it gives itself."[6] Generally, then, in Cameroon and by extensions sub-Saharan Africa, rulers and ruled follow the logic of "conviviality," sharing the same images and idioms, as they inhabit the same episteme. As Mbembe stridently put it, "Those who laugh, whether in the public arena or in the private domain, are not necessarily bringing about the collapse of power or resisting it,"[7] making it "unnecessary to insist, as does Bakhtin, on oppositions (dédoublement) or, as does conventional analysis on the purported logic of resistance, or disengagement, or disjunction. Instead, the emphasis should be on the logic of "conviviality and the dominated within the same *episteme.*"[8]

As others have pointed out, there appears to be a disproportionate pessimistic bent to Mbembe's analysis of the African postcolony as he appears to leave no room for incompleteness or undecidability fracturing domination. His conceptualization of power in the postcolony leads him, like Habermas, to encounter it only in terms of juridical power, negativity, and domination, if not repression and restriction. For the postcolonial state's power ostensively creates only a "world of meanings all its own, a master code which in the process of becoming the society's primary central code, ends by governing the various logics that underlie all other meanings within that society."[9] This is radical pessimism to be sure, which overshadows Bakhtin's pivotal point in his historicized account of folk culture: that folk culture goes beyond simply a negative critique of the social order, containing within it also the possibilities for *imagining* a utopian alternative by inversion of values. Such a utopian world is one "in which anti-hierarchism, relativity of values, questioning of authority, openness, joyous anarchy and the ridiculing of all dogmas hold sway, a world in which syncretism and a myriad of differing perspectives are permitted."[10] By contrast, Mbembe trains his gaze on the negative sides of laughter, "its derisiveness and its futility." For as Karlström put it, "His Africans are either dupes of the State episteme or strategic actors seeking to get what they can from the state."[11] But what is Mbembe's broader project, and what gives it its universal appeal beyond the postcolony that Africa represents? Summarily, as this chapter's epigraph suggests, Mbembe seeks to go beyond both essentialist and anti-essentialist accounts of Africa and Africans, which fail to offer insights into how Africans live, how they "exercise their existence." That is to say, Mbembe seeks neither to essentialize the Africans nor to simply contextualize or trap them within disciplinary approaches (whether structuralist or rationalist), nor, as in contemporary political theory, to turn them into "the mute subjects of investigation, unable to be heard in response to these methodologies."[12] His task therefore is to attempt to situate Africans as entangled within a difficult, even brutal postcolonial existence, as fairly autonomous subjects.

In spite of the limits of his discussion of the mirror of African existence that "reflects a figure that is in the present yet escapes it,"[13] and despite his critique of Foucault as a theorist preoccupied with hybridity, fluidity, and negotiations, Mbembe's analysis still raises vital questions about *how* subjects (in this instance the African state and its subjects) are embedded and entangled in (a hollow and repressive) power. And, consequently how, or in what manner, must the former slave, for the sake of the subject, seek to escape or cross it. While Mbembe tends to read this pivotal life movement of political transformation through Hegelian lenses and to truncate vital aspects of the nature of the complex processes of subjects' struggles for meaning and transformation, his book critically sets the stage for a further interrogation of these processes wherein power (and time) is entangled with its subjects. In other words, it behooves those of us interested in social processes to generate questions and analyses that seek to ferret out the particularities about the way subjectivities, whether in colonial, postcolonial, or global practices of "exercising existence," play and interplay in postcolonial entanglements as guided by certain (and varying) sovereignties of the imagination, for remapping modern state spaces and subject places and for transfiguring one's place-in-time.

Consider here the Jamaican figure of the *ruud bwai* (rude boy). In opposition to the "system," he is seen as the embodiment of resistance against the disciplinary powers of the state. David Scott reads the *ruud bwai* through Foucault's optic of "ascetical" practices of self-fashioning:

> The figure of the *ruud bwai* disrupts the dominant regime of cultural-political truth that bodies are to be educated into a particular raced/classed regime of sensibility, breeding, and conduct. It constitutes a site of internal *danger* to the norms of bourgeois-liberal civility. *Ruud bwais* self-fashioning constitutes a practice of the self by means of which the

(typically) young, working-class male refuses the disciplined body of postcolonial order, refuses to be a "docile body" available to be worked over by capital, to be worked over by the police, or to be counted by the statistical ideologues of representative democracy. Rather than to submit to these disciplinary regimes the *ruud bwai* sets out to take a hold of the body's energies himself and to impose upon it a new regularity, a new order, a new set of rules and values, a new pattern of pleasures. And central to this new order of the body is precisely the cultivation of an agonism, a decidedly truculent rhythm, and a menacing surface that tears the edges of the governing classed/raced cohesion.[14]

I have no quarrel with this perspective, except insofar as it narrowly reduces oppositionality to the disciplinary dictates of a monolithic nation-state order and governing elite, whose political party power exploits also very much contributed to the formation of the *ruud bwai* ascetic-aesthetic, and who deliberately exploited it. Is there a relationship between political *gunmanism* and the "new order" that *ruud bwaism* represented? What is excluded from Scott's analysis is how this *ruud bwai* "self-fashioning" involves an acquiescence to gang discipline,[15] and the refashioning of a certain style, fabricated from global filmic cowboy images and exploits. Scott takes the official state pronouncements about sacred identities at face value. He fails to recognize its other informal, less visible side, its duplicitous production of the profane, the *ruud bwai*. It is a modern image, not the figure of the Maroon-affirming opposition in flight from the plantation. The *ruud bwai* image might well be celluloid, to be sure refashioning a different, profane identity, much resembling Ivan in the Jamaican film *The Harder They Come*—a spaghetti Western gunman. It is as if the "unsubjugated" body, since Scott is reading bodily performance here, is an automatic rendering of an absolute opposition. It is as if the disciplinary tactics of state and political party don't work through and with these performances of unsubjugated bodies, even creating them for political nonstate activity. Inattention to these other aspects of *ruud bwai* "culture" leaves Scott open to the charge of a certain kind of *ruud bwai* romanticizing (through a Foucault analytic), which in the essay he disavows. But the questions that Scott raises are pivotal. "How is it possible to practice freedom within the prevailing relationships of power, within the prevailing hierarchies of civility and citizenship?"[16] This is really the pivotal point that Mbembe also grapples with in his text, even though he remains steeped in a melancholic analysis of the disempowering agony of Africans "living in the concrete."

How are people "exercising their existence" given this global interweaving of modern economies and societies which, as Saskia Sassen posits, happens in the context of "new geographies of power," unmooring identities and reforming states throughout the world? And how do these conditions reverberate through the post-Creole imaginations of postcolonial peoples? Or rather, how do these readings and interpretations constitute elements of their imagination? Though the Caribbean region is replete with ambivalent, multitextured gestures, images, works of art, and organic theatrical productions,[17] I will scrutinize one ambivalent popular cultural response: the group referred to on television as "Lucians," operating out of St. Lucia in the Caribbean's Windward Islands. I would like to read the Lucians' performances as representing an intersection of Creole projects, for making a place which, in this instance, enables a critical stance toward the state's project for governing space and opens up fields through which denunciations can be inserted, even as it reaffirms some of the state's tenets as well. Put another way, what the group seeks to do is capitalize on the state's hobbled governance project, provoking its further fragmentation and disabling, or rather its destabilization, while nevertheless affirming it—a negative affirmation of sorts but not one in the register of open resistance.

Lucians challenge the reforming state by questioning elites' exclusionary authoritarian practices, even as they reproduce an elitism similar to that of the state's project for producing the Creole nation-state. The group at once utilizes the vocabularies, idioms, and symbols of the state, itself reflective of earlier forms of creolity, but through satire, slapstick comedy, and social commentary it challenges the ways in which earlier forms of *creolization* gave rise to a particular national imagination and critically comments on the conduct of the state as reflected primarily through the practices of its institutions and its political strategies.

Disparaged by notable sections of the middle class and spurned by government officials, the group emanates from the cultural politics of Caribbean youth. Its practices reveal some of the strategies employed by people to mitigate the pace, quality, and intensity of change (most often termed as a lack of and absence of change) in a particular locality. I would therefore like to treat them as a manifestation of a species of ambivalent and obliquely oppositional, expressive culture, operating within the field of popular culture, laying claim to a certain idea of global locality whose significance lies in the revelations the group engenders about ideas of nation, community, and the search for a different kind of local identity that could usher in new thoughts about inclusionary democratic forms of governance and lifestyles, many of those disallowed and disavowed under older forms of creolity. *Lucians'* immanent critique of the state expresses, then, an open-ended critical consciousness that is multidirectional in its objective and insinuations. It allows nationals the space to "play themselves" by invoking the imagery of an unfiltered, or rather unedited or minimally edited, reality. This allows people to engage in behaviors that appear unregulated or seemingly unscripted and to deliberately speak "nonsensically," to bait the listener with excessive sexual innuendos, and to loosen their bodies in ways deemed shameful and embarrassing to the nation-state's notions of respectability and good character—in short, to performatively dis-connect from the nation-state's "imagined community," at least in part.

Referring to the overuse of the concept of "popular" and its consequent meaning, García Canclini writes:

> We need to apply to the term "popular" the "philosophical prophylaxis" that Fredric Jameson once proposed for the words power and body. Stop using them for ten years. Nevertheless, because in the name of the popular, museums will continue to be founded and television programs, books and symposia created, perhaps it would be better to accept that the popular is a field of dispute and negotiation over social meaning. It therefore seems far more fruitful, rather than elaborate a theory of popular culture, to examine the ways in which this rhetorical figure reveals itself in conflicts and negotiations.[18]

Bearing in mind Canclini's frustrations and provisos, I attempt in this chapter "to deconstruct the various strategies of those who stage the popular" and to examine popular expression "within the social structures of power."[19] Attention is directed first to the context of the region's reorganization of state, economy, and Creole forms of sociality out of which the multidirectional popular form that Lucians represent emerges. That is, the emergence of this form of expressive culture is linked to the structural effects of globalization on the island and to the promise that it carries to remake national identities independent of the economic and cultural projects of the developmentalist state. Both state institutions and people are placed thereby in an embattled situation, contextualized by the unraveling and remaking of key aspects of the national project. I want to add here that it is not as if the glaring contradictions of this "imagined community" surfaced since the 1980s, when the implementation of the neoliberal economic project began, but rather that the stresses and strains under which Caribbean states are placed as a result of that order make the masking over of contradictions and differences impossible to sustain. Moreover, competing discourses outside (globally and regionally) and within the nation-state breed contention. The center, as William Butler Yeats might have written of the region, cannot hold.[20] Yet the precursor for such a crisis was already rooted in the character of the Creole nation-state's project of nation building, as I discuss below.

(UN)MAKING NATION-STATES IN PROCESSES OF DEVELOPMENT

As a number of analysts have argued, West Indian nationalisms and the state Creole projects moved along a trajectory that combined the project of state building with the welfarist concerns of the working peoples. Consider that political parties in the Anglophone Caribbean either received a fillip from trade union mobilization or were closely aligned with them, providing a somewhat contractual relationship between worker and middle-class nationalist and laying the basis for the characteristic political party-state hegemony in the region. It has been argued that this feature of West Indian nationalism, this social bargain was the basis for the region's peculiar brand of parliamentary democracy, at least until the 1980s. Addressing this issue, Jorge Dominguez argues:

> Statist bargains on behalf of democracy sought to provide gains for the great many, the worker and the business owner, while exporting the costs of running such states to the international community via commodity prices or foreign aid. Parties were the institutional brokers for such distributive politics; allegiances to them depended to a large degree on the expectation of particularistic benefits. These states by and large did not threaten the society's habits of resistance in religion, or property ownership.[21]

As others have pointed out, this relationship was fraught with conflict, which Dominguez refrains from acknowledging. He is correct in stressing the extent to which the making of modern subjectivity in the region involved ostensibly a mutuality of agendas. Such institutions and discourses about state and society were forged within and against the backdrop of the constitutive emergence of messianic decolonization movements promising to transform colonial subjects into citizens of sovereign nation-states. And this decolonialist move was proclaimed as the ultimate opportunity to realize their potential as human beings in the world and their proper presence and place in the world.

The paradox, however, is that though nationalists presumed a priori that such a place was already there, their brand of nationalism and the historical moment they occupied were themselves intrinsic to the creation of those very social spaces, which then became reified in their resistance to flexibility in changing them when challenged. National creolizing, or rather nationalizing Creole projects, had the effect therefore of tethering or fixing certain ideas of nation to citizenship and to the sense of place deemed desirable in these territories and in the world. But neither ideas about nations nor the national and Creole projects designed to underscore those ideas operated without passive or active silencing of alternative projects, as many have pointed out.[22] Such silencing served to produce, in the Foucauldian sense, various knowledge and power complexes and called forth certain kinds of conduct, though oftentimes the associated material practices of these more or less silenced alternatives (often transformed) continued to be practiced in other places overtly or surreptitiously. In these processes of subjectification and othering, economic development projects were instrumental and creative in the ideological exercise of turning subjects into citizens, that is, into particular kinds of citizens. In this context, nationalist development policy operated at two levels, one legitimizing the idea of the state and, at the same time, the other creating and attempting to control the conditions under which working peoples existed, forming, at the very least, their various mappings of ethnic, class, and gender identities. Such a dynamic process, however, is conducted through a veritable *politics of the cross*, which, to restate, is the lateral intersection of complex sociocultural maneuvers (that is, people's critical mimetic mo(ve)ments) with those topologies of governable space which are partially mediated through states and state-sanctioned institutions.

In the ongoing processes of development and within the current era of globalization there exists an array of mechanisms that both the state elites and the populace have employed to maneuver within globally articulated local spaces, despite its plethora of contradictions and systemic unevenness.[23] Significantly, neither the populace nor political elites have sought to dispense with the notions of nationalism or national development of the nation-state, even though they have been placed under enormous strain and their interpretations are increasingly at odds. Elites seek to rehabilitate these notions and reshape them according to the economic and cultural, global and local, trends. This means that state formation is an ongoing project carried through the various tributaries of *creolization*, as its legitimation via varieties of Creole nationalism and tropes of citizenship renders the stakes in *citizenness* a malleable and historically contingent exercise. The idea of citizenness (as discussed earlier), however, exceeds the "liberal notion of the citizen simply as an individual holder of rights protected by the state to a normative ideal, that the governed should be full and equal participants in the political process."[24]

The Creole nation-state's struggle for citizenship and national development, in contrast, tends to represent the struggle for hegemony and "national culture." Forged from systems of slavery and indentured labor, with complex histories of resistance, the formation of nation-states in the Anglophone Caribbean, a mid-to-late-twentieth-century phenomenon, is inseparable from notions of modern freedom and sovereignty, which take as axiomatic the capacity of states to chart their own development. Consequently, more often than not, as many have observed, what emerges as national culture, even national character, silences and excludes alternative perspectives given the hegemonic propagations of identity, sovereignty, and freedom. Yet even a hegemonic culture is open to challenge, ensuring the partiality and therefore ongoing status of cultural identity formations.[25]

In a somewhat paradoxical manner, given the political models upon which national elites drew, individual freedoms were linked with those of the emergent postcolonial state. Mobilization for sovereignty was based on promises of national development. Cultural practices for citizenness were incorporated into or marginalized by this project, eliding forms of otherness that could ultimately pose challenges to the political inventions of national community. Yet the promise of development and of sovereignty, "to be our [Caribbeans'] own masters," along with notions of respectability, convinced many West Indians of the possibility of a shared national identity that could sustain imaginations of proper presence or homely dwelling spaces. Therefore, the idea and practice of development cannot be extricated from a politics of place and from the cultural constructs of citizenship and nationalism propagated by state elites and practiced by elements deemed respectable. The lure of citizenship and its link to a will to place, as guided by the post-Creole imagination, pulled people into the orbit of the development project to the extent that it seemed the harbinger of the necessary conditions of citizenship or modern freedom. Nonetheless the attachments to the Creole nation-state's project of development were contingent and versatile ones, routed through topologies of governable spaces. A certain kind of particularization of the universal is thus a germane aspect of Caribbean creolization practice and its politics of space and place.

Against this perspective I now wish to explore the efforts of the Lucians' challenge to the Creole state's projects of politics and sovereignty and development.

THE FLIGHT INTO AN ENTANGLED MODERNITY AND THE FORGING OF A SENSE OF PLACE

Several years ago urban middle-class and upper-middle-class young men emerged on the St. Lucia cultural scene under the name Lucians to call attention to the general sociocultural and political conditions on the island. Using an independent television station, they produced shocking skits, interviews, and biting commentaries on the politicians of the day. They wove themselves into the popular imagination of St. Lucians in provocative ways. Their interviews with ordinary St. Lucians on subjects as diverse as sex, mathematics, and folk festivals embarrassed and mocked the national image, highlighting the discrepancy between it and reality, and in the process revealed the hollowness of pronouncements of national unity. These interviews revealed that nationals disagreed on far more issues and interpretations of national history than had been imagined. They underscored that parades, ceremonies, festivals, and other rituals of the nation-state were spectacles open for interpretations in excess of those officially given. People's understanding of popular phrases varied widely. Functional illiteracy was far higher than imagined: the icons of the nation, the flag, the popular name of the island, Helen, and its history were misunderstood, misrecognized, or pointedly ignored or even distanced. Central to the Lucians' television shows was the lampooning of politicians and their policies. In one skit depicting political corruption, a special password was needed to enter a swinging party. Passwords referred to comments on the state of the economy, for example, "bananas is dead," referring to the negative effects of the World Trade Organization's policy concerning the island's banana industry. But these could not gain one entrance to the party, while "jobs for the boys, contracts" won instant access to the "party of politics." Relying on these shock techniques, members of the group, in particular its leader, were seen in various stages of undress on television, poking fun at middle-class Creole notions of respectability.

In 2001, just before the national election, Lucians formed a formal political party called the STAFF party (the acronym for the French Creole phrase "sous tout après fête fini": all drunk after the party is over). STAFF puns intentionally on both the high consumption of alcohol during electoral hustings and the name given to employer-organized Christmas parties. Ordinarily staff parties are considered bonuses, ranging in size and sophistication from enterprise to enterprise and designed to build workplace morale and to welcome the festive season symbolizing employers' concern for employees. The STAFF party's political symbol was a rum bottle. Such punning points to a grand conspiracy on the part of political and economic elites. It is entertainment that both masks and reveals the extent to which people were being manipulated in instances of conviviality.

The STAFF party held at one meeting reputed to have attracted one of the largest crowds in the island's political history, roughly five to six thousand people, most of them young. The group commandeered a public square renamed Independence Square two decades ago, after its colonial name, Sir William Peter Boulevard, became politically inappropriate. They had none of the usual political party giveaways, like rum, fried chicken, T-shirts, and other trinkets regarded generally as bribes, and proceeds from the Heineken beer sold at the political meeting went to the Aids Action Foundation. As one newspaper columnist put it,

> Convinced that politics in the Country was a "chicken and rum" affair, wherein politicians indiscriminately made any and every unfulfillable promise to their constituents while keeping them sated and intoxicated with food, drink and music, Hunte decided to illustrate to the public exactly what he thought it was they were being submitted to, by taking the whole thing to extremes: the mock candidates on his TV platforms

made the most outrageous, ridiculous promises to their viewing audience while waving rum and beer bottles.[26]

The lampooning of politicians was mixed with discussion of what the Lucians group felt was needed for the country. Performers strutted across stage making ridiculous promises to the populace. They promised to transport beaches to inland parts of the island to develop the tourist industry. They wanted to place air conditioners under breadfruit trees, so that people would feel cool. They planned to enlarge potholes (holes in the roads, caused by erosion) in an urban community so that tourists might be ferried from one to the other. All these gimmicks played on the impossible promises that define the electoral strategies used to hustle votes in a parliamentary democracy. Focusing on such overtly ridiculous promises also called into question the obsessive state preoccupation and development of the tourist industry, an industry which Terry Nichols Clark notes is becoming the most profitable strategy adopted by cities worldwide to replace declining manufacturing and industrial sectors.[27] Interspersed with this spectacular performance were public service messages encouraging people to vote for their party of choice, emphasizing that their vote was theirs and that they could place their Xs wherever they chose, that they should not be fooled or fall for political bribery. This was defensive posturing designed to call attention to the seriousness of the carnivalesque presentation of politics. Ironically, it mimicked the realpolitik of the electioneering of political parties in the region.

MIMICRY AND THE STAGING OF A
DIFFERENT BUT SIMILAR TRUTH

Though Lucians were critiquing the formal aspects of politics, calling on candidates to run for the toilet seat on account of what went on in parliament, theirs could hardly be interpreted as a rejection of political form, reject though they might the procedures and conduct usual to that form. Lucians wanted reforms; reforms might be called "structure-producing," insofar as they would have an enduring effect upon state institutions.[28] They wanted politicians to concern themselves with the *real* problems of the nation. Exposing the corruptness of the political system is not automatically a call to dismantle it; it is a call to rehabilitate it, to overhaul one element of the state machinery, in order to heal the nation's schisms. The state is important to this venture, its apparatuses necessary to mitigate its own ill health. "We are calling on them," say Lucians, "to get their act together, because politics is the most powerful medium in our culture at this time. It is practically the only game in town."[29]

Lucians are concerned with provoking sociocultural questioning and a new political consciousness. "We need to think and know about 'our' national identity," asserts Hunte, producer of *Lucians* and leader of the STAFF party, implying the need to open up discussions about the ways in which power has been mobilized to generate social and economic inequalities. "Society has no sense of itself," he claims. "Partisan politics have hijacked the process of national identity. Party shirts are like gang colors, that's why we have no national identity. There is no more first world anymore, you are either on the same page as the States [the United States] or you are not," he avers. The *Lucians* series targets people in the upper echelons of society, deemed ignorant, "to inform them about who they are dealing with. To get these people to understand the backwardness of the nation. Where we are at." Hunte speaks of people at the top needing to "evolve," to realize that they are not far removed from the people at the bottom, "though they pretend they are."[30] "Elite St. Lucians are too busy working within old paradigms. We need to catch up with the speed of the rest of the world," he says. He compares St. Lucians with people in overindustrialized countries, who, he claims, "can follow the geometric patterns across the grass without walking in the mud. Both educated and uneducated St. Lucians lack that discipline or ability to obey rules." Hunte's tone, therefore, is as authoritarian as the political elites whom he criticizes and challenges. The criticism of the state, of the politicians, is redirected at the nation itself. A nation that lacks something.

In the nation's televised display its "imagined community" is questioned.[31] Echoing the U.S.–produced *Saturday Night Live*,[32] the series lampoons and subverts the idea of imagined community, pointing to its schisms, its doubleness, its untenable hybridities, and its duplicities through constructive mimicry and mockery to stage and highlight the fact that St. Lucians are not "up to scratch." It is local globalized theater mobilized in protest and counterprotest.[33] The message is that too many St. Lucians "are out to lunch," doomed to underdevelopment. They have different interpretations of popular phrases, and they sell their souls to political elites for fried chicken, rum, and "bon temps." They lack a cohesive national identity.

Departing from other portrayals, Lucians portray the nation by what it lacks. It is nevertheless rectifiable. "If only people understand where we need to get and fast we can develop our own resources." "Why is the government unwilling to develop hemp?" Hunte asks. "Why let their agendas be set by the United States. South Africans are developing hemp, and they saw it here. They got their ideas from a visit to St. Lucia by one of their ministers."[34]

In their heyday Lucians ranked among the most popular local television productions; its ambiguous appeals and protests seem to be unlike any other protest in the island's history. It is not a strike; it is not about performing banned "culture"; it is not directed at undermining the state or seeking to replace its officers. That was the more radical option that erupted elsewhere, as evidenced in the army mutiny in Trinidad and Tobago in the 1970s.[35] The incipient guerrilla movement there also sought to destabilize and replace the liberal decolonizing state. The black power movement in the 1960s was a sociopolitical movement with distinct objectives at once cultural and political, which questioned the continuing socioeconomic inequalities felt among the black poor and the continued reliance on Eurocentric standards of culture and respectability. Also, leftist politics facilitated the rise of revolutionary Grenada in the late 1970s, as well as its demise in 1983, which was compounded by the U.S. military invasion. But in St. Lucia, members of the radical group The Forum, who resisted certain state policies in the late 1960s and early 1970s (for example, foreign ownership of land and hotels), became incorporated in the state, carrying on similar policies. The Workers Revolutionary Movement (WRM), a Marxist nationalist grouping of the late 1970s, also fizzled out, with many of its male members joining the "new" Labour Party.[36] However, several former St. Lucian government officials served in various capacities in Grenada's People's Revolutionary Government.

CULTURAL POLITICS STAGED

Even though not engaged directly in oppositional politics, Lucians' engagement with the governing projects of the state reflect the staging of cultural politics, to be understood here as "the process enacted when sets of social actors shaped by and embodying different cultural meanings and practices come into conflict with each other." Such a definition, the anthropologists Sonia Alvarez, Evelina Dagnino, and Arturo Escobar assure us, "assumes that meanings and practices—particularly those theorized as marginal, oppositional, minority, residual, emergent, alternative, dissident, and the like, all of them conceived in relation to a given dominant cultural order—can be the source of processes that must be accepted as political."[37] Moreover, they argue, "Culture is political because meanings are constitutive of processes that, implicitly or explicitly, seek to redefine social power. That is, when movements deploy alternative conceptions of woman, nature, race, economy, democracy, or citizenship that unsettle dominant cultural meanings, they enact a cultural politics."[38]

Though cultural politics generally refers to social movements, particularly emergent ones, its fundamental concerns are with the rise (and demise) of public spheres in the wake of the state reorganization and of the neoliberal globalization project that has seemingly allowed for greater space for amorphous social expressions which, like social movements, enunciate or interlocute with received cultural notions of citizenship, though focusing not on individual rights but rather more on other liberal ideas such as membership and participation, within territorial spaces, and nation-states.[39] These political and cultural interpellations are the new fragmented registers of democracy which may or may not be linked to renewed attempts at nation building. Projecting partial and spasmodic coherencies about political culture, state policies, and national socioeconomic and cultural formatting, members of such groupings constitute and reflect at once the unraveling threads of the current national and neonational state project and its Creole connivances, giving rise to new forms of ethical political constituencies.

Lucians in staging their version of cultural politics are comically oppositional. The group expresses this opposition ambiguously via the politics of alterity, utilizing transnational subversive forms a là *Saturday Night Live* with polysemous messages to and about "the nation." Lucians, though middle class, engage poorer classes, resembling the tactics of early national elites who "lowered" themselves to working peoples to seek their approval to win their votes and to loosen colonialism's political hold on the region. It is a group with its own sense of what the nation needs, like the early male nationalists who spearheaded the decolonization struggle.

Jamaica's Norman Manley in the 1930s reportedly told the Jamaican working peoples, "My head is wiser than yours tonight."[40] The region's history is replete with examples of privileged middle-class young men exposing ordinary people to the public gaze and the interests of elites, whom they claim are oblivious about the level of "evolvedness" of their constituents. Lucians is no different: "It is about telling people, that if you decide to clean a wall and paint it, and say don't mess it up, people will mess it up." It is a protest that plays on, or complements and counters, the "national distaste" for male homosexuality, constituting the woof and weft of a good part of local culture. During the STAFF party's spectacular launching, men were masked as women and feigned copulation on stage, suggesting that the nation is being screwed by politicians and keeping with the common conception of gay sex. Lucians toy with domestic violence. Men masked as women ran around the stage beating masked men with pots, to the crowd's loud approval. It is masculinist, to be sure, but it also implicitly critiques the island's gender constructions and the relationships which facilitate spousal abuse. As in old-style political parties, no women are present, not at the STAFF party's public shaming of the island's electoral politics, and certainly not on its list of forwarded candidates. If numbers measure a political party's openness to representation by women, the STAFF party's gender politics appears as regressive as that of those whom they ridicule. Three official political parties presented women. The ruling party had two; the official opposition, three; and a newly formed alliance party, four. Nor do women play central roles in the Lucians' television performances. If they appear at all, they tend to serve as props, or they are merely interviewed on the streets. Men produce the series. This is oppositional masculinist politics, certainly, but it defies an easy paradigmatic fit, given some of the more subtle critiques of macho masculinity produced by Lucians. Nevertheless, this masculinist production is lodged within a certain acceptance of the politics of the "post-colonial" state. As Anne McClintock reminds us,

> No "post-colonial" state anywhere has granted women and men equal access to the rights and resources of the nation state. Not only have the needs of "post-colonial nations" been largely identified with male conflicts, male aspirations and male interests, but the very representation of "national" power rests on prior constructions of gender power. Despite most anti-colonial nationalisms' investment in the rhetoric of popular unity, most have served more properly to institutionalize gender power. Marital laws, in particular have served to ensure that for women citizenship in the nation-state is mediated by the marriage relation, so that a woman's *political* relation to the nation is submerged in, and subordinated to, her *social* relation to a man through marriage.[41]

Hence the mimicry, representation, and indeed masking of gender politics through which Lucians' own immanent critique is rendered.

A FEW SMALL NIPS OR DEEP CUTS

Does this biting critique, though encased within the "idioms, symbols and episteme" of opposition and resistance, represent "a few small nips, or does it slice deep into the national body?" Will it cause severe injury, even as it presents itself as entertaining spectacle? That depends on the state of the body or on the body of the state. This section's heading takes its name from a Frida Kahlo painting which I came across in Herrera's eponymous biography.[42] In this painting, *A Few Small Nips*, a woman's body lies lifeless on a single bed. It is covered with stab wounds. Even the painting's frame is splattered with blood, making more ironic the painting's title. A man stands at the side of the bed, his shirt stained with blood, in his right hand a bloodstained knife—Frida Kahlo's artistic rendition of the woman's husband, the murderer. Herrera explains that Kahlo got the idea for the painting from a newspaper story of a man who murdered his wife by stabbing her twenty times: in his defense he claimed that it was only a few small nips.

During my interview with Hunte,[43] I was thinking about this painting, as Hunte seemed perplexed by the barrage of vitriolic criticism that his group had attracted. He seemed to think that *Lucians'* carnivalesque comedy differed little from the comedy performed elsewhere, as in *Saturday Night Live*. Only a few nips, was what he was thinking. Nips were only warnings. Perhaps Kahlo's subject did not really want to kill his wife. Perhaps he was not aware of the deadly or deathly (death of a sacred subject) effects of his "playful" stabs. Were the Lucian young men just playing around, unaware of the lethal aspects of their jokes? Were they having gendered fun at the nation's and women's expense? Like *Saturday Night Live*, STAFF party and the *Lucians* series were not a big deal to the performers, and because of this belief, the criticism stunned them. They were horrified at the response of the political elite, journalists, and culture producers surviving on government subventions. One columnist noted of the STAFF party,

> Already they have ignited a debate about alcoholism, ignorance and how ruthlessly we ridicule each other, in this society. They have pointed out how not degrading, but uplifting the portrayals of women on television

are. Most importantly they have tapped into the violent, existential, alcoholic, uninformed energy of The New Majority. They don't represent all the truth about the youth, but that doesn't make what they portray any less true.[44]

Another stated that organizing the STAFF party

> wasn't an easy task: the other political parties resented being caricaturized, and their supporters tried to resist the farcical entity into the serious democratic process. They went on air, making an effort to convince the populace that the STAFF party was making a mockery of the system. That Hunte and his colleagues were encouraging the youth to despise the process and by so doing, were deepening the apathy which the young people were already demonstrating.[45]

Addressing a press conference on the formation of the STAFF party, St. Lucian prime minister Kenny Anthony said, "This can be a very dangerous thing to do. Any purported political organisation that seeks to engender cynicism in the political process, as distinct from *political theatre,* that clearly ought not to be encouraged."[46]

How he defined political theater is anyone's guess. Although the Lucians were dismissed as a bunch of idiots, jokers, and dangerous people playing around with serious issues, as a bunch of young fellows with "false consciousness" unaware of the implications of their televised theater, nevertheless, no one could dismiss the fact that on one Saturday night these "jokers" had assembled some 3,000 young people who "filled the William Peter Boulevard, jammed the side streets, overflowed into Constitution Park in a solid, enthusiastic mass"—the largest gathering ever for a political event in Castries"[47]—to satirize and ridicule the political system, government corruption, broken promises; to show in vivid detail how St. Lucians were being "screwed" by the system. It did not help their political credibility that all Lucian candidates lost their deposits at the polls, their foolishness and "pappyshow" confirmed. *Balle fini, violin en sac* (The party is over, the violin is packed). The space that Lucians turned into a cultural political theatrical arena of opposition was reclaimed by the real politicians. But STAFF party's ideas continue to be interwoven in Lucians' television production series, where the idea was born. They have a carnival band and are thinking of new and spectacular ways to shame or expose the nation, ways that embrace, toy with, share, condemn, and disavow certain kinds of political practices.

DEMOCRATIC ANTAGONISMS

How do we read this perplexing carnivalesque counterconduct, which even as it criticizes and questions the orientation and tenor of national politics, particularly its electoral procedures, and the empty political promises that constitute its tactics, as well as the tenor of traditional social identities and roles and the idea of the nation as "imagined community," nonetheless affirms them, utilizing the authoritarian voice of political leadership and of its homophobic practices? This is "hysterical realism," a phrase taken from a critic's characterization of Zadie Smith's brilliant novel *White Teeth* and the more recent *Autograph Man*.[48] Hysterical is intended in two senses here: derision that cries out via individual and group exhibitionism, and a source of hilarity. But it goes beyond that.

Chantal Mouffe argues that "one must determine what conditions are necessary for specific forms of subordination to produce struggles that seek their abolishment."[49] "As long as equality has not yet acquired (with the democratic revolution) its place of central significance in the social imagination of Western societies, struggles for this equality cannot exist." In this Mouffe distinguishes between democratic struggle and democratic antagonism:

> Democratic antagonisms do not necessarily lead to democratic struggles. Democratic antagonism refers to resistance to subordination and inequality; democratic struggle is directed toward a wide democratization of social life. I am hinting here at the possibility that democratic antagonism can be articulated into different kinds of discourse, even into right wing discourse, because antagonisms are polysemic. There is no one paradigmatic form in which resistance against domination is expressed. Its articulation depends on the discourses and relations of forces in the present struggle for hegemony.[50]

But it seems that the antagonism that is expressed within Lucians' street and TV performances ostensibly relate less to group or individual suffering at the hands of the nation-state than to appeals for a different kind of nation-state. These constitute not only an identification but also a disenchantment with the official direction of the nation, and this Lucians attribute to an out of touch governing elite.

The expressive practices of Lucians constitute forms of cultural entanglements that allow for a new kind of political initiative, but not necessarily as Bhabha would have it, representing a "new" "third space," or even entirely progressive.[51] Their participants engage in a playful but stinging critique of the state and of the nation, though they do so while recognizing the state's authority, or its "vertical encompassment," to the population, standing above society, as Akhil Gupta and James Ferguson have highlighted elsewhere.[52] And I should add that they do this from the relatively safe vantage point of the middle class. Such polyvocal carnivalesque forms resonate with Achille Mbembe's analytical construct of the "*time of existence and experience, the time of entanglement,*"[53] which speaks of time lived in its multiplicity and hence to a certain kind of disarticulation within lived time spaces," ensuring their partiality, incompleteness, and inherent undecidability. Thus, while not a Bakhtinian counterculture, Lucians' staging of cultural politics furthers the idea of dialogue as critical to these "state-in-society" relations and their continual transformations, as Migdal would say. One can argue that the derision, ribaldry, and humor actually represent a certain kind of dialogue, even as they highlight its absence in the imagined community.

The Lucians' performance is best interpreted within the context of such entanglements. The group's entanglement here refers to the gestures of modern connection, the attractiveness of development à la developmentalist state, the idea of the possibility of catching up, of "being on the same page as the [United] States." Ensconced within the metonymy of this phrase are registers of self-sufficiency, that is, of development options for "ourselves."[54] The performance of identity and of culture by Lucians undermines the fixedness of national identity by its revelation of endless diversity, doubleness, and ambivalences of its meanings by all those interviewed on the Castries' streets. It hollows out the meaning of national identity created in an earlier phase and context of creolization and still prevalent today in much of the region, though increasingly under challenge.[55]

St. Lucia's national cultural policy seeks to preempt such disharmony and fragmentation within its cultures of power by according the political directorate superordinate influence over the text and even context of the island's cultural processes.[56] While stressing the importance of diversity, criticism, and individual contribution to the transformation of St. Lucian culture, it is the directorate which seeks to ultimately oversee the correct practice of it. The image it projects is that it knows what's best for the nation and that it acts in the interest of the nation and society.

Despite the dismissal of the Lucians by political elites, local journalists, and regional academics, beneath the group's theatrical skits lies the rejection of a possible connection between their fantastic performance and previous struggles for inclusion, now finding voice again among the ruins of development's earlier promises. Neither riotous nor overtly politically rebellious, neither the familiar petition nor picketing as we know it, Lucians represent a grasp for citizenness, not of the legal variety denied by the colonial polity but rather a form of "citizenship" beyond decolonization's pathetic exclusions and the time-worn promises to link national development to the emancipation of the individual and to state sovereignty. Its television productions seem to scream: "I don't want to be respectable (like that) anymore! Let me the man run to the bathroom, pull down my silk underwear and sit on the toilet, and screw up my face, in full view of a TV audience, let me talk nasty, ask women what kind of sex they want, wash underwear and hang it out to dry, to poke fun at the idea of a 'Man you Must' [a man who does women's bidding]. A man like that is like a reindeer, he in da forest with endless horns. He getting endless horns."[57] Such a man is a cuckold. It is as if these performances render a significant public wonderment: "Where has striving for a certain sanctimonious and intolerant respectability got the region and its inhabitants?"

The production of cultures is a global or rather doubly articulated phenomenon. Each place is not the same, and so histories have to be unbundled as identities are unmoored and remoored.[58] In this instance, we need to examine closely the ideas of citizenship spawned by the decolonization movement: the partial silencing of alternative viewpoints; the hegemonies that defined and displaced national characteristics; political and economic elites' version of community; and the multiple versions of the national character that have emerged over time. Certainly the postcolonies instituted rights, but these rights were guaranteed through specific practices of citizenship. If you fell outside those boundaries that formally mapped one's place in time—for example, if you did not practice respectability in a Creole Anglo-Saxon kind of way, particularly if you were brown or black—then you did not place or properly belong.

A DIFFERENT VERSION OF
BELONGING AND IMAGINING

In this context of competing notions of belonging, place, and the character of community, analyzing this popular performance necessitates focusing on the politics of the postcolonial state, the ideology and practices of the decolonization movement, and the mechanisms through which national communities have been shaped. This point is well made by Virginia Dominguez in her discussion of what Israelis designate as culture (Tarbut) and heritage (Moreshet). She argues that the contest is over the privileged place of the European or Ashkenazim in Israeli history versus that of the Sephardim.[59] In spite of the affirmation of the peoplehood of Jews, the national culture "remains prey to internal contradictions which may give rise to contestation." "Zionism," she explains, "privileges the secular interpretation of Jewish culture, affirming the disproportionate contribution of the European Ashkenazim over those of Sephardic Jews. Sephardic Jews take the positive aspects of the meaning of heritage, structuring Jewish culture and identity around Judaism, considering discrimination faced at the hands of Ashkenazim."[60] But contest within society can take place around any issue, so long as certain people feel marginalized and/or threatened. Consider that even in a more or less racially homogeneous sociocultural space, such as St. Lucia, such a moment resulted in anything but equal standing for Creole citizens, no doubt stimulating Lucians' interrogation of the idea of "imagined community." What were the procedures of such imagining? How many versions existed and why? Under what conditions?

Lucians of course are not the Zapatistas of Chiapas.[61] They do not constitute a political movement, nor do they exemplify a social or political movement; they have neither organizations nor distinct political aims. They do not, like the Zapatistas, constitute a "political movement" of excluded citizens, like Mayans, like Aborigines, like too many U.S. minorities who continue the age-worn refrain of Sojourner Truth, "Ain't I a Woman-[Man]?," who through their pained appeals and practices provide an example of an "alternative nationalism," an ambivalent belonging to an enduringly racialized nation-state.[62] They are not, like the Zapatistas, building cultural spaces with which to redefine the nation, expanding the boundaries of nationalism, citizenship, and political society—at least not directly. Their protests have not, like the Zapatistas,' spawned cyberprotests, beyond the limits of their sited geographies.[63] They are not antiliberal insofar as liberalism posits a relationship between the individual and the state in which the former is to be protected from the latter through sets of procedures based on rights. Instead, their counterconduct is jocular; it satirizes within the episteme of a paradigm of socioeconomic and cultural development put in place by the postcolonial state, whose elites are being scrutinized by larger numbers of its nationals on the island and within the Caribbean diaspora. This jocularity, this conviviality cannot be described as zombification, in the sense of Mbembe's postcolony, nor is it resistance in the sense of affirming an alternative.

Yet Lucians are engaged in highly textured, ambivalent visioning of a more democratic community, one which embraces a certain kind of critical albeit ambivalent dialogue. Their carnivalesque performances are immersed and rehearsed in their sense of hi/story, which is "western and modern," as well as the Caribbean's historical condition, though lived differentially, transterritorially, and even intraterritorially, considering the linked histories of world geographies and places.[64] They constitute a moment in the production and undermining of a particular Creole tradition, and their ambivalent voices ring out above the battering of Windward Island States from the neoliberal challenge, fostered in the wake of structurally adjusted economies and the global institutionalization of the "new geography of power."[65]

Like a majority of the world's peoples, Lucians' situation, their entangled habituses, are being recomposed under the neoliberal economic project, and the cultural exchanges that global awareness facilitates. All kinds of people, even the middle classes, live in the interstices of these "present spaces." All kinds of agendas veer zigzaggedly toward a questioning of things as they were made to be. The pursuit of collective and individual sovereignty of the imagination finds compatible, incompatible, and contradictory existences. Is it any wonder that popular culture presents seemingly incomprehensible performances, and that its multi-accentuated content is at once its style?[66]

The observations that I make here are not about cultural performances emerging in the context of the power vacuum that is supposedly created in the wake of a declining state. States are not declining in the sense of losing their power or relevance in the populace.[67] In fact, given the increase in the number of government-connected non-governmental organizations (NGOS), it might simply be that governable spaces are being reconstituted even though not directly led by traditional state institutions that "stand above" the people.[68]

Fragmentary sociocultural responses have surfaced in the wake of the economic globalization project. These have rearranged the state, shuffled social relationships within the nation, and brought into sharper relief latent schisms within the national community. To be sure, what little state control existed has been further loosened, though it still remains. As Stuart Hall would say, "The state is not about to apologize for its egregious errors and leave the stage";[69] its officials too are engaged in new forms of ambivalent hybrid performances and institutional presences designed to regain the state's symbolic legitimacy as the *only* game in town, or at least the one with the most power to shape the nation's cultural and economic agendas, including its paths of creolization and related histories.

The West Indians' peculiar brand of nationalism has required that the nation as a unit become the equal of metropolitan nations, or of those like Singapore.[70] Mimicry? Perhaps, but one also invested in a critical mimesis of styles and forms of power, and thus not simply passive but rather more a movement for an agentive and creative or productive mimicry. Indeed the pursuit of development, though rooted in the idea of economic autonomy, also embodied the notion of a multifaceted way of being. Development included civilization, respectability, metropolitan and cosmopolitan similarities, and indeed a proper presence for the nation and citizens. It was the modern vehicle through which a certain creolity instrumentalized itself using technologies of government.

Development so absorbed, disseminated, and naturalized into the project of Creole citizenship guides the ways in which it, and ideas like it, became incorporated into the imaginaries of community and individual, making it possible to imagine communities as national, and state formation as a condition of that possibility. Citizenship, development, and the nation thus became triangulated into a relatively seamless strategy for remapping the present that was used by nationalizing elites as a mode of decolonization. Nevertheless, it was always challenged, even if only from within its projects and vocabularies.

Development projects influenced the culture at large and, in the context of state formation and reconstitution, recomposed spaces, replacing, displacing, and accommodating earlier forms of Creole modern subjectivities and insinuating branches of the state into the production and the lives of its people and vice versa. Caribbean decolonizing states are embedded in, and outcomes of, creolizing cultures.[71]

Lucians can be understood as one urban response to a dislocated state, a weakened body unhinged from the socioeconomic and cultural possibilities associated with older forms of Creole development. This partly explains the recurring but differentially expressed refrains of the group. They target, namely, (1) electoral politics, (2) development, and (3) the legitimacy of the state. Ultimately, Lucians want the reorganization of the entire state and a different relationship to development; they want to experience different state spaces and subject places. It is the same cry of banana farmers on the island. Theirs is an ambivalent appeal for the state to get out of the business of production, but not entirely, should the banana farmers require their assistance. A large constituency of Windward Island farmers has opted to remain in the system and for the moment is happy to be there without the overbearing presence of state institutions and personnel. At the same time, the farmers have accommodated to the Darwinian tone of globalization and are prepared to try their hands at being "the fittest." New farmer-controlled enterprises portray the state as inefficient and incompetent, using language similar to that of WTO, World Bank, and U.S. trade officials, who advocate the supremacy of the market as policy determiner par excellence. For them, the state has mishandled the banana industry and private enterprise is required to restore managerial credibility and profitability: "What is needed is effective production organization and coordination, driven by the private entrepreneur's stimulation of market demands, which is to be found locally, regionally, and internationally."[72]

Though it would be problematic to see Lucians' cultural politics as seeking a kind of radically emancipatory politics, it is fairly safe to argue that Lucians dabble in, or rather seek to open up, spaces for the existence of counter-hegemonic ideas, laden with suggestions about the reorganization of community, nation, and citizenship. The stage on which they perform represents an open space in a place or public sphere, where connections and opportunities are closing, even for middle classes, for those who may have assiduously followed the tenets for proper Creole presences as enunciated by the state. Such new open spaces may be inhabited by different discourses and practices. They are an indication that in the face of globalization, or even before it had more forcefully intertwined itself in the regulatory policies of the state, the nationalist project had engendered multiple contradictions onto the spatial templates for its subjects/citizens. Promises of national and individual redemption have been unmasked, reinterpreted, and represented ludicrously. Indeed, it might be legitimate to argue that the neoliberal globalization project has added fuel to the fire, but even as it excludes and as much as it resembles an imperial project, it has nonetheless provided many disenchanted Caribbeans with the spaces that they craved to begin to voice their discontent and to create the context of struggle, entangled though they may be in modernist projects of mapping the present.

AN UNFINISHED GENESIS OF THE IMAGINATION

The questions I began with in this chapter related to Mbembe's critical interrogation of how people are exercising their existence and whether social processes created possibilities for new forms of democratic governance and of belonging to the nation-state. In this regard we may ask: Do Lucians' performances succeed at "cultivating forms of ethical political practice" that will promote a responsiveness to "exclusions and injuries produced by the existing shape of the political community?"[73] Undoubtedly we are witnessing new forms of creolity that thrive on, and are produced by, elements of the "new" global spaces, facilitating its manifold cultural presences but hardly foreclosing on a certain interpretation of local agency, some of whose practices recall earlier Creole carnivalesque performances. But the question still remains open. However, I will not join the chorus dismissing Lucians as pure "pappyshow," or worse, as empty national mockery.[74] What is important is that we not lose sight of the multifarious ways in which the globalization project is being facilitated, received, engaged, enacted, and performed in several sites, reconstructing the terrain on which *creolization* proceeds as well as shaping its substance; and in this specific case leading to a carnivalesque quest for more open dialogic relationships between marginalized citizens and political and economic elites. There is no stopping "dis here" Carnival.

FIVE

"GENS ANGLAISES"

Diasporic Movements Remixing the World
with Post-Creole Imaginations

So you have seen them
with their cardboard grips,
felt hats, rain-cloaks, the women
with their plain
or purple-tinted
coats hiding their fatten-
ed hips.
These are The Emigrants
On sea-port quays
at air-ports

anywhere where there is ship
or train, swift
motor car, or jet
to travel faster than the breeze
you see them gathered:
passports stamped
their travel papers wrapped
in old disused news-
papers: lining their patient queues.[1]

The image of bags and baggage in the lives of people is a common and everyday one. At airports, railway and bus stations, refugee streams, shelter seekers, dislocated people, people on the move—all carry baggage. In many instances they also carry their lives, and their past experiences in the confines of a single suitcase. Yet this everyday and somewhat frequent image plays such a significant part in our lives. Baggage is always associated with comings and goings, arriving and departing, beginning and ending—and it can be experienced at any point in our lives—as children, youth and adult. It is also associated with happiness and sadness, with success and failure, with hope and despair, with birth and death—not one of us has at sometime or the other not carried baggage that relates to some kind of memory.[2]

TRANSNATIONAL STUDIES, whether in the form of border studies or of various diaspora studies, reveal the ways in which ordinary people straddle many locations with their movements, practically subverting neat political topographies of "imagined communities" and forcing a reimagining of the national. Such reimagining disturbs institutional and discursive elements of political and social cultures, most notably the nation-state's creolization projects. The new social fields that are created by such strategies of transnational and global mobility, difficult for authoritative (statist) elements to police, have challenged the primacy of the states' role in the guidance and formation of particular creolized identities. However, what is often not foregrounded in these studies is the fact that these practices of mobility are still invested in the politics of place and the refashioning, redeeming, or rehoming of the spaces of the nation-state and its cultures of citizenship, difference, and temporality.

Faced with the impact of the West's globalization project, and recognizing like Hannerz and others its hybridized or polyvalent cultural Creole convivialities,[3] I am concerned, however, that transnational studies too often focus on resistance and the "subversion" of state narratives of nations in a celebratory fashion, overlooking the ongoing conservative influences that may underpin the formation of transnational identities, different from, though often seeking covalence with, the nation-state. As Hilbourne Watson put it, "The cultural logic of the nation-state dictated that in order to become a person one had to be a national and that set the universal in conflict with the particular: nationalism plays a key role here and beyond."[4] Nonetheless, careful attention should be paid to these home-making practices of power in which subjects are caught up, as well as critically invested in, in order to consider the specularities of presence called forth in playing out tropes of citizenship, that is, seeing "how modernity's individual subject, agent, sovereign being, self-interested person, is being produced and reproduced" as part of this "imagined community" through the inner and outer exercising of existence in complexly mapped social and cultural fields.[5]

The idea of "imagined community," though associated with the formation of nation-states, can forge other kinds of nonstate-led social and political communities based on a host of distinctions. In the aftermath of a nation-state configuration, say, in colonial polities, even as older loyalties are undermined or grow useless, individuals may still coalesce around different forms of nationalism, territorially rooted, or even unrooted, as in the case of Armenians. And even without the "benefit" of nation-states, nationalism or feelings of loyalty toward a particular territory can flourish in de facto colonial places in postcolonial contexts. This is certainly the case of Puerto Rico, where versions of nationalism compete for authenticity in relation to the island. Both on the mainland United States and the island, Puerto Ricans celebrate their adherence to the particularities of place, even as such performances have become hotly contested sites signifying specific identities. By themselves and in combination, however perceived, family, nation, and nation-state may therefore serve as powerful instruments and magnetic memories that constantly root and ground the individual despite transnational locations. Even so, a nationalist's desire for sociocultural autonomy or freedom, if not counterhegemony, over her or his personal sphere will influence the texture of transnationalism, infusing and warping it with expectations first experienced in the originary location. Yet this coagulation of (Lefebvrian) spaces is seldom remarked upon as transnationalism; it is most often perceived as "a step in the right direction," away from the nation's constraints, as if transnationalists move to locations devoid of state presences. The problem with these perspectives is that they continue to measure movement in a binary oppositional relation to the nation-state, as if the latter constituted the only constraint or irredeemable institution or practice within an individual's social life world.

As many have concurred, the Caribbean is an international locale, a series of spaces whose cultural imaginaries include multiple assumptions of travel so that migration has to be figured as central to the formation and sustenance of nations and states and their disruptions as well. But not all travel or journeying is celebratory or entirely transgressive, as some analysts have assumed. All (citizen) ships are not made from the same material and cultural bodies, and all the passengers do not all have similar motives or imaginations. Indeed, migration of Caribbeans to the "motherland" often carried with it a certain amount of dread, and migration of Haitians in rafts to the Bahamas and the Florida keys "provide a somber counterpoint to more celebratory theories of travel and diaspora, by highlighting the underside of these processes."[6] Moreover, Caribbean history is replete with instances of state encouragement of nationals' migrations, given the inabilities of the former to provide them with adequate levels of economic support. Consider the domestic labor schemes, the outcome of a collaboration between Canada and Caribbean states which resulted in thousands of young women employed as domestics in Canadian households. Also consider the U.S. farm labor schemes that facilitate the migration of thousands of Caribbean nationals to work on American farms. James estimates that by the end of the postwar period, "over 40,000 workers from the Bahamas, Jamaica, Barbados, St. Vincent, St. Lucia and Dominica were in the U.S. under the scheme."[7] The high rates of growth experienced during Puerto Rico's Bootstrap economic programs were premised on the state-encouraged migration of tens of thousands to the U. S. mainland. However, as Ramón Grosfoguel recounts, although Puerto Ricans migrated as U.S. citizens, they were incorporated as veritable second-class citizens, becoming akin to "a distinct racialized minority," distinguished from other minorities including Asians, blacks, and Chicanos.[8] Consider, too, nation-state–sanctioned tourism the second or first industries for many Caribbean states whereby nations are encouraged to see and sell themselves through the eyes of white foreigners. Indeed, tourism depends on the sale of national patrimony in transnational markets, yet this openness also accommodates a further thickening of the routes and spaces of Caribbean social life, with such deepening entanglements making for shorter bridges of flight.

As I recount these hi/stories or "human identity stories," I am concerned that the metaphor of travel not be overused to suggest that fixedness is its opposite, contrasting location, or perhaps more importantly, that travel not be always read as involving a loosening of connections, a footlooseness that makes the idea of originary location redundant. Some of these concerns have been raised in the context of anthropology's attempt to come to terms with the connotation of fixedness that the concept of culture conveys. Clifford's rectification of this connotation construes traveling as normative. He even argues that dwelling or staying might be conceptualized as exceptional, at least in the conventional sense of these terms. In other words, transnational experiences have increasingly become integral elements of people's cultural personae. In response to this, Homi Bhabha and Stuart Hall support the consciousness of travel or traveling cultures but warn against the overemphasis on travel to the exclusion of dwelling. As Bhabha responded, "I really want you to talk about the place of a lack of movement and fixity in a politics of movement and a theory of travel."[9] I want to rephrase Bhabha's concern here, to address not fixity or "lack of movement" as a field of spatial relationships but rather as a constant reinvention of the spacings or mappings of the local and national against what might be seen as nonnational, nonlocal, and even global and transnational spaces. My aim here is to bring the literatures of transnationalism, diaspora, and migration together to make a case for a less binary approach to travel and "dwelling" or to link travel to a politics of "dwelling," though I am aware that the quest of writers like Clifford, Robertson, and others is to pry loose the field of anthropology from its approach to culture as a bounded and stable set of practices. But I make these points to gesture to the meaning of these phenomena of staying and moving as regenerative principles underlying processes of creolization that are being crafted by the double-articulating movements of diasporas remixing the world, their world, and convoluting those knots of presence in that dynamic "time of entanglement." Transnationalism as considered here, then, regrounds and sustains the individual in altered states of power and subjectivity through its accommodations of his or her quest for the morphogenesis of cultures of power.[10]

By grounding, I mean to make an analogous gesture toward the multipurposive strategies of provision grounds, those grounds which were spatially removed from plantations and which slaves bargained with to retain elements of an unproscribed freedom of sorts. Tomich argues that these grounds "offered a space for slave initiative and self-assertion that simply cannot be deduced from their economic form. Through them, the slaves themselves organized and controlled a secondary economic network that . . . allowed them to begin to construct an alternative way of life that went beyond the plantation."[11] Whereas early forms and processes of creolization received a boost from and subverted plantation or plantation-related regimens, insofar, say, as access to provision grounds repositioned the slave within the plantation regimen and, later, small plots of land repositioned the newly freed within the plantation system, the colonial state and the Atlantic economy generally; transnational groundings serve as sites of Creole subversion and accommodation as well. Such provision grounds, therefore, performed multiple functions: first, grappling with the present and its mappings, that is, seeking to maneuver within the material and cultural circumstances of the present moment; and second, treating "the present" as a step with which to negotiate the future and not really as an end in itself. Options were opened up by these grounds but their presence did not break entirely from all the elements of plantation control or from its local and global capitalist production rhythms. In a similar fashion, one may argue that the transnational grounding prepares the transnational citizen to negotiate with altered (nation) states from a stronger position, even as it alters such nation-state spaces and reanimates efforts to negotiate and/or transcend those conditions, processes, and outcomes. The transnational embodies sociocultural exchanges, given her or his contact with others. And these exchanges result in the alteration of ideas and the acquisition and alteration of the uses of material and cultural objects, all of which carry with them their hi/stories, their displaced or (re)placed past identities.

UNTHINKING TRAVEL AND FIXITY
AS AUTONOMOUS CONDITIONS

The problem in grappling with the stultifying effects of the binary of travel and dwelling and substituting travel for fixity as a strategic means to get beyond it, at least as Clifford uses it, is that even as he recognizes the role of memory in "fixing" people to or at certain locations, he fails to explore how the imagination of those places travels. What I assert here is that the idea of belonging to a certain nation, however imagined or by whom, is a powerful fix on peoples' *sense of themselves and their place* as they travel. I want to emphasize that this "fix" does not invariably represent a stasis as in a photographic image. Even so, photographic images are literal snapshots, moments that index a given state, a present. But we can never know the entire life of the person in the snapshot. Memories and cultural artifacts function similarly, and likewise selectively; thus they are a partial recognition of the familiarity of "originary" place. It is something captured in memory that is not to be equated with all of the nation-state narrative. It is a certain kind of familiar and basic maneuvering that resonates in the field of culture. As people travel or migrate they carry various quantities and different kinds of cultural and physical luggage from their originary home locations. These operate as signs with which to read, write, explore, dwell, accommodate, connect, disconnect, and even ostensibly (not just ambivalently) resist certain aspects of the "hosts' *own* cultures" of power. Much of this interaction takes place unconsciously, as migrants get into the nitty gritty of surviving, making the most of what they have, find, and keep. Let us say everyone carries cultural "suitcases" of sorts. We are mostly unaware of the contents within those suitcases, but we may clue in, and as Irit Rogoff notes, oftentimes these suitcases represent other critical aspects of such travel or migration, beyond the personally scripted narrative. I will return to this point later.

However, it should be noted that such movement takes place within a hierarchical global system, more evident in its economic distinctions (say, between a North and South, broadly speaking), where color racisms and sexisms might be treated differently but accorded a similar status, however different the location (from "originary" to "new" place). This is borne out in the Haitian person's observation of the racial and class inequities that he or she encounters in the land of opportunity, despite its seductive appeal.[12] The Haitian's cry that she does not want "to be black again" is not a rejection of a black consciousness per se but, on the contrary, a deep recognition and a memory of social place in a specific spatial positioning and a response to being "fixed" relationally into an inferior social location that leads the poor Haitian to hope to permanently dis-locate in a land that famously promises freedom and individual rights.[13] In the United States, itself a complex diasporic habitus (despite its seductive promises) whose imperial and colonial politics have contributed disproportionately to the refurbishment of the Atlantic's racialized and gendered infrastructure, the Haitian finds herself/himself still having to engage in a personal politics that involves a renewed affirmation of a black self, indeed a redefinition of subjectivity—of Haitianness and ultimately of blackness. Oftentimes the Haitian, in an effort to resignify the self, joins those enduring multifaceted struggles of African Americans, the locally despised marginals. For racialization of Caribbeans generally has been an enduring colonial and postcolonial feature of the world economy, even in those overly industrialized countries where they (most former colonial powers of the region) are deemed citizens.

CULTURAL SUITCASES: THE BAGGAGE OF BELONGING

I return now to this idea of suitcases or luggage, which I appropriate from visual culture's alleged fascination with the propositions, albeit binary, of the suitcase as symbolizing expectations, utopic dreams as well as nostalgia toward lost worlds, and perhaps tolerated displacements. As Rogoff summarized luggage's currency within visual culture:

> Primarily [either] it has served as the signification of utopian beginnings—such as those accompanying the triumphant claims of immigration to the "new world"—or it has represented doomed journeys of annihilation, of no return. Operating fairly strictly within such binary constraints which serve by necessity to produce one another, "luggage" within this traditional signifying system seems to have served to affirm national entities and narratives as well as national borders by working back to originary moments of flight, expulsion, ejection, annihilation and crossing over.[14]

When Rogoff raises these issues of representations of suitcases in visual culture, she does so in order to situate and frame her intention of moving beyond these binary imaginings. For her visual culture's focus on suitcases is a case of the sign masking the social relations of positionality within which it is embedded. A somewhat asymmetrical relationship exists between sign and signifier. Both speak to the unequal playing field that is the outcome of the circulation of global capital as well as systems of political and cultural domination. I want to shift laterally (from these visual cultural analytics), to associate suitcases with their physical and symbolic properties. I want to entertain the idea that suitcases can be opened and closed, their contents usually removed, relocated, or lost, as more items are accumulated. Within the suitcases are meaningful artifacts made so by the national and personal places they occupied (past or present) in the location from which the traveler comes but also those others that are carried to negotiate unanticipated conditions. The latter are the representations of the transnational received and reinterpreted through a national's experience, or the results of how the nation-state *presents* itself transnationally. Once removed from their "original" location, they cannot be experienced in the same way, a point that Hall and others have made in different contexts.[15] Thus, it can be said that the relocated artifacts of the person or nation have become somewhat dislocated, even as they attempt to anchor the elusive familiar. Therein the idea of nationness, like the nation itself which is constantly in a state of flux and change, becomes malleable and capable of being transformed. Yet elements of the national identity, which is a recognition of an original homeland, however differentially spatialized, mediate this transnational space. This play on or of nation is crucial to routing and rooting the transnational experience. Though she treats the local, global, and international as separate spheres instead of constitutive domains, Mary Chamberlain's point is still germane. As she says,

> Whatever the reason for migration, migrants come from somewhere. They arrive with a cultural suitcase, made locally. They arrive caught in the tension between the global and the local, between the international and the national, between *their* idea of the global and *their* idea of the local. They are not acultural itinerants, international vagrants, with no fixed abode, but rational human beings driven by complex, and mobile strategies, fretworks of dreams and aspirations, calculations and plans,

obscure directives and unarticulated responses, changing and changed by their journey.[16]

Literally and metaphorically, the biographies of Haitians in *The Butterfly's Way* disclose those suitcase contents that these transnationals carry when they travel.

The contents of Maude Heurtelou's suitcases included

the talcum powder on my nightstand, which the vendor at the Iron Market in Port-au-Prince had wanted no payment for because I was leaving for university abroad. The multicolored kite that decorated my wall was made twenty years before by the neighborhood shoeshine man, who had presented it to my mother thinking she was carrying a boy. An unknown artist had sculpted the metal sheet lantern by my window. The small wicker basket in the corner of my room had carried dried Ilan Ilan flowers from my middle school in Port-au-Prince. The embroidered pillowcase where I rested my head each night was made by hand in the mountains of Jacmel. It was embossed with my great grandmother's initials and passed down from my grandmother, to my mother, and now myself. My rubber sandals, a gift from my friend Marie, reminded me of traveling Haitian feet, steady firm, and purposeful in their gait.[17]

Heurtelou took her suitcases and their contents to her new location in Quebec City. As she put it:

After more than two decades from Haiti, I still reach out for my suitcases, both physical and cultural, for all of the items in them, linked as they are to memories and traditions, that have helped me, and still continue to help me survive the immigrant life. However, my suitcase has now expanded with a few more items gathered from other cultures, with the letters and photographs of the friends I have made in Guatemala, Canada, and Florida, with their stories, and languages, and traditions that have slowly merged into my own: the particular lilt of Guatemalan Spanish that I eventually mastered, the hand-made fabrics from San Andrés, the *cabane à sucre* parties in Quebec City, where I indulged in maple syrup candies out on the street, along with the other residents, natives, and immigrants alike. What my own cultural isolation as an immigrant in these places has taught me is that I am part of a living culture that in no way stops being a part of me, even when I am not completely immersed in it. With everything I do and say, I am perpetuating that culture, enriching it, modifying it when necessary, but contributing to its regeneration. My suitcases, both physical and cultural, have always, and will always, make me proud of my culture. They are perhaps a microcosm of what I am missing living abroad, but will never completely lose.[18]

REMAKING THE NATIONAL

This chapter therefore explores how travelers,[19] particularly working-class, rural land-based working people, a group overlooked in the literature on diaspora—whether journeying to the Atlantic, Mediterranean, or Pacific from the Caribbean, or from the rural to the urban and back—carry cultural and mental suitcases of the familiar. From the repository of the daily familiar, they "choose" those practices and relationships they wish to preserve and to remember in their new spatial locations. At the intersection of the unfamiliar and the familiar, the outer and the inner, is a ground as fertile, and likely representative, as that between the imbricated national and the transnational. How else to explain the key elements of national culture which persist inventively—even as their institutional homes are dismantled—than through the transnationals' continued practice of an identity which assumes a certain kind of identification with forms of nationhood, even when state propagated?

Though of a different provenance, my argument bears some relevance for literary theorists' ideas about "writing the nation" or for that matter unwriting the nation; it is not reducible to these themes. What I seek to discuss are the ways in which transnationalist practices can reinforce notions of nation or displace and replace them, as people relocate from "periphery" to "center" and back, temporarily or permanently, physically or through subjective memory travel, or those relayed, as exemplified by Audre Lorde's recollection of Carriacou through her parents' references.[20] In other words, as Stuart Hall said of diasporic identity, it is never quite finished.[21] But which identity is? Transnationals return to a remembered originary location, but no one, or place, remains quite the same. That is to say, people thus placed may constantly revise notions of national cultural practices, and though they undermine its selective originary conceptions, they may never be too far removed from the changing nation or from state pronouncements and interpretations of the nation. In this sense, a people's creolization project need not sever itself from a nation-state's technologies of government for fixing creolization performances of place to be transformative.

The entangled practices of "fixity" in "diasporic mo(ve)ments" of place, and relatedly space, that I have in mind here parallel the analytical observations made by Bhabha in his discussion of "dissemiNation" and the complex articulations required to sustain signifying regimes of representation caught up with fantasies of origin and identity (or with sovereign ideals of citizenship in the city-citizen game of modernity).[22] My concern here, however, is to trace the doubleness in writing the nation by unthinking travel and fixity as autonomous contesting conditions, and by linking "the cultural construction of nationness" with those sets of (re)homing practices, exercised by the returning traveler, through which the " scenario of articulation" of the nation is recursively formed and transformed.[23] Thus, even as I seek to redirect our attention to the imaginaries of nation, the ensuing discussion calls attention to an elusiveness of this memory, this imagining, and also to the fact that its points never remain in the same location even when memory recalls. What I would like to convey is the (re)orientation to location that endures, the strength of which depends on how social and individual experiences are played out, when one acts to move away from it. In coming to terms with these interlocuting practices of travel, the novelty of this chapter lies in its attention to the home-coming traveler rather than the outbound migrant, and the former's constituting and reconstituting influences in forming a transnational social field from his or her originary but transnationalized home. I would like to explore these points with the following anecdote and draw out even further the renewed nationalist implications that might get buried with the current fascination of "traveling cultures."

REWORKING THE NATION THROUGH
TRANS-NATIONALIZING

While working on a land registration project, thanks to the University of Madison's Land Tenure Center, I was able to return to St. Lucia and serve as a team leader, analyzing the impact of a USAID (United States Agency for International Development) land registration program. The program represented the first stage of a new land policy designed to mobilize key segments of the populace, many of them family land heirs, to combat the contrived "underproductive" use of family land. Because much land on the island had been communal or family owned, many St. Lucians are reluctant to engage in its commodification. Yet many have been forced to do so. I do not want to give the impression here that family land was ever completely outside the market economy. In fact it was created by an earlier form of market economy in the postemancipation era. I would like to treat it as one type of response to an older form of modernity, generated within the context of nineteenth-century plantation agriculture. By that I mean that land generally was instrumental for the acquisition of status and respect—a strategy toward a more empowered citizenship or citizenness, as I stated earlier. No doubt it yielded economic benefits and shaped a certain kind of maneuver within a society where power was used abusively for the most part. Working people exported crops cultivated on it and serviced the moral economies of their households as well. Family land provided working people with the provision to procure other produce, for example, ground provisions and fruits, and it was also a space where their animals could graze. No doubt the key to family and community stability lay in the procurement of land.

Such land was a dynamic institution which, while promoting a particular form of life or lived experiences, lends itself to its own transformation because of its members' desire to participate in alternative or newer forms of a liminal modernity. That is to say, its alleged sacrosanctity was always open to interpretational (as well as intergenerational) shifts resulting in changes in its symbolic, familial, and economic values. It no doubt provided working people with the means to live territorially and deterritorially at home and abroad, so that certain "traditions" were maintained and simultaneously undermined and transformed. Although much family land might have been noncommodifiable, its heirs still retained connection to the machinations of capital in its various economic and sociocultural configurations.

I became the tenant of a St. Lucian couple who had spent, as they put it, "over thirty years" living in England. Jack and Judith both worked for a hotel, though Judith, intermittently a part-time worker, had cared for Jack's three children born in London and her six left in St. Lucia, whom they sent for later. Upon their return to St. Lucia, they built two houses. One of the houses they lived in; the other, on the same property, they rented out. A typical example of rural St. Lucian architecture, Jack's and Judith's house was small and wooden, with four rooms and a front veranda, with an indoor toilet, an outdoor shower, and an outdoor kitchen equipped with a small propane gas stove, as well as a coal-pot, a supply of coal, and a low basement, referred to as a cellar. Opulent by rural standards, their second house had four bedrooms, a large indoor bath and toilet in addition to an outdoor shower, and came fully furnished, including a refrigerator and propane stove in the indoor kitchen. I stayed in this house for four months.

During that time, Jack, Judith, and I communicated mainly in French Creole, more familiarly known as patois, as they could not, or rather would not, speak standard English, a curiosity which aroused my interest. I discovered that the couple had succeeded for those thirty years to move not only exclusively within the Caribbean diaspora but among members of a small group from rural St. Lucia and of fellow Toulons. This group reinforced a particular kind of St. Lucian nationality, French Creole being its defining component. Because English had become the language through which they negotiated their occupational and market-related activities, they preferred to converse with each other in French Creole. Furthermore, French Creole set them apart from other Caribbeans and West Indians, a subset of a diasporic community of distinct membership, thereby easing their return to St. Lucia and subsequent retirement in the early 1980s. Jack's and Judith's two houses were built on family property, a source of keen familial animosity. Not only had Judith surveyed the family land (an unusual act even for the late 1980s) but she had carved out an individual share, diminishing the extent of the whole. Soon after I moved in she not only considered selling another piece of her land but tried to convince other family members to do the same. She had dismembered the land, she said, because it was in a state of gross neglect. She wanted to both cultivate it and safeguard it against other heirs' encroachments, specifically that of her "wayward" nephew, who lived on the property. She often reminded me that she had done what any English person would do. Observations such as "en L'Angleterre, yo pa-a faire so ahn" and "beche en L'Angleterre pa-a fé sa" punctuated her conversational rationalizations (in England that is not the way things are done; white people in England don't do that).[24] "Land worked for people, not people for the land," she once claimed. Furthermore, the money the land made allowed them to live a decent life. These were radical views in Toulon, where 58 percent of all land was held by families and any women owners had their families to thank for the "privilege." In a survey conducted in 1987, 40 percent of those interviewed were adamant about the sacrosanctity of family land, 21 percent said they would sell it for a good price, and 26 percent claimed they would have to consult with the family before considering the idea.[25] Madame Judith was a keen observer of what worked for English people in England. Having learned a new approach to family land ownership, she implemented these ideas in a way that in part reconstituted her homeland, remade the local, reconstituted the nature of her fixity, or her place, encouraging other members of her family to reinterpret and renew older Creole traditions of making place. Since 1987, an even more vibrant land market has taken shape on the island. Out of 129 parcels of land whose records I examined in the land registry, 15, ranging in size from 0.05 to 7 hectares, had been sold, with one sold several times. Land was also sold to family members and heirs, suggesting consolidation among family members, perhaps a recycling of the family land tradition, but most certainly the pervasiveness of freehold tenure at the expense of family land.[26]

PRACTICING NATIONAL BELONGING THROUGH FAMILY

This anecdote suggests that facility in English is fair to high among Caribbean immigrants, particularly St. Lucian ones in England, even those who migrated in 1960, when the island's illiteracy rate was roughly 43 percent. But I am not so much concerned with the presence or absence of French Creole as with a lifestyle that bears consideration for those engaged in mapping transatlantic, transnational, or transcultural identities and the cultural politics they enact. Madame Judith's story opened up an area for research into Caribbean nationals who have returned to their original homelands: "returnees," "expatriates," "returned nationals," or "English people (gens anglaises), and facetiously, "ain't its," as they are variously called.

For the first ten months of 1960, 43,450 West Indian migrants arrived in England. Indeed,

In 1955, migrants coming from the Caribbean to Britain numbered 27,550. By 1960, the numbers of Caribbean migrating to Britain had risen to 49,650; and the rate had increased to 66,300 during the following year. By the time the Commonwealth Immigrants Act was passed in 1962, limiting immigrant entry, the number of arrivals had decreased to 31,800. After this, Caribbean arrivals numbered only 3,241 in 1963, peaked at 14,848 in 1965 and began falling rapidly to less than 10,000 in the average year.[27]

Douglas Midgett estimates that many of the roughly 10,000 St. Lucians who left for England did so in 1961, just before the 1962 Commonwealth Immigrants Act, the intention of which, as is well known, was to curb primary immigration from black and brown Commonwealth countries.[28] In his budget address in 1960, the administrator of the colony stated that by the end of November 1959, 860 persons had left St. Lucia for the United Kingdom, "in search of employment or to join their relatives."[29] Moreover, he added that "there was continued demand for St. Lucians for employment overseas, from St. Croix, Antigua and the United States, the latter of which started in 1951. Migrants had remitted over $400,000 to the island in the form of savings in addition to the direct remittances made by workers to their dependents."[30] Swithin Schouten, in founding a new political party on the island in 1960, declared that the self-government of the St. Lucia Labour Party was a sham and used it as an example of growing disillusionment among the island's population concerning the fact that "over 1000 St. Lucians at a cost of over $300,000 of solid cash have left for England in the past six weeks alone."[31]

The island administrator's upbeat contention was that "agricultural land is changing hands and new capital is being brought into the country to modernize our methods of cultivation and production." Furthermore, "Small industries are springing up around us as well as new buildings which all point to the birth of a new era of progress." In reality, however, employment was scarce and the island was poor. The colony's budget in 1960 was only $5.6 million, of which over $4 million came from local revenue, $1.7 million from a grant in aid from the federal government, and $172,703 from colonial development and welfare schemes.[32] Moreover, the island's economy was in transition. King sugar, its main crop, was rapidly declining, with a shortfall of 1,483 tons from the year before; so too were the secondary crops of cacao and copra.[33] In this transition, bananas, which would emerge as the substitute for sugar—the island's new monocrop—were not yet a fully developed endeavor, though expectations for its success ran high.[34]

Many working people who left St. Lucia were unskilled artisans who had been unable to find jobs on the island or had low-paying jobs. But among those who left were nurses, civil servants, teachers, farmers, and secretaries. One retired nurse who migrated to St. Croix in the U.S. Virgin Islands told me that when she left St. Lucia she earned one Eastern Caribbean dollar a month!

Working people responded to the call from the passing empire for workers to rebuild England. Several returnees located in the south of the island referred to this English demand for workers, combined with their inadequate jobs or their unemployment, as the reason for their departure from the island. They became the first member of their families to leave or followed in the wake of the earlier migration of family members. As St. Lucia was a colony at the time, St. Lucians traveled with British passports, so it was possible to be "British and St. Lucian at the same time," one person said.[35]

Given Caribbeans' long-standing tradition of physical flight and the conditions of uncertainty in many parts of the region, travel (for example, to places such as Panama, Cuba, Costa Rica, the Dominican Republic, Trinidad and Tobago, the French and English Guianas, and Dutch Curacao and Aruba) and the association of travel with personal advancement appeared inevitable. One migrant in Frank Abenaty's sample expressed it thus: "It's just that if you wanted to achieve a profession you had to come to England . . . We thought that it [Great Britain] was the centre of our cultural heritage. We sang patriotic songs on Empire Day and things like that. So this was the seat of culture; you couldn't go anywhere else. If you went to America all you had was an American degree, which was not considered the same as the British at that time."[36] West Indians who migrated did not have a pan-Caribbean identity but insular ones, leading them to migrate to areas where their fellow islanders had settled. Researchers have highlighted such clustering. According to Peach, for example, Dominicans and St. Lucians settled in the Paddington area, Grenadians in Hammersmith and Ealing, Antiguans were in Hackney Waltham Forest, and Montserratians settled in Stoke Newington.[37] Jamaicans, on the other hand, were in Brixton. Even so, many islanders like Jack and Judith formed even smaller clusters of regions within islands. Peach observed that migrants from Anse la Raye and Canaries, two neighboring districts, preferred Paddington, while those from Choiseul settled mainly in East London. Migrants from the capital city of Castries resided in South East.[38] These areas were open areas, through which various Caribbean and other subjectivities and histories intersected and mingled.

Caribbean migrants to Great Britain worked in hotels, restaurants, hospitals, sewing factories, laundries, transport, and rail, swept the streets, held a host of other jobs. Some studied in British universities or polytechnics, but most were working people. One respondent said that no sooner had she arrived in England than she sought work three days after. She worked once as a ward orderly. In her words,

> When I went there as a ward orderly, looking at the state of the place in the kitchen, you couldn't drink water. We take knives and scraped all the kitchen everywhere on every ward, we used to take turns clean all the walls, the floors where everything becomes white. We cleaned a lot. Then the white people start to see the dirt on the floor. They start saying, oh you didn't clean that, but before we came they never saw the dirt. We used to laugh [at the situation].[39]

Dissatisfied, they sought better job situations as they tried to survive in a harsh England.

One younger respondent said that what struck her about England when she left her Dominican village, following her parents who had left earlier, was:

> Doors being shut. You go into an apartment, and you have to close the doors behind you. Also the crowdiness of the rooming house. I always thought, why leave the Caribbean where you have so much freedom, and come to this place where you have to share a kitchen. I realized right there and then, that I wanted to return.[40]

Mr. Roberts agreed:

> Listen, if I had purchased a round trip ticket, believe you me, I would not be talking to you now. I had a one-way ticket and could not return. But I wanted to turn right back and come back. I don't know how we survived. I learnt the word "hate" in England. It is exactly what it says in the English dictionary. Hate amongst both blacks and whites. Once you get in England it becomes a reality.[41]

And so there was always a sense of home, or more homely spaces as well as family, left behind. The idea of returning home shaped their transnational experience but also presented opportunities to remake that original home as well. Put another way, deterritorialization reinforced their proprietary conception of territorial belonging through "familial ethnicities," but changing ones. They sent money home, securing their homeland connection but making demands and communicating their expectations. One respondent said that she dated only men who wanted to return. "If the man was not interested in returning, there was no point in seeing him. I wanted someone who shared my desire to return."[42] "To be a St. Lucian is being home; being in my village, being me, being ourselves. I have always been proud of being a St. Lucian."[43]

Being a St. Lucian is not a nation-state designation, at least it was not then, given the colonial status of the island. It referred to community, a particular experience of community and identity. Time spent in England, much longer than they anticipated, involved a conscientious economic effort aimed at returning home. Life for working people was different than it was for the students and the male political figures frequently discussed in diaspora studies. Whereas a number of students and politically conscious male migrants busied themselves with political affairs, associating with C. L. R. James, joining Pan African movements and anti-racist causes, and so on, the working people of the Caribbean worked at procuring economic improvements and, the women especially worked at maintaining the stability of their families and households in England and St. Lucia, keeping alive the dream of return.

But this condition was experienced by many Caribbeans in England. A Barbadian friend and colleague whom I showed an earlier draft of this chapter wrote:

> I relate in a very personal way to some of the issues you raised. I have two brothers and one sister living in England: one brother has lived there since 1956, the other since 1961, and my sister since 1970. The family connections with Barbados have remained fundamental and integral in spite of time and distance: this is about connecting transnational spatialities, I think. Both brothers helped to finance my high school education with their remittances. We have remained in very close contact over these years, visiting, telephoning, discussing family matters in Barbados, purchasing land there jointly, renting it, dealing with ailing parents, supporting them financially until the end and financing their burials, etc. Clearly for all of us as children, there was never a question of remaining connected transnationally. My visits to the UK have exposed me to

relatives, in-laws, friends who carry on as though they did not leave rural Barbados, but whose lifestyles are not Barbadian and whose social connections, eating habits, ways of preparing meals, celebrating Xmas, etc. after 40 years remain as culturally connected as ever. Of course, my siblings' children are Brits with semi-Bajan accents and as deeply rooted in British culture as in transnationalized Bajan culture.[44]

One gens anglaise recalls,

While you are living in England, mentally you feel as though you are in St. Lucia, because one always has plans [to return] because while you are there, you are working, you are making preparations so that one day you will be able to return home and live an independent life. It is also physical, because from time to time, one leaves England and comes here on holiday, on business, if you like, buying properties, making preparations. Because you will tend to return home for good one day. That cannot be done just like that; you are working on a daily basis, gathering whatever you can financially, to put aside, so that one day you can return. Most of us are looking forward to retiring one day. I am contented now. I am enjoying the fruits of my labor now.[45]

In the 1980s, as members of the St. Lucia Association, gens anglaises raised funds holding dances and other events for the purchase of an ambulance for Canaries and La Fargue. They networked to find out the most essential need of the island and sent boxes during times of need; for example, when a hurricane devastated the island, they sent food and clothes.

Conscious of themselves as people from a particular colonial place with its colonial projects, gens anglaises of St. Lucia, with their personal histories or ontological narratives set within the sociohistorical colonial and postcolonial templates of public narratives, wove their transnational desires and expectations into a multiplex task of bettering themselves, their families, and their country.[46] As one respondent put it, "I know how St. Lucia was when I left. The whole of St. Lucia was in the same predicament. Times were hard for most people."[47] Under those circumstances, maintaining the St. Lucian relatives was crucial. It was, as Stephan Palmié posited in relation to Caribbeans living in New York, that England served as the St. Lucians' periphery of sorts.[48] However, it is a periphery that registers different meaning at different times, and to which immigrants add and take away. In other words, migrants have a critical approach to this periphery which allows them the wherewithal to relive and return to a transfiguring core in their rerouted lives.

GOING HOME AGAIN TO A (RE)MOVING COMMUNITY

In reconsidering the relationship between territorialization and deterritorialization, Jonathan Schwartz tells a story about Boris, who worked as a janitor in Canada and spent some time in Macedonia, his original home. Boris was constructing a car park near his home. And to complete the job a large plum tree had to be cut down and its roots removed. Schwartz observes that "the work of removing roots in Boris's case was also a way of deepening roots in the place." The anecdote about Boris's plum tree might indicate the resilience, not the frailty, of the root metaphor in an understanding of migrants' and villagers' exchanges. Schwartz concludes,

> The obverse symbolic—cutting away the actual roots in order to make space for other roots—underlines the plurality and simultaneity of fields in the migration process. Our study continues to be that of territorialization, but instead of reifying or essentializing the "two ends of the migration chain," the village and metropole can be experienced "in the making." Rather than merely deconstructing "roots," we can also perceive how the horticultural metaphors are practiced and, thereby, how they shape meaning of our informants' identities.[49]

This is a critical point. Both village and metropole are "experienced in the making," rather than seen as distinctive ends of a pole representing territoriality and deterritoriality.

Many transnational St. Lucians have returned, distinguishing themselves by the houses they build, many large and opulent. A few have been particularly enterprising, setting up small factories, performing their trades, and employing small numbers of St. Lucians. All of this is noticed and constantly remarked upon by other St. Lucians, the "true" locals. For example, they might be reminded facetiously, by a shop clerk or a clerk at a government office, that things in St. Lucia work differently. "This is not England you know. You are in St. Lucia now," one gens anglaises remembered being told by an office clerk.

The process of rerooting more often than not is trying. Local St. Lucians retain skepticism toward transnationals. For them, transnationals reinforce a certain kind of locality by others, which, when compared with theirs, seems to the locals to be less authentic. In other words, difference is perceived as inauthentic—those who "stayed" are skeptical about those who left. In 1978, as the government and people readied themselves for political independence, which was expected the following year, those resident in England expressed their anxiety at being deprived of their British citizenship. Several letters appeared in the local press, and the high commissioner's office in London was flooded with concerned inquiries. In response to this, one writer of a facetious column, "En Passant," in the local newspaper declared:

> St. Lucians living in England must be happy now that St. Lucia's independence has been delayed. This gives them more time to enjoy their cherished status as "Englishmen." Incidently people are wondering if the Premier's suggestion to woo St. Lucians living abroad back home after independence includes those St. Lucians living in England. People have their doubts that the St. Lucians in England can be brought back home— not the way these fellars enjoy being "Englishmen."[50]

But they have returned. On their return, gens anglaises reroot themselves in St. Lucia variously. Whereas before their departure they lived as extended families on family land, sharing labor, goods, and other services, now many do not. In one community in the south, one respondent recalled how close knit the people there were:

> Cachilet community are always together always close. If you hungry you just tell someone you had nothing and everybody would send food for you. That's how we lived in Cachilet, in my days when I was young. [If] You sick everybody would come around—bringing medicine and taking your clothes to wash, cleaning the house. That's how we lived for generations. Because Cachilet people were from one family.[51]

They no longer live this way. But several family members who never left the island occupy various lots on her family land in Cachilet. One respondent said that she would support the selling of family land if the elders agreed to it. As much of this land is not occupied, or too distantly located, selling it, she said, would be an option.

In the community of Yonkers Town in the south, which has roughly two hundred houses, residents have established one of the more well-organized and structured communities on the island. Though the community consists of other St. Lucians, it is the "English" people who dominate the association, and it is they who fight for services within the community. It is a distinctive community, with well-paved streets named after the flora and fauna of the island—a distinctive gesture. A long battle was required to obtain these services. The Yonkers Town Association (YTA) was set up as a result of close contact with a government minister who, as the representative for the area, convened the meeting at the behest of Mrs. Roberts, the prospective leader of the association. She felt sufficiently concerned about the association being treated as an English-people project, so the larger constituency connection provided her with the cover to launch it. The association has raised funds through a variety of ways, including beach-bashes, country and western dances, and flower shows. Influenced by their English experience, they wanted a well-organized neighborhood, good roads, drainage, and named streets. They later worked on a park and playing field for the community.

For gens anglaises, only upon returning to the island did they realize their difference from the "local" St. Lucians. Their transnationalized status, honed by the practice of being St. Lucian in England, was different from that of those on the island. It is this relationship that led to mixed feelings of being at "home." Perceived as different and operating accordingly, gens anglaises say they are overcharged for services because of their "ex-pat" (expatriate) status. Services are more expensive in their communities. Gardeners and other service people charge more to work in that community. Vendors overcharge. And gens anglaises believe that local St. Lucians bear more than a little resentment toward them. "Wherever you see someone complaining about a particular service, a particular attitude, generally about a certain way of doing things—that person is bound to be someone from abroad," said one respondent. "It is just that for so many years, we have been exposed to a different way of doing things."[52] Most migrants left in their early twenties during the 1960s, young enough to unlearn, relearn, and readapt to a new cultural milieu. In the Yonkers Town Association, the gens anglaises say they get things done. They, more than the locals, can be counted on to fulfill their obligations. They learned these ways in England and grew to appreciate punctuality, order, structure, and organization. In fact several said that they were drawn to the Yonkers community because it resembled an English community, with its street names and numbered houses.

Karen Fog Olwig, in addressing the "disjuncture and transience" attributed to transnationals generally, argues that despite the fluidity of life, cultural sites perform the work of rooting deterritorialized Nevisians. "Disjunction and transience" are not acceptable concepts with which to view Nevisians. Olwig posits that "by focusing on the global relations which generations of people have developed and sustained at the same time as they have maintained a presence in their local island society, it is possible to detect the existence of institutions of some permanence. These institutions have accommodated the local and global conditions of life presented to African-Caribbean people and provided significant and stable points of cultural identification."[53] In this rendering of permanency, the question of fixity emerges as a static positioning. Yet nothing or no one on the island of Nevis, or elsewhere for that matter, stands still and maintains the same relationship over time. This change in relationship is precisely what happened in the case of the gens anglaises. Inhabiting a different relationship to the island and its institutions, including the acknowledged Creole custom of family land and family members, gens anglaises find themselves engaged in an informal study of various social relationships on the island. Outside of family land, few such institutions exist. Like researchers, they must look for signifiers to proceed along a certain route, if their rerooting is to be successful or not too trouble prone.

Karsten Pærregarrd argues that, like anthropologists, natives also analyze their cultures. The people we study act as "outsiders" and "insiders" as well. Migrants carry ideas about their homelands that are mutable, with and within them. They experience the homeland differently.

The invention of a Tapeño culture and the creation of a Tapeño identity is the result of a complex process of negotiation between different forms of representations, and that the actors in this process are made up of villagers, migrants, the rest of the Peruvian society as well as by the anthropologist. Moreover migrants' inventional practice represents an implicational counterpart to the life of the people living in the village as much as the anthropological project does. Migrants not only possess an intimate knowledge of native life (along with their fellow villagers), they are also involved (along with the anthropologist) in a continuous process of understanding and interpreting it and, ultimately, changing it.[54]

To return to their native land, so to speak, requires much adjustment and the success of it depends on correct analysis of a changed and changing locale, one which the local St. Lucian is at pains in his or her interaction to point out is not the same as that in England and elsewhere—it is fixed as a changed St. Lucia. One respondent, who was running a small factory, put it this way:

> You don't just come back without a plan. You have to have done your homework. A lot of people who left came back thinking that they were going to be recognized as having made it abroad—they believed that they were going to set the pace for others to follow—only to find that when they return vast changes have taken place. Some of their friends who stayed evidently did very well. They live in bigger houses, they drive a fancy car, and dress better. Since they cannot compete, they return.[55]

Transnational Caribbeans, by their multiple insertions into the scales of the modern represented in industrialized and agrarian spaces, are constantly analyzing their location, their place(e)s, comparing and contrasting the two lives, a critical exercise in the rerooting. For they are now identified with two or more locations to which they can never really *totally* return. Gens anglaises are conscious of the benefits of living in the English welfare state: the benefits for the unemployed, the national health care, the support for mothers with children, the ease with which various services are accessed. The English state controls but it also delivers. All of that is lost in the return to St. Lucia, which can ill afford a welfare status similar to that of Great Britain. One respondent complained about what she saw as the disjuncture between the government and the people, which was not good for the island.

> St. Lucia is going three steps forward, and two steps backward. The people are not supporting the government. They are constantly dissatisfied with the government, always complaining. If they give them a job, they are wasting the government money. Even my car [a Toyota], they never have parts for it. I have to send for parts abroad. They are afraid of their own shadow. If they buy one part, they not buying two. Parts take six months to come. They are afraid to stock up.[56]

CROSSING BORDERS: TURNING TRANSNATIONALS
INTO ALTER-NATIONALS?

In Caryl Phillips's *State of Independence,* Bertram, the protagonist, has returned from England and is seeking to reroot himself within the community. He wants to invest in a business, with the help of his old school friend, now a minister in the government. He is rebuffed by Jackson, who says:

> You English West Indians should just come back here to retire and sit in the sun. Don't waste your time trying to get into the fabric of the society for you're made of the wrong material for the modern Caribbean. You all think too fast and too crazy, like we should welcome you back as lost brothers. Well, you may be brothers alright, but you lost for true for you let the Englishman fuck up your heads.[57]

It is a contestation between authenticities—the real West Indian versus the "traveler" who has become different from the local perspective, or rather from the way in which local is constructed by those who stayed, the more or less lateral Creole contestation, where one seeks to become the measure of "real" localness, the presentness of the local. Fitting in or rather fitting back in is rife with tension, especially as it comes up against a shifting hierarchy of statuses based on the stayed and the traveled.

Migrants' return often goes with scant state support, especially as they have yet to form formal associations actively pursuing their interests. Though they are transnationals and transculturals, the return to the island involves a border crossing, into the space of the (re)imagined national community made evident by the grudging concessions which both the state and fellow citizens allow. The state defines "returning nationals" accordingly,

> a) a citizen of Saint Lucia by birth, of eighteen years and above, returning to Saint Lucia to settle after a minimum of ten years residence abroad; b) a citizen of Saint Lucia by descent who is eighteen years and above who is coming to Saint Lucia to settle, after a minimum of ten years residence abroad; or c) an alien spouse of a citizen of Saint Lucia by birth or descent, coming to Saint Lucia to settle after a minimum of ten years residence abroad.[58]

Returning nationals have first to encounter customs, the main state institution whose personnel regulate the quantity and type of goods and household effects that they can bring into the state duty free. A gen anglaises can't simply pack up every conceivable item used during his or her stay abroad. This is the most ironic part, because the list of allowable items restricts the migrant's lifestyle. Customs regulates what is required to live in the state and restricts household effects accordingly. For example, a returning migrant is allowed three lamps and one of each of the following items: couch, video recorder, video camera, liquor trolley, microwave oven, stove, refrigerator, electric opener, kitchen scale, electric knife, and blender, as well as "one motor vehicle per family of a returning national whether the motor vehicle is used or new, provided the CIF value of the motor vehicle does not exceed US$15,000.00." Returnees may also bring in a limited quantity of heavy duty tools which they may require for their occupation.[59] Moreover, these concessions are conditional. A returning national who does not comply with the rules of citizenship stands to lose all of these concessions: "Immediately following [his or her] return to Saint Lucia, [anyone who] returns abroad and resides outside Saint Lucia for a continuous period exceeding three months, loses his or her privileges under the Second Schedule to the Act, and is liable to pay all taxes waived for him or her under the Second Schedule to the Act."[60]

Though there is an official in the Ministry of Foreign Affairs who ostensibly focuses on the affairs of returning nationals, there is no systematic program dealing with them. In other words, except for matters concerning the returning nationals' household effects, no other service is provided, for the status becomes invisible once he or she complies with local rules and regulations. Returning nationals are not considered people with special problems, in need of special attention. They are left to their own devices, to integrate themselves back into the changed social spaces of the nation-state and cultural ideas about the ideal citizen, the sacred identity.

Diasporic cultures, at least postcolonial ones, grow along shifting national lines, whether actual or perceived; and the people who engage in these cultures remap traditional political geography by their migrations. With regard to the project of globalization, this remapping has caused the obsolescence of some state functions, for instance, the economic provisioning of the homelands for citizens and families. As many studies demonstrate, Caribbeans have always been a highly mobile population, even during the restrictive times of slavery. Caribbeans have always transgressed the sort of tightly demarcated, socially constructed and scripted spaces in which official national narratives co-opt individual identity, and vice versa. Even "Indians" and some "mixed-race" groups of the region—those not popularly associated with movement—migrated. As Charles Carnegie notes, the very narratives which elicited transgressions obscured historical accounts, in which only the groups disruptive enough to enter such narratives were remembered as revolutionary or rebellious, for example, the Maroons. The singling out of such groups by nationalists and scholars, Carnegie notes, silences the role of "Indians" and some "mixed-race" groups, who, because movements for them was commonplace, were able to aid the Maroons in their escapes. Such methods also belittle the general prevalence of movement. Even so, the performative hi/stories of peoples of the black diaspora forged these routes which nonetheless rely upon a rootedness, that is, fixing yet liminal performative practices articulating the projects of nationness changed through such practices. Paradoxically then, the rootedness of traveling moves within these routes of transnationalism. Transnationalism may therefore be said to be the rhizome in and through which certain kinds of "flexible citizenship(s)" or nationalisms are lived.[61] The flip side also works. This refers to the ways in which locals, while staying put spatially, may live (inter)nationally. I have in mind the multiple ways in which localisms, or national expressions, are rejected outright or enriched by outernationalisms, as in the case of Manthia Diawara's Motown-style groups in Mali, James Ferguson's cosmopolitans of Zambia, and Elvis's presence in Zanzibar as recounted by Ahmad.[62] In all of these cases, subjects occupying national space subverted and pluralized those territorial spaces, nurturing new kinds of expectations, as they tapped into outernational ideas about identity and being—even if that meant that they were "copying" copies, the echo-sounds of geographically disparate yet entangled temporalities. Choice national images were constantly refurbished by outernational images, which undermined or altered states' and accepted ideas and concepts of what constituted the national character. In the best of cases, these contradictory or contesting images may simply coexist.

These studies cited above reveal implicitly the need to dislocate the notion of the making of "the nation" from bounded and singular places. The task here recalls several analysts' appeals to reconceptualize the practices of "stateness," that is, to treat the institutions for the making of "the nation" as elements that legitimize, propagate, and promote particular (Creole) projects of identity that strive to sensitize national imaginaries to the state's more or less vertical demands and presentations. However, a condition for the success of this kind of cultural project, for mapping the present, is the constant surveillance of dangerous narratives and acts that oppose, or are perceived thus, by offering workable alternatives to those authorized. But such surveillance can only be partial. States can never entirely undo the different or entirely undermine alternative symbols or expressions, although at times they too frequently appear to resort to murder, ethnic cleansing, and genocide. States being inherently bounded in their power and projects rely on masking narratives that perform the task of imagining certain kinds of communities that can exist only relationally, contained in notions of "us" versus "them," or authentic versus inauthentic.[63] But even those narratives are historically bound, producing particular temporalities through which only certain subjectivities can be realized.

Efforts to grapple with these related histories of states and subjects are conveyed in transnational studies, which stress multiple attachments of nationals. In reference to the Caribbean, Duany argues that "transmigrant communities are characterized by a constant flow of people in both directions, a dual sense of identity, ambivalent attachments to two nations, and a far-flung network of kinship and friendship ties across state frontiers."[64] Cultural mobility and hybridity seem to replace political geography as the preeminent constitutive elements of an identity brokered between a country of origin and a host. But not exactly. Basch's, Schiller's, and Szanton Blanc's careful study notes that, since the 1960s, Haitian and Antillean transmigrants in the United States have paid more attention to social and political projects in Haiti and the Antilles. Furthermore, constructs of color, class, and culture they imported from their home islands in the form of cultural practices have become the prism through which they see and respond to the shifting cultural sands of the United States. As the authors note in the Antilleans' case, the proliferation of transnational organizations variously contending with nationalist dreams was not propelled solely by West Indian migrants' involvement in nation-building processes.

> Closely intertwined with the increasing transnationalism of Vincentian and Grenadian voluntary organizations, these public expressions of identity also were linked to the hegemonic contention around race and ethnicity that began to take place in the United States in the mid to late 1990s. . . . The effect of these shifting hegemonic processes in the United

States and the Caribbean was to create a layered immigrant political community in which the immigrants began to see themselves as Vincentian or Grenadian and West Indian, constructs that had cultural, nationalist, and ethnic meaning.[65]

According to the specificities of racialized sociocultural relations in the United States, nationalists' dreams varied; many of those relations were read through immigrants' experience of habituses, to use Bourdieu's concept.[66] Transnational locations often undermined the kind of persistently colonial nation which denied all its citizens full individual rights, a critical component of their flight to modernity. I will return to this construct shortly.

This is evident in the nationalist scoring of transnationalist positions characterized by Haitian women's organizations, members of which mobilized their transnationalist location to undermine the nation-state's exploitation of women's vulnerable social position. Charles credits the women of the Haitian diaspora in North American communities with the strengthening and shaping of the Haitian women's movement on the island. The formation of Haitian women's organizations in the United States took place within "a clear collective consciousness of *being Haitian,* reinforced by language, a strong nationalism and a distinct identification of Blackness. This uniqueness found expression in numerous Haitian clubs, student organizations, churches, political groups, community organizations, and private businesses. Since the 1980s, many other voluntary associations have emerged to reinforce Haitian ethnic identity."[67] Though Haitian women's organizations like RAFA (Rally of Haitian Women)—formed in 1973 to become, in Montreal in 1979 Valiant Women, and in New York, UFAP (Union of Patriotic Haitian Women)—adopted the overthrow of the Duvalier regime as their objective, they eventually focused "specifically on women's issues, especially the problems encountered by women when working within the national political organizations, within their households, and in the societies to which they immigrated and settled."[68] In the late 1980s, at least 60 percent of the members of such groups as Fanm D'Ayiti (Women of Haiti), Comité Feminin, and Kay Fanm were residents of North American communities. With Duvalier's overthrow, many of the women who had participated in transnational organizations returned to Haiti to deepen the democratic process. Charles's study highlights the transnationalist dynamics of nationalist interventions, also demonstrating the uses of gender in the construction and destruction of a certain national identity, making way for a regeneration of dispositions, practices, perceptions, and performances of this identity.

"Settled" diasporan communities do transpose national with transnational concerns. Milagros Ricourt's study of the Dominican community of Washington Heights raises questions about the impact of the generational divide among diasporan Dominicans.[69] She concludes that those transnational studies which see the reference point of immigrants as "an ambivalent attachment to the host society and a persistent outlook toward the home island, as well as family networks that cut across geopolitical boundaries, describe incompletely immigrants' practices." Ricourt's study of older and second-generation Dominicans highlights a process of "distanciamento," a distancing from island politics and a recognition of permanency of their stay in the United States. Though the rise in the number of Caribbeans acquiring American citizenship transforms the political and cultural landscape of certain places, New York, for instance, it seems to me that every migrant population has its moment of distanciamento, and migrants who are systematically discriminated against, as are Dominicans, continue to seek affirmation of their identities, or rather place, in those cultural symbols associated with island homes. In the early phases of migration, West Indians distanced themselves from their island homes' colonialist racism. Because the New York Democratic Party offered participatory politics denied them at home, they used it to express their political identities. As a result they identified socially, politically, and culturally as part of black America, but this slackened with the onset of political independence and statehood.[70] Certainly the current proliferation of Caribbean political representatives in the boroughs of New York suggests an enduring intersection of national and transnational concerns.

Posing the dynamics of a diasporic community in terms of transnationalism versus Americanization is not likely to bear much fruit, however, considering the oppressive conditions, racial and otherwise, that Dominican and Caribbean working peoples face in the United States, not to mention that most Caribbean immigrants still have families in the islands. Nevertheless, Ricourt's study and others call attention to importance of the generational divide assessing the waxing and waning of transnationalism's intersection with nationalist concerns. Only long-term studies that historicize transnational influences upon nationals, at home or abroad, can tackle these issues.

One way to investigate the intersection and overlap of transnationalism and nationalism is to assume or acknowledge that a certain amount of slippage occurs between the nation's creolization projects and the individual's personal experience, which is itself constructed from a grab bag of national narratives, some of which may marginalize or accommodate the national subject's reinterpretations, given his or her social position within the topologies of nation space. In analyzing these state and society relationships and slippages, I find it useful to draw upon Gramsci's concept of hegemony (further elaborated by Raymond Williams), to see specifically how ideas can be transposed from the state level to the personal level.[71] In particular, dominant state practices may be seen as produced through a certain kind of culture making at the level of the institutions of official governance, facilitated by the enactment of various legislation and policies. This may accommodate or facilitate the conjoining of agendas or their co-option to merge the distinctions at varying moments between the projects of states and the personal agendas of citizens.[72] The ways in which specific state-directed *cultures of power* are elaborated provides a framework for linking state practices with "nation" and "individual" or citizen-signifying fields. These relationships are multiple, layered, complex, open, and yet familiar. Elaboration of the narratives of the familiar, of the habitus, the diasporic habitus, can aid us in disclosing the transnationalized guises of nationalist yearnings, along with their personal connection. They also provide clues as to how rhizomic rootedness is preserved in disturbing or refreshed ways, in performances of transnationalization and vice versa, and how these operate as mechanisms to undermine the "coloniality" of their Creole powers and place.

Mary Chamberlain's study of narratives of Barbadian migrants to Britain and their return to the island provides contextually rich evidence by which to interpret such transnational and national connections. More to the point, her study shows the ways in which the nation is fixed, unfixed, imagined, and even unimagined. The diverse oral histories and life stories that Chamberlain gathered reveal a rich fascinating cultural history, through which larger narratives of nations, states, and travel take shape. These fascinating stories evince a transnationalism lived through the national prisms of color and class, themselves reflections of global systems and anchored in common beliefs about upward social mobility that migration often makes possible.[73] They record how contact among families was maintained and against that constitutive backdrop what might have happened to these national artifacts. As demonstrated in earlier migration studies, remittances helped members migrate and helped sustain island-based relatives on Barbados:

> With each remittance, contact was maintained. Just as family-support enabled the migrants to leave, so migration assisted in the maintenance of family at home, ensuring family loyalty and identity across the generations, and across the seas. This may account for the ultimate return of family members to Barbados, which, in turn, became incorporated in the family model of migration. The family demonstrated a positive disposition to migration, and a determination to maintain family links and unity throughout migration. This was a family which, as Olive said, "love to travel."[74]

I consider this practice, this ideology of travel, pervasive in Caribbean culture. It reveals an outernationalization of the Caribbean national(s) (nationally anchored practices) as well as a nationalization of the outernational, registering the intertwined bricolage inherent to lived spaces of modernities. Importantly, my Judith and Jack anecdote highlights their agency in selecting in accordance with their personal agendas. Perhaps, as Chamberlain put it,

> The family in terms of both its structure and directives, may, [therefore] offer a key to understanding change. The clues to this lie within memory in its twin role as agent of socialization and historical evidence. The migration narratives demonstrate the historical importance of collective memory. Individual memory is, moreover, always collective, for it contains, and synthesizes, the memories of previous generations. As an active ingredient in socialization it influences the behavior and actions of successive generations.[75]

But these memories, these traditions, never remain quite the same.

As a deeply embedded practice in the Caribbean, such migration highlights the tension in the very designation—Caribbean culture, with its assumptions of boundedness and distinctiveness. Both Chamberlain's migration narratives and the Jack and Judith story presented earlier disclose vital elements of moving cultures—as Clifford puts it, traveling as intrinsic to cultures—but also, with varying degrees of success, the ambivalent attempts of people to root or interpret such practices in a particular notion of the "nation-state." Clifford's warning to anthropologists in particular to see cultures as unstable and unbounded refers in principle to the actual physical movements, the connections that people have beyond the localized, as was the practice of traditional ethnography. As has been shown, the Caribbean region is the site of engagement with the global, and therefore always open to transnational and translated transactions. But what is interesting is how, in spite of this global imperative of Caribbean existence, certain notions of community, of country, of particular practices continue to ground these traveling cultures, in the fabric of the identities of these traveling, traveled people. Herein lie clues to threshing out the shifting expressions of Caribbean cultures, insofar as state narratives and the challenges that they engender provide Caribbeans with a sense of community, more or less. The experiences that flow from this earlier imagined community provide the basis for a transnational existence, or several different kinds of them depending on Caribbeans' various accommodations and rejections of aspects of state and antistate narratives of national identity.

In the light of the Jack and Judith story, and the reading of spaces in the Chamberlain study, it would seem that the spawning of the transnational presence of Caribbean people has led to the dynamic construal of the nations and their state spaces as a source of a familiar and familial historicity. In other words, the existence of the nation provides Caribbeans with a place of return, a reference point, a rootedness before or after their transnational sojourns. This is a crucial point. And it enables a fuller reading of "Americanity," the concept deployed by Quijano and Wallerstein which embraces "Caribbeanity," its peoples, and their flight to modernity in the crucible of the violence of a New World historicity shaping tragic absences—e/raced presences and elided "pasts" (as discussed in chapter 3).

The above point strongly supports an interpretation of the Caribbean's lived experiences as a liminal movement that its peoples have staked through spaces and places; that is, through their transnationalized "societies," "politics," "economies," "geographies," and "cultures," despite the several violences they have endured from being entangled in "modern" systems of production and their cultural creations. In the case of the Caribbean, then, its traditions have always been liminal creations bridging critical mimetic mo(ve)ments, even as they pursue liminal mo(ve)ments beyond and through the several spaces of various places.

Rethinking "the flight to modernity" now conveys at once a sense of physical *and* liminal movement, a journeying from place to place and the rehoming of present spaces given a politics of mapping the present, largely through a project of Westernization. Nonetheless, the fashioning of modern sociocultural spaces entailed the incorporation of an array of various cultural influences coming from diverse areas, not least Creole Europeans in the Americas and their colonial counterparts, as well as those from the former homelands of Africa, India, China, and so on.[76] The uneven pace and the circumscription of choices (made so by the then-emergent world domination by European nation-states)[77] meant that constructions of self, community, and place would be heavily influenced by the *presences* of Old World offerings, which were themselves transformed by a dynamic process of capitalism. A different kind of space emerged, to be sure, but one which Caribbeans were as much a part of as they had been placed apart from, and one that they were themselves creators of, despite their inscripted status as consumers of ideas, objects, and interpretations. Performative nationalisms, as particulars and transnationalisms, should therefore be understood within this complex, doubled, and dynamically folding process of *creolization*.

CONCLUSIONS

This brutish yet hopeful ritual of crossing, which translates people through modern spaces and entanglement and which founded Americanity, perhaps, then, helps to explain the basis of a traveling culture such as the Caribbean. Yet the current focus on travel and transnationalism misses a crucial dimension of travelers. That is the extent to which they and Caribbeans alike enact rituals of rootedness through which the trip is experienced. Because many immigrants today build social and cultural fields that ground themselves like rhizomes even as they cross geographic cultural and political borders, in critically exploring the effects of cross-cultural fertilization and political alliances, we need a methodology which assumes the intersections of transnationalism, nationalism, and the repositories of the familiar, which assumes in effect cross-cultural wombs of a liminal modern space, given the experiences of mapping the present.

Another issue shadowed in this discussion relates to the implication of transnationals in the project of rehabilitating the nation-state, through their renewal of "modern" and state-derived notions of nation. If, with all the speculation about the decline of the nation-state, the idea of the state is still not as senile as the state institutions that seek to realize and stabilize their powers in the world, we may fruitfully ask several questions. For example, in what new ways have diaspora transnationals been drawn into or out of the refashioning of modern cultures of power, and with what consequences for themselves and their states' erstwhile imagined communities and statist national projects? How do these entangled processes affect citizens' dynamic yet rhizomically rooted concepts of their place-in-time? How do such subjects effect changes of state or national narratives and their own remappings of the present, in hegemonic spaces of the modern? What new *Weltanschauungen* have emerged whereby transnationals might (re)locate themselves?

Though the couple I mentioned earlier returned to St. Lucia with firm alternative ideas about rural St. Lucian architecture and land use, the thirty-plus years they spent in England changed them, as it did the gens anglaises and the Barbadian returned nationals. They were able to use the (seemingly) English way of life as a reference point to negotiate the changed and changing island-national space, and their places within it. I would like to say that a newer more useful form of creolization came up against older versions, and Jack and Judy reinterpreted that tradition within the context of their present needs and desires, one of which was, surely, a strong desire to return home, again. The circle of migration was not as concrete as it appeared on a common map. But even maps themselves only rehabilitate political conceptions of space. Jack's and Judith's migration was interrupted by slippery cultural memories, experiences, and concepts of self in relation to communities and newer forms of "culture" and cultural exchanges.

National identities cannot be essentialized, any more than transnational liberties can exist without bounds or bonds. And modernities' expressions and practices are constantly contested, their demise, transformation, or morphing hastened more often by those who dwell in multiple locations here and there, with their various modalities of the here and the there. These transnational practices of *creolization* by the Caribbean diaspora are deeply entangled exercises of existence that are expressed in a politics of making place. The unity is submarine. We can thus catch glimpses of similar movements elsewhere in the Americas in Laurier Turgeon's discussion of how Amerindians used beads from elsewhere in reshaping their identity:

> With the subsequent increased exchange of goods, movement of populations and intercultural tensions, Amerindians adapted their forms of representation to the changing context and reconstructed their identity with beads of the other, for incorporating the other was a means of regenerating the self. Contact brought about a fundamental shift from an identity grounded in self to one constructed from the (re)sources of the other.[78]

This observation, reconceptualized within the context of the issues of transnationalism, migration, and the remaking of self and community as presented here, is troubled nonetheless by a particular mapping of the present whose price has been a certain distancing, rupturing, and severing of connections construed within another temporality—one which no longer uniquely frames their time of existence and experience. The dynamic processes of *creolization* addressed in this chapter tell the stories of transnationalized citizens who are remixing and moving the world with their post-Creole imaginations. And indeed, they are stitching together—through critical mimetic mo(ve)ments, diasporic habitusees, and typographies of place—complex relational histories of the present, and perhaps a future. . .

SIX

AN EBAY IMAGINARY IN
AN UNEQUAL WORLD

Creolization on the Move

Many communitarians seem to believe that we belong to only one community, defined empirically and even geographically, and that this community could be unified by a single idea of the common good. But we are in fact always multiple and contradictory subjects, inhabitants of a diversity of communities (as many really, as the social relations in which we participate and the subject-positions they define), constructed by a variety of discourses and precariously and temporarily sutured at the intersection of those positions.[1]

La créolisation n'est pas une fusion, elle requiere que chaque composante persiste, meme alors qu'elle change déjà.[2]

From there to here,
From here to there,
Funny things
Are everywhere.[3]

THE SECOND TIME I spoke with King Arthur it was drizzling lightly in the schoolyard where we sat, in Garrisons.

"Give thanks to Spaulding," King Arthur said. "Is he who bring pipe water and electricity into the area."

He pointed to the "high-rise" where he lived and commented that it was good to live there, that there was no place else he would rather be. He had lived there for forty-five years, in an area dotted with so-called high rises, or low-income housing, named after distant countries and cities: Angola, Havana, Brooklyn, Zimbabwe. King Arthur felt safe in garrisons. I, on the other hand, had a taxi waiting.

In the old days, "the bush days," "the rough days," King

Arthur explained that you "had to go to stand-pipe [and] fill up your drum to take a bath. So it was not easy dem days." He pointed out to me evidence of the old days, a shack here, a dark place there. "Give thanks to Spaulding," he said again.

Anthony Spaulding was the Peoples National Party's (PNP) representative for the area in the 1970s, an outspoken supporter of Democratic Socialism in Jamaica.[4] It was he who was responsible for bringing garrisons out of darkness by providing it electricity, he who, in King Arthur's opinion, conjured from squalor, civilization.

King Arthur was celebrating his fifty-third birthday. Three years ago, on his fiftieth birthday, he had changed his name from Sir Arthur to King Arthur. The young people who knew him were especially pleased by the change and took up the new name with glee. He had acquired the name "Sir Arthur" in school, and it seemed to him appropriate that he should have acceded to that highest of ranks at a time in his life when he was happy with "where he reach right now." He was working for the PNP, responsible for tending the plants in garrisons, a job of which he was very fond.

King Arthur was a Rastafarian. I learned this the first time I met him, a year earlier, outside the football stadium in Garrisons. I had noticed a Toyota parked nearby emblazoned with the name KING ARTHUR. That logo had its effect, and it was not long before I introduced myself to the man himself, and King Arthur had invited me to admire his assortment of objects with which his car was adorned. There were pink torn-up baby dolls. There was a photograph of Norman Washington Manley, founding father of Jamaica, and one of Marcus Garvey (the Jamaican pan-Africanist who mobilized millions of African descendants to imagine themselves as members of one community). There was a red-and-black Garrisons' football flag. There was the Jamaican flag. And there was a flag bearing Haile Selassie's image, as well as a photograph of the man. The man? King Arthur assured me that "the emperor used to go to church and praise God like any other man," but he was less willing to venture an opinion regarding Haile Selassie's death, a word King Arthur did not use. He was also unwilling to discuss the relationship between his faith and his avocation. I made a note to press that point at a later date.

"Man to man is so unjust," he said to me, citing Bob Marley. The objects in his car, he added, pointing to the limbless baby dolls especially, "keep [me] company in this unjust world." "And the red, yellow, and green representation of Africa dangling from his rear-view mirror? I asked him, reaching out to touch it. His sister lives in Ethiopia, he said. She left the Trench Town area when Haile Selassie came to Jamaica in 1960 proffering "repatriation" and land grants to Jamaican citizens. She and her Jamaican husband have six children, he said, "three princesses and three princes born in Ethiopia!"

I had been reading Achille Mbembe's *On the Postcolony*. Rich in observation and in rhetoric, the book had made a deep impression on me. It was Mbembe's Africa and the idea of time, as lived in entanglement, that I pictured as King Arthur described all the many objects in his car relating to that continent and disconnected from it as well. There was nothing that one could describe as continuous or discontinuous memory of Africa here or not there. But I was also intrigued by King Arthur's reconstitution of space that went along with his realignment or dislocation of time. For contrary to the general middle class public's view that such an inner city place was a space of disharmony, to King Arthur it was a place he would not leave for any other deemed safer or friendlier.

When I met King Arthur again, a year later, he had added to this odd assortment of objects the flag of the Jamaican Sunshine Girls, the name of Jamaica's world-ranked netball team. The island was hosting the World National Netball Championships for twenty-six international participants, and King Arthur wished to show his support. He wished to give me a flag to allow me to do the same, but I declined.

I was thinking about these objects, and King Arthur guessed as much. They make him happy, he said. They are the things he wants to have around him, he said: they help him to escape, if he must. Here was a Japanese car filled with stuff from various places and times mobilized in the name of happiness, in the attempt to suppress or reflect the reality of living in a certain place, on a certain island, in a Jamaica that is now. They were recycled objects coming from various elsewheres particularized by their histories, in the Atlantic and beyond it, reinvested with various meanings. Those meanings sometimes clashed, at least in the minds of those conscious of their originary contexts, even objectives. Even the name "King Arthur," for instance: was it conjured against a token of the 1970s programs of Jamaicanization, West Indianization, and Socialism?[5] "Nanny fe we queen" (Nanny is our queen) had defiantly adorned the walls of the gated university when Queen Elizabeth visited in 2002, and now here was this man, this nationalist, postnationalist, colonial, postcolonial King Arthur.[6] Was the title "king," in keeping with the Maroon queen tradition playing on a fantasized and legendary rebellious past? Or did it represent the mere acceptance of, and even King Arthur's return to, everything *royally* rejected by the PNP earlier, except empire?[7] Whatever the reason, it is certain that King Arthur—a complex man, ostensibly an informal horticulturalist, caretaker of a small green section of a PNP inner city constituency—had hobbled together a set of objects which appealed to his sense of self, his pursuit of a certain sensibility of personal sovereignty.

All of these items from disparate places, and times, assembled in a very colorful car suggested a desire to be seen, perhaps a play for an untimely hypervisibility, through a chaotic "cutting of a particular style" and a fashioning of *difference* for his own place, his own identity, using the tactics of bricolage. King Arthur's idea of style, and its inherent constructedness through the "cut and mix," resonate well with Dick Hebdige's notion of (sub)-cultural style as "the process of meaning-construction" and not the end product.[8] The King Arthur story is also suggestive of an approach to making place that is open ended and encoded in spatial practices that reflect Glissant's "poétique de la Relation," at once a theory of the spaces of the Caribbean and its Creole practices, as well as an intervention against linear readings of time and space. The interpretive movements being stitched together by King Arthur for his "scene of presence" thus seem to favor a reading of time and space that is indexed (as the epigraph from Glissant above suggests), by entanglement, non-synthesis and unpredictable movement, in short, "chaos." In his discussion of Glissant's later texts, Nicholas Coates makes the compelling argument that chaos theory underpins Glissant's emphasis on relationality, rhizomatic conditions, and open systems, or rather the openness of "tout-monde" as a "chaotic" (cultural and social) space. Chaos here is not about anarchy, but rather an appeal to recognize the complexity and sensitivity of dynamical systems, and in particular to sustain the relations of the specific to the whole, of rooting with *errance,* in the general interpretations of the processes of the (social) whole. Accordingly, for Glissant, "le chaos n'est pas 'chaotique.'"[9] Instead, as Coates argues, "The virtue of chaos as a theory, lies in the fact that it re-affirms *Relation.* . . . Rather than abstract essences, then, it is ultimately the necessary interaction between all the elements in a given system, together with the dynamic movement between *lieu* and *globalité,* which governs the identity of elements, none of which can safely be discounted."[10] This position parallels my own in the chapter, which shares Glissant's emphasis on openness, flexibility, and a soupy fluidity. It reflects most centrally our joint concern about the relationality in processes of becoming vis-à-vis being that implicates a state of "worlding." Moreover, his concept of Relation points quite definitely to a politics of space and place, and to the inherent uncertainties unsettling the idea of absolute space underpinning the West's colonial project as well as the project of Negritude—at least insofar as both occupy a similar terrain of discovering a universal, whether it be in terms of "whiteness" or universal "blackness" in the space of a "lost Africa."[11]

Building on Glissant's compelling perspective, I would like to develop this reasoning by arguing that *creolization*, as it has emerged in the Caribbean and in the Americas generally, should be further understood as entailing a duality of space, mapped over the relational topologies of global and local spaces and double articulated within diasporic traditions or habituses, but going beyond them as well. I wish to underscore the vital importance of this perspective on creolization by highlighting the deficiencies in the prevailing contention over the general versus the particular status of the experience of creolization in the modern world. I will do this by highlighting the binaristic thinking that still haunts these critiques and by drawing attention to, or rather reemphasizing the question of "newness," raised in chapter 1. More specifically, I wish to point to the particular ontological conditions framing the quest for newness, spatial hi/stories making place in the world, and consider the practical and polemological methodologies through which such difference has been, and is being, pursued and appropriated.[12]

These considerations are pivotal yet are either overlooked or inadequately engaged in the debate regarding whether creolization is a general property of the global, or a specific property of the local (Caribbean) and as such a type of originary historical phenomenon marking oppositional cultural difference. They are likewise inadequately engaged in the debate on the politics and nature of diasporas. Indeed, in these debates the central referents raised posing questions about cultural change and difference, namely, creolization and diaspora, need to be rethought, along the lines proposed in chapters 1 and 2. This is because, I argue, the contentions have largely revolved on the basis of a one-sided concreteness being granted to these phenomena. I turn now to develop these points.

BEYOND THE GLOBAL AND LOCAL:
CREOLIZATION'S LINKED LOCATIONS IN
THE POST-PLANTATION ERA

The specter of localness as fixed historical site is the present ghost that haunts critiques suggesting that creolization can only spring forth from plantation places, that it belongs here and can't be seen there. (Let's ignore for now the well-known fact that urban slavery was a common phenomenon even in those places where plantations were dominant, as advanced in chapter 1.) I do not mean to suggest that there is nothing unique about Caribbean history and culture. But the point I wish to make is that it is a uniqueness that is locally sited and enacted but not necessarily locally derived. This is by no means an attempt to deny the agentive qualities of the Caribbean person either but merely to suggest that to speak of Creole subjectivity and cultural practices only in the sense of localized forces leaves out the extent to which the Caribbean person and place were always "double articulated," to use Doreen Massey's term in a different context. Massey posits that notwithstanding the fruitful discussions of globalization, migration, and cultural shifts, the idea of place was still quite essentialized, that even sophisticated theorists conceived place as Being rather than becoming. Massey argues that such characterizations of place as "Being" "are all attempts to fix meanings and often to enclose them too: to give places single, fixed identities and to define them as bounded and enclosed, characterized by their own internal history, and through their differentiation from 'outside.'"[13] It is the centrality of this "Being" to the analyses of Caribbean creolization that I interrogate.

Creolization as a process of a particular projection of culture-power in the Caribbean and the Americas generally, within the context of Atlantic slavery and indentureship, no doubt gives the Caribbean within the Americas its special historical and cultural character. Thus, as has been pointed out by a number of historians, the Caribbean was central to the forging of the modern Atlantic economy through its role as a producer of sugar with African slaves, later with Indian indentured servants, and other migrants, Portuguese, Chinese, Javanese, Middle Eastern Jews and Arabs, and if, like Charles Wagley, we include Brazil, particularly its North Eastern section, Japanese, all of whom serviced in one way or another the slave/sugar industry in Plantation America.[14] In the face of asymmetrical power, people seek to build places of comfort, with found materials, as Marx would say, and I would add discourses, interpretations, and various symbols. They attempt to transform conditions, set in motion new processes, borrowing from various places and utilizing multivalent strategies and styles which destabilize given spaces and temporalities, a process Marx failed to dwell on in his discussion of capital's homogenizing tendencies.

It is not surprising, then, given this history of entanglement within the region, that it is now being presented as a harbinger of the cultural fusions or practices of hybridity that are said to characterize the social and cultural face of contemporary globalization. In particular, the concept of creolization has been controversially appropriated to refer more broadly to the sociocultural fusions and cultural pastiches now held to be characteristic of various parts of the world economy. While certainly limited in its power to describe the nature of social life in contemporary globalization, and while also overshadowing the political processes at work in these cultural encounters and convivial practices, this current deployment of the concept may nonetheless prove itself useful, at least to the degree that it helps to dislodge the reading of the *creolization* processes through a specifically plantation fulcrum. And it may likewise be useful to the extent that it helps to highlight parallel sociocultural networks and relational constructions that extend within and beyond, and sometimes in spite of, the constraining originary locations of identities, ethnicities, and experiences. Moreover, such a new usage of the term would perhaps provoke an extension of the discussion of creolization beyond former plantation societies, beyond the Caribbean and the Americas, as it should be. Certainly, people across the world increasingly exhibit an "eBay imaginary," with the ability to enlarge choice sets, more prevalent now than before, though such choices are construed within, and constrained by, the context of particular socioeconomic and cultural, class, and racial positionings in spaces crisscrossed by diverse diasporic practices.

Accordingly, there should at the very least be a dialogic relationship between diaspora and Caribbean creolization studies, as the former decenters the static meaning of place, while the latter acts to represent particular dynamic roots and routes of creolization that shape and are shaped by the post-Creole imaginations. Furthermore, *creolization* studies also offer a means for grappling with the "une poétique de la Relation" articulating *le lieu* and *le globalité*, place and space. This dialogic relationship thus offers possibilities for contemplating the global articulations of creolization writ large, as well as possibilities for enabling an attention to creolization's articulations of the global. These I will consider now, as evidenced materially and discursively among mainly Afro-populations.

CONSIDERING AN EBAY IMAGINARY

In a review of new science fiction writing, Fredric Jameson described the style of the genre as an "eBay imaginary." He cites a description from one of the books under review in support of his analogy:

> a fresh fruit T-shirt, her black Buzz Rickson's MA-1, anonymous black skirt from a Tulsa shrift, the black leggings she'd worn from Pilates, black Harajuku school girl shoes. Her purse-analog is an envelope of black East German laminate, purchased on E-bay—if not actual Stasi-issue then well in the ballpark.[15]

Jameson goes on to comment:

> An eBay is certainly the right word for our current collective unconscious, and it is clear that the references "work," whether or not you know that the product is real or has been made up by Gibson. What is also clear is that the names being dropped are brand names, whose very dynamic conveys both instant obsolescence and the global provenance and neo-exoticism of the world market today in time and space.[16]

This "eBay imaginary" is thought to pervade the current deployment of the concept of creolization, whereby everyone more or less enjoys equal access to a buffet of cultural offerings from which one may choose whatever suits one's fancy.

Charles Stewart and Mimi Sheller, for example, have both commented on the resurgence of terminology like creolization, syncretism, and hybridity given the new anthropological interest in "how local communities respond to historical change and global influences."[17] Previously such terminology was utilized by Sidney Mintz and Richard Price to describe the creation of New World identities and cultural forms.[18] Thus, as argued by Kamau Brathwaite, Sidney Mintz, and Richard Price (whose perspectives were animated by the contentious debates about acculturation, deculturation, and retention), the conditions of slavery and the mixing of Africans with different groups led to the emergence of new cultural forms, namely, Creole cultural formations, and concomitantly the process of creolization. They meant to stress the agency, the active struggles, negotiations, and creativity of a people living in the jaws of slavery, going beyond the Herskovitsian idea of African survivals and retentions.[19] In contrast, globalization studies have tended to generate widespread use of the concept of creolization as a descriptor of a "late modern" condition or have deployed it as a heuristic device for apprehending the nature of cultural contact, exchanges, and appropriations. For example, the anthropologist Ulf Hannerz, cautioning about globalization literature's primary focus on the economic and political concerns, appealed for "an anthropology of structures of meaning."[20] Hannerz uses the term creolization to describe the value of "indigenous" and "imported" "culture." However, in undermining such binarisms as Western and non-Western, traditional and modern, he reintroduces them and embraces a one-directional movement of culture, by his singular reference to a Western versus a non-Western "indigenous" culture and his pronouncements about the center's role in disseminating culture.[21] There is little room for the kind of south-south creolization such as has occurred, for instance, in the spread of Rastafarianism from Jamaica to Africa and beyond, nor for the kind of cross-cultural contact that emerges within the social interstices of territories, which is how the term has been deployed in an Afro-American plantation setting. Hannerz's perspective therefore begs the question of the rationality of this lopsided relationship, which nonetheless results in the whole world being creolized, as Hannerz suggested in another article.[22] Statements like "the whole world is Creole," or Clifford's "we are Caribbeans in our urban archipelagoes"[23] tend to erase the particularities of people and places and the pervasiveness of the operations of power and its subjects. While immensely attractive in the wake of the intensification of cultural contacts occurring within globalization's time-space compression, a defining trait of the modern condition, there is no doubt that this construal of creolization, combined with ideas about syncretism and hybridity, elides important dimensions of the nature and process of globalization. Accordingly a critique of these appropriations is in order.

Rejecting these anthropological and cultural perspectives advanced by globalization studies, Espelencia Baptiste sees as pivotal to creolization or the development of Creole cultures the transportation of people, namely, Africans, Indians, and Chinese, to the region as labor. The labor organization of the plantation, the production of commodities under a specific regime, is therefore central to Creole cultural creativity. For Baptiste, the absence of this origin is therefore untenable in global discourses of creolization.[24] Mimi Sheller, too, seeks to locate creolization within the context of a plantation-derived dynamic.[25] Sheller speaks of the Caribbeans in the Caribbean in the 1970s, framing Creole in terms of conflict, and in the 1980s in terms of subversion and oppositionality. She concludes that, insofar as the anthropologists and the cultural theorists do not stress these aspects of power and conflict alongside cultural production, they are akin to "pirates on the high seas of global culture."[26] Sheller believes that the concept of Creole has been appropriated as a free-floating signifier of the border-transcending encounters of globalization and wants it to be reclaimed. In other words, creolization is not translatable without its specific Caribbean referents. She proposes that we adopt Richard Burton's perspective, which attends to the power and class dimension of creolization by referring to Afro-Creole, Euro-Creole, and Meso-Creole, in order "to maintain an awareness of the differences in class power along a cultural (and racial) continuum, involving conflict and contention across many borders."[27]

On another point, in a critical essay Aisha Khan, angling from a different vantage point, posits that the arbitrary use of creolization to refer to celebratory cultural models (not processes) overlooks the fictional claim of the Caribbean as a master symbol of cultural mixing. Thus, *creolization* as *a model,* and the Caribbean as a place which mirrors the future of the world, overlooks the exclusions and silences that its practices and ideological claims have engendered in the region. Despite their longstanding genealogy in the region, Indo-Trinidadians or East Indians have been excluded from Creole narratives.[28]

These criticisms highlight the silencing power of identity narratives which have structured and influenced the choices of people everywhere, not least in the Caribbean. My discussion is intended to supplement these critiques, but from a vantage point which (1) eliminates the analytic of binarism that informs most critiques; (2) stresses the inherent utility of the term in light of the multiplication of Creole situations that researchers now map across the globe; and (3) re-emphasizes the need to reinscribe the notion of how power influences the choices and directions of creativity (as in artistic product) in terms of *self* and *place.*

Though advancing a vital point about the erasure of power in the popular treatment of creolization as creative synthesis or syncretism, critics nonetheless, perhaps unwittingly, reaffirm creolization as a separable and bounded experience of time and space. They emphasize its plantation genesis, portray Caribbeans as peripheral subjects "consumed" by others, as if the region, inequality notwithstanding, has not itself a history of consuming other places in order, ironically, to reassert their presence through acts of creativity. A certain kind of locale privileging sneaks in with the critical indignation which serves, unwittingly perhaps, to set apart the region in the "time of entanglement" that marked the eruption of global processes reassembling the world, its peoples, their presents, and their cultural practices. Burton's propositions, endorsed by Sheller, do not avoid that pitfall. Indeed, they end up bringing in neoplural society through the back door,[29] by their imputation of autonomously produced spheres of creolization. The assumption of creolization as founded there, originally fixed "here," this locale, sets up a crudely oppositional relationship upon an imbricated and relational local and global, one that lends itself to a misrecognition of the relationality of time-space processes producing the spaces of localities and globalities at once. That is to say, each of these groupings that Burton identifies was created in relation to the other, and *all* elements participated, though not on equal terms, in the modern project of remapping the present—resulting in the propagation of several marginalizations in and across time, space, and geography, marginalizations that gave rise to the manifold struggles for self, place, and presence and to spatial repositionings that constituted the basis of the cross-cultural social and political process of creolization, here and elsewhere, even "over there."

The implicit global versus local positioning that is being engendered in the debates on the nature of the creolization process thus yields a problem for apprehending the relational hi/stories or spatial ontologies that have been and are being secreted in processes of creolization. One implication of this problem, derived from the covert binarism in play, lies in the analytical closure it generates when it comes to grasping the forces invested in *tout-monde*, in "une poétique de la Relation" articulating *le lieu* and *le globalité*, place and space. For while it may be wrong to proclaim "the-world-in-creolization" (since that effaces the crucibles of power in the world), it seems impossible to deny a process of "creolization-in-the-world," one that is always on the move shaping post-Creole imaginations and the related physical and psychic itineraries for place, given the pervasive condition of unhomeliness.

In the underlying flat reading of the politics of place, this debate may reintroduce the idea that Mintz and Price dismissed, which is that master/ slave power dynamics were total and that the spaces given through the plantation were the sole platform on which the soil of cultural creativity, or rather a politics of place, could be feasibly mounted. In *The Birth of African American Culture*, Mintz and Price argue that the master's monopoly of power was constrained, since in many critical ways he was dependent on the slaves, since the latter was plantation labour and intrinsically important for the production of agricultural commodities for export. Thus, while the societies were deeply divided by status, occupation, physical type, and much else, the continuous interaction of members of various groups on many levels, and in many different ways, forged a complex interdependence.[30]

Accordingly, while not here endorsing the simple view of creolization as mere mixture, at the same time one should be careful not to displace its power dynamics into the ghetto of the plantation space. Rather, one should consider the myriad ways in which the cut and paste of *creolization* bespeaks a wrestling with global power relations by people's real and imaginative journeying across different "scenes of presence." In eliding the relational as well as multistaged, multiplaced, and multispaced dynamics of the processes of selective creation and cultural struggle, critics may very well end up undermining the complexity of the process of creolization that they seek to underscore.

The point I am stressing here turns on always seeing the constructedness of the global and the local in the stitches of time being affected and effected in complex *creolization* processes. In particular, it behooves one to treat the experiences or hi/stories that are being read through the optic of the global and local as being quintessentially relational spheres, mutually constituted and contested cultures of power. As long as the image of creolization remains bound to a plantation-slave imaginary, bound to geography, it becomes too limited to address *creolization processes*, not to mention present, post-Creole imaginations. Tied to the plantation as origin, and to limited outcomes, usually cultural forms and practices, such constructions are too linked to the plantation society thesis, now intellectually debunked but continuing to live vicariously in the popular intellectual imagination, that is, in the imagination of journalists, politicians, academics, and others. What I am suggesting is that specific notions of conflict, agony, displacement, dismemberment, and alienation associated with the creolizing Caribbean New World diasporas, seem bogged down in an analytic that privileges locale, and a singular temporality associated with the early formation of the Americas. Consider here, for example, Stuart Hall's reading of Caribbean identity as necessitating the mapping of power through a dialogic stance in order to appreciate "how the colonized produce the colonizer." Yet, tellingly, he still leaves Caribbean people as seemingly transfixed "conscripts of modernity" or of a contemporary "mapping of the present." He thus states that there was a

> co-presence, interaction, interlocking of understandings and practices, often [in the Caribbean case, we must say always] within radically asymmetrical relations of power. It is the disjunctive logic that colonization and Western modernity introduced into the world and its entry into history constituted the world after 1492 as a profoundly unequal but "global" enterprise and made Caribbean people what David Scott has recently described as "conscripts of modernity."[31]

But this so-called conscripted Caribbean globality is insufficiently plowed by existing analysis, nor are its multitemporal rhythms being adequately teased out. And even though the nationalism of the 1960s, 1970s, and 1980s introduced a whole new set of power relations in the region, reshaping the way in which culture was thought and even practiced, it is a tendentious temporality, situated within a broader canvas of the politics of mapping the present, a politics of time, space, place, and the (cultural) body that largely, but not wholly, is stitched together by a modern economy of power: modern governmentality.

Our attention to the dynamic of *creolization* processes has thus to incorporate the forming of relational hi/stories through a politics of space and place. Moreover, with regard to Mbembe's "time of entanglement," I treat *creolization* experiences as signified and constructed through both global and local conditions of space that situate experiences both here (dis-ordered in time) and there (dis/ordered in space).

In these debates, which are essentially over the ontology of creolization processes and experiences, perhaps what should be stressed are the pervading presence of this *contingent* mapping of the present, its hegemonic shaping of cultures of power, and the multiple strategies invoked to unsettle, transform, and transfigure it. Perhaps, then, what should be stressed are the chaotic spatialities of sociocultural strategies which seek to create new or different spaces within the context of the various configurations of modern social power. And perhaps what should be focused on in characterizing *creolization* experiences are the assertions and affirmations of a will to place and the post-Creole imagination. This will to place intimates our manipulations of the right and aesthetic to belong, to place, wherever sited, as de facto or de jure citizens in the varied practices of becoming in the world. In other words, as the ideas developed in chapters 1 and 2 suggest, *creolization* was and still is an emancipatory project inextricably tied to the (un)making of modern subjects and the homing of modern freedoms. Thus, the double-articulated making of place is always fundamentally linked to the mapping and remapping of the present and, relatedly, the making and unmaking of complex subjectivities. Such processes involve pastiche tactics, the deployment of ready-made elements drawn from the various fragmented histories and larger contexts in which people have been embedded, but going beyond those conditions as well. Fleeing the plantation thus becomes critical to rethinking the experience of *creolization* as a global as well as liminal politics, and also as a globalizing phenomenon incorporating geographies and being influenced by the chaos of relational spatial hi/stories. To continue this project of fleeing the plantation, I now wish to turn to the task of trying to intellectually mine the dialogic relation that lies between creolization and diaspora studies and that connects them to the question of newness, or the production of radical difference in the world.

(DIS)ARTICULATING DIASPORAS

A good starting point from which to approach this issue of "newness" and difference (an issue, I might add, that lies at the heart of the heat of existing debates on creolization), is through the concept of diaspora. Its utility stems from the fact that the experiences of diasporas have been associated with the decentering of the nation-state and those practices directed at monopolizing processes of identity creation. Furthermore, as Meighoo argues, the concept of diaspora itself is best grasped as a "signifying practice" through which particular culturally specific identities are (re)formed *to create* certain meanings.[32] The idea of diaspora thus facilitates an optic that destabilizes the overdeterminism of locales through its focus on global processes, imaginations of diverse places, as well as on the plurality and flexibility of traditions, communities, and temporalities. It allows for movements beyond absolutisms, as Gilroy argued, and captures the modes of feeling and choices, the multiple practices and styles and the shifting identities that its constituents draw on from plural arenas that may incorporate but go beyond racial or ethnic social locations and representations, as I think King Arthur's objects reveal. In other words, the study and examination of diaspora, in theory and practice, allows for a line of escape from national and ethnic overdeterminations which disable the analysis of new and different social practices that occur outside of certain territorial places, spaces, and ethnicized identities.

In my rereading of *creolization* through the analysis of diasporic practices and habituses, the orientations that I critically engage in this chapter are those which conceptualize diasporas as constituted by homeland attachments and which lend themselves to singular imaginations of a given condition, in this case a condition of blackness. These "Africa-linked diasporas" may be contrasted with those other diasporas that seek to reconstitute homelands, like Sikhs and Kurds.[33] One must admit, however, that the idea of reconstituting homelands cannot be entirely discounted insofar as practices sometimes seek to alter negative perceptions of particular homelands in search of "proper presence."

Through this critique I reaffirm and reconsider strategies for fleeing the plantation (both as metaphor and method) and the historically fixed setting generally acknowledged as the originary location of Creole as well as "black" identities and Caribbean/American Creole practices. The chapter thus argues for the idea of a post-plantation thinking of creolization to be introduced as a much-needed critical process to erase the ethnic essentialisms that several diaspora studies reproduce, however unwittingly, in terms of experience, identity, and responses to cultures of power. In contrast, I consider treating diaspora as a practical and polemological methodology rather than a condition or transfixed state of being, but I also recognize diasporic communitarian formations as a practice contained within, though also fractured by their inherent identitarian instabilities. Of course, this latter point is a recognition of the well-known fact that identities are always under construction, reconstruction, and morphing. Thus, as Brent Hayes Edwards posited, grappling with diaspora "forces us to articulate discourses of cultural and political linkage only through and across difference in full view of the risks of that endeavor."[34]

As stated earlier, the idea of diaspora, when deployed as an analytical tool, offers a perspective that decenters the nation-state as the source of identity and culture, a perspective that at its best speaks to contingencies, unessentialisms, and transnational dynamics. More often than not, however, the diasporic perspective enunciates the "traditions" of a black transnational community, mapped along a political consciousness, for example, Garveyism or pan-Africanism, or along certain events which recognize the global remaking of a stigmatized blackness and the attendant negotiations within conditioning culture systems. This is compounded by the idea of diaspora as a determining condition of being. African diaspora studies have thus been criticized for their inability to get beyond a black essentialized subject, as that subject is now being defined less by its association to a naively represented "African homeland" than by its racialized subjectivity and the "diverse set of social, political and cultural elements which influenced how people of African descent were able to make their history."[35] In this regard there has been a marked shift toward a rereading of blackness and diaspora through a poststructural rethinking of these black diasporic subjectivities, as seen for example in Paul Gilroy's and Stuart Hall's efforts to de-essentialize "black" identity while at the same time stressing its relationship to diverse "living memories" of "the past."[36]

Michael Hanchard's work has also sought to introduce the problem of a racial temporality, which describes a temporality that locks black subjects into a lagged time, from which there seems no escape and which acts to homogenize black subjectivity and its politics as well.[37] In other words, for Hanchard, the racialization of people of African descent has worked to create time lags that define and sustain their subordinate position globally. Unfortunately, in his use of this concept of "racial time" to explore how such temporal lags structure politics, particularly in the Americas, Europe, and other postcolonial places, there is no attention to difference, no recognition of the play of *différance*, and no attempt to allow for the presence of multi-temporalities inhabiting those habituses given in racialized modes of governmentality. When applied to particular historical moments, the inherent determinism of Hanchard's racial temporality excludes the possibility of diaspora time being itself a historical and social relationship and a signifying practice articulating diaspora experiences, as Meighoo argues, which unsettles given and overdetermined structures, positions, and temporalities. In other words, insufficient recognition has been given to Barthold's point that "being black may very well imply dwelling in a perpetually contingent state of time,"[38] even if that "possibility is not necessarily equivalent to actuality."[39] Accordingly, she suggests that "from one point of view, the history of black people during the past millennium has been the history of a people's rebellion against the uncertainties of time, a balancing act of circumstance and heritage that viewed closely, assumes heroic proportions, both in Africa and in the New World."[40] From this perspective, the history of black people records a story of them exceeding and criticizing those hegemonic temporalities, making for a "standing in line" and "waiting in line" generally, and also points to a possible disruption of a particular time line.[41] There is thus an incompleteness to the time line when lived by black bodies that itself contributes to the fungibility and indeed mobility of black presences against the limits of dis-placements in creolized subjectifications associated with the making of modern power.

Plural temporalities mark the ontological complexity of postcolonial times. Nevertheless, perhaps Hanchard's aim may be best seen as more an effort for identifying the temporal mappings and constraints that condition the experience of black subjectivity. Hanchard would perhaps suggest that one should treat "racial time" as the ostensive overarching analytical frame being given for "being black" in the present, a temporal double bind through which other temporalities are ineluctably entangled. "Racial time" is thus a time which is to be wrestled with for its restructuring, for refolding or refashioning, depending on the variation in the geographic and time-spatialization of black subjects and on the variety of their post-Creole imaginations. But this revised interpretation softens but hardly erases the overplayed constraint built into his deployment of the concept even though he successfully highlights the fixing tension in the play of time.

Apart from these issues, diaspora studies also have tended to suffer from a limited attention to issues of gender, class, transgenerational, as well as interethnic and intraethnic conflicts and configurations. Thus, as Anthias points out, "The lack of attention given to transethnic solidarities, such as those against racism, of class, of gender, of social movements, is deeply worrying from the perspective of the development of multiculturality, and more inclusive notions of belonging."[42] Further, as Patterson and Kelley in their critical essay on diasporas also warned, "Neither the fact of blackness nor shared experiences under racism nor the historical process of their dispersal makes for community or even a common identity."[43] The attempts to treat diasporas as bridges or forces for a certain essentialized notion of community through "shared" identity or history is thus founded on multiple fault lines that undermine these ways of understanding the nature and dynamics of diasporic practices. Instead of seeking to salvage this framework, then, perhaps greater attention needs to be paid to the complex temporalities and strategic affinities at play in the productions of diasporic social forms. To underscore this point, in what follows I highlight one example of how a diaspora becomes-vis-à-vis-Being through the elective affinities being engendered for the productions of place and presences in the Americas.

On the Nicaraguan coast a consciousness of self as that which constitutes a placement and displacement of black consciousness is filtered through an assertion of Creole, signifying here an attachment to the chaotic pragmatics of a cut and paste identity, in a small but historically significant mixed-race population. As Edmund Gordon shows, these Creole identities are contradictory and shift depending on how Creoles view the power dynamics of the moment as constructed within the relationships they have with the Nicaraguan central government. Among these Atlantic Coast Creoles, an "African" identity is there and not there, but mostly not there, or expressed with and bridged through other racial presences, which may strengthen or erase it variously.[44] But none of the identities that these Nicaraguan Creoles call forth seems stable. And all seem to play with and resist codification in their crisscross performatives of place and space. They are what Bill Maurer, in another context, would call "creolization in redux," moving in, between, and through identities, themselves unfixed, and using them as technologies to negotiate various official disorders that constrain their claims to belonging to states here or there.[45] I will return to this idea later.

Nicaraguan Creoles see themselves as Jamaican descendants, and as heirs to a superior British colonial culture. They value their knowledge of English over their Spanish-speaking mestizo compatriots, who themselves play racial games which constitute black as inferior. Among these Creoles, the Garvey movement had its adherents in the 1920s, and the civil rights struggle and the black power movement in the United States resonated with them in the 1970s. There were local Rastafarians among them who suffered repression at the hands of the revolutionary government. In recent times, they have adopted the Miskitu identity, as they make claims on land owner-ship as indigenous people.[46] Thus, on Nicaragua's Atlantic coast, the dias-pora is constituted through a politics of place that moves with the imagina-tions of post-Creole home spaces, and one that also moves cultures of power, morphing them strategically and pragmatically, with reference to diverse claims to cultural variants on a spectrum of Creolisms. In this way then the Nicaraguan Creoles move themselves along national, racial, ethnic, and indigenous paths as strategies to engage, contend, or leverage a mestizo-dominated nation-state, whose functionaries (even the revolution-ary ones) have largely resisted or barely accommodated Creole claims of belonging.[47] Each of these cultural styles of identity complements, overlaps, and competes with others, allowing thereby for a repositioning of selves in excess of any assumed social location and enabling the hope of staying ahead of the times, or, for that matter, simply sustaining the pragmatic necessity of zigzagging in and out of (the) times.

Taking these sociocultural variations into consideration, if the diaspora as a lens is widened and the presuppositions for a racial community based on the violence of slavery in the plantation system are understood merely as tendencies, then it will be realized that diasporas are really methodologies that pragmatically reconstitute open-ended "structures of feeling," subjec-tivities, temporalities, and imaginations, in order to allow for the expression of place. These social coalitions forged in the crucible of a violent hi/story, a violent space and time, have roots in the plantations but are rooted and routed elsewhere as well. They remain as dynamic adaptive social forces for the projects of making place and spatial hi/stories and thus are extended to the post-plantation processes of creolization. Thus, in fleeing the plan-tation, diasporic forms, practices, methodologies, and processes must be grasped as dynamic phenomena actually and potentially creative of new traditions. And they may be credited as being concerned with the possibili-ties for sustaining, wittingly or unwittingly, emancipatory and perhaps redemptive projects that slip in and out of presently given representations, hi/stories, and blacknesses, in the struggles for (re)mapping the present. I now wish to complete this discussion by turning the lens on the role of popular culture in animating a critique of African diaspora and how it may support a vision of post-present space-time possibilities, perhaps in order to, as Bhabha suggests, "touch the future on the hither side."[48]

John Akomfrah's nonlinear multitemporal documentary *The Last Angel of History* traces an imperfect hi/story in which past and future inform each other and interpellate the present, in a way that calls together that space-time represented by science fiction as well as by techo-funk: the psychedelic funk of Sun Ra's big band and Arkestra sonic sounds emanating from the condition of alienation, displacement, cultural dislocation, estrangement, and otherness in the United States. The past, like the future, is portrayed in a series of disjunctured images of Egyptian and African folklore, fragmented politicized images of Africans and African Americans shown demonstrating or performing. While the present is the space of fragmentation, the ever-present future is captured as endless frontiers, like outer space, the great unknown that conjures up imaginative, unidentifiable objects and projects, alternative moments and states of being. Lee Perry, the Jamaican reggae producer, bedecked in his custom–made space outfit, spinning, twisting around, searches silently; meanwhile Sun Ra performs intergalactic, extraterrestrial sounds. Akomfrah's message is that here there are independent black musicians, unbeknown to each other yet creating space-time sounds, which echo similar themes. In the film George Clinton pleads ignorance. He's heard the name Lee Perry but does not know of his work. Amid these images, two critics and science fiction writers, Octavia Butler and Ishmael Reed, raise interesting questions about science fiction's relation to the black condition. Reed shares Akomfrah's position that "the Black experience is science fiction,"[49] as does the critic Greg Tate. To paraphrase Reed, "Black people are alien; we [black people] are not believed. Life is normal in this country [the United States]. Police don't plant evidence. They don't lie. Drug dealers are called here to make appointments, before they [the police] execute them. So the African American experience is a far out experience. We certainly have more credibility in Europe."[50]

The film implies that techno music emerged out of the ruins of a decayed, deindustrialized Detroit—the Detroit of Motown, a future past, the sound most identified with modern black Americans. In the film one critic dwells on the irony of techno's birth and says, "Isn't it strange that computers [which] were used to aid and abet the military-industrial complex of World War II, and subsequently that technology mutated, evolved and diversified to such a degree that African American and young black British musicians can use computer technology to construct a soundtrack at the end of the industrial epoch, can use technology as ways to create sonic worlds. Some of these sonic worlds will secede from mainstream or be antagonistic toward it." Techno is "neither street nor stage," a music critic states. In the techno world, sampling consists of an Afro-futurism which digitizes race memory, "collapsing all eras of black music on a chip in endless referencing."

A poignant and touching moment in the film occurs when the "first black American" astronaut talks about his heritage and how when he traveled into space he carried a flag representing all the countries of Africa, which he later took to Africa to show the people, saying, "Look what we did together—what we accomplished together." In the familiar optic of the diaspora this is the moment when nationalism becomes irrelevant. In this narrative, the U.S. African American embraces a larger community, accommodates a broader ideology of communitarianism, namely and usually an uncomplex pan-Africanism, but one of recognition, a technology and rationality of brotherhood.[51]

As a rejoinder to Jeffrey Skoller's argument that the film's nonlinear flight through history is evocative of Walter Benjamin's metaphorical image of history as an angel who while flying into the future looks back at the past—an idea considered literally and unproductively in the film *Sankofa*—I would argue that the documentary in question is also about how the imperfect past-present-future provides a unique vantage point from which to view "the past."[52] The somewhat tendentious narration within the documentary suggests a contested past/future that is informing the past/present and post-Creole imaginations even as it recomposes and remaps the juxtaposition of tradition and the modern. In the film, the critics and musicians recount and recompose their presence within this space-time and stress continuity of black/African traditions and conditioning in the hegemonic systems of power implicitly defined as embodied elsewhere. But in seeking to align their presence to an interpretation of the past, another storyline emerges, which subverts this earlier account. It is one which is not so much about the past per se but, as Michel-Rolph Trouillot would say, about how the present directly speaks to those lived and unsettling demoralizing experiences and sustains their acknowledgment.[53] Moreover, this other narrative introduces tensions with the narrative of continuity as it goes beyond the present to envision a future, which secedes from a past or, at any rate, a particular grasp of it. It suggests the possibility that such experiences of the present always embody an imagined but uncertain or opaque future.

Central to the film's discourse is the "black condition" in the United States, a condition construed as alien, as science fictional, but with a futuristic presence which goes through and transcends the elements of the real horrors of the past, in living through the horrors of the present but also moving beyond them as well. This attention to the future suggests that the horrors, which are pervasive experiences in the present, are reshaping "black lives" and forging communities, and beyond particular representations of racial recognition or identification. But the production of that new something is not *determined* by that hi/story. Although the narrators' angle imposes a mapping of black racial connectedness, based on an objectified black essentialist presence, the commentators, in seeking to draw upon this deterministic reading, also offer vital clues suggesting the ways in which the "othered" black subjects constantly strategize to undermine the stability of such othering. The connection which they seek to make, rhetorically at least, is tied to those essentializing diaspora studies that demonstrate a notion of an "imagined community" beyond the nation-state boundaries that emerged in the context of hegemonic structures of a racialized world— an imagined world unified by a sense of black victimization that shares a consciousness of blackness.

Akomfrah's film discloses that Detroit's deindustrialization (particularly registered by the decline of its reputation as the Motor City) closed down opportunities for its more vulnerable citizens but also opened up new avenues for them to express their musical, human, and racial consciousness that transcended by liminal acts the latter as well. What they produced in their own words was not anything resembling what was "stereotypically black" but something else, nonetheless authentic to a particular interpretation of "black" traditions, however dogmatic that interpretation may seem with respect to an Afrocentric consciousness. I am using the concept of "authentic" here in Trouillot's sense—a present consciousness of the wrongs and inequalities of the present.[54] To be sure, this is a post-plantation creolization —a process not confined only to Detroit-based techno music, but operant in a globalized world experienced both as threat and as challenge, and ultimately as opportunity. For what the musicians of techo reveal is a process of reckoning with the past that does not allow its overdetermination of their futures. This hardly means that they are not aware of it, or that others, particularly the past and present determinations by dominant others, do not attempt to misrecognize and derail their sovereignties. What my interpretation points to is that these musicians, if not the critics, are moved by the imagination of a post-Creole future space (place) or the beyond of a future time, and not just a past present.

For the Caribbean, the story of Jamaican (writ large Caribbean) music gives pause to discussing Creole culture by constantly looking back, seeing such processes primarily through a plantation prism whose centrifugal points include the plantation and a certain Africa everywhere. Garth White, for example, speaks authoritatively about the influence of rhythm and blues on the development of Jamaican music. White argues that "although Black American dance styles very popularly accompanied Afro-American tunes, there was much room for extemporizing; indeed even while utilizing black American steps, the black Jamaican would include an element peculiarly his or hers." Therefore,

> Although one can claim "distinctly Jamaican" for some of the dance features of the Jamaican poor right through their history, one is most certainly aware of the susceptibility of the Jamaican populace to influence by outside forms especially when that "outside form" had familiar elements or elements which could logically be added or developed out of its then present practice.[55]

While White and others cite music's malleability, its "hybridizations," and its appropriations as a condition of possibility for new sonic worlds, they also reference the necessary improvisations that are needed to move beyond a certain time-space. In other words, the chaos of double-articulated mo(ve)ments is a condition of futures, and within these futures are the possibilities for overtaking pasts (which may be indexed through faint or partial and living memories) and redeeming a genealogy of the present diasporic subjects work to create newness in the world. Or, as Gilroy would remind us, these subjects, faced with the twinning of lived and systemic crises in modernity, work for a politics of transfiguration, and not just a politics of fulfillment.[56]

DIASPORIC CREOLIZATION:
ECHOES OF SOUND-PRACTICES

Louis Chude-Sokei, referring to the echoes of sound across the Atlantic, makes a similar claim, like Gilroy, to sounds as creating "alternative public spheres." In the context of the cross cultures of the black diasporic styles, "nothing ever ends up anywhere; instead echoes merely ricochet off sources and each other. And as we know, sound waves, when not captured by a receiver, head off into space and follow the still reverberating aftereffects of the big-bang."[57] These echoes do not stay within these racial interstices, however. Nor are these all racialized in similar ways with similar racial effects. Differences, that passive representation of others, as well as *différances*, obtain.

Consider the urban black American music genre hip-hop, with its roots in the inner-city toaster reggae in Kingston and among Puerto Ricans in the Bronx, which now arcs across the Middle East. Stripped of its origins and dismembered in Israel it feeds the righteous cause of right-wing Israeli youth, appealing to the state to give peace a chance. What will happen to this genre and to the Israeli diaspora as hip-hop appeals to left-wing youth, who equate their plight with those of "niggaz," more often than not, the subject of hip-hop rhythms? How will sonic rhythms and messages re-sound across the Mediterranean and Indian oceans? What kind of politics will it support, considering its routes/roots and its momentary resting places?[58] What tone will be recognizable; what message, what condition, what differences? How will it reverberate as it re-echoes in its reformed originary spaces? What different geographies, spaces will it map? What new technologies of mimicry and critical mimesis might arise?

Indeed, insofar as mimicry refabricates and reinvents post-Creole cultures, it does so selectively, productively adapting and changing the sites and echoes of sounds and other cultural practices.[59] As key to *creolization*'s reproduction of forms seemingly outside the nation-state, mimicry's meaning will derive from the context in which social relationships, bearing that which is mimicked, take place. Thus, a good part of the post-plantation flights of creolization takes place within an enlarging global analytic of modern power, oppressive in a different sense than the plantation, challenging and even liberating in others, closely resembling processes that others describe in Latin America and Africa. Popularized by Caribbeanists and demarcating an element of the uniqueness of Caribbean empowerment and survival practices, creolization, like diasporization, touches many places.[60] Considering that plantations and the Caribbean were part of a wider socioeconomic and cultural complex in which people constantly appropriated, borrowed, mimicked, and echoed warping and juxtaposing temporalities, post-plantation creolization processes are therefore suggestive of the different technologies of being and becoming operating in an unevenly linked modern system of sociocultural sovereignties: modern governmentality.[61]

GLOBALIZED INEQUALITIES: UNDANCEABLE RHYTHMS?

Beyond these easily grasped improvisations of musical rhythms, in a highly unequal global world, the disjunctures between the possibilities and seeming impossibilities for human, or at least the subject's, development are immense. In some cases these disparities, discrepancies, and asymmetries produced in globalization appear to be growing. These conditions of inequality lead one to consider the issue of how certain cultural practices, including those appropriated spaces forged and distinguished in their locales by "scenes of presence," are being drafted and revised to respond to restructured socioeconomic developments, often with the collusion of incapacitated or rather differentially capacitated states, expected to perform to the beat of globalization. These considerations of the impact of capitalism's simultaneous forays into homework, various forms of casual work, and wage work, of the creation of various kinds of workers are often being thought through literatures that focus on the coexistence of various times. For example, in voicing his concerns that history relies on linear time to the exclusion of all other, Dipesh Chakrabarty laments the exclusion of cultural practices that operate outside of (linear temporal experiences) historical time. Chakrabarty argues for a perspective that incorporates the notion of plural temporalities, that is, of different times existing simultaneously.[62] In the context of neoliberal economic processes, this means, for example, that we consider various strategies of temporality that may be at work in the various kinds of sociocultural responses to capital but treat them neither as residual precapitalist phenomena nor necessarily as overdetermined by capitalist social relations. Accordingly we should consider these practices existing paradoxically inside and outside capital and as negotiating spaces and places through and against it, as I have illustrated in chapter 3 in particular. These practices constitute people's negotiated responses, from not one but many different locations, like the infinite adaptations within the voodoo religion practiced away from its New World location in the global city of New York.[63] Neoliberal capital has thus occasioned and been accompanied by cultural transformations as people of all socioeconomic and cultural persuasions engage with its knowledges, institutions, and cultural impositions. This is especially the case now, when the capacities of nation-states to promulgate their cultural and economic programs have been severely challenged, if not undermined, and altered.

Economically the deepening influence of the market and the restructured relationships among and within nation-states have introduced new strains of capitalism, which engender an enticing, repulsive, powerful consumer hustle-culture, which in turn produces forms of work that for many are alienating, debilitating, and insecure but for others are promising outlets for the realization of their new sovereign selves. In any case, many states, individuals and communities are unable to resist or offer alternatives to those cultures of consumption and work, promoted within the world economy. But individuals do counteract and participate, albeit at varying levels, in these various global dynamics, so this is hardly a passive postdialectic operation, making the issue of how power operates and is conducted within these arenas critical.[64]

On the shadier side of globalization in the Caribbean, the severe erosion of the sugar industries, the overripening of banana economies, the general decline of agricultural and manufacturing complexes, the sweatshop nature of its export-processing industries, the indiscriminate spread and shift in tourism toward packaged deals—all this has meant the substantial reorganization of systems under which creolization of a particular type thrived. The widespread emergence of heritage tourism, for example, has resulted in the commercialization and ultimate transformation of Creole cultural forms. Like every other part of the world, the region now has significant sections of its population in the informal sector, engaged in all forms of hustle, while some remain in the formal sector. From being the world's most modern location of production, the Caribbean and too many parts of the Americas are becoming critical as places of consumerism and are now highly networked by cell phones and used cars re-exported from Japan. Informal activities have superseded the formal sector, and remittances estimated in

1996 at US$2.4 billion and nearly twice that in 2001 made the Caribbean and Latin America critical recipients of such flows. Remittances globally represent US$100 billion, of which Latin America and the Caribbean receive some 22 percent.[65]

Framed in terms of the rise of poverty and of the machinations of capital and labor and accompanied by an inquiry into how the poor survive (or what alternative mechanisms of survival exist), as I have stated elsewhere, the rationalization of informal studies has failed to address the question of power.[66] The question of power concerns itself with how states and capital influence the choices and cultural practices of the populace and, in this instance, how they determine the sites available to that populace shaping forms of informality and the associated cultural forms and practices. As one study which looks at the responses of peripheral peoples to incursions of mining capital in New Guinea contends, the Guineans' cultural responses and the constructions of their subjectivities and interests are structured not only by a creative "hybridity" (based on local traditions) of the kind that generates complex forms of oppositional cultural-political engagement but also by the cultural policy of a multinational corporation intent on promoting and othering native Guineans, who must struggle within and against those identities that recast them and their various emancipatory projects.[67]

These negotiations constitute a politics of neoliberal governmentality, a morphing politics of the cross, at the center of which is a conflict over meaning and control over traditional modernisms, both of which are under reconstruction. It is important to examine such issues of power in studies of how various types of Creole cultural forms adapt, resist, or generally renegotiate the influences of capital, in formal and informal settings and in the social and material conditions in which cultural expressions are produced and renewed. As the emergence of *Lucians* discussed in chapter 4 demonstrates, new opportunities also present themselves for the practice of the sovereignty of self inculcated within and through the "sovereignty of imagination."[68] This is not only a Caribbean condition, for the struggle to overcome the stultifying constraints of otherness when wearing its familiar identitarian garbs is a condition manifest in the more vulnerable parts of the world economy, including key sections of global cities, where various migrants are found.

CONCLUSIONS

Lest we forget, I have cited these examples of life in the contemporary moment of globalization processes in order to reemphasize the argument that, despite differentiated histories and changing ways of becoming-vis-à-vis-Being in the world, there is an underlying and highly demanding political rationality of modern governmentality that is impacting the economies and cultures of *tout-monde.* The Caribbean is no exception. Immanuel Wallerstein speaks of the assertions of alternatives that obtain within the registers of class, gender, and race as antisystemic movements conditioned by the world economy.[69] But this perspective erases the view from within the constituent parts of the global, erasures that are critical for understanding the minutiae of determinations. Robertson offers a different perspective, one which seeks to debunk the idea of the world economy's monopoly over local determinations. He concludes that "it is a massive, twofold process involving the *interpretation of the universalization of particularism and the particularization of universalism.*"[70] What Robertson offers here is a way of grappling with globality and locality, not as distinct and autonomous spheres but mutually imbricated and foundational to the rise of the Atlantic world economy, since the seventeenth century and the formation of Europe and those others "without histories." Considering its incorporation and colonization as a complex of plantation, sugar, and slavery, within this incipient world economy of modernity, the Caribbean was a pivotal location for the elaboration of these global forces.[71]

Thus, as Glissant and others have argued, the experiences of creolization can be treated as a worlding phenomenon, operating through a specific mapping of modernity, a specific mapping of the present and its particular cultures of modern power. The diverse peoples who occupy different positions, express different places, and dwell in diverse locations within a *globalité*, though they share power unequally, have furthermore increasing access to an "eBay imaginary," not necessarily in terms of the brand names but, like King Arthur, in terms of the symbols and styles representing social and cultural power and their trappings that expand their seductions, induce desires, and facilitate escapes. Each subject in renegotiating his or her relation to modern power, and in intervening in the chaotic system of *tout-monde*, tries to create new cultural forms, maneuvering within the mapping of culture systems and its given state spaces and subject places constraining and enticing ways of being in and through the world. This is a necessary dwelling with power, despite the violent processes of othering to which he or she may be subjected.

It cannot be emphasized enough that the present relations of power pervasively operate to make available or unavailable certain choices and therefore structure incompletely possibilities for place and presence. Indeed, in Orwellian speak, all Creoles are equally mapped, but some are given more space than others and deemed more present than others.[72] However, within the overarching cultures of power conditioning creolization processes and diasporic tendencies, all the subjects of the present who share, produce, and unsettle these spaces of power will make (depending on their sociocultural positions) different yet related journeys, within and across the more or less racialized spaces of plural temporalities, and will seek different (im)possibilities for post-Creole hopes of homing modern freedoms.

RETHINKING CREOLIZATION
THROUGH MULTIPLE *PRÉSENCES*

Masks, Masquerades, and the
Making of Modern Subjects

There is an opportunity here for actually putting forward a representation of culture as something profoundly incoherent and internally conflicted, something that goes beyond relations to dominant cultures of colonialism, where the dominant / dominated model is much too simple. So it seems to me that in relation to three really burdensome models: the impositions of geography, of geographical location; the nation-state and local identity; and the legacies of colonialism that established a binary opposition with colonial powers, creolization makes it possible to put forward precisely the kind of incoherences that will undo all three in the plight of cultural representation.[1]

> Drum stick knock
> And the darkness is over me
> Knees spread wide
> And the water is hiding me
> Limbo
> Limbo like me.[2]

THE APPROACH ADOPTED here extends the creolization debates beyond the confines of the colonial era and destabilizes their favorite intellectual points of departure, their resting places in the plantation, slavery, the immediate postemancipation era and indentureship, even as we seek to address the fundamental socioeconomic and cultural transformation under way in former plantation societies. The arguments here underscore how changes attendant to processes of globalization have refurbished and undermined *creolization projects* that have brought the region and its people deeper into the ambit of the economy of power, and not just the world economy, as the setting and outcome of the modern Caribbean's placements. Insofar as these processes obtain elsewhere, yet are connected, as are those places where Creoles resettle in migrant, even diasporic communities, then the *creolization* dynamic and the post-Creole imaginary's reach, are global projects and processes, making the Caribbean only one particular site. Moreover, reflections on the current claims about contemporary globalization and the propositional globalizing processes of *creolization* allow us to feed forward earlier practices of subject-citizens into these debates in order to recontextualize our understanding of contemporary strategies of maneuver. And, in particular, they allow us to see the interdependent practices of global and local place making, in its diverse locales, as unstable sociocultural maneuvers and positions subject to an eBay (and post-Creole) imaginary. These maneuvers express the dynamics of various limboing strategies that inhere in the relations subject-citizens have with the institutions and representatives of modern social power in moving creolization processes.

This epilogue synthesizes and presents the book's arguments for decentering the traditional focus of creolization discourses on the Caribbean, plantation, and, in part, even the "black Atlantic," while being critical of those deployments of the creolization motif in contexts where power is erased. Thus, as deployed in this text, we have signaled our flight from the plantation by our rewriting of Creolization/creolization with the double C (capital and lowercase), henceforth *creolization*, to call attention to the nature of the ontological complexity of those dynamic experiences "that endlessly rework and transform the cultural patterns of varied social and historical experiences and identities."[3] In particular, these processes are conditioned by a spatial politics of mapping the present, that is, by and large, but not wholly, ordered by the rationalities of modern governmentality which constrain and excite contesting projects for crossing through seas of present hi/stories (human identity stories). But, in all this, we argued that Caribbean sociocultural productions are pivotally about assertions of self, affirmations, or rather, a *will to place, inducing a journeying from place to place.* Such hi/stories are characterized by multiple, overlapping, and often conflicting, post-Creole imaginations for homing modern freedoms and hence for stimulating the morphogenesis of given cultures of power, with its entangled temporalities, in the enduring hope of realizing vital (yet elusive) dreams of future time, proper presence, or post-Creole home spaces. At stake then in these triple articulations of place, space, and the present are our Creole subjects, routing through modern space yet with cultural bodies rooting in the multiplicity of diasporic habitus that they compose, recompose, and transpose for the making and unmaking of their times, spaces, places, and (cultural) bodies.

As in Caryl Phillips's *Atlantic Sound*, in this text there is a repeating stress on the politics of homing modern freedoms, through practices which seem to animate a politics of masking and masquerade, in the critical mimetic mo(ve)ments for place and, relatedly, space. For his part, in his capacity as a traveler, tourist, ship's passenger, and dispersed if not displaced British person, visiting Atlantic ports implicated in eighteenth- and nineteenth-century mercantile, early colonial slave-driven forms of globality, Phillips lays emphasis on the steadfastness of contemporary cultural parochialisms, which seemingly (dis)place a political consciousness of "blackness" among Atlantic peoples. In contrast, though similarly engaged in a politics for, and analysis of, the processes for (re)homing, spaces, places, and the present, Paul Gilroy stresses the sensibility of a shared community, albeit not around any commitment to pure tropes of identity, and uses the ship as a metaphor to emphasize the routes, displacing or rather rerouting the roots, of "black" identity.

These very different aspects of the politics of "homing" and its "cultural investments" help to underscore a central plank of the position of this text, which is to highlight the importance of the different contexts through which the processes of making spaces and places may be experienced and read. Thus, despite the common denominator of an attention to "black" subjects and the politics of place, or presencing, with Phillips's *Atlantic Sound,* belonging is seen as localized in Liverpool in a fashion that revises, or rather silences, particular aspects of its Atlantic connectedness, in contrast to Gilroy's story of an antagonistic indebtedness which highlights it. A specifically spatialized place-based racism is thus bracketed from its black Atlantic connection despite the diasporic displacement that links people, blacks and others, along the contours of particular forms of modern social power, underscored by slave/plantation histories.

In engaging with these discourses, this book has generally privileged a more complex view of *creolization* in examining the cultural practices that attend the plural diasporic habituses of the Atlantic, and it has sought to demonstrate how collective national histories are lived personally, as well as how transnational experiences critically reshape national lives, individual sensibilities, and collective spaces.[4] This approach problematized the making of place(s), and relatedly space(s), and called for a perspective that embraces a model of *relational histories*, linking places and spaces that have been entangled in a politics of mapping the present. This, we argued, is vital to an understanding of *creolization* as embedded in a politics of place that extends beyond the black Atlantic. Given the importance of the duality of space, or *une poétique de la Relation*, it must be emphasized here that while our perspective allows for a fleeing of the plantation, this *relation* or condition of *spatial duality* in the making of hi/stories, places, and spaces implies that there are ontological and epistemological limits on reading *creolization* across time and space. That is, the relational ontologies of space oblige sensitivity to the interpretive limits of a particular model of *creolization* addressing processes that are embedded in complex yet contingent times, spaces, and cultural bodies, processes which set real grounds for the negotiating and navigating, or even refusal and voiding, of the chains of modern freedom. This caveat is undoubtedly inescapable, even if the analytical frame of the model itself, as the politics and processes of selective creation and cultural struggle, may have general analytical appeal and may point in the direction of genealogies of creolization experiences in the seas of present hi/stories.

To explore the dimensions of the post-Creole imagination, we proposed a method (outlined in chapter 1 and sketched in chapter 2) that recognizes and acknowledges relational economic histories within the present world system. Though originally deployed in debates about modes of production versus market determinism—the dynamic of internal development, on the one hand, and the deterministic impact of the external, on the other— Tomich calls for a method that "presents a unified, multidimensional and relational approach" to Atlantic history, which was a point of inspiration for the elaboration of our model of *creolization*. Like Tomich, then, we seek to express a "unified, multidimensional and relational approach" to the deeply layered and entangled social history of *creolization*—that generic but concrete process of making modern subjects. This text, however, has offered to explore more deeply the strategic power relationships embedded in the making of place(s) and giving rise to the experiences of *creolization* as a multidimensional process of selective creation and cultural struggle.

Thus, in grasping and theoretically elaborating on the nature of *creoliza-*

tion processes, our argument has been that one needs to shift from a focus on "the power of economy, "that is, the capitalist world economy, to that of the "economy of power," or modern governmentality. Our approach thus stresses the inner and outer localities of the global, and vice versa, as fundamentally interconnected processes, through the production of economies of power, and its foldings of the present. These relationships constitute, so to speak, a process whereby *creolization* moves through the world—a world that is caught up in the forging of the hi/stories and identities of people and places. In other words, there is a phenomenon which one might call "creolization-in-the-world" which is implicated in the projects of spatial hi/stories, an open-ended politics of making modern subjects. In this sense, our arguments draw upon an older conceptualization of the dynamic nature of locales as being generally entangled in transnational and modern spaces, hence the view of the Caribbean region as a modern transnational space prominent in the work of Mintz and Price, and as critically extended in the later perspectives of Paul Gilroy and Sassia Sasken. A key point of departure for this work, though, is the analysis of the concepts of space, place, and modernity and the distinctive conceptualization of the latter as a complex process lived as a "time of entanglement," through which there are the productions of space, translations of place, the movements from place to place and their imbrications with the manipulations of citizenship in the present, as rooted and routed by the creolizing will to place.

This text has thus strived to offer new analytical and methodological insights to help further examine processes of globalization, and it may thus provide a useful perspective from which to reflect upon world system versus culture debates, as manifest, for example, in Anthony D. King's edited collection *Culture, Globalization and the World-System*. In that book, analysts grappled with how to construe the historical intertwinement of the world without privileging the power of the economy or "culture." But invariably, as even critics within the book pointed out, the perspectives offered in it end up treating the global and the local *as already* constituted locations, wholes, or totalities where the economy and culture still compete as separate spheres linked by analytical conjunction rather than by some process of integration. Moreover, as Janet Wolff notes, the multiple referents attached to a loose concept of "culture" fail to bring clarity to the problem of how to bring in "culture" as an explanatory variable in seeking to better grasp the dynamics of social processes.[5] Hence there seems to be a discourse that unwittingly "confuses a variety of processes, practices and levels of analysis" that are implicated in these social processes.[6] Part of the problem here is that the various efforts being put forward in the King text lacked any clear position on the underlying ontological conditions and processes being expressed in the constitution of the social world and its mode of formation and transformation. One bold initiative of this book is precisely to lay bare certain theoretical perspectives on the constitution of human and social becoming vis-à-vis being-in-the-world and its interdependency with cultures of power, or the virtual mapping of the present. In outlining our method, we drew principally on Lefebvre's analytics of (social) space read laterally with Deleuze's thinking on "the fold," and Wilson Harris's engagements with the "wombs of space." We also drew on Heidegger revisited through Derrida's ruminations on place/presence, time and Being, as well as the (later) Foucault, Glissant, and other poststructuralist-inflected readings of "the social," "power," "culture," "time," and "place" in "scenes of presence." This revisiting of contemporary philosophical reflections was furthermore supplemented by an insistence on considering ontology not as mere metaphysical speculation, or hard-core thesis of being-in-the-world, but rather, as Stephen White argues, as a need for sustaining weak affirmations in order to come more fully to terms with the reality that we inhabit.[7] Hence our unabashed openness to realist points of view, even where we were critical of certain positions held in these contributions. Our realist orientations were filtered *primarily* through the works of Trouillot, Glissant, Tomich, Massey, Mbembe, Bourdieu, Lefebvre, Foucault, and (recent) critical realist theories of social ontology and process. These perspectives, while bearing their own tensions and limitations, may (as shown by this work) be critically and reflectively integrated in a way that holds together insights needed for systematically differentiating amongst the elements *composing* and *articulating* the interrelationality of connectedness (and disconnectedness) in certain social spaces.

Undoubtedly, one of the problems hampering thinking about complex processes of sociocultural change, such as *creolization*, has been the fragmented explorations provided in treating systematically related processes. And, relatedly, the tendency to continue thinking of it as one-time, one place *cultural possession* of some bounded sets of cultures that could be essentially described and known at a single point in time, with a narrow spatial slice into a convoluted reality. These tendencies may reflect the influence of imposed disciplinary boundaries, or unconscious or hidden ontological scripts as well as political prejudices or ideals. Or they may simply be due to the inescapability of our bounded rationality, and hence ultimately, one's embedding in specific epistemological limits, as conditioned by one's state of being in time and space. To the extent that these problems exist, at least in these senses, one's analyses will be limited in conceptual and explanatory reach, as reflected in an inadequate theorization of the complexity of sociocultural transformations that inhere in the modern context of globalization.[8]

In this book, the question of citizenness—that is how people fashion themselves, creating and morphing elements of habituses in which they find themselves—has been taken as a central element for understanding processes of *creolization*, routed and rooted by the will to place and the post-Creole imaginary for proper presence. Yet only recently has this received the attention it deserves in the literatures on creolization. We argue, however, that it is pivotal to grasp these liminal dialectics of (re)homing place, in order to deepen one's understanding of Caribbean sociocultural practices of "*creolization* in an unequal world." The book, through chapter 5, also explores and theorizes an approach to territorialization or localization as a phenomenon that is being articulated within processes of deterritorialization mediated by the politics of negotiating the relation between power and its subjects. These trans/nationalizing and (re)homing processes are intrinsic to the pursuit of various kinds of (re)rootedness and routedness that take place in the Caribbean region and elsewhere. In this sense, we recompose current debates about globalization and localization by revealing practices and processes that go beyond the postulations of false-dichotomous locations, and replace it instead with "une poétique de la Relation"—a cross-cultural poetics evocative of co-relational and intertwined histories. It is, as Rogoff's words in the first epigraph to this epilogue suggest, an attempt to recognize the presence of such sociocultural incoherencies, yet supplemented by the effort to theorize these strategies relationally through an optic which views them as liminal processes and politics, for effecting critical double mo(ve)ments and double articulations. These processes of staking place and presence, or of homing modern freedoms, act to re-configure diasporic and nondiasporic habituses, as well as the state spaces and subject places expressing cultures and spaces of power. This largely occurs through an imagining of the nation's symbolisms as mechanism of, and for, social empowerment.

The seas of *creolization*'s hi/stories have indeed been violently charted through neoliberalism's biopolitical strategies within globalization and conducted by the cultural bodies of subject populations, albeit morphed by their circuits of places as guided by their will to place. Accordingly, processes of cultural morphogenesis are the seas of our spatial hi/stories which are moving time, space, and our Creole subjects from place to place. Unsurprisingly, then, the everyday politics of *creolization* practices, of making spaces and (re)homing places, is linked to the pervasiveness of migrant populations from the South to the North, within the South as well, the information technology revolution, the transnational flows of popular culture, the dispersal of financial global-city networking, and indeed to cacophonous assemblages of modern space, the site of globalization processes that will obscure, escape, disturb and refold the governing procedures of any single state.[9]

These social and cultural mo(ve)ments of *creolization* practices effected through the double articulation of space and place produce a complicated plurality of temporalities and styles of identity that enable people, as both creators and consumers of modern state spaces and subject places, to maneuver and move, that is, transfigure their place-in-time. As shown in chapter 3, the politics and practices of accommodation coded in the desire to belong, or the will to place, engendered strategies that allowed Creole subjects to utilize global relationships to reposition themselves locally and transnationally. Contextualized within "Western" projects of modernization and progress, Caribbeans' insertion into the sociocultural ideological constructions of "the West" were nonetheless veritable challenges to their spatial marginalizations enacted within the Caribbean locale. But seen from a global economy scale, these acts enabled their incorporation within processes of economic and sociocultural development that drew them even further into the ambit of "Western" projects for mapping time and space and, more important, induced them to "read" (in a de Certeau's fashion) their futures within such processes and beyond them as well. Seeking to reshape and influence the socioeconomic and cultural coordinates of their world, Creole colonial citizens have thus engaged in several practices to root and indeed reroute themselves in the Americas and beyond. Consider also the seemingly contradictory and ambivalent practices and approaches toward rootedness—seen through the optic of rhizomic rootings and routings—and its endowment of possibilities and limits as exemplified by the gens anglaises, the subject of chapter 5. The desire to place, to re-create their own world, to (re)home spaces of belonging, is thus certainly critical to understanding the nature of *creolization* and post-plantation *creolization* processes.[10]

However, while this mobility and the critical mimetic mo(ve)ments of subject populations are crucial to the morphing of cultures of power, and without seeking to conceptualize the nation-state "as the horizon for *any* form of politics that adopts the life-processes of the working classes as its point of departure,"[11] it can still be argued that despite its partial displacements, decline, and transformation, the biopolitical policies of state institutions continue to play vital roles in bridging the effects of modern governmentality and thus in *formally* linking citizens to developments transnationally.[12] More often than not, state elites and others achieve this in the name of nationalism and under the dispensation of what constitutes *the* national character and national good. One of the effects of this "poétique de la Relation" has been that the *state* of state institutions serves as a measure of the *changing* socioeconomic and socio-cultural relationships, *and possibilities*, underway in diverse places. State-in-society relationships thus continue to be part and parcel of the process of disturbing the governmentalization of the state, as well as the society or its peoples, and must be kept as a critical element that inflects processes of *creolization* and the dynamic possibilities for re-mapping the present, or re-calibrating one's place-in-time.

As we have witnessed since the inception of the so-called postcolonial period, that is, in the aftermath of political sovereignty and in these en-tangled times-spaces of modern governmentality, both citizens and states have been actively engaged in negotiating the terms and conditions of the present, as fundamentally pivoted or navigated through the spaces of Creole citizenship. This has led to a process of destabilizing older forms of Creole culture and relationships to the nation and nation-state and setting the conditions for the rise of new cultural forms and, ultimately, the remapping of the present or the restructuring of its times of entanglement: past times re-membered, future time imagined, and interstitial, liminal presents.

However, as the chapters in this book show, both states and their subjects are actively repositioning themselves within the vortices created by the ab-sences, or rather dis-placements, of older traditions of governance that sanctioned proactive forms of development, more or less, and defined cit-izenship in terms of one's affinity to nation and the much-vaunted national development.[13] It was that spirit which symbolized the interconnected relationship between the sovereignty of place and that of individual, more or less. However, at another level, the histories of *creolization* as articulated in projects of nationality, and indigeneity, have ensured the marginalization of many citizens considered not quite Creole enough, or who for whatever reason have not availed themselves of the fruits of the Creole nation-state. This holds for non-Caribbean subjects as well. Consider the trumpeting of mestizaje that defines Latin countries' ethnic blend. Mobilized for such hegemonic purposes, creolization-masking projects thus engineer a strategic biopolitics in adapting modern governmentality to its subjects, who wittingly or unwittingly maneuver within, or become entangled with, these masquerading essentialisms depicting identity, time, place, and cultures. Such masking practices, as Gerard Aching comments, "articulate degrees of recognition, misrecognition and non-recognition between masked subjects and viewing subjects."[14] But even for those included in the register of the Creoleness of the state, maintaining the masks and masquerading as the subjects have been difficult. As such, these masking projects, though laced through by unequal power relationships, are continuously disturbed through what, following Pelton, may be referred to as the *liminal state*.[15] This refers not so much to a determinate phase in a ritual transition but rather to "a source of recreative power,"[16] a power that, as Austin-Broos comments, is an index of "a permanent possibility in social life."[17] In particular, as Aching suggests in his reflections on Glissant's idea of the nature of Creole form, creolization can be viewed as a politics of covert disclosure wherein rituals of performative masking become the means whereby agents seek transformations of sacred and profane visibility and indeed a *présence*, "disclaiming social irrelevance, and expressing a desire for engagement."[18] Thus, Creole subjects, just like Anansi, the spider trickster in the folklore of the Akan group of Twi-speaking people, seek to enlarge and transfigure their place in the world through the liminal state and the liminal performative. Indeed, as Austin-Broos further comments, in "Pelton's description of Anansi's liminality, two aspects are especially important: the idea of liminality as a total state and the idea of liminality as an idiom of performance."[19]

Citizenship, then, or rather the desire for citizenness, mobilizes a liminal dialectic of presencing. Citizenship's ideological claims of being inclusionary by and large ring hollow in the face of the exclusionary device of mapping the present through strategies of nation building, imagined communities, and so on—that is, through homemaking strategies which perpetuate the idea of both heterogeneity and homogeneity by states of exception, exclusions, or, more generally, a politics of "othering." The many mottos which proclaim variously "out of many one," nonetheless, paradoxically seek to integrate through exclusionary practices, which in turn elicits a variety of counterconducts, strategic double movements, or a tactical limboing of modern governmentality, in the hope of alternative and more empowering presents/places, or for proper scenes of presence in public spheres.

As shown in chapter 4, however, though these counterconducts may challenge the undemocratic practices engaged in by governing regimes, such protests themselves need not be entirely democratic or liberatory. In short, the new cultural politics that critics generate and engage in may draw upon some authoritarian and even singularly masculinist performances common to the sociocultural practices of particular places—somewhat akin to placing new wine in old containers. But even as these reinforce and embrace different exclusionary tendencies, they nonetheless point out critical caveats, even absences, in the democratic procedures and general practices of nation-states. The ambivalences internal to contesting individuals, organizations, and cultural groupings reveal the uncertainty of the postcolonial period and its openness to diverse multidirectional challenges and accommodations. For there are no guarantees to the establishment of any particularized community, or public, or the practices that transpire within these imagined communities, making even the unrealizable possible. The experiences under postcolonialism and even under the project of neoliberal globalization, as under colonialism, have thus served largely to reconfigure rather than replace the core significance of the state-in-society relation for mediating the will to place, albeit in contexts that are reworking the city-citizen, shepherd-sheep biopolitical games of inseparable autonomies.

It is useful, then, to see state-in-society relations through a lens of *creolization* and Creoles' critical mimetic mo(ve)ments for re-staking and homing proper presence, as this helps to further interpret and examine the ways in which states have implemented neoliberal policies emphasizing some elements over others, even as multilateral organizations push for wholesale adoptions of such an ideology.[20] In this way, it is possible to historicize, or situate, the *creolization* process and the strategies of post-Creole imaginings within a dynamic global analytic, while at the same time maintaining the focus on concrete and shifting patterns and forms of state power articulated relationally through space and place and enacted relationally through diverse strategies of inclusion and exclusion, or diverse politics of (re)homing or homemaking-staking place, in search of "proper presence."

Within these constitutive developments worldwide, not least the various "original" Creole locales, and through a discussion of the Caribbean *creolization*'s local and global coordinates, this book thus advances a broader approach to the study of sociocultural histories of Caribbean places. But even as one focuses on the Caribbean Creole and post-Creole imagination, it is recognized that these arguments and observations have been made especially for, and of, the postcolonial condition in Africa. As Paul Tyambe Zeleza posited of the African postcolonial state: "The state undergoes a miraculous metamorphosis from being the incarnation of the colonial evils of oppression and exploitation into the personification of the postcolonial possibilities of freedom and equality. This re-imagination facilitated the authentication and authorization, domestication and Africanization of the state as a set of practices and processes, ideas and interests."[21] In both Africa and the Caribbean, in the period of structural adjustment and now neoliberal globalization, citizens confront, challenge, and manipulate state institutions that are increasingly questioned in terms of their ability to deliver goods and basic services of the kind enabling the nurturing of respectability and national character that its officials never tire of trumpeting, now doing so nostalgically. Given the ongoing renegotiation of definitions of governance and citizenship, each constituency vies for power and for control of, if nothing else, the discourses of the public sphere, canceling out and installing temporary hegemonies over governable spaces. As Achille Mbembe put it:

> The postcolony is made up not of one coherent "public space," nor is it determined by any single organizing principle. It is rather a plurality of "spheres" and arenas, each having its own separate logic yet nonetheless liable to be entangled with other logics when operating in certain specific contexts: hence the postcolonial "subject" has had to learn to continuously bargain [*marchander*] and improvise. Faced with this . . . the postcolonial "subject" mobilizes not just a single "identity," but several fluid identities which, by their very nature, must be constantly "revised" in order to achieve maximum instrumentality and efficacy as, and when required.[22]

Mbembe's observations about Africa reinforce this book's sentiment related to the connectedness of *creolization, as a politics of making place,* and postcolonial conditions globally. His arguments about the postcolony in some ways resonate within the postcolonial histories of the Caribbean. The similarity of these conditions across the world and the imaginations and imaginaries that they spawn, particularly among former colonial, now postcolonial worlds, suggest a basis for Philip McMichael's comparative method encapsulated in the phrase "incorporated comparisons," of the kind that recognize the unity of the world economy regardless of the differentiated (but linked) histories of places, paying particular attention to conflicted processes that define the creolization processes elsewhere. Michel-Rolph Trouillot reminds us that, by definition, histories are open-ended and certain of heterogeneous outcomes and therefore are constantly open to challenge.

The acts of re-making selves and places under new and different conditions and social coordinates may destabilize and dislocate older received notions and practices of *creolization.* By dislocate, I mean in the sense of partly replacing them in an imaginary that offers possibilities exceeding the imaginaries of state elites and other citizens. Against this backdrop, the simple and specious interpretation of the flower festivals as one of mindless imitation, or the general charge of mimicry by a cartoonist of St. Lucia's newspaper, ironically called the *Voice of St. Lucia,* misses the point as noted in chapter 3. Refurbished forms of *creolization* challenge, play with, appropriate, and subvert the older localized Creole givens, by "detour, evasion, mimicry, by subverting the cultural dominant from below, by appropriation, translation, and expropriation."[23] But this is not simply an interplay between the dominant and the subordinate in a war of position. It is a process that straddles and borrows from a spectrum of classes and places. Consider the appropriation of *Saturday Night Live* styles by Lucians and the images, styles, and sounds of rap, hip-hop, dancehall, and gospel, ubiquitous across unequal global spaces. These improvisations are pervasive throughout the Americas and beyond wherever power subjugates or invokes differences.

Lucians' satirical performances in the Caribbean, discussed in chapter 4, can be effectively juxtaposed to the controversial U.S. documentary *Paris Is Burning.* In the latter, performed by marginalized gay black and Latino U.S. Americans, the artists disavow the exclusions of powerful white U.S. America and enact the excesses of power and style of that class with the scant resources at hand. In the words of Roger Ebert, the film depicts "the successful attempt by outsiders to dramatize how success and status in the world often depend on props you can buy or steal, almost anywhere—assuming you have the style to know how to use them."[24] It doubled also as the subversion of an elitist practice of the celebration of luxury and power. Yet it was also a reinforcement, a legitimization of the aesthetic values of a particular bourgeois and white lifestyle but lived and experienced differently. In that sense it was an improvisation not dissimilar from the labor strategies of the enslaved and indentured, who were not, as stated before, always preoccupied with Massa's grand designs, despite his disproportionate sway over their lives.[25] They were as interested in refashioning and mimicking an existence—a making of themselves—within the interstices of the very violent exercise of power, generally, and thus, as proposed by George Lamming, exercising a "sovereignty of the imagination," in the sense of "choosing and making and remaking that self which you discover is you."[26] But the critical mimesis that these forms entailed was meant for a production of newness typified by liminal acts.[27] Consider the vogue dance, developed among gay subalterns in *Paris Is Burning*, which was at once affirmative of the old but refreshing it as well, so much so that it is then absorbed as new by the establishment.

The continual refashioning of pasts, presents, and *présences* to engage the future is thus critical to defining the Caribbean's modern colonial and postcolonial condition. But this engagement need not be exercised within nor strategized from familiar Caribbean locales, which in any case represent the various workings of transnational and global. As emphasized throughout this book, *creolization* processes have always been structures of practical activity entailing a *messianicity*, even when routed through the configurations of the present's dis-ordered *présences*. Thus, in engaging with this chaos, other places are re-membered in (re)homing place following the violence of uprooting, but they are not necessarily recalled as a nostalgic refuge from a frightening present or indeed future but rather are evoked as a strategy to confront the changing time-spaces of modernity and its increasingly global publics.[28] Reconsider here for a moment the impact of the growth of the Haitian diaspora in the United States, and within it the rise of new feminist politics mobilized against the Duvalierist regime, which succeeded in establishing Haiti's first democratically elected government, that of Jean Bertrand Aristide. According to Carolle Charles, the post-1986 development of Haiti's women's movement was rooted in the gendering of state violence under the Duvalierist regime, which led to "change in state gender policies redefining women as political subjects and the transnationalization of Haitian women's struggles with the massive movement of international migration."[29] Both of these components reflect the context, condition, and the imagination of the changing nature of Creole citizenship within and to the Haitian nation-state. These transnational activities of Caribbeans result in critical changes among citizens within communities, as well as in their relationship to the state. They result in the creation of new *présences* at particular sites.

In this sense, as stated in chapter 5, the rerouting and rooting of Caribbean citizens, for the most part within and outside the multiple locations of the North Atlantic facilitates a different "poétique de la Relation" within the nation-state. While deteriorating socioeconomic conditions within Haiti made it urgent for Haitians within the U.S. diaspora to consider action in transforming the spaces within the nation-state through more or less democratic political struggle, other Caribbeans reposition this relationship differently. Even so, these strategies and tactics operate and maneuver within certain notions of place and belonging, calibrated by the remembrances of, or the imaginative enactment of, spatial hi/stories for times yet to come, for a future-present time.

As emphasized in this text, the motifs of fleeing and homing are important analytical registers for rethinking the processes and politics of *creolization*. The various chapters have shown that even when confined by the plantation in slavery and the hierarchical sociocultural registers of postemancipation, Creole citizens always sought to flee the plantation in order to vivify alternative possibilities of dwelling. The structuring power of globalization's economic forces reinforce and reconfigure the region's vulnerabilities but also opens up liminal spaces for some of its transnational citizens to create distance from the demanding performative strictures of nation-states, although many still adhere to and observe some of those sacred rituals of citizenship. In these demanding politics of the cross—where agents creatively negotiate vertical demands while navigating for horizontal necessities—something different, something new is created well beyond the conservative dynamics evident in the push and pull of any locale or histories where people route and root to express the sovereignty of their imagination.

Observations of Caribbeanists on the recreolization of Puerto Ricans on the U.S. mainland are useful here. Juan Flores speaks of the new entangle-ments and new creolized identity as indicative of the rebirth of creolization within the diasporas of the United States. With half of Puerto Rico's popula-tion living in the United States and grappling with issues of racism, na-tionality, and pan-Latin identitarian tendencies, new poetry takes these issues as its focus, using English, Spanish, and SpanEnglish mixed codes. According to Flores, the diaspora culture remains rooted/routed to its an-cestral culture leading to an unsettling recreolization. As he puts it:

> One of the most unsettling and consequential aspects of the diasporic perspective, then, of this recoiling diaspora vengeance, is créolité as rear-ticulated Africanization, a redefined relation to blackness and to African heritage, including the African moorings and blackness in their own Puerto Rican background culture and its history. This newly defined cultural nexus is most striking, and troubling to the conservatively con-ceived national culture, in its reference to the relationship to African Americans, and the strong class dimensions which are implicit in that affiliation.[30]

Flores's salutary reinterpretation of Hall's components, *présence américaine* (which in Hall's conceptualization refers to the site of the New World location, and his passing reference to native peoples), refocuses attention on the influence of the U.S. *présence américaine* and the influence of African American cultural practices upon Caribbean cultural forms and expres-sions, given the fact that the United States is home to Caribbean Creoles. His idea sets the imagination beyond the originary *présences* that con-stituted the bulk of *creolization* of a certain period, to contemporary varying conditions, which (re)produce different cultural forms within a transna-tional Atlantic (and its beyonds) *présence américaine*.

The circulation of Puerto Ricans within and to the United States and back to Puerto Rico makes for an interesting comparison between the return of mainly older Caribbean migrants from Britain and the United States, with their different understandings of cultural practices. How its bearers relate to older transnational island forms of creolization would make a fruitful study. Schematically dealt with in chapter 5, the return of "gens anglaises" is fraught with resistance and tension. Black British identity relocated back home results in a certain reconstitution of rootedness, the recreation of different localities, sure indicators of the blurring of the boundaries of global and local, and of *creolization* here and there.

In this context, the idea of a stabilizing local might be seen as an enactment of a desire to perform a certain elusive authenticity, a sovereignty of imagination apprehended in the relations between returned migrants and those who experienced particular kinds of global discourses and practices within the spatiotemporality of the homeland islands. These tensions are channeled through the familiar hierarchies (and processes) of gender, race, and class, like neighborhoods, as seen in chapter 5, but now operating in different registers, not least reconstituted rurals and urbans. To be from a particular neighborhood anywhere carries its distinguishing baggage, where the gens anglaises live. Wanting to return to the local, to return home, comes at a price, but seems an ineluctable step in the Creole line of escape for proper presence and dwelling places.

Speaking of local in relation to artistic production in the Americas, Gerardo Mosquera posits that much of it is local, in the sense "that it is the result of artists' personal and subjective reactions to their contexts, or because it seeks a cultural, social, or even political impact in their milieus."[31] Trapped within a language that inadequately captures the movement of entanglement of space and time, but wrestling within it to capture these processes, Mosquera continues:

> These artists are frequently well informed about other contexts, about mainstream art, or are also looking for an international projection. Sometimes they move in and out among local, regional, and global spaces. Usually their art is not bonded to nationalistic modernism or to traditional languages even when it is based on vernacular culture or specific backgrounds.[32]

Local, then, simply refers to the agentive features of action emanating from a certain place and time. Even so, neither the local, the regional, nor the global represents distinct locations. They are complexly entangled "vernacular modernities" that give rise to certain perspectives, sociocultural tensions, and various cultural practices. These deliberations underscore Rogoff's remarks about the concept's possibilities for articulating incoherencies about "culture" generally. As she says, rather than a model characterized by situational harmonies, "creolization makes it possible to put forward precisely the kind of incoherences that will undo all three in the plight of cultural representation."[33] But Rogoff's use of the term "undoing" should not be understood as the complete withering away of these boundaries materially, or even within peoples' imaginations, but rather, an allusion to their tenuousness and their openness to myriad possibilities that involve their unmaking and remaking and the strategic (discursive) essentializing that sometimes obtains even as lives are experienced practically. This is a point made by several analysts noted especially in chapter 6.

To be sure, localization forces contributing to this destabilizing view of "culture" are always pitted against those which seek to homogenize space, place, and nation in exclusionary ways. Consider the role of culture producers sanctioned by nation-state institutions. For example, the current calls within the Caribbean region for states to take control of "cultures" produced within the region unwittingly refer to acceptable, therefore sanctioned profitable forms of such practices. Creole citizens do not stand objectively outside of these tendencies. Certainly, many resist, but significant numbers, albeit ambiguously, partake of these homogenizing tendencies intrinsic in the debates about citizenship and national character, thus reifying local sociocultural structures, while performatively exceeding them—making for the experience of multiple tensions as mediated by these crisscrossed positional ties and permutations of experiences.

All of this suggests that the post-Creole and postcolonial imagination operates without guarantees for any particular kind of community; rather, it enlarges community and allows for its continual extension and multiple expression through a plurality of diverse communities. Transnational historical tendencies jostle contradictorily and in synchronicity with localized and national ones, making for heterogeneous moments in which place becomes territorially important, imparting to citizens identities that exclude other places and people seemingly important to their collective historical or nonhistorical consciousness. Now more than ever, global conditions linked to various desires assemble disparate Creole populations within unhomely homelands, across and beyond the Atlantic world. Juan Flores is indeed correct in his claim that discussions of *creolization* necessitate the incorporation of diasporas, which as was suggested in chapter 6, are really methodologies that pragmatically reconstitute open-ended structures of feelings, subjectivities, temporalities, and imaginations, in order to allow for the expression of place. The formation of the Caribbean and therefore its *creolization* processes has always been transnational. At the same time, the conditions within which "cultures" are reformed and refurbished take place within contexts that override the singularity of a *given* place and time yet at the same time make it seem urgent, even necessary. This is the paradoxical global.

In that sense approaching issues of universalisms' relationship to particularisms central to globalization studies can be done through the optic of "une poétique de la Relation"—a cross-cultural poetics as conducted through processes of *creolization* and the multiple practices and strategies of maneuver for homing modern freedoms. This requires, as Flores astutely noted, grappling with several more *présences* than those offered either by the specifically island-Caribbean context or, I should add, also by the binds of ethnic originaries.[34] It requires, too, that we flee the historical and intellectual constraints of the plantation's centrality to *creolization*'s processes—substituting a thorough understanding of the material and discursive, even ideological conditions that structure people's choices and seek to shape the sovereignty of their imagination, by the politics of mapping the present. I hope that this book is a step toward this fruitful flight, perhaps even a mo(ve)ment in the "Creole line of escape."

PREFACE

Tanya Shields was very helpful in referencing some of these poetic associations with the image.

1 Derek Walcott, "The Sea Is History," in *The Star-Apple Kingdom* (New York: Farrar, Straus and Giroux, 1979), 25.

2 Grace Nicholls, *I Is a Long Memoried Woman* (London: Karnak, 1983).

3 I am of course here thinking of Édouard Glissant's redeployment of Gilles Deleuze's and Félix Guattari's concept of the rhizome as a way of envisioning the nature of social life and cultural transformation processes, or, as he stated, as a way of addressing his "real subject—the entanglement of world wide relation." Glissant saw the rhizome's errant rootedness—"a network spreading either in the ground or in the air, with no predatory rootstock taking over permanently"—as the essential principle supporting the "Poetics of Relation, in which each and every identity is extended through a relationship with the Other." Édouard Glissant, *Poetics of Relation,* trans. Betsy Wing (Ann Arbor: University of Michigan Press [1990] 1997), 31, 11.

4 Irit Rogoff, "Open Session: Modernity, Creolization and Globalization," in *Créolité and Creolization,* ed. Okwui Enwezor et al. (Ostfildern, Germany: Hatje Cantz, 2003), 102.

5 Wilson Harris, "The Limbo Gateway," in *The Post-Colonial Studies Reader,* ed. Bill Ashcroft, Gareth Griffiths and Helen Tiffin (London: Routledge, 1995), 378–82.

6 Glissant, *Poetics of Relation.*

7 Christopher Cozier is a Trinidad and Tobago–based artist. I thank him for allowing me to use this image.

8 Homi Bhabha, *The Location of Culture* (London: Routledge, [1994] 2004), 367.

9 From David Eggers's *What Is the What* (San Francisco: MacSweeny, 2006).

10 Excerpt from Kamau Brathwaite's, "The Emigrants," *The Arrivants* (London: Oxford University Press, 1973).

11 See Achille Mbembe, *On the Postcolony* (Berkeley: University of California Press, 2001), 15.

12 Email conversation with author, ca. early 2007.

13 Konte, like the La Commette and the Bèlair, are considered to be African-derived and European-derived dance forms.

14 I do address some of these issues in my book *Negotiating Caribbean Freedom: Peasants and the State in Development* (Lanham, Md.: Lexington Books, 2005). There I wrote about how such romanticization missed the realities of state/peasant relationship in the context of a globalized region.

15 Michaeline A. Crichlow and Patricia M. Northover, "Power and Its Subjects: Development Dilemmas, Post-colonial Re-structuring of Rural Spaces/Places/Identities and State Reconfiguration," Eleventh World Congress of Rural Sociology, "Globalization, Risks, and Resistance," Trondheim, Norway, July 25–30, 2004.

16 The Race Space Place project received funding from the Provost's Common Fund in 2006. It is an ongoing project that aims to incorporate other worlds besides the Atlantic. For a sense of the project, see http://www.jhfc.duke.edu/racespaceplace.

17 The year-long reading group under the auspices of a larger project, "Race, Space, and Place: The Making and Unmaking of Freedoms in the Atlantic World and Beyond," culminated in a symposium held April 13–14, 2007.

18 See Patricia Northover with Michaeline A. Crichlow, "Freedom, Possibility and Ontology: Rethinking the Problem of Competitive Ascent in the Caribbean," in Clive Lawson, John Latsis, and Nuno Martins, eds., *Contributions to Social Ontology* (London: Routledge, 2007), 207–30.

PROLOGUE

1 Edward Kamau Brathwaite, "Caribbean Man in Time and Space," *Savacou* 11–12 (1975): 1.

2 Saurabh Dube, *Stitches on Time, Colonial Textures and Postcolonial Tangles* (Durham, N.C.: Duke University Press, 2004).

3 David Harvey, *The Condition of Postmodernity* (Oxford: Basil Blackwell, 1990);

Saskia Sassen, "Spatialities and Temporalities of the Global: Elements for a Theorization," *Public Culture* 12, no. 1 (2000): 215–32.

4 Nicholas Thomas, *Colonialism's Culture: Anthropology, Travel and Government* (Princeton: Princeton University Press, 1994), 105. What is disclosed here are the problems associated with totalizing concepts, and a method that at once grasps the relation between conceptual apparatuses and the histories they seek to evacuate.

5 Still, such movement as experienced in one locale, however differentially adapted, and dare I say creolized, is fundamentally structured by the dynamics of the world economy.

6 Richard Price, "The Dark Complete World of a Caribbean Store: A Note on the World System," *Review* 9, no. 2 (fall 1985): 217.

7 Richard Price seeks to explain the historical moment in which the Creolité of the Martiniquan intelligentsia appears: see Richard Price, *The Convict and the Colonel* (Boston: Beacon Press, 1999); Richard Price and Sally Price, "Shadow Boxing in the Mangrove," *Cultural Anthropology* 12, no. 1 (1997): 3–36.

8 I was commissioned to carry out a study the results of which were published in 1994 as *Land Use and Land Tenure Patterns in the Windward Islands: An Analysis of the Agricultural Sectors of Martinique, St. Vincent Dominica and Grenada, 1970–1990* (St. Augustine, Trinidad: Caribbean Network of Integrated Rural Development [CNIRD]).

9 Michel-Rolph Trouillot, *Peasants and Capital: Dominica in the World Economy* (Baltimore: Johns Hopkins University Press, 1988).

10 Lila Abu Lughod, "The Romance of Resistance: Tracing Transformations of Power through Bedouin Women," *American Ethnologist* 17 (1990): 41–55.

11 Consider the strategies of Nicaraguan Creoles that are invoked depending on the community's needs and their relation to the state policies. See Edmund T. Gordon, *Disparate Diasporas: Identity and Politics in an African-Nicaraguan Community* (Austin: University of Texas Press, 1998). Also see Arturo Escobar, "Cultural Politics and Biological Diversity: State, Capital, and Social Movements in the Pacific Coast of Colombia," in *The Politics of Culture in the Shadow of Capital*, ed. Lisa Lowe and David Lloyd (Durham, N.C.: Duke University Press, 1997), 201–26.

12 I use "moral economies" in Karl Polanyi's sense, referring to householders who produce primarily for their own household purposes rather than the market. See Karl Polanyi, *The Great Transformation: The Political and Economic Origins of Our Time* (Boston: Beacon Press [1957] 1977).

13 Capturing this idea is the somewhat crude phrase "the personal is the political."

14 Some analysts even interpret informality in parts of the Caribbean as intrinsic to Creole cultures. Katherine Brown, for example, attempts to eschew informality as a product of survival strategies and relate its occurrence in Martinique to the "trickster, cunning and opportunist" cultures of slaves, part of the strat-

egies of resistance against the slave master, the colonial, and now the colonial postcolonial power as in the case of Martinique. Informality occurring there can be explained by a "cognitive system of débrouillardism." Brown, *Creole Economics: Caribbean Cunning under the French Flag* (Austin: University of Texas Press, 2004). Also see "Creole Economics and *Débrouillard:* From Slave-Based Adaptations to the Informal Economy of Martinique," *EthnoHistory* 49, no. 2 (September 2002): 373–403. In these formulations the binaristic model of either/or is reconstituted linearly from Anansi to the contemporary Spider people, yet the interpretation makes the whole world seem palpably Creole and Martiniquais! But the question unanswered is how are Martiniquais different from other people elsewhere, where these same processes have been occurring?

15 I have sought to highlight these politics of "rural othering" in M. Crichlow and Patricia Northover, "Power and Its Subjects: Development Dilemmas, Post-Colonial Re-Structuring of Rural Spaces/Places/Identities and State Reconfigurations in Contemporary Globalization Processes," paper presented in Trondheim, Norway, 2004. There has been a virtual industry in the literature on informality. The titles are too numerous to mention here. But see the bibliography and the articles generally in *Informalization: Process and Structure*, ed. Faruk Tabak and Michaeline Crichlow (Baltimore: Johns Hopkins University Press, 2000).

16 WIEGO, http://www.wiego.org/, 2–4.

17 Consider that staying at home, not working outside of it, was a position pursued by black women, desiring human existences; this idea is captured in Paula Giddings, *When and Where I Enter: The Impact of Black Women on Race and Sex in America* (New York: Bantam Books, 1984).

18 Mary Chamberlain, *Narratives of Exile and Return* (New York: St. Martin's Press, 1997).

19 Orlando Patterson, the John Cowles Professor of Sociology at Harvard University, was the featured lecturer at Jamaica's celebration of forty years of independence on October 16, 2002: "Emancipation, Independence and the Way Forward." Patterson stated: "Again, we can follow India's lead and stop complaining about a brain-drain of our nurses. Instead, we should invest heavily into training as many thousands as the U.S. and Canadian economy needs. Nurses are known to be among the most active members of the transnational community. They keep close ties with the island and often send their children back to be brought up here. In a few short years they pay off the entire cost of their education with their remittances, and like Indian programmers in Silicon Valley, provide net earnings of thousands of dollars each year over the course of their working lives. And when they retire they typically return home and spend their savings and social security earnings in Jamaica. What is true of nurses is only a little less true of teachers: another area of great shortages in America. Our expenditure in tertiary training then, should emphasize those skills and professions that offer the best prospects for graduates to be employed both here as well

as in the transnational system." See Michaeline A. Crichlow, *Negotiating Caribbean Freedom: Peasant and the State in Development* (Lanham, Md.: Lexington Books, 2005), especially the epilogue.

20 "PM proposes Training Pact with US," Jamaicaobserver.com, October 3, 2003.

21 Ibid.

22 Nigel Bolland, "Creolization and Creole Societies: A Cultural Nationalist View of Caribbean Social History," in *Questioning Creole: Creolisation Discourses in Caribbean Culture*, ed. Verene A. Shepherd and Glen L. Richards (Kingston: Ian Randle Press, 2002), 33.

23 Steve Pile, "Opposition, Political Identities and Spaces of Resistance," in *Geographies of Resistance,* ed. Steve Pile (London: Routledge, 1997), 16.

24 Melville Herskovits, *The Myth of the Negro Past* (Boston: Beacon Press, 1958).

25 Herman Bennett, "The Subject in the Plot: National Boundaries and the 'History' of the Black Atlantic," *African Studies Review* 43, no. 1 (April 2000): 101–24.

26 Jean Besson, *Martha Brae's Two Histories: European Expansion and Caribbean Culture-Building in Jamaica* (Chapel Hill: University of North Carolina Press, 2002). The concept of culture building used here, and by anthropologists elsewhere, like in the work of Sidney Mintz and Richard Price and others, I find problematic, for it conveys an architectural concreteness, unchanging edifices, in the midst of transculturality and flexibility.

27 Aisha Khan, "Journey to the Center of the Earth: The Caribbean as Master Symbol," *Cultural Anthropology* 16, no. 3 (2001): 271–301; Percy Hintzen, "Race and Creole Ethnicity in the Caribbean," in *Questioning Creole: Creolisation Discourses in Caribbean Culture*, ed. Verene A. Shepherd and Glen L. Richards (Kingston: Ian Randle Publishers, 2002), 92–110. See also the discussions sparked by Viranjini Mujnasinghe's "Theorizing World Culture through the New World: East Indians and Creolization," *American Ethnologist* 33, no. 4 (2006): 549–62. Most of this critical work has focused on Trinidad and Tobago.

28 Hintzen, "Race and Creole Ethnicity in the Caribbean"; Nigel O. Bolland, "Creolisation and Creole Societies: A Cultural Nationalist View of Caribbean Social History," in Shepherd and Richards, eds., *Questioning Creole*, 15–46.

29 Hintzen, "Race and Creole Ethnicity in the Caribbean," 93.

30 As Percy Hintzen notes, though enormously influential, this ideological creolization project registered unevenly across the national terrain, serving as a precursor and infusion into the national project uniting and dividing disparate people on the basis of ethnicity.

31 Eric Williams quoted in the *Trinidad Guardian,* 1967.

32 Mr. A. A. Thompson, identified as minister without portfolio in the PNM government in 1964. *Trinidad Guardian,* 16, no. 3 (1964).

33 Susan E. Craig, *Community Development in Trinidad and Tobago: 1943–1973: From Welfare to Patronage*, working paper (Kingston: Institute of Social and Economic Research, 1974), 54–55.

34 Ibid., 57.

35 Michael Hanchard, *Orpheus and Power: The Movimento Negro of Rio de Janeiro and São Paulo, Brazil, 1945–1988* (Princeton, N.J: Princeton University Press, 1994).

36 I refer here to the ways in which the present recuperates the past, that the critiques of Lucians reflect more than simply a genuflection to a past but a constant reliving of it in various versions of the present and its structuring of their futures. This idea is part of what Pierre Bourdieu meant by the conditioning of habitus. Pierre Bourdieu, *The Logic of Practice*, trans. R. Nice (London: Polity Press, 1990), 53–56. See also Gareth Williams, "Subalternity and the Neoliberal *Habitus*: Thinking Insurrection on the El Salvador/South Central Interface," *Nepantla: Views from South* 1, no. 1 (2000): 130–70. Williams offers a critical reading of twenty-two-year-old Salvadoran Solórzano's tale of the meaning of her life as a gang member in Los Angeles.

37 Nicholas Thomas, *Colonialism's Culture: Anthropology, Travel and Government* (Princeton: Princeton University Press, 1994).

38 This point is elaborated in Crichlow, *Negotiating Caribbean Freedom*.

39 I say some, since I believe that ideas of development that underpinned that project are still fairly intact in the imaginations of citizen-subjects. Which is to say that belief in the transformative power of the state, in the ability of state elites to "do something," even to perform miracles, still obtains among significant sections of Caribbean populations.

40 The term "eBay Imaginary" is appropriated from Fredric Jameson, in "Fear and Loathing in Globalization," *New Left Review* 23 (September–October 2003): 105–14. Jameson was discussing the style of new science fiction writing. See chapter 6 for a fuller discussion of how I use the term.

41 See, for example, Norman Girvan, *Aspects of the Political Economy of Race in the Caribbean and in the Americas* (Mona: Institute of Social and Economic Research, 1976).

42 Stuart Hall, "Cultural Identity and Diaspora," in Jonathan Rutherford, ed., *Identity: Community, Culture and Difference* (London: Lawrence and Wishart, 1990), 225–37.

43 Achille Mbembe, *On the Post Colony* (Berkeley: University of California Press, 2001).

44 Michel-Rolph Trouillot, *Silencing the Past: Power and the Production of History* (Boston: Beacon Press, 1997), 146. Though raised in a different context in a discussion of the meanings of the proposed Disney theme park on slavery and the idea of authenticity, these words are salient in this context.

45 This is not intended, of course, to let, say, Christianity and Christians off the hook. For instance, how might we view Christians, or the long history of Chrisitianity pockmarked by episodic violences of its adherents, and Christian politicians who preach love but are producers of massive suffering of all kinds?

46 Obika Gray, "The Jamaican Lumpenproletariat: Rogue Culture or Avatar of Liberation," *Social and Economic Studies* 52, no. 1 (March 2003): 1–33. For a

fuller discussion of Gray's development of the idea of the predator state, see idem, "Predation Politics and the Political Impasse in Jamaica," *Small Axe: A Caribbean Journal of Criticism* 13 (March 2003): 72–94.

47 Chakrabarty speaks of the perils of European historicism which would grasp these as premodern or even prepolitical forms. Speaking of historical time as out of joint with itself, he states: "I take gods and spirits to be existentially coeval with the human, and think from the assumption that the question of being human involves the question of being with gods and spirits." See Dipesh Chakrabarty, *Provincializing Europe: Postcolonial Thought and Historical Difference* (Princeton: Princeton University Press, 2000), 16.

48 See Glenn A. Elmer Griffin, "Come, We Go Burn Down Babylon: A Report on the Cathedral Murders and the Force of Rastafari in the Eastern Caribbean," *Small Axe* 21 (October 2006): 1–19; "Jah" is the Rastafari's idea of God.

49 In Griffin's account, the two men speak the powerful lyrics of reggae superstars (for example, Bob Marley and Peter Tosh) to outline their vision of suffering and redemption. According to Griffin, "The killers were frustrated by the incapacity of the existing Rasta structures in St. Lucia to image a cultural and political world much different from the one they occupied." Ibid., 16.

50 I am developing this idea of morphing from Margaret Archer; see chapter 2.

51 One is thinking here of Trouillot's discussion of the Disney theme park on slavery. See Trouillot (1995).

52 Stephan Palmié, *Wizards and Scientists: Explorations in Afro-Cuban Modernity and Tradition* (Durham, N.C.: Duke University Press, 2002).

53 Lauren Derby, "Haitians, Magic, and Money: *Raza* and Society in the Haitian Dominican Borderlands, 1900–1937," *Comparative Studies in History and Society* 36 (1994): 488–526.

54 Caryl Phillips, *The Atlantic Sound* (New York: Alfred A. Knopf, 2000); Paul Gilroy, *The Black Atlantic: Modernity and Double Consciousness* (Cambridge: Harvard University Press, 1993).

55 Erna Brodber's work, animated by Zora Neale Hurston's almost caricatured view of Jamaican males of the 1930s, shows the complex ways in which Jamaican mibrants grappled with issues of resettlement and their foreign experiences. Her study "A Profile of Jamaican Men" (unpublished manuscript, ca. 1970s) consists of 200 interviews with male migrant returnees born between 1893 and 1900. It was a response to Hurston's and Clarke's anthropological observations about absent Jamaican males in rural households. See also Erna Brodber, *Standing Tall: Affirmations of the Jamaican Male: 24 Self-Portraits* (Kingston: Sir Arthur Lewis Institute of Social and Economic Research, 2003), and idem, *The Second Generation of Freemen in Jamaica, 1907–1944* (Gainesville: University Press of Florida, 2004). Unfortunately, none of the aforementioned works by Brodber foregrounds or interweaves critiques of Hurston's or Clarke's anthropological assumptions. Also see Mary Chamberlain, *Narratives of Exile and Return* (London: St. Martin's Press, 1997); and John Western, *A Passage to*

England: Barbadian Londoners Speak of Home (Minneapolis: University of Minnesota Press, 1992).

ONE   LOCATING THE GLOBAL IN *CREOLIZATION*

Lloyd Best, a Caribbean philosopher and economist, was a critical founder of the New World group that sought to unthink the colonial paradigms of development and sociocultural being in the Caribbean. If any Caribbean person spoke to the issue of "fleeing the plantation," it was Lloyd Best, with his relentless scholarship and academic and public offerings, especially through his magazine *Tapia*, dedicated to unveiling key elements of the deterministic properties of the plantation on our collective psyche and suggesting ways to move beyond them, through the practice of certain kinds of freedoms. We write in this unsettling tradition and dedicate this chapter to his memory.

1 Wilson Harris, "Creoleness: The Crossroads of a Civilization?" in *Caribbean Creolization: Reflections in the Cultural Dynamics of Language, Literature and Identity*, ed. Kathleen Balutansky and Marie-Agnès Sourieau (Gainesville: University of Florida Press, 1998), 24.

2 Dale Tomich, "Atlantic History and World Economy: Concepts and Constructions," *ProtoSociology: An International Journal of Interdisciplinary Research* 20 (2004): 102.

3 Édouard Glissant, *Caribbean Discourse: Selected Essays,* trans. Michael J. Dash (Charlottesville: University of Virginia Press, 1989), 221.

4 Kathleen Balutansky and Marie-Agnès Sourieau, Introduction, in *Caribbean Creolization*, 3. Two recent texts that also provide excellent coverage of the issues relating to the use of the concept of "creolization" are Okuwi Enwezor et al., eds., *Créolité and Creolization* (Ostfildern, Germany: Hatje Cantz, 2003); and Verene Shepherd and Glen Richards, eds., *Questioning Creole: Creolizing Discourses in Caribbean Culture* (Kingston: Ian Randle and Oxford: James Currey, 2002). See also Charles Stewart, "Syncretism and Its Synonyms: Reflections on Cultural Mixture," *Diacritics* 29, no. 3 (1999): 40–62.

5 For a critical reflection on the idea of the "Caribbean," see Antonio Gaztambide-Giegel, "The Invention of the Caribbean in the Twentieth Century," *Social and Economic Studies* 53, no. 3 (2004): 127–57.

6 See, for example, O. Nigel Boland, "Creolization and Creole Societies: A Cultural Nationalist View of Caribbean Social History," in Shepherd and Richards, eds., *Questioning Creole*, 15–46. Also see Percy Hintzen, "Creoleness and Nationalism in Guyanese Anticolonialism and Postcolonial Formation," *Small Axe* 15 (2004): 106–22; and Rex Nettleford"s reflections on Caribbean culture in "Caribbean Culture: Paradoxes of the 1990's," in *Caribbean Public Policy: Regional Cultural and Socio-economic Issues for the 21st Century*, ed. Jacqueline Braveboy-Wagner and Dennis Gayle (Boulder, Colo.: Westview Press, 1997), 73–89.

7 See, for example, Shalini Puri, *The Caribbean Postcolonial: Social Equality, Post/Nationalism and Cultural Hybridity* (New York: Palgrave Macmillan, 2004); Deborah Thomas, *Modern Blackness: Nationalism, Globalization and the Politics of Culture in Jamaica* (Kingston: UWI Press; Durham: Duke University Press, 2004); and Patricia Northover and Michaeline Crichlow, "Freedom, Possibility and Ontology: Rethinking the Problem of Caribbean Ascent," in *Contributions to Social Ontology*, ed. C. Lawson, J. Latsis, and N. Martins (London: Routledge, 2007), 207–30. Of course the intellectuals' participation in partisan political agendas has also been signaled as one of the limits of the deployment of the concept of Creole, creolization, and its relatives; see in this regard, for example, Richard Price and Sally Price, "Shadowboxing in the Mangroves," *Cultural Anthropology* 12, no. 1 (1997): 3–36, and Mimi Sheller, "Creolization in Discourses of Global Culture," in *Uprootings/Re-Groundings: Questions of Home and Migration*, ed. S. Ahmed, C. Castaneda, A. Fortier, and M. Sheller (Oxford: Berg, 2003), 273–94.

8 Percy Hintzen, "Race and Creole Ethnicity in the Caribbean," in Shepherd and Richards, eds., *Questioning Creole*, 92–110. For a critique of the gender and ethnic biases of creolization discourses, see Heather Smyth, "Roots beyond Roots: Heteroglossia and Feminist Creolization in Myal and Crossing the Mangrove," *Small Axe* 12 (2002): 1–24; and Aisha Khan, "Journey to the Center of the Earth: The Caribbean as Master Symbol," *Cultural Anthropology* 16, no. 3 (2001): 271–97.

9 Lloyd Best, "West Indian Society One Hundred and Fifty Years after Abolition: A West Indian Re-Examination of Some Classic Theories," abridged version of public lecture delivered at the University of Hull in 1983.

10 The idea of the "modern" has been largely articulated through discourses on modernization and capitalistic development processes. Accordingly, it has been principally conceptualized in terms of the temporalities of types of societies, the forms of their institutions, and the structure of normative expectations. This can be seen in the significant emphasis on modernity as history and pattern, which has been subject to an intense debate targeting the premise of linear temporalities and the evacuation of difference and agency. See, for example, Bruce Knauft, ed., *Critically Modern: Alternatives, Alterities, Anthropologies* (Bloomington: Indiana University Press, 2002).

11 To reference "theory" or the "theoretical" has become almost politically incorrect in recent times—not without good reason since the term had become deeply corrupted with the hegemonic rise of a variety of positivisms and their images of science. However, before we succumb to the temptation to annihilate or move beyond theory, in exclusive favor of the contexts of experience or praxis, we wish to recover use of the term albeit without adherence to positivists' binary canons of science. We thus persist in an engagement with "theory," as an interpretive analytic; as the grounded activity of critically thinking about things, conditions, and processes in the world; as an exercise in understanding,

without guarantees, that participates in the remarkable quotidian acts of producing a symbolic world, for getting through the world.

12 A seminal effort to shift the terms of discourse to recognize the spatiality of the modern has of course been offered by David Harvey, *The Condition of Postmodernity* (Cambridge, Mass.: Blackwell, 1990). However, we will be adopting a different tactic in theorizing the production processes of modern spaces, by seeking to move somewhat away from the heavily geographically inscribed and Marxist-inflected reading he offers in that comprehensive, important, and pathbreaking text.

13 See David Hoy, *Critical Resistance: From Poststructuralism to Post-Critique* (Cambridge: MIT Press, [2004] 2005), 189.

14 The notion of emergence here is used to refer to the "entry of forces," as suggested by Foucault in "Nietzsche, Genealogy, History," in *The Foucault Reader*, ed. Paul Rabinow (New York: Pantheon Books, 1994), 76–100, 84. Foucault also, somewhat elusively, suggests regarding a space of emergence as a "*non-place*," perhaps to intimate its liminal state as a portal, gateway to and between times and places, and perhaps also to point to it as a contested and undecided (or undecidable, neither appropriated nor dominated) and thus open-ended time-space of being. Given Foucault's methodological leaning as well, this rendering of emergence would act to distance its use away from teleological models of emergence, and perhaps also from invisible hand models of spontaneous order; see Edna Ullmann-Margalit, "Invisible-Hand Explanations," *Synthese* 39 (1978): 263–91. Thus, emergence as used above in the Foucauldian sense also seems to suggest a need for models of process, causal analysis, or generation that eschew closed, totalizing, or deterministic systems. See, in this regard, the elaboration on emergence, from a "dialectical critical realist" perspective, by Roy Bhaskar, *Dialectic and the Pulse of Freedom* (London: Routledge, 1993), 49–56.

15 We extract this concept from Wilson Harris's text *The Womb of Space: The Cross-Cultural Imagination* (Westport, Conn.: Greenwood Press, 1983). He uses this concept to explore cultural space as "the womb"—the place and body of grounding—for and of, cross-cultural creativity that cuts across chasms of difference to produce genuine change in ontologies of being. Elsewhere, he writes of "space as the womb of simultaneous densities and transparencies in the language of originality," intimating a growing complexity in his conceptualization of the folding nature of "space." See Harris, "Creoleness," 26.

16 Jacques Derrida, *Margins of Philosophy*, trans. Alan Bass (Chicago: University of Chicago Press, 1982), 13.

17 Sylvia Wynter, "Unsettling the Coloniality of Being/Power/Truth/Freedom: Towards the Human, after Man, Its Overrepresentation—An Argument," *New Centennial Review* 3, no. 3 (2003): 257–337.

18 Gilles Deleuze, *The Fold; Leibniz and the Baroque*, trans. Tom Conley (Minneapolis: University of Minnesota Press, 1993).

19 John Roff, "Gilles Deleuze," *The Internet Encyclopedia of Philosophy* (2006), http://www.iep.utm.edu.

20 See Viranjini Munasinghe, "Theorizing World Culture through the New World," *American Ethnologist* 33, no. 4 (2006): 549–62.

21 See Stephan Palmié, "Creolization and Its Discontents," *Annual Review of Anthropology* 35 (2006): 433–56. It may be noted here then that our deployment of a concept of creolization does not rest methodologically upon, nor does it extrapolate any kind of reading of processes of "cultural" change through linguistic models and frameworks. Further, it does not seek to provide another overgeneralized analytic of modernity but rather seeks to *unsettle* understandings of the phenomenon derived from the matrix of the plantation.

22 An affirmation as defined by Deleuze is "to release, to set free what lives": Gilles Deleuze, *Nietzsche and Philosophy* (1983), quoted in David Hoy, *Critical Resistance: From Poststructuralism to Post-Critique* (Cambridge: MIT Press, [2004] 2005), 24.

23 Quoted in Stuart Elden, *Mapping the Present: Heidegger, Foucault and the Project of Spatial History* (London: Continuum, 2001), 20.

24 Ibid., 20.

25 Again, in this unusual writing, we wish to draw attention to the ontological interdependencies in, or foldings of subject being, by introducing the citizen-subject, as persons qua S/s/objects. "Being" a subject entails then not just the articulation of spaces representing "the Subject," or the subject of power, but, of equal importance, it also presupposes the conduct of the material forces of differential bodies. Bodies, the object media for social life, refer here not just to physicality but also to cultural bodies, in the Nietzschean sense, of "a social structure composed of many souls," quoted in Hoy, *Critical Resistance*, 47. For a further discussion of the body as culturally embedded, see Hoy's interesting analysis of the Nietzschean "body" as "a multiplicity of interpretations" or an entanglement of "felt texts," 47–53. And for a relatively recent and excellent review of the analysis of the body in social and cultural anthropology, see also Stephen Van Wolputte, "Hang On to Your Selves: Of Bodies, Embodiments and Selves," *Annual Review of Anthropology* 33 (2004): 251–69.

26 Françoise Vergès suggested the idea of bricolage for interpreting creolization processes as an "ethics of borrowing and mimicry"; see Vergès, "Kilter Kreol: Processes and Practices of Créolité and Creolization," in Enwezor et al., eds., *"Créolité" and Creolization*, 179–84. The idea has since been interestingly elaborated upon by Wendy Knepper in "Colonization, Creolization and Globalization: The Art and Ruses of Bricolage," *Small Axe* 21 (2006): 70–86.

27 The use of the concept "bridging" here is meant to evoke its multiplicity of meanings, in several contexts, ranging from media and technology studies to social capital and poetic studies, while still signaling an attachment to its dominant sense of use as something that links and connects spaces and places. A remarkable grappling with the metaphorical powers of the bridge is provided

by the American poet Hart Crane in his classic "The Bridge" (1930), *The Complete Poems of Hart Crane*, ed. Marc Simon (New York: Liveright Publishing, 1986), 43–44.

28 Karl Marx, "The Eighteenth Brumaire of Louis Napoleon," in *The Marx-Engels Reader*, ed. Robert Tucker, 2nd ed. (New York: Norton, 1978), 595.

29 Elden, *Mapping the Present*, 3. This project of spatial history is discussed by Elden as a critical thread linking Heidegger's and Foucault's work. It is a thread that also connects diverse modern thinkers on the relation between time and space, most notably present in Lefebvre, Deleuze, Derrida, and Homi Bhabha. It is indeed a multiple and rich vein of thought that underpins postcolonial- and poststructuralist-inflected Marxist studies. Within Atlantic space this question of the relation between time and space is evident in the works of C. L. R. James, Franz Fanon, Wilson Harris, Kamau Brathwaite, Derek Walcott, Stuart Hall, Sylvia Wynter, Dale Tomich, Édouard Glissant, Michel-Rolf Trouillot, Sidney Mintz, Richard and Sally Price, and Paul Gilroy, to highlight a prominent few. For a rich discussion of the notion of space in contemporary literature of the French Caribbean, with a focus on Condé, Chamoiseau, and Glissant, see N. Coates, "Gardens in the Sands: The Notion of Space in Recent Critical Theory and Contemporary Writing from the French Antilles" (2001), http://web.mac .com/nick.coates.

30 We agree with Roger Brubaker's and Frederick Cooper's arguments that in making reference to notions of identity, one needs to remain sensitive to its elusiveness as an analytical concept and vigilant against reifications; see their essay "Beyond Identity," *Theory and Society* 29 (2000): 1–47. Yet it remains a central category of practice in today's modern times, staking out claims to places as well as proper place in the negotiations of recognition (self-recognition and recognition by others), and the politics of making newness. Accordingly, as pointed out by Craig Calhoun, a continued analysis of "identity-talk," and its spaces of politics, seem inescapable in one's investigations of the projects of history making and its interweaving levels of social, political, public, bodily and biographical life formation; see Craig Calhoun, *Social Theory and the Politics of Identity* (Cambridge, Mass.: Blackwell, 1994). See also Akhil Gupta and James Ferguson, eds., *Culture, Power, Place: Explorations in Critical Anthropology* (Durham, N.C.: Duke University Press, [1997] 2001).

31 Michel-Rolph Trouillot, "Culture on the Edges: Caribbean Creolization in Historical Context," in *From the Margins: Historical Anthropology and Its Futures*, ed. Brian Keith Axel (Durham, N.C.: Duke University Press, 2002), 199.

32 We've suggestively here turned the title of Ulf Hannerz's article "The World in Creolization," *Africa* 57 (1987): 546–59, on its head. Hannerz's adoption and use of the concept of creolization stems, he argues elsewhere, less from an engagement with the Caribbean as "New World" phenomena than through his encounters with the Creole linguistics analytic. See Ulf Hannerz, "Theorizing through the New World? Not Really," *American Ethnologist* 33, no. 4 (2006): 563–65.

33 The concept of writing a "history of the present" was introduced by Foucault to mark first his own shift in historical method, from the seemingly sanitized analytical tracking of the artificiality of knowledge productions to the genealogical method, which meant "the union of erudite knowledge and local memories which allows us to establish a historical knowledge of struggles and to make use of this knowledge tactically today"; see Foucault, "Two Lectures," in *Power/Knowledge: Selected Interviews and Other Writings by Michel Foucault, 1972–1977,* ed. Colin Gordon (New York : Pantheon Books, [1972] 1980), 83. His second purpose was to signal the need for a shift from the "archeological space" of history as an objective container of events marking the unfolding of lawful progress to the "genealogical space" of political methodologies and processes in making present histories. Thus, as Rizvi comments, Foucault rejects both "romantic history (history based on the past) and teleological history (futuristic history), and conceptualizes the present in terms of incorporating both past and future"; see Ali Muhammad Rizvi, "Reading Elden's Mapping of the Present," *Cosmos and History: The Journal of Natural and Social Philosophy* 1, no. 1 (2005): 179.

34 In their introduction to *Foucault and Political Reason,* Andrew Barry, Thomas Osborne, and Nikolas Rose comment on the trend for "grand theory" as typified in what they see as "numerous ambitious theses about our world, its nature, its pasts and its futures" and urge for the eschewing of such desires; see *Foucault and Political Reason* (Chicago: University of Chicago Press), 2. The target for their concerns was efforts at *actual writings* about a present "in which modernity takes on the status of a comprehensive periodization; an epoch, an attitude, a form of life, a mentality, an experience" and where critiques tended toward a "reciprocal totalization." That is, the new vernaculars of critique are seen as being engaged in a similar attempt to grasp "the essence of an epoch." Our approach here bears much sympathy for this caution being clearly sounded by Barry et al., yet this precaution should not be read as a stipulation against theorizing "the present." Rather their warnings are against the erasure of the multiplicity of imagined histories that characterize the politics of the present, or, as they say, bid "to introduce an 'untimely' attitude in our relation toward the present. Untimely in the Nietzschean sense: acting counter to our time, introducing a new sense of the fragility of our time, and thus acting for the benefit, one hopes of a time to come" (5).

35 See Foucault, "Nietzsche, Genealogy, History," in *The Foucault Reader,* ed. Paul Rabinow (New York: Pantheon Books, 1984), 76. For very good discussions of Foucault's method of genealogy, see Hubert Dreyfus and Paul Rabinow, *Michel Foucault: Beyond Structuralism and Hermeneutics* (Chicago: University of Chicago Press, [1982] 1983), chap. 5, and Mitchell Dean, *Governmentality: Power and Rule in Modern Society* (London: Sage Publications, 1999), chap. 2.

36 The concept of liminality, being betwixt and between, at the point of a threshold, or crossroads of transformation, is a powerful idea that has been deployed

in a range of practices, including art, religion, anthropology, psychology, philosophy, cultural studies, and social theory. The concept was analytically developed through the field of religious studies and anthropology in the seminal works of Mircea Eliade, Victor Turner, Arnold van Gennep, Asmoron Legesse, and Robert Pelton, in the effort to grasp the power of African folkloric heroes and ritual processes of transformation. See Robert Pelton, *The Trickster in West Africa: A Study of Mythic Irony and Sacred Delight* (Berkeley: University of California Press, [1980] 1989). It plays an important role in poststructuralist analysis and in particular postcolonial theory. The specific notion of a "liminal dialectics," however, has also been put forward by Sylvia Wynter in outlining her philosophy of freedom and "becoming human" in the world. See Neil Roberts, "Sylvia Wynter's Hedgehogs: The Challenge for Intellectuals to Create New 'Forms of Life' in Pursuit of Freedom," in *After Man, towards the Human*: *Critical Essays on Sylvia Wynter,* ed. Anthony Bogues (Kingston: Ian Randle Press, 2006), 157–89. As noted by Roberts, Wynter's "liminal dialectics" refers to "the dialectical tensions among those who are liminal heretics and others representing the non-liminal status," 182. Our view of a process of "liminal dialectics," however, is read through our model of creolization, which puts forward the analogy less in terms of a kind of Kuhnian revolution and rather more in terms of a "politics of transfiguration," a concept entertained by Nietzsche and also in Gilroy's *Black Atlantic.* See Tracy Strong, *Friedrich Nietzsche and the Politics of Transfiguration* (Urbana: University of Illinois Press, 2000), and Gilroy, *The Black Atlantic,* 37. For us, like Gilroy, this politics of transfiguration suggests an emphasis on the emergence of "qualitatively new desires, social relations, and modes of association" (ibid.).

37 See Homi Bhabha, *The Location of Culture* (London: Routledge, [1994] 2004), 324.

38 See Donald Moore, *Suffering for Territory: Race, Place and Power in Zimbabwe* (Durham, N.C.: Duke University Press, 2005).

39 Elden, *Mapping the Present,* 49.

40 This effort may be seen also as a way of critically developing Gilroy's project in *The Black Atlantic,* which makes an intervention for creolization studies, through his engagement with the debate on cultural nationalism, in order *to displace* closures expressed in attachments to monolithic ethnicities and nationalisms. See *The Black Atlantic,* ix, 202. The "double consciousness" perspective read for the "Black Atlantic" is, of course, a variant on the theme of creolization as a New World phenomenon, first articulated by Sidney Mintz and Richard Price, *The Birth of African-American Culture: An Anthropological Perspective* (Boston: Beacon Press, [1976] 1992). There, the authors qualify the anthropologist Melville Herskovitz's view that Afro-American culture was mainly African cultural survivals, and this led to the continuity-discontinuity identity debates on creolization and relatedly diaspora, which have tended to reflect all the pitfalls of the essentialist–antiessentialist dialectic that engulfs identity discourses. See Chris-

tine Chivallon, "Can One Diaspora Hide Another? Differing Interpretations of Black Culture in the Americas," *Social and Economic Studies* 54, no. 2 (2005): 71–105; also consider David Scott's reflections on Mintz's reading of the Caribbean in "Modernity That Predated the Modern: Sidney Mintz's Caribbean," *History Workshop Journal* 58 (2004): 191–210. The continuity-discontinuity debate also pervades the literature on modernity, with a similar dialectics of identity/non-identity playing itself out there as well; see Bruce Knauft, ed., *Critically Modern: Alternatives, Alterities, Anthropologies* (Bloomington: Indiana University Press, 2002).

41 In posing this question about the creolization process we are thus seeking to critically develop a line of inquiry set out by Foucault in "The Subject and Power," where the goal is "to create a history of the different modes by which, in our culture, human beings are made subjects." This work of turning human beings into "subjects" has been intensely explored by Foucault in the study of the sciences, its dividing practices and the ways in which a human being can "turn him or herself into a subject." See Foucault, "The Subject and Power," in *Michel Foucault: Beyond Structuralism and Hermeneutics*, ed. Hubert Dreyfus and Paul Rabinow (Chicago: University of Chicago Press, [1982] 1983), 208.

42 See Homi Bhabha, "How Newness Enters the World: Postmodern Space, Post-colonial Times and the Trials of Cultural Translation," in *The Location of Culture*, 212–35.

43 Dale Tomich, "Atlantic History and World Economy," 102.

44 Gilroy, *The Black Atlantic*, 198.

45 We are referencing here Rebecca Scott's idea of freedom, where she focuses on the ways in which freedom was constructed within the present constraints that people of color in Louisiana and Cuba faced. In coining this phrase used by physicists, Scott uses it metaphorically. In her words, the phrase "helps to convey the way in which two broadly similar systems can evolve over time into dramatically different end states . . . Even if initial conditions are comparable, and even though the processes of change themselves can be seen to be governed by causation against a similar background, evolution over time possesses certain genuine degrees of freedom." See Rebecca J. Scott, *Degrees of Freedom: Louisiana and Cuba after Slavery* (Cambridge: Harvard University Press, 2005), 6.

46 The quote is from Tomich, "Atlantic History and World Economy," 102.

47 See Margaret Archer, *Realist Social Theory: A Morphogenetic Approach* (Cambridge: Cambridge University Press, 1995).

48 It should be emphasized here that we are *not* relying on Archer's notion of culture system—the set of things that are intelligible and are shaped by logical relations between them, which is taken as parallel to Popper's World Three. Our notion of culture is a system of relations entailing both social movements of life and practices of representation, whether textual or not. Moreover, we do not subscribe to a view that communities are constituted by a "shared culture that shapes the individual and makes him or her a replicate in miniature of the

whole" but rather that they are shaped by "the ongoing debate over what shared culture is, . . . the inherited symbolic system does not determine who will win in any given conflict, but it directs community members to 'what is worth fighting about' "; see Neil ten Kortenaar, "Beyond Authenticity and Creolization: Reading Achebe Writing Culture," *PMLA* 110, no. 1 (1995): 31–32. Our "culture system" concept is thus more in line with Foucault's concept of "discourse," where he states that "discoursing subjects form a part of the discursive field—they have their place within it (and their possibilities of displacement), and their function (and their possibilities of functional mutation). Discourse is not a place into which subjectivity irrupts; it is a space of differentiated subject positions and subject functions." See Foucault, "Politics and the Study of Discourse," in *The Foucault Effect: Studies in Governmentality*, ed. Graham Burchell, Colin Gordon, and Peter Miller (Chicago: University of Chicago Press, 1991), 58.

49 An early effort to understand the way in which the social histories of the Caribbean are shaped by the presence of modern governmentality can be found in David Scott, *Refashioning Futures: Criticism after Postcoloniality* (Princeton, N.J.: Princeton University Press, 1999). Our own efforts at grasping the nature of creolization as shaped by modern governmentality involve a rather different elaboration of this phenomenon and its engendered processes, as outlined in our sketch of a method.

50 Trouillot, "Culture on the Edges," 190.

51 Ibid., 197.

52 Ibid., 198.

53 Ibid., 201.

54 Félix V. Matos Rodríguez, "Quién Trabajará? Domestics, Urban Enslaved Workers, and the Abolition of Slavery in Puerto Rico," in *Slavery without Sugar: Diversity in Caribbean Economy and Society since the 17th Century,* ed. Verene A. Shepherd (Gainesville: University Press of Florida, 2002), 248–71.

55 Ibid., 252.

56 This work demonstrates the disparity between the colonial's intent or idealism and the actual practices that ensued in different spaces, particularly in urban areas. Cities, for example, had a different population ratio of slaves to planters than plantations. Also there were large numbers of free people as there were slaves intermingling in these spaces. Consider the even closer juxtaposition of wage and slave labor, especially within the confines of a very small island. See Anne Pérotin-Dumon, *La ville aux îles, La ville dans l'île: Basse-Terre et Pointe-à Pitre, Guadeloupe, 1650–1820* (Paris: Editions Karthala, 2003).

57 Zambos were the offspring of Africans and Indians in Mexico. Palmer states that such progeny drew their cultural persuasions from their African and Mexican parents and from Spaniards but adds, "Because Zambos were more likely to be reared by their mothers, it may be guessed that they were influenced and shaped by them culturally," 128. Colin Palmer, "Afro-Mexican Culture and Consciousness during the Sixteenth and Seventeenth Centuries," in *Global Dimensions of*

the *African Diaspora*, ed. Joseph E. Harris (Washington, D.C.: Howard University Press, 1993), 125–36.

58 Mintz and Price, *The Birth of African-American Culture.*

59 John Thornton, *Africa and Africans in the Making of the Atlantic World, 1400–1800* (Cambridge: Cambridge University Press, 1998), 192.

60 Ibid., 195.

61 Ibid., 196. Thornton concludes: "Even if owners really did hope to randomize slaves, however, it might prove impossible to do this effectively. Of course, such a strategy would be immediately limited by the relative lack of diversity among arriving Africans, so that at best one might have seven different groups—perhaps an effective deterrent to rebellion with the side effect of limiting the growth of an African culture."

62 Paul E. Lovejoy and David V. Trotman, "Enslaved Africans and Their Expectations of Slave Life in the Americas: Towards a Reconsideration of Models of 'Creolisation,'" in Shepherd and Richards, eds., *Questioning Creole*, 86.

63 "Informal," "informality," and "informalization" used throughout the text refer to those areas of economic activity which are associated with casual employment, family, or personal and social relations. More often than not these enterprises and persons associated with them operate outside formal connections to state or other forms of capital. These enterprises are usually articulated with formal ones and play a significant role in creating employment and income generation. In this way they are critical to socioeconomic development especially in places where states can no longer provide basic services for local populations. For a fuller discussion of this, see, for example, *Informalization: Process and Structure*, ed. Faruk Tabak and Michaeline Crichlow (Baltimore: Johns Hopkins University Press, 2000).

64 Saurabh Dube, *Stitches on Time: Colonial Textures and Postcolonial Tangles* (Durham, N.C.: Duke University Press, 2004).

65 Edward Kamau Brathwaite, "Caribbean Man in Time and Space," *Savacou* 11–12 (1975): 1.

66 Charles V. Carnegie, *Postnationalism Prefigured: Caribbean Borderlands* (New Brunswick, N.J.: Rutgers University Press, 2002). While we agree with the thrust of Carnegie's general argument, we believe he fails to explore the meaning of dwelling in these migratory movements. A certain approach to dwelling may have the strange effect of linking the agendas of the subaltern with those of the nation-state. Also, we think there is need to discuss the extent to which informal nationalisms that exist parallel to official ones are integral to the lives of transnationals and intersect with the formal ones. See, for example, Thomas Hylland Eriksen, "Formal and Informal Nationalism," *Ethnic and Racial Studies* (January 1993): 1–25. Eriksen shows how this coeval phenomenon operates in Trinidad and Mauritius.

67 Gaspar argues, "The Cape Verdeans projected an argument of Atlantic significance that the Antigua authorities had no difficulty understanding, particularly

where their own interests and those of the British Atlantic community were concerned." See David Barry Gaspar, "Subjects to the King of Portugal: Captivity and Repatriation in the Atlantic Slave Trade (Antigua 1724)," in *The Creation of the British Atlantic World: Anglo-America in the TransAtlantic World*, ed. Elizabeth Mancke and Carole Shammas (Baltimore: Johns Hopkins University Press, 2005), 93–114.

68 Linda M. Heywood, "The Angolan-Afro-Brazilian Cultural Connections," in *From Slavery to Emancipation in the Atlantic World*, ed. Sylvia Frey (London: Routledge, 1999), 16.

69 Ibid., 10.

70 This idea was prompted by Flávio Gomes, "Other Black Atlantic Borders: Escape Routes *Mocambos*, and Fears of Sedition in Brazil and French Guiana (Eighteenth to Nineteenth Centuries)," in *New West Indian Guide* 77, nos. 3–4 (2003): 253–87. Gomes writes about the Maroon communities, *mocambos*, living on the border of Brazil and French Guiana and their frequent crossings in search of freedom against the constitutive backdrop of "internationalism."

71 Brathwaite, "Caribbean Man in Time and Space."

72 Ibid., 11.

73 Ibid.

74 Ibid.

75 Glissant, *Caribbean Discourse*, 66.

76 Ibid., 67.

77 We have in mind specifically David Parker's incorporation of the concept of habitus in the context of diasporic experiences to explore the everyday experiences of the Chinese in Britain, through the optic of the Chinese takeaway. See Parker, "The Chinese Takeaway and the Diasporic Habitus: Space, Time and Power Geometries," in *Un/Settled Multiculturalisms: Diasporas, Entanglements, Transruptions*, ed. Barnor Hesse (London: Zed Press, 2000), 73–95.

78 One is mindful of David Harvey's *Spaces of Hope* (Berkeley: University of California Press, 2000).

79 See especially Brent Hayes Edwards, "The Uses of Diaspora," *Social Text* 19 (2001): 45–73, elaborated in Brent Hayes Edwards, *The Practice of Diaspora: Literature, Translation, and the Rise of Black Internationalism* (Cambridge: Harvard University Press, 2003), and Paul Gilroy's *Black Atlantic*, in particular chap. 6. Also, for an excellent discussion of the work that invocations of diaspora have tried to accomplish, see James Clifford, *Routes: Travel and Translation in the Late Twentieth Century* (Cambridge: Harvard University Press, 1997), 244–77.

80 Pierre Bourdieu, *The Logic of Practice* (London: Polity Press, 1990), 53–56.

81 Michael Hanchard, "Afro-Modernity: Temporality, Politics and the African Diaspora," *Public Culture* 11, no. 1 (1999): 245–68. But these temporalities are hardly even or uniform across diasporic space.

82 See Parker, "The Chinese Takeaway and the Diasporic Habitus."

83 María Josefina Saldaña-Portillo noted that the colonial system completely re-

structured the indigenous life-worlds, but "to the degree that indigenous communities produced meaning and value in excess of Spanish techniques of governmentality, they also produced a cultural formation that exceeded colonialism's subalternized category of the Indian." She notes that this is not a "pure other to colonialism" but rather that colonial techniques of governmentality gave rise to "new and resistant indigenous identities . . . and new political and cultural indigenous communities." See "Reading a Silence: The 'Indian' in the Era of Zapatismo," *Nepantla: Views from South* 3, no. 2 (2002): 290.

84 An emphasis on "movements" or "movements in meaning" as practices that transform the "scenario of articulation" is of course a key feature of poststructuralist readings of social history; see Homi Bhabha, *The Location of Culture*, 312. The issue of exploring the hows of this movement in "difference," "as what travels in diaspora," is also taken up by Edwards, *The Practice of Diaspora*; see also his response to reviews of this text in "Pebbles of Consonance: A Reply to Critics" in *Small Axe* 17 (2005): 135–49.

85 Drewal's discussion of Yoruba practitioners in New York is useful here not in its elaboration of diasporic practices per se but because of how it opens up the structured nature of the habitus toward an understanding of the excesses that may be performed which go beyond extant pedagogical positions or cultural locations. See Drewal, "Nomadic Cultural Production in African Diaspora," in *Diaspora and Visual Culture: Representing Africans and Jews,* ed. Nicholas Mirzoeff (London: Routledge, 2000), 115–42.

86 Ibid., 122.

87 Michel-Rolph Trouillot, "Theorizing a Global Perspective," *Crosscurrents* 4, no. 1 (1996): 5, http://web.jhu.edu.

88 Michel-Rolph Trouillot, *Peasants and Capital: Dominica in the World Economy* (Baltimore: Johns Hopkins University Press, 1988).

89 There is a growing literature on the transformation of the nation-state generally. With reference to the Caribbean, see especially Clive, Y. Thomas, "Globalization, Structural Adjustment and Security: The Collapse of the Post-Colonial Developmental State in the Caribbean," *Global Development Studies* 1, nos. 1–2 (1998): 67–84; Fitzroy Ambursley and Robin Cohen, *Crisis in the Caribbean* (New York: Monthly Review Press, 1983); Michel-Rolph Trouillot, *Haiti: State against Nation: The Origins and Legacy of Duvalierism* (New York: Monthly Review Press, 1989); Michaeline A. Crichlow, *Negotiating Caribbean Freedom: Peasants and the State in Development* (Lanham, Md.: Lexington Books, 2005). Many of these positions are of single countries or have to be teased out because they are embedded in interpretations of the political, the social, and democracy generally. As will be seen throughout the text, we have made use of much of the historical, anthropological, cultural, and philosophical literature pertaining to this subject.

90 Sayyid makes the argument for the Muslim *Umma* as a political diaspora, considering that it is a community of shared beliefs and given its marginaliza-

tion within the Western-led globalization project. See S. Sayyid, "Beyond West-phalia: Nations and Diasporas—the case of the Muslim *Umma*," in Hesse, ed., *Un/Settled Multiculturalism*, 32–50.

91 Malcolm Waters, *Globalization* (London: Routledge, 1995), 65.

92 Ibid., 62–64.

93 Kenichi Ohmae, *The Borderless World: Power and Strategy in the Interlinked Economy* (London, 1991), referenced in Ray Kiely, "Globalization: Post-Fordism and the Contemporary Context of Development," *International Sociology* 13 (1998): 96. Also see Nigel Harris, *The End of the Third World: Newly Industrializing Countries and the Decline of an Ideology* (Harmondsworth, Middlesex: Penguin, 1986).

94 Giovanni Arrighi, Beverly J. Silver, and Benjamin D. Brewer, "Industrial Convergence, Globalization, and the Persistence of the North-South Divide," *Studies in Comparative International Development* 38, no. 1 (spring 2003): 4, 18. These conclusions are echoed by other recent studies of spatial inequality; see, for example, Nancy Birdsall, "The World Is Not Flat: Inequality and Injustice in Our Global Economy," Ninth Annual WIDER lecture, 2005, http://www.cgdev .org. With respect to the Latin American and Caribbean regions, see the Inter-American Development Bank report, "Social Cohesion in Latin America and the Caribbean: Inequality, Exclusion and Poverty in Latin America and the Caribbean: Implications for Development" (2003), http://europa.eu.int.

95 Ulf Hannerz, "Scenarios for Peripheral Cultures," in *Culture, Globalization and the World-System*, ed. Anthony D. King (Minnesota: University of Minnesota Press, 1997), 107–28.

96 See Tabak and Crichlow, *Informalization*.

97 Jim Davis, "Rethinking Globalisation," *Race and Class* 40 (1998–99): 44. The images cascading across U.S. television screens in the wake of the Hurricane Katrina disaster are significant reminders about the large enclaves of poverty and substandard living standards that pervade the lives of vulnerable citizens.

98 Saskia Sassen, "Spatialities and Temporalities of the Global: Elements for a Theorization," *Public Culture* 12, no. 1 (2000): 219, 221.

99 For example, see Fernando H. Cardoso, and Enzo Falletto, *Dependency and Development in Latin America* (Berkeley: University of California Press, 1979). Also see G. Palma, "Dependency: A Formal Theory of Underdevelopment or a Methodology for the Analysis of Concrete Situations of Underdevelopment?" *World Development* 6, nos. 7–8 (1978): 881–924; Celso Furtado, *Obstacles to Development in Latin America* (New York: Doubleday, 1970); Furtado, *Development and Underdevelopment* (Berkeley: University of California Press, 1964); Andre Gunder Frank, *Capitalism and Underdevelopment in Latin America: Historical Studies of Chile and Brazil* (New York: Monthly Review Press, [1969] 2004); James Petras, *Class State and Power in the Third World with Case Studies on Class Conflict in Latin America* (Montclair, N.J.: Allanheld Osmun, 1981);

Norman Girvan, *Foreign Capital and Economic Underdevelopment in Jamaica* (Kingston: ISER, UWI, 1971).

100 Saskia Sassen, "Women in the Global City: Exploitation and Empowerment," http://www.lolapress.org.

101 Edgardo Lander, "Eurocentrism, Modern Knowledges, and the "Natural" Order of Global Capital," *Nepantla* 3, no. 2 (2002): 250–51.

102 Roland Robertson, *Globalization: Social Theory and Global Culture* (London: Sage, 1992); William Roseberry, *Anthropologies and Histories* (New Brunswick, N.J.: Rutgers University Press, 1989); Ulf Hannerz, *Cultural Complexity: Studies in the Social Organization of Meaning* (New York: Columbia University Press, 1992).

103 Hannerz, *Cultural Complexity*, 87.

104 Robertson, *Globalization*, 100.

105 Eric Wolf, *Europe and the People without History* (Berkeley: University of California Press, 1982), 23.

106 June Nash, "Ethnographic Aspects of the World Capitalist System," *Annual Review of Anthropology* 10 (1981): 408.

107 Sidney Mintz, "The So-Called World System: Local Initiatives and Local Response," *Dialectical Anthropology* 2, no. 4 (1977): 254–55.

108 Ibid.

109 Arjun Appadurai, *Modernity at Large: Cultural Dimensions of Globalization,* Public Worlds, vol. 1 (Minneapolis: University of Minnesota Press, 1996).

110 Eric Wolf, "Distinguished Lecture: Facing Power—Old Insights New Questions," *American Anthropologist* 92, no. 3 (1990): 587.

TWO   CREOLE TIME ON THE MOVE

1 Doreen Massey, "Double Articulation: A Place in the World," in *Cultural Identities in question,* ed. Angelika Bammer (Bloomington: Indiana University Press, 1994), 117.

2 Michel Foucault, "The Subject and Power," in *Michel Foucault: Beyond Structuralism and Hermeneutics,* ed. Herbert L. Dreyfus and Paul Rabinow (Chicago: University of Chicago Press, [1982] 1983), 216.

3 Henri Lefebvre, *The Production of Space,* trans. Donald Nicholson-Smith (Malden, Mass.: Blackwell Publishing, 1991), 408.

4 Achille Mbembe, *On the Postcolony* (Berkeley: University of California University Press, 2001), 1.

5 We draw mainly on Dale Tomich, "Worlds of Capital/Worlds of Labor: A Global Perspective," in *Reworking Class: Cultures and Institutions of Economic Stratification and Agency,* ed. John R. Hall (Ithaca, N.Y.: Cornell University Press, 1994), 287–311. Philip McMichael expresses a similar perspective in "Incorporating Comparison within the World-Historical Perspective: An Alternative Comparative Method," *American Sociological Review* 55 (1990): 385–97.

6 While the world system perspective's pivotal categories of core, semiperiphery, and periphery collapse the distinctiveness of social relations, treating them in a functional manner to the market which it privileges as the main locus of change, modes of production privileges production in a separatist fashion which obscures the ways in which the market works to unite different but connected labor processes simultaneously across diverse geographies.

7 Tomich, "Worlds of Capital/Worlds of Labor," 303.

8 Ibid., 307.

9 Ibid.

10 Ibid., 308.

11 Roland Robertson, *Globalization: Social Theory and Global Culture* (London: Sage 1992), 184.

12 Dale Tomich, "Small Islands and Huge Comparisons: Caribbean Plantations, Historical Unevenness, and Capitalist Modernity," *Social Science History* 18, no. 3 (1994): 339–58.

13 Richard Werbner, "Multiple Identities, Plural Arenas," in *Postcolonial Identities in Africa*, ed. Richard Werbner and Terence Ranger (London: Zed Books, 1996), 2.

14 Juan Flores, "The Diaspora Strikes Back: Créolité in the Hood," in *Créolité and Creolization,* ed. Okwui Enwezor et al. (Ostfildern: Hatje Cantz, 2003), 170.

15 Those who proclaim the end of development have focused on the breakdown of the apparatus which accompanied these ideas in the postwar period. They have not considered sufficiently the extent to which states and people continue to clamor and perpetuate elements of this era. Considering that no era is ever completely superseded, this linear trajectory of postdevelopment continues to live on in such a way that it has become identified as an emancipatory device among Caribbeans who wish for a return to that era. Some of these ideas have been tackled in Michaeline Crichlow, *Negotiating Caribbean Freedom: Peasants and the State in Development* (Lanham, Md.: Lexington Books, 2005). For a position on postdevelopment, see Arturo Escobar, *Encountering Development: The Making and Unmaking of the Third World* (Princeton, N.J.: Princeton University, 1995); idem, "Imagining a Post-Development Era? Critical Thought, Development and Social Movements," *Social Text* 31–32 (1992): 25. To be sure, elements of such a critique emanated from the 1970s Caribbean left, when they referred to development along a noncapitalist path requiring a strong centralized role for the state elite. It could be argued that they too were seduced by the development discourse. For a perspective on this, see María Josefina Saldaña-Portillo, "Developmentalism's Irresistible Seduction: Rural Subjectivity under Sandinista Agricultural Policy," in *The Politics of Culture in the Shadow of Capital,* ed. Lisa Lowe and David Lloyd (Durham, N.C.: Duke University Press, 1997), 132–72.

16 The example of the "banana wars" highlights the difficulties and transformations that have befallen farmers and parastatal organizations. See, in this regard,

Steve Striffler and Mark Moberg, eds., *Banana Wars: Power, Production and History in the Americas* (Durham, N.C.: Duke University Press, 2003), as well as Michaeline Crichlow, "Neo-Liberalism, States, and Bananas in the Windward Islands," *Latin American Perspectives* 30, no. 3 (2003): 37–57.

17. This mantra "world class or no class" was carried in the budget address of Jamaica's minister of finance Omar Davies, May 1, 2002, p. 3. See especially the last chapter in Crichlow, *Negotiating Caribbean Freedom*.

18. For an account of Central America, see Laura Putnam, *The Company They Kept: Migrants and the Politics of Gender in Caribbean Costa Rica, 1870–1960* (Chapel Hill: University of North Carolina Press, 2002); Velma Newton, *West Indian Migration to Panama, 1850–1914* (Kingston: ISER, 1984).

19. Gilroy, *The Black Atlantic: Modernity and Double Consciousness* (Cambridge: Harvard University Press, 1993), 40.

20. A "culture system" here may be defined as "the signifying system through which necessarily (though among other means) a social order is communicated, reproduced, experienced and explored" (Raymond Williams); or as "a set of material practices which constitutes meanings values and subjectivities" (Glenn Jordan and Chris Weedon), both quoted in *Cultures of Politics and the Politics of Cultures,* ed. S. Alvarez, Arturo Escobar, and Evelina Dagnino (Boulder, Colo.: Westview Press, 1998), 3.

21. See, in particular, Glissant, *Caribbean Discourse: Selected Essays,* translation and introduction by Michael J. Dash (Charlottesville: University of Virginia Press, 1989); Edward Brathwaite, *The Arrivants: A New World Trilogy* (Oxford: Oxford University Press, 1973); and Wilson Harris, "The Four Banks of the River of Space," in Wilson Harris, *The Carnival Trilogy* (London: Faber and Faber, 1993), 267–427. For a detailed and engaging discussion of the Caribbean scholarship addressing the "complex dialogue between space and being," in the formation and negotiation of the Caribbean's becoming, or "opening up of identity," see Nicholas Coates, "Gardens in the Sands: The Notion of Space in Recent Critical Theory and Contemporary Writing from the French Antilles" (2001), 18, 20, http://web.mac.com/nick.coates.

22. See Ato Quayson, *Calibrations: Reading for the Social* (Minneapolis: University of Minnesota Press, 2003), xi. In that text Quayson offers a reading practice, calibrations, a "form of close reading of literature with what lies beyond it as a way of understanding structures of transformation, process and contradiction that inform both literature and society," xi. For a recent discussion of his work and approach, see *Research in African Literatures* 36, no. 2 (2005).

23. Kristen Simonsen, "Bodies, Sensations, Space and Time: The Contribution from Henri Lefebvre," *Geografiska Annaler, Series B: Human Geography* 87B(1) (2005): 6.

24. Lefebvre, *The Production of Space*, 39.

25. Ibid., 38.

26. The interpellation of mappings of spatial sites by imaginations of power is a

central characteristic of modern capitalistic systems as advanced largely in the works of the Marxist geographer David Harvey.

27 Edward Soja, a postmodern geographer, has also been leading the charge in examining the politics of space and place, especially with regard to urban space. See Soja, "Writing the City Spatially," *City* 7, no. 3 (2003): 269–81.

28 This is a critical theme of the work of plantation theorists, such as Lloyd Best and George Beckford, who pointed to the ways in which the political imagination of economic geography configured the Americas' social, economic, and physical landscapes. See Michaeline Crichlow, "Plantations," in *International Encyclopedia of the Social Sciences,* 2nd ed., ed. William Darity (Farmington Hills, Mich.: Macmillan, 2007). The structuring of the countryside by the cultural politics of producing sacred and profane identities through rural spaces, and dualisms of productive/urban versus unproductive/rural has also been explored in E. Melanie Dupuis and Peter Vandergeest, eds., *Creating the Countryside: The Politics of Rural and Environmental Discourse* (Philadelphia: Temple University Press, 1996). In a conference paper, we have also explored this issue through the idea of a process of "rural othering." See Michaeline Crichlow and Patricia Northover, "Power and Its Subjects: Development Dilemmas, Postcolonial Re-structuring of Rural Spaces/Places/Identities and State Reconfigurations in Contemporary Globalization Processes," presented at the Eleventh World Congress of Rural Sociology, Globalization, Risks and Resistance, Trondheim, Norway, July 25–30, 2004.

29 The emergence of anthropology as a discipline and the rise of creolization and diasporic studies have played critical roles in these racial and cultural stereotypes connected to specific places and sites, see, for example, Kevin Yelvinton, "The Anthropology of Afro-Latin America and the Caribbean: Diasporic Dimensions," *Annual Review of Anthropology* 30 (2001): 227–60. Petrine Archer-Straw also emphasizes the ways in which notions of blackness and Creole identity are entangled in a discourse on primitivism; see "Paradise, Primitivism and Parody," in Enwezor et al., eds., *Créolité and Creolization,* 63–76. Of course, the literature on "producing" the nation is voluminous but see in this regard Manu Goswami, *Producing India: From Colonial Economy to National Space* (Chicago: University of Chicago Press, 2004), and especially Thomas Blom Hansen and Finn Stepputat, eds., *Sovereign Bodies: Citizens, Migrants, and the States in the Postcolonial World* (Princeton, N.J.: Princeton University Press, 2005). This text explores and questions, in the aftermath of 9/11, the relations between state, territory, and sovereignty, and thus the nature, configuration, constructions, and contestations of subject spaces.

30 Donald Moore, Anand Pandian, and Jake Kosek, "The Cultural Politics of Race and Nature: Terrains of Power and Practice," in *Race, Nature and the Politics of Difference,* ed. Donald Moore, Jake Kosek, and Anand Pandian (Durham, N.C.: Duke University Press, 2003), 40.

31 Lefebvre, *The Production of Space,* 37.

32 Ibid., 37.

33 Gilroy, *The Black Atlantic*, xi. See also Antonio Benítez-Rojo, another social theorist who also compellingly draws out the thesis of space as product-rhythm in his emphasis on the spatial rhythms of the Caribbean in *The Repeating Island: The Caribbean and the Post Modern Perspective*, trans. E. Maraniss (Durham, N.C.: Duke University Press, 1996), 78–81.

34 David Scott, *Conscripts of Modernity: The Tragedy of Colonial Enlightenment* (Durham, N.C.: Duke University Press, 2004).

35 See Sibylle Fischer, *Modernity Disavowed: Haiti and the Cultures of Slavery in the Age of Revolution* (Durham, N.C.: Duke University Press, 2004), 36. Fischer is making an important point here, even if the issue may be one of relative emphasis in the end.

36 The "Derridian trace" refers to "the pure movement which produces difference. *The (pure) trace is différance*. It does not depend on any sensible plentitude, audible or visible, phonic or graphic. It is, on the contrary, the condition of such a plenitude." Jacques Derrida, *Of Grammatology*, trans. Gayatri Spivak (Baltimore: Johns Hopkins University Press, 1997), 62.

37 Homi Bhabha, *The Location of Culture* (London: Routledge, [1994] 2004), 19–21.

38 Quoted in Gilroy, *The Black Atlantic*, 202.

39 See Jacques Derrida, "Différance," in Derrida, *The Margins of Philosophy*, trans. Alan Bass (Chicago: University of Chicago Press, 1982), 3–27.

40 Ibid., 13.

41 See Homi Bhabha, *The Location of Culture*, 2.

42 Ibid., 205.

43 Moore, Pandian, and Kosek, "The Cultural Politics of Race and Nature," 2.

44 Gilroy, *The Black Atlantic*, 202, 191.

45 Bhabha, *The Location of Culture*, 367, 364.

46 Foucault, quoted in Iain Mackenzie, "Limits, Liminality and the Present: Foucault's Ontology of Social Criticism," *Limen* 1 (2001): 12, http://www.mi2hr/limen. For us, this phrase helps to highlight the ways in which "being-present" is always coincident with "middle passages" and a struggle with, and for, boundaries of difference. The phrase was being used elsewhere by Foucault to depict the circumstance of the madman in society as like one cast adrift on a boat and "being a prisoner in the midst of what is freest, the openest of routes; bound fast at the infinite cross-roads."

47 Bhabha, *The Location of Culture*, 26.

48 Lefebvre, *The Production of Space*, 41.

49 Nikolas Rose, *Powers of Freedom: Reframing Political Thought* (Cambridge: Cambridge University Press, 1999), 33.

50 See Lefebvre, *The Production of Space*, 37. Our extrapolations in the passage are a way of expanding the meaning intimated in this quote. It is consistent with Lefebvre's immediately following comment that space is always a "present space."

51 Richard Price, "The Miracle of Creolization: A Retrospective," *New West Indian Guide* 75, nos. 1–2 (2001): 35–64.

52 Quoted in ibid., 47.

53 Quoted in ibid., 48–49.

54 Tim Inglod, *Evolution and Social Life* (Cambridge: Cambridge University Press 1986), 293.

55 Tim Edensor, *National Identity, Popular Culture and Everyday Life* (Oxford: Berg, 2002), 37.

56 See Michel Rolf-Trouillot, "The Otherwise Modern: Caribbean Lessons from the Savage Plot," in Bruce Knaft, ed., *Critically Modern: Alternatives, Alterities, Anthropologies* (Bloomington Indiana University Press, 2002), 223–24.

57 See Lefebvre, *The Production of Space*, 39.

58 Ibid., 191.

59 Ibid., 31.

60 Ibid., 165.

61 Michel Foucault, *Society Must Be Defended: Lectures at the Collège de France, 1975–76*, ed. Mauro Bertani and Alessandro Fontana, trans. David Macey (New York: Picador, [1997] 2003), 59.

62 See Anibal Quijano, "Coloniality of Power and Eurocentrism in Latin America," *International Sociology* 15, no. 2 (2000): 215–32, as well as Doreen Massey, *For Space* (London: Sage, 2005), and Trouillot, "The Otherwise Modern."

63 Michel Foucault, "What Is the Enlightenment?" in *The Foucault Reader,* ed. Paul Rabinow (New York: Pantheon Books, 1984), 39.

64 See, in particular, C. L. R. James, *The Black Jacobins: Toussaint L'Ouverture and the San Domingo Revolution* (New York: Vintage Books, [1963] 1989); Sidney Mintz, "Enduring Substances, Trying Theories: The Caribbean Region as Oikoumene," *Journal of the Royal Anthropological Institute* 2, no. 2 (1996): 289–311; David Scott, *Conscripts of Modernity*; and Sibylle Fischer, *Modernity Disavowed*.

65 For a discussion of the home-staking tactics in these entangled processes of "writing the history of the present," see Donald Moore, *Suffering for Territory: Race, Place, and Power in Zimbabwe* (Durham, N.C.: Duke University Press, 2005). Our approach shares many of the ideas of that text, which offers to read the politics of the Kaerezi district in Zimbabwe through the themes of governmentality, race, and place and which stresses the feature of *entangled times and spaces*. Our text shares the perspective of examining practices of place making, especially in colonial and postcolonial spaces, through their imbrications with modern governmentality. But we wish to provide a closer examination of the dynamics of the processes mediating its constituting, locating, and configuring, as well as its reconstituting, reconfiguring, and relocating, in order to better grasp the character of the struggles shaping and moving the mapping of the present. We hope we are not read as implying a monolithic conception of power, the political, or the present time into analyses of the modern. Certainly,

as far as possible, we wish to eschew the temptation to actually write the present, which is the complaint that has been levied against texts such as David Scott's *Conscripts of Modernity* (2004) and Michael Hardt and Antonio Negri's *Empire* (Cambridge: Harvard University Press, 2000). The complaint here concerns the way that these works seem to lean heavily toward a singular reading of the present, even as they seek to explore the residual spaces for freedom in acting against the grain of a "government of freedom," either from the political enigma of the "multitude" or by asking new questions from "tropes of tragedy." We prefer to lay the emphasis on the entangled and vexed liminality of this contingently emergent and strategically moving modern space, and its foldings of the present.

66 See Paget Henry, "Wilson Harris and Caribbean Poeticism," in Henry, *Caliban's Reason: Introducing Afro-Caribbean philosophy* (London: Routledge, 2000), 90–114.

67 Saurabh Dube, *Stitches on Time: Colonial Textures and Postcolonial Tangles* (Durham, N.C.: Duke University Press, 2004), 12.

68 Édouard Glissant, *Poetics of Relation*, trans. Betsy Wing (Ann Arbor: University of Michigan Press, [1990] 1997).

69 See Elden, *Mapping the Present*, chaps. 2 and 3, but especially pp. 34–43.

70 Ato Quayson, *Calibrations*, xxxii.

71 Quoted in ibid., xiii.

72 David Harvey, *The Condition of Postmodernity* (Oxford: Blackwell, 1990).

73 Derrida offers to highlight this central concept briefly as "the ineluctable" in his opening comments on Lacoue-Labarthe's critical deployment of this concept; see Derrida, "Introduction: Desistance," in Philippe Lacoue-Labarthe, *Typography*, ed. Christopher Fynsk (Stanford, Calif.: Stanford University Press, 1989), 1, 5. Lacoue-Labarthe uses it to capture the sense of an "impossibility in consisting," a "deconstitution" (116, 174). This notion is in several respects similar to Judith Butler's analysis of detachment that occurs in processes of desubjugation, which involves that the self "risks its deformation as a subject" by asking "Who will be a subject here, and what will count as a life?" Quoted in David Couzens Hoy, *Critical Resistance: From Poststructuralism to Past-Critique* (Cambridge: MIT Press, [2004] 2005), 96.

74 Wilson Harris, "Creoleness: The Crossroads of a Civilization?," in *Caribbean Creolization: Reflections in the Cultural Dynamics of Language, Literature and Identity*, ed. Kathleen Balutansky and Marie-Agnès Sourieu (Gainesville: University of Florida Press, 1998), 31.

75 It is often overlooked in reading Foucault that in his discussion of governmentality he was less concerned with "the plurality of forms of government and their immanence to the state" but was rather more interested in the fact that "among all these forms of government that interweave within state and society, there remains one special and precise form . . . the particular form of government that can be applied to the *state as a whole*" (our emphasis); see Foucault,

"Governmentality," in *The Foucault Effect: Studies in Governmentality,* ed. Graham Burchell, Colin Gordon, and Peter Miller (Chicago: University of Chicago Press, 1991), 91.

76 See Thomas Lemke, "Foucault, Governmentality and Critique," presented at the "Rethinking Marxism" conference, University of Massachusetts, Amherst, September 21–24, 2000; http://www.thomaslemkeweb.de.

77 Ibid., 2–3.

78 Thomas Lemke, "The Birth of Bio-Politics: Michel Foucault's Lecture at the Collège de France on Neo-Liberal Governmentality," *Economy and Society* 30, no. 2 (2001): 191.

79 Michel Foucault, "Politics and the Study of Discourse," in Burchell, Gordon, and Miller, eds., *The Foucault Effect,* 61.

80 A "law of tendency," that is, the exercise of a certain causal power, is arguably equivalent to Foucault's notion of power as a "way of acting upon an acting subject or subjects," or his interpretation of power relations as " intentional and non-subjective"; see Michel Foucault, "The Subject and Power," in *Michel Foucault: Beyond Structuralism and Hermeneutics,* 2nd ed. (Chicago: University of Chicago Press, 1983), 220. The notion of a "law of tendency" is distinguished in critical realist discussions from "tendency laws," as the latter refers to a constant conjunction of events, or regularity laws, and thus presupposes closed systems. See Tony Lawson, "Tendencies," in *The Edward Elgar Companion to Economic Methodology,* ed. J. Davis, W. Hands, and U. Mäki (Cheltenham: Edward Elgar, 1998).

81 Foucault, "Governmentality," 89–90.

82 For a general analysis of governmental technologies shaping modern social life forms, see Rose, *Powers of Freedom*; see also Mitchell Dean, *Governmentality: Power and Rule in Modern Society* (London: Sage Publications, 1999).

83 Aihwa Ong, *Neoliberalism as Exception: Mutations in Citizenship and Sovereignty* (Durham, N.C.: Duke University Press, 2006), 4.

84 Michel Foucault, "Right of Death and Power over Life," in Rabinow, ed., *The Foucault Reader,* 265. For a recent discussion of the implications of the biopolitical for "forms of life" and temporal being-in-the-world, or the "politics of life" in contemporary contexts, see the special issue of *Polygraph,* "Biopolitics, Narrative, Temporality," ed. Rodger Frey and Alexander Ruch, *Polygraph* 18 (2006).

85 See, for example, Kenneth Surin, "Post-Political Citizenship," in *Polygraph* 15–16 (2004): 47–57.

86 Dean, *Governmentality,* 47.

87 See Donald Moore, *Suffering for Territory*; Dube, *Stitches on Time*; Werbner and Ranger, eds., *Postcolonial Identities in Africa*; and Leela Gandhi, *Postcolonial Theory: A Critical Introduction* (New York: Columbia University Press, 1998).

88 See, for example, Gerard Aching, *Masking and Power: Carnival and Popular Culture in the Caribbean* (Minneapolis: University of Minnesota Press, 2002);

Adam Lively, *Masks: Blackness, Race and the Imagination* (Oxford: Oxford University Press), as well as Tejumola Olaniyan, *Scars of Conquest/Masks of Resistance: The Invention of Cultural Identities in African, African-American and Caribbean Drama* (New York: Oxford University Press, 1995).

89 Gunter Gebauer and Christoph Wulf, *Mimesis: Culture-Art-Society,* trans. Don Reneau (Berkeley: University of California Press, [1992] 1995), 3. "Mimesis" here is not used as a synonym for strategies of mimicry although it may entail such. Rather, we wish to speak to the "breadth of the concept" as masterfully elaborated by Gebauer and Wulf in this classic text.

90 Quayson, as outlined in his introduction, conceives of mimesis largely through the representational work of art—dramatic, literary, or otherwise. These works of art are vital, however, for one's complex engagements with reality as they provide a "transitional object-process" for negotiating "our alienations from reality." Quayson, *Calibrations,* xxv.

91 Aching, *Masking and Power,* 4–5.

92 Ibid., 5.

93 Edensor, *National Identity, Popular Culture and Everyday Life,* 58.

94 Ibid.

95 Foucault quoted in Mitchell Dean, "Demonic Societies: Liberalism, Biopolitics and Sovereignty," in *States of Imagination: Ethnographic Explorations of the Post Colonial State,* ed. Thomas Hansen and Finn Stepputat (Durham, N.C.: Duke University Press, 2001), 41.

96 James Ferguson and Akhil Gupta, "Spatializing States: Toward an Ethnography of Neoliberal Governmentality," *American Ethnologist* 29, no. 4 (2002): 981.

97 Joel Migdal, *State in Society: Studying How States and Societies Transform and Constitute One Another* (Cambridge: Cambridge University Press, 2001).

98 Dean, "Demonic Societies," argues for an interpretation of Foucault's comment on the demonic coupling of these two games as the attempt to combine "sovereignty and biopolitics," where "biopolitics refers to the relationship between the government and the population" (45, 47).

99 Foucault, "Governmentality," 103.

100 See, for example, Ferguson and Gupta, "Spatializing States," for an elaboration of the new tactics of neoliberal governmentality, or systems of governance, which they view as separate but not separated from state power.

101 Our idea of a mimetic mo(ve)ment was provoked by Sean Lokaisingh-Meighoo's creative reading of diaspora as "diasporic mo(ve)ment" and as a style or "signifying practice" of identity formation. See his "The Diasporic Mo(ve)ment: Indentureship and Indo-Caribbean identity," CERLAC Working Paper Series, September 1998, http://www.yorku.ca/cerlac.

102 In a critical essay against the superficial deployment, or political capture, of the concept of "creolization," Mimi Sheller provocatively recasts creolization as "a theory of uprooting/regrounding [which] allows for a dwelling in migration predicated upon the imaging of 'routes' not simply away from home, but also

towards homes, and the imagining of 'roots' not simply as origins but as claims to belonging." See M. Sheller, "Creolization in Discourses of Global Culture," in *Uprootings/Regroundings: Questions of Home and Migration,* ed. Sara Ahmed, Claudia Castañeda, Anne-Marie Fortier, and Mimi Sheller (Oxford: Berg, 2003), 286. This perspective fits very well with our own conception of creolization as a "journeying from place to place" and a "homing of modern freedoms," albeit drawing on different sources of inspiration for the expression of a similar optic. The imagination of a state of "unhomeliness" is also critical to Homi Bhabha's reading of the postcolonial condition in *The Location of Culture,* which for him reflects a movement (desired or not) into a liminal space, an uncanny and often disorientating space. Or, as he states, "the unhomely moment relates the traumatic ambivalences of a personal, psychic history to the wider disjunctions of political existence"; see 15. Of course, the concept of home, or home spaces, is also a dominant theme in classic Greek mythology, inspiring a masterful reinterpretation of Homer and Odysseus by Derek Walcott in his epic poem *Omeros* (New York: Farrar, Straus, Giroux, 1990). It is also deployed in the analysis of diasporic movements, in feminist as well as Marxian political analysis, with the latter pivoting on a theme of alienation; see in particular Clifford James, *Routes: Travel and Translation in the Late Twentieth Century* (Cambridge: Harvard University Press, 1997); and Quayson, *Calibrations.* Within the context of debates on creolization, we are thus in a sense revisiting this well-traveled and worn concept of "homing."

103 Rose, *Powers of Freedom,* 31.

104 Ibid., 32.

105 Ibid.

106 Ibid., 33.

107 As Foucault elaborated, "Governing people, in the broad meaning of the word . . . is not a way to do what the governor wants; it is always a versatile power equilibrium. With complementarity and conflicts between techniques that assure coercion and processes through which the self is constructed or modified by himself." Quoted in Lemke, "Foucault, Governmentality and Critique," 4–5.

108 Critical realism is a wide ranging philosophical paradigm that stretches over several disciplines and sets itself up against the philosophical traditions of positivist philosophy, inclusive of the so-called Popperian post-positivist tradition based on falsification principles of rational belief, as well as against the contemporary waves of radical constructivism, or strong relativism, as well as varieties of postmodernism. The hallmark of critical realism is its insistence on the need for principles of ontological realism and truth, albeit reformulated to acknowledge the varieties of realist and truth theories, and its advocacy of methodological principles consistent with effective social scientific explanation in open systems, that is, systems outside of experimental control and that are constituted through intentional human agency. For elaborations of the critical realist perspective, see Andrew Collier, *An Introduction to Roy Bhaskar's Philosophy* (Lon-

don: Verso, 1994); I. Cruickshank, *Realism and Sociology: Anti-Foundationalism, Ontology and Social Research* (London: Routledge, 2007); and M. Archer, R. Bhaskar, A. Collier, T. Lawson, and A. Norrie, eds., *Critical Realism: Essential Readings* (London: Routledge, 1998).

109 Margaret Archer, *Realist Social Theory: The Morphogenetic Approach* (Cambridge: Cambridge University Press, 1995), 201.

110 Roy Bhaskar, *The Possibility of Naturalism* (London: Routledge, 1979).

111 Archer defines SEPs as being "irreducible to people and relatively enduring . . . specifically defined as those internal and necessary relationships which entail material resources, whether physical or human, and which generate causal powers proper to the relation itself" (*Realist Social Theory*, 177). In other words, a structural power is a social power that is exercised through social being and acts with a certain intensity in a certain direction in constraining or enabling the actions and experiences of the subjects in their social relationships.

112 Mbembe, *On the Postcolony*, 16.

113 See Stuart Hall, "Old and New Identities, Old and New Ethnicities," in *Culture, Globalization and the World System: Contemporary Conditions for the Representation of Identity,* ed. Anthony King (Minneapolis: University of Minnesota Press, 1997).

114 Limbo is a part of a festive dance popular throughout the Caribbean. It is believed that limbo was born on the slave ships from Africa. Captive slaves, hands and feet bound in chains which were attached to an iron bar, to limber up their stiff cramped limbs devised a competitive exercise to see who could pass beneath the iron bar without touching it with their bodies. Inspired by Atau Tanaka's bio-electronic dance/music form, where music is created through the muscles of the body connected into an electronic net/web, a soundnet, Ryuta Imafuku links this remarkable performance to the creative performance history of the body (the expressive media of rhythm, sounds) that limbo remembers. But, as Imafuka brilliantly highlights, in remembering history, limbo also recreates it through a form of mimetic play reflective of the powers of Anancy or "the Trickster," a spider hero of West African tribal folklore (Ananse), who is able to transform negative states and the world he inhabits to advantage. See Ryuta Imafuku, *Music of the Spider: A Sonic History of Muscles,* www.cafecreole.net. In the remembered strategy space of limbo, the powers of Ananse thus survived Middle Passage trauma, to become celebrated in an "Afro-Caribbean aesthetic of play" as a symbol of the liminal politics of subversion and transformation by Afro-Creoles. See Dianne J. Austin-Broos, *Jamaica Genesis: Religion and the Politics of Moral Orders* (Kingston: Ian Randle Publishers; and University of Chicago Press, 1997), 46; see also Barry Chevannes, "Ambiguity and the Search for Knowledge: An Open Ended Adventure of the Imagination" (Inaugural Professorial Lecture, University of the West Indies, Mona, March, 2001). However, Pelton describes the trickster as "more than a symbol of liminal man. It seems closer to the truth, to say rather, that the trickster is a symbol of the liminal state itself and of its

permanent accessibility as a source of recreative power." Ananse is thus a *meta-morph* "because he belongs to many worlds, he is a transformer." See Robert Pelton, *The Trickster in West Africa: A Study in Mythic Irony and Sacred Delight* (Berkeley: University of California Press, 1980), 35, 36. Limbo is thus deeply symbolic of the liminal processes of change being articulated in the practices of creolization and its critical mimetic mo(ve)ments for homing freedom—processes which, like limbo, also carry deep memories of a body politics engraved in the mapping of the present. See in this regard S. Stanley Niaah, "A Common Genealogy: Dance-hall, Limbo and the Sacred Performance of Space," *Discourses in Dance,* no. 2 (2004): 9–26. Liminal processes of transformation were first discussed in the area of shamanic and initiatory transformation, which are sacred "rites of passage." Victor Turner described these rites of passage as "marked by three phases: separation, margin (or limen) and aggregation. The first phase of a separation comprises symbolic behavior signifying detachment of the individual or group either from an earlier fixed point in the social structure or a set of cultural conditions (a "state"); during the intervening liminal period, the state of the ritual subject (the "passenger") is ambiguous; he passes through a realm that has few or none of the attributes of the past state; in the third phase the passage is consummated." Quoted in Pelton, *The Trickster in West Africa*, 33.

115 According to the observations of R. E. Dennet, who studied West African folklore, religion, and culture of the nineteenth century, albeit from a very colonial perspective, a Lembe is a bracelet connected to a marriage rite that has been associated with the Bantu and Yoruba spiritual practices and philosophy; see http://www.sacred-texts.com. A Lembe, as noted by Brathwaite, also refers to "the opening of the gate of water into a new experience," which parallels the limbo ritual as a movement toward a resurrection, an entering into a transformed state of being. See *Three Caribbean Poets on Their Work: E. Kamau Brathwaite, Mervyn Morris, Lorna Goodison,* ed. Victor Chang (Mona, Jamaica: University of the West Indies, Institute for Caribbean Studies, Faculty of Arts and General Studies, 1993), 22.

116 Barnor Hesse, "Diasporicity: Black Britain's Post-Colonial Formations," in *Un/Settled Multiculturalisms: Diasporas, Entanglements, Transruptions,* ed. Barnor Hesse (London: Zed, 2000), 116.

117 Ibid., 117.

THREE "DIALECTICS OF RESISTANCE"

A version of this chapter appeared in *Contours: Journal of the African Diaspora.* I have dealt with some of these issues in my book *Negotiating Caribbean Freedom: Peasants and the State in Development* (Lanham, Md.: Lexington Books, 2005). Much of the research for this article was facilitated by Old Gold, International Travel, and Arts and Humanities grants from the University of Iowa. Research time spent at the Obermann Center for Advanced Studies at the University of

Iowa provided the space for me to rework this chapter. I thank Glen Richards for his helpful editorial suggestions.

1 Doreen Massey, "Double Articulation: A Place in the World," in *Displacements: Cultural Identities in Question*, ed. Angelika Bammer (Minneapolis: University of Minnesota Press, 1994), 117.

2 Achille Mbembe, *On the Postcolony* (Berkeley: University of California Press, 2001), 196.

3 The thoughts of de Certeau in his seminal text *The Practice of Everyday Life* are an important source of inspiration for this chapter, in particular his emphasis on "a dwelling" and "forms of 'the dwelling'" that dynamize and secrete the given spaces of "being-in-the-world"; see *The Practice of Everyday Life* (Berkeley: University of California Press, [1984] 1988), 52, 55. Indeed, this text is indebted to his critical insights and engagements in social theory, but we have sought to make further and different distinctions on the central concepts of place and space that he works with in his text, hence his bracketing in chapter 2. Yet while differing in our strategy for engagement with social theory, and while differing in our modes of addressing the relationship between space and place, we believe that certainly our notion of "place" introduced in chapter 1 can be said to be consistent with his thinking on "space," while the concept of "mapping the present" discussed in chapter 2 seems to parallel his notion of the fiction of "une place proper," "un lieu proper," "une economie du lieu proper" (44, 49, 55).

4 Mimi Sheller, "Creolization in Discourses of Global Culture," in *Uprootings/Regroundings: Questions of Home and Migration*, ed. Sara Ahmed, Claudia Castañeda, Anne-Marie Fortier, and Mimi Sheller (Oxford: Berg, 2003), 277, 276.

5 Bénédicte Boisseron, "A Creole Line of Escape: A Story of Becoming-Dog," *Contemporary French and Francophone Studies* 10, no. 2 (2006): 205–16. See also Homi Bhabha's discussion of "unhomely lives," which he defines as the "paradigmatic colonial and post-colonial condition," in *The Location of Culture*, 13–25.

6 Shalini Puri, *The Caribbean Postcolonial: Social Equality, Post/Nationalism and Cultural Hybridity* (New York: Palgrave Macmillan, 2006); Kevin Yelvington, *Producing Power: Ethnicity, Gender and Class in a Caribbean Workplace* (Philadelphia: Temple University Press, 1995); David Scott, *Refashioning Futures: Criticism after Postcoloniality* (Princeton, N.J.: Princeton University Press, 1999); Richard E. Burton, *Afro-Creole: Power Opposition and Play in the Caribbean* (Ithaca, N.Y.: Cornell University Press, 1997); and Karen Fog Olwig, ed., *Small Islands, Large Questions: Society, Culture and Resistance in the Post-Emancipation Caribbean* (London: Frank Cass, 1995).

7 Burton, *Afro-Creole*, 7.

8 Karen Fog Olwig, "Cultural Complexity after Freedom: Nevis and Beyond," in Olwig, ed., *Small Islands, Large Questions*, 100–120.

9 Aníbal Quijano and Immanuel Wallerstein, "Americanity as a Concept, or the Americas in the Modern World System," *International Social Science Journal* 44 (November 1992): 549.

10 Ibid. Consider that the U.S. part of the Americas "was the first state in the modern system to enact formal segregation, as well as the first country to park Native Americans into reserves."

11 Ibid., 552.

12 John Thornton, *Africa and Africans in the Making of the Atlantic World, 1400–1800*, 2nd ed. (Cambridge: Cambridge University Press, 1998).

13 I am thinking here particularly of the recent texts on Indo-Caribbean creolizations, and the debates within, say, Trinidad. See Viranjini Munasinghe, *Calalloo or Tossed Salad: East Indians and the Cultural Politics of Identity* (Ithaca, N.Y: Cornell University Press, 2001). Also see Tejaswini Niranjana, "Left to the Imagination: Indian Nationalisms and Female Sexuality in Trinidad," *Small Axe* 2 (September 1997): 1–18; idem, *Mobilizing India: Women, Music, and Migration between India and Trinidad* (Durham, N.C.: Duke University Press, 2006).

14 In 1989, at a UNESCO conference held at the University of the West Indies, St. Augustine, in Trinidad and Tobago, Kusha Haraksingh delivered a paper on the construction of citizenship by East Indians in Trinidad. Although I felt that the paper had too many silences about the contested quality of citizenness by Indo-Trinidadians, the discussion opened a different perspective for imagining the ways in which Indo-Trinidadians sought to carve out spaces of comfort under a trying colonial project, in a place they called home.

15 In Fanon's perspective there is a hybrid and ambivalent relationship that defines the native's relation to the settler. His notion that the native wants what the settler possesses is open to material and metaphorical interpretation. See Frantz Fanon, *The Wretched of the Earth* (London: Grove Publishers, 1963).

16 Lloyd Best, "The Mechanism of Plantation-Type Economies: Outlines of a Model of Pure Plantation Economy," *Social and Economic Studies* 17, no. 3 (1968): 283–326.

17 During the heyday of the French Revolution, the island experienced somewhat of an early emancipation in 1793, which led slaves to abandon estates, leaving many to collapse.

18 See Yvonne Acosta and Jean Casimir, "Social Origins of the Counter-Plantation System in St. Lucia," in *Rural Development in the Caribbean,* ed. Patrick I. Gomes (New York: St. Martin's Press, 1985), 34.

19 Dale Tomich, *Slavery in the Circuit of Sugar: Martinique and the World Economy, 1830–1848* (Baltimore: Johns Hopkins University Press, 1990), 6.

20 Edward Braithwaite, *The Development of Creole Society in Jamaica, 1770–1820* (Oxford: Oxford University Press, 1971); Ulf Hannerz, "Scenarios for Peripheral Cultures," in *Culture, Globalization and the World-System*, ed. Anthony King (Minneapolis: University of Minnesota Press, 1997), 107–28.

21 Speaking in a different context (in a direct challenge to the notion of tradition conceptualized in the Afrocentric historical interpretations) of the diasporic sensibility, Paul Gilroy argues that "black political countercultures . . . grew

inside modernity in a distinctive relationship of antagonistic indebtedness." See *The Black Atlantic*, 191.

22 James Clifford, *Routes: Travel and Translation in the Late Twentieth Century* (Cambridge: Harvard University Press, 1997); King, ed., *Culture, Globalization and the World-System*; Eric Wolf, *Europe and the People without History* (Berkeley: University of California Press, 1984).

23 To be sure, there are distinctions when land-based working people become visible in the postemancipation period. For example, they make a staggered appearance in Guyana. In Jamaica, they appear immediately at the end of slavery.

24 Carl Stone, "Political Aspects of Post-War Agricultural Policies in Jamaica," *Social and Economic Studies* 23, no. 2 (1974): 145–75; Ramon Grosfoguel, "De-peasantization and Agrarian Decline in the Caribbean," in *Food Agrarian Orders in the World-Economy*, ed. Philip McMichael (Westport, Conn.: Praeger, 1995), 233–53.

25 Sidney Mintz, *Caribbean Transformations*, 155.

26 Ibid.

27 George Beckford, *Persistent Poverty: Underdevelopment in Plantation Economies of the Third World* (Oxford: Oxford University Press, 1971); George Beckford and Michael Witter, *Small Garden Bitter Weed* (London: Zed Press, 1982); Kari Levitt and Michael Witter, eds., *The Critical Tradition of Caribbean Political Economy* (Kingston: Ian Randle Publishers, 1996).

28 For a useful critique of this folkoric tendency, see Roland Littlewood, "History, Memory and Appropriation: Some Problems in the analysis of Origins," in *Rastafari and other African Caribbean World Views,* ed. Barry Chevannes (Syracuse: Syracuse University Press, 1995), 233–52.

29 Lila Abu Lughod, "The Romance of Resistance: Tracing Transformations of Power through Bedouin Women," *American Ethnologist* 17 (1990): 41–55.

30 See Homi K. Bhabha, "Signs Taken for Wonders: Questions of Ambivalence and Authority under a Tree outside Delhi, May 1817," in *Race Writing and Differences,* ed. Henry Louis Gates Jr. (Chicago: University of Chicago Press, 1986), 163–79. Bhabha's constructs, ambivalence, hybridization are useful as lens through which we can view the range of dispositions of colonials and the colonizers.

31 Ibid., 180.

32 Sidney Mintz, "Was the Plantation Slave a Proletarian?" *Review* 2, no. 1 (summer 1978): 95.

33 This is an adaptation of Aimée Césaire's and Leopold Senghor's metaphor used by Hall. See Stuart Hall, "Cultural Identity and Diaspora," in *Identity: Comunity, Culture, Difference*, ed. Jonathan Rutherford (London: Lawrence and Wishart, 1990), 230. Hall uses the concept of *présence américaine* to call attention to the representation of Native Americans, e.g., Arawaks, Caribs, Tainos, Amerin-

dians, but only in passing. It is the New World space that he wants to see as the place of culture building or creolization. Although I see this as a vital *présence* in the Caribbean, I prefer to use Quijano's and Wallerstein's construction of Americanity referring to the Americas in the modern world. Although I use Hall's constructs, I am conscious of the limitations of his présences in constructing a changing Caribbean identity. Even as he makes pivotal points about the discursive nature of traditions, and the constancy of change in Caribbean cultural identity, I think his formulae are quite limited and reproductive of a monolithic Africa and Europe. In other words, I think his stress on the verticality of power relations hardly captures the horizontal production of differences among non-European populations in the region. Moreover, he ignores completely the experience of Indo-Caribbeans and others.

34 In Stuart Hall's words, "The 'New World' *Présence* America, *Terra Incognita,* is therefore itself the beginning of diaspora, of diversity, of hybridity and difference, what makes Afro-Caribbean people already people of a diaspora"; "Cultural Identity and Diaspora," 234.

35 Quijano and Wallerstein, "Americanity as a Concept," 550.

36 Ibid.

37 See Akhil Gupta and James Ferguson, "Beyond Culture," in *Culture, Power, Place: Explorations in Critical Anthropology,* ed. Akhil Gupta and James Ferguson (Durham, N.C.: Duke University Press, 1997), 33–51.

38 Roy Augier, "Before and After 1865," *New World Quarterly* 2, no. 1 (1965): 34. See also Douglas Hall, *Free Jamaica, 1838–1865: An Economic History* (New Haven, Conn.: Yale University Press, 1959).

39 In his study of Dominica, Trouillot nuances the argument that former slaves in the postemancipation period left the plantations in droves. Instead he finds that they were very selective about which plantations they were going to work on and which they were boycotting. See Michel-Rolph Trouillot, "Labour and Emancipation in Dominica: Contribution to a Debate," *Caribbean Quarterly* 30, nos. 3–4 (1984): 73–84.

40 Swithin Wilmot, "From Falmouth to Morant Bay: Religion and Politics in Jamaica, 1838–1865," *Social History Workshop* 8–9, Papers Session 3: Religion and Society (November 1985): 2.

41 Karl Marx, *Grundrisse: Foundations of the Critique of Political Economy*, trans. Martin Nicolaus (New York: Random House, 1973), 325–26.

42 Douglas Hall, *Free Jamaica*, 158.

43 Ibid.

44 J. W. Hinton, *Memoir of William Knibb* (London, 1849), quoted in Gisela Eisner, *Jamaica, 1830–1930: A Study in Economic Growth* (Manchester: Manchester University Press, 1961), 211; Douglas Hall, "The Flight from the Estates Reconsidered: The British West Indies, 1838–1842," *Journal of Caribbean History* 10–11 (1978): 7–24.

45 Douglas Hall, "The Flight from the Estates Reconsidered."

46 Walter Rodney, *The History of the Guianese Working People, 1881–1905* (Baltimore: Johns Hopkins University Press, 1981).

47 Eisner, *Jamaica*. Eisner's use of the concept of smallholder relies on size rather than on qualitative relationships within and among households. Thus it embraces holders with properties of fifty acres and more and much less.

48 The cultivation of ground provisions served a dual purpose. First, it supplemented the household income as it lowered the cost of production, and second, its consumption covered those areas of subsistence where wages fell short.

49 Douglas Hall, *Free Jamaica*, 192.

50 Smallholders grew a variety of crops at the same time, a practice that, given current ecological concerns for the destruction wrought by the cultivation of single crops, has only recently gained support.

51 Roberts states that banana cultivation was responsible for significant internal migration of working peoples to the eastern parishes of St. Thomas, Portland, and St. Mary and also tremendous infrastructural development of those areas. See George Roberts, *The Population of Jamaica* (Millwood: Kraus Reprint, 1979). See also Thomas Holt, *The Problem of Freedom: Race, Labor, and Politics in Jamaica and Britain, 1832–1938* (Baltimore: Johns Hopkins University Press, 1992).

52 Lila Abu Lughod, in "Romancing Resistance," shows that what passed for resistance in Bedouin society was not applicable as such in a broader Egyptian context. There it became part of the gendered hierarchy.

53 Eisner, *Jamaica*, 234–35.

54 See Holt, *The Problem of Freedom*, 349.

55 Ibid.

56 Ibid., 353.

57 According to Marshall, planters saw the system of *metayage* as a "desperate expedient" "which would enable them to retain ownership of their estates and secure some profits from them during a period of depression. They adopted a system which would allow them to pay wages in kind rather than in cash; the labourer now in 'partnership' rather than in wages, shared with the planter the risks, expenses and profits of sugar production. The labourer now supplied all the manual labour necessary for the cultivation, reaping and manufacture of the canes grown on a plot of land loaned to him by the planter; the planter supplied carts, stock and machinery for the manufacture of the sugar; and the sugar produced was shared between them." See Woodville Marshall, "Metayage in the Sugar Industry of the British Windward Islands, 1838–1865," in *Caribbean Freedom: Economy and Society from Emancipation to the Present: A Student Reader*, ed. Hilary Beckles and Verene Shepherd (Kingston: Ian Randle and James Currey Publishers, 1993), 64.

58 Woodville K. Marshall, "St. Lucia in the Economic History of the Windward Islands: The Nineteenth-Century Experience," *Caribbean Quarterly* 35, no. 3 (1989): 30.

59 Ibid., 32–33.

60 See Charles V. Carnegie, *Post Nationalism Prefigured: Caribbean Borderlands* (New Brunswick, N.J.: Rutgers University Press, 2002).

61 Many planters for the most part controlled the terms of the contract and could manipulate returns to the peasantry. Nonetheless there also occurred among the generally disadvantaged peasantry the transition from subsistence production to petty commodity production for some of them. Michael Louis, "'An Equal Right to the Soil': The Rise of a Peasantry in St. Lucia, 1838–1900" (Ph.D. diss., Johns Hopkins University, 1982), 79.

62 See Theodore Draper, "Don't Tread on Us," review of *A Struggle for Power: The American Revolution* by Edmund S. Morgan, *New York Review of Books,* March 21, 1996, 17.

63 They lamented, "Most of us, through much difficulties [*sic*] have purchased land, and portions of these are in canes, others in coffee, cotton, and provisions; and we hope by these means to subscribe for the education of our children, and support the Public Institutions, as we hitherto have done. But there are some who lurk in secret places to plunder, when good men have gone to take their rest—too lazy to work for themselves. The law punishes them, however, when they are overtaken [*sic*] we are lacking a continuous and remunerative labour, and hence we have to pick out for ourselves such employment as will pay us best, looking for better days when our clothing and food will be reduced, as the present prices are intolerable. Your excellency, the difficulties to obtain land to cultivate extensively, and the overrunning by cattle, our provision fields—the owner having no fences to keep them from trespassing—fill the country with abandoned fields, and hereby want and destitution. The state of the by-roads which lead to the small freeholders and taxpayers' cottages, are uncared for, and in the most deplorable condition—some resembling goat tracks, and not ways for human beings. We speak out now, because we know Your Excellency will do all in your power." Quoted in Hall, *Free Jamaica*, 195.

64 Louis, "'An Equal Right to the Soil,'" 75.

65 Ibid.

66 Ibid., 101.

67 Clinton Hutton, "Colour for Colour, Skin for Skin: The Ideological Foundations of Post-Slavery Society, 1838–1865, the Jamaican Case" (Ph.D. diss., University of the West Indies, Mona, 1992), 161.

68 Holt, *The Problem of Freedom*, 301.

69 Ibid.

70 Ibid.

71 Holt, *The Problem of Freedom,* chap. 7, discusses how Canada became "white" and qualified for concessions associated with white citizenship denied darker peoples of the empire.

72 Swithin R. Wilmot, "From Bondage to Political Office: Blacks and Vestry Politics in Two Jamaican Parishes, Kingston and St. David, 1831–1865," in *Jamaica in*

Slavery and Freedom, ed. Kathleen E. A. Monteith and Glen Richards (Kingston, Mona: University Press of the West Indies): 319; idem, " 'The Old Order Changeth': Vestry Politics in Two of Jamaica's Parishes, Portland and Metcalfe, 1838–1865," in *Before and After 1865: Education, Politics and Regionalism in the Caribbean,* ed. Brian Moore and Swithin Wilmot (Kingston: Ian Randle Publishers, 1998), 101–11.

73 Kevin Gaines, *Uplifting the Race: Black Leadership, Politics and Culture since the Turn of the Century* (Chapel Hill: University of North Carolina Press, 1996). Ideas about uplift and the role of a talented black elite, "the talented tenth," were also propagated by W. E. B. Du Bois in *The Souls of Black Folk* (New York: Signet, 1982).

74 Glen Richards, "Friendly Societies and Labor Organisation in the Leeward Islands, 1912–19," in Moore and Wilmot, eds., *Before and After 1865*, 138.

75 Ibid., 142.

76 Terence Ranger notes that Europeans who observed the creolized performances of the peoples of the East African coast ("as dummy battleships were towed through the streets of Mombasa, or marchers dressed in the full ceremonial uniform of the House of Lords paraded through Lamu") could not figure out whether it was a mockery of them or "a tribute to white power." Referencing the anthropologist Clifford Geertz, he concludes that it was both. "They combined the wink with the strut." See Terence Ranger, "Postscript: Colonial and Postcolonial Identities," in *Postcolonial Identities in Africa,* ed. Richard Werbner and Terence Ranger (London: Zed Press, 1996), 276–77. These "separate systems" are counterposed as the egalitarian of the implied authentic Caribbeans versus hierarchical of the colonial. For a discussion of this perspective, see Acosta and Casimir, "Social Origins of the Counter-Plantation System in St. Lucia."

77 Peter Wilson, *Crab Antics: The Social Anthropology of English-Speaking Negro Societies in the Caribbean* (New Haven, Conn.: Yale University Press).

78 See Shalini Puri, *The Caribbean Postcolonial.* See especially chap. 4. Puri's take on this issue is necessary, and I share her concerns, but she comes to this question from a critique of cultural studies, and I from "folk/peasant/working peoples' studies." Moreover, because I am interested with how the "politics of the cross" is staged and negotiated, how to historicize space and spatialize history in the analysis of Caribbean cultural practices, my project differs from hers.

79 Michael G. Smith, *Plural Society in the British West Indies* (Berkeley: University of California Press, 1965), 9.

80 For a discussion of the ideological and historical premises of M. G. Smith's plural society, see Don Robotham, "Pluralism as an Ideology," *Social and Economic Studies* 29, no. 1 (1980): 69–89; also David Scott, "The Permanence of Pluralism," in *Without Guarantees: In Honour of Stuart Hall,* ed. Paul Gilroy, Lawrence Grossberg, and Angela McRobbie (London: Verso, 2000), 282–301.

81 Sidney Mintz and R. Price, *Birth of African American Culture* (Boston: Beacon

Press, [1976] 1992); Lawrence Levine, *Black Culture and Black Consciousness* (Oxford: Oxford University Press, 1977); Don Robotham, "The Development of a Black Ethnicity in Jamaica," in *Garvey: His Work and Impact*, ed. Rupert Lewis and Patrick Bryan (Mona: ISER and Extra Mural Studies, 1987), 23–38.

82 Karen Fog Olwig, "Village, Culture and Identity on St. John, V.I.," in *Afro-Caribbean Villages in Historical Perspective*, ed. Charles V. Carnegie (Kingston: ACIJ, 1987), 20–44.

83 Maroons were escaped slaves who established communities on the outskirts of plantations. Accompong, a Jamaican community of runaway slaves, signed a treaty with the British in 1739 that allowed their legal existence. Such villages had distinct locations, but they were not isolated from the rest of the population. The treaty accorded them 1,500 acres and in the 1950s they were given access to 7,000 acres by the colonial regime. See Barbara Klamon-Kopytoff, "The Maroons of Jamaica: A Historical Study of Incomplete Politics, 1955–1960" (Ph.D. diss., University of Michigan, 1973).

84 Michael Louis suggests that the organization of these communal communities may partially explain the high level of solidarity against colonial policy.

85 African immigrants surfaced in many islands of the Caribbean Basin. Many writers have shown how "African" culture received a boost from new free African migrants arriving during the late nineteenth and early twentieth centuries.

86 Interestingly, Antonio Benítez Rojo, in his discussion of Caribbeanness, suggests an island continuum of African cultures. Speaking of Cuba as representing an Antillean island where African influence was and remains profound, Benítez Rojo argues, "Before the formation of what we could call a Cuban national culture a phenomenon that occurred later under the Plantation it is possible to imagine a type of creole culture characterized by the variety of its local manifestations but also, above all, by the participation of the Negro, slave or not, in conditions advantageous to him as an acculturating agent." He concludes, "In my opinion, one has to conclude that the Negro slave who arrived at a Caribbean colony before the Plantation was organized contributed much more toward Africanizing the creole culture than did the one who came within the great shipments typical of the Plantation in its heyday." Antonio Benítez Rojo, *The Repeating Island: The Caribbean and the Postmodern Perspective* (Durham, N.C.: Duke University Press, 1992), 69–70.

87 For example, Antigua and Barbados represent islands that had little independent space from the plantations and the hegemony of the planter class and the colonial state.

88 Interview of Ms. Bouty, in *Oral and Folk Traditions of St. Lucia*, Cultural Heritage Series No. 1, ed. Joyce Auguste and Muriel Gill (Castries: Camdu, Ministry of Education and Culture, Saint Lucia, 1986). Transcription of an oral interview from the Oral Historical Project of the Folk Research Center of St. Lucia. Dates unknown.

89 On winks and struts, see Clifford Geertz, *Interpretation of Cultures* (New York: Basic Books, [1973] 2000). My own interpretation of cultural practices eschews

the idea of autonomous relativism. These cultural practices warrant "thick description," one that rejects facile binaries and even dialectical outcomes, but as this text underscores, the Caribbean is a Western project.

90 James Ferguson discusses the styles adopted by urbanites in Zambia; in this case "strategies of survival under compulsory systems" constitute the compulsory economy of rural-urban relations in the deteriorating economic space of late-twentieth-century Zambia. See *Expectations of Modernity: Myths and Meanings of Urban Life on the Zambian Copperbelt* (Berkeley: University of California Press, 1999), 99.

91 La Maguerite is celebrated on October 17 and La Rose on August 30.

92 Henry Breen, *St. Lucia: Historical, Statistical and Descriptive* (London: Longman, Brown, Green, Longmans, 1844; Frank Cass, 1970), 191–92.

93 Michael Louis, " 'An Equal Right to the Soil,' " 131.

94 Ibid.

95 Ibid., 128.

96 See Brackette Williams, " 'Ef Me Naa Bin Come Me Naa Been Know': Informal Social Control and the Afro-Guyanese Wake, 1900–1948," *Caribbean Quarterly* 30, nos. 3–4 (1984): 26; idem, *Stains on My Name, War in my Veins: Guyana and the Politics of Cultural Struggle* (Durham, N.C.: Duke University Press, 1991), for a discussion of the intersection of status systems and racial hierarchies, especially chaps. 6 and 8. With "inequality," Williams is contrasting communal practices with those advancing notions of self-advancement that lead to uneven advancement in the community.

97 Ernestine Kolar. "Sklaverei, emanzipation und Freiheit" (Ph.D. diss., Universität Wein, 1985), 562, 563. Kolar notes how the laboring population sacrificed to equip the Anse La Raye Catholic church, even going so far as to subscribe funds "to procure from France the usual pompous ornaments and sacred vases generally used in the Roman Catholic churches."

98 Ibid. Also Henry Breen, letter to the governor, December 31, 1860 (unpublished), Folk Research Center of St. Lucia.

99 Patrick A. B. Anthony, *The Flower Festivals of St. Lucia* (Castries: Folk Research Center, [1985] 1990), 11.

100 Ibid.

101 I am reminded here of James Scott's discussion of the way in which pomp and ceremony serves as a public transcript that performs dominance. See his *Domination and the Arts of Resistance: Hidden Transcripts* (New Haven, Conn.: Yale University Press, 1990). These particular roles and performances serve to construct consent and acceptance, as well as provide the templates for mockery. See also Lauren H. Derby on the use of parades by the Dominican dictator Raphael Trujillo, "The Dictator's Seduction: Gender and State Spectacle during the Trujillo Regime," in *Latin American Popular Culture: An Introduction*, ed. William Beezley, and Linda A. Curcio (Nagy: SR Books, 2000), 213–41.

102 Daniel Crowley, "La Rose and La Marguerite Societies in St. Lucia," *Journal of American Folklore* 71 (1958): 543.

103 Ibid.

104 Ibid.,

105 Breen, *St. Lucia,* 200–201.

106 From all accounts, women were particularly susceptible to the values and mores of colonial elites.

107 *Abwe:* A French Creole or patois name no doubt having its origins in the French word *boire,* meaning "to drink."

108 Simmons commented that " Dr. Daniel Crowley, and anthropologist to whom I introduced this custom in the heights of Dennery, at Aux Lyons, wrote afterwards in *Caribbean Quarterly* 4, no. 2 (December 1955), although it (the ceremony) continued for 12 hours, no sign of drunkenness was visible/until dawn. My comment on this is that Crowley was not visible until dawn, for he succumbed four hours earlier, replete with the 'well-cooked meal of Portage yams, rice, and a ragout of beef.' " Harold Simmons, "Notes on Folklore in St. Lucia West Indies for Members U.S. Volunteer Peace Corps" (unpublished manuscript, ca. 1960), 4–5.

109 Gordon Rohlehr, "Caribbean Folk Media and Social Protest: Calypso and Reggae" (unpublished manuscript, ca. 1980s). See also the CD collection *Music from Trinidad: The Golden Age of Calypso,* ed. Phillipe Zani (Paris: EPM, 1996).

110 Gaspar argues that large numbers of slaves known disparagingly by the British as brigands fought with the French against the British capture of the island, such that war shaped the affairs of the island between 1789 and 1814. These former-slave republicans, believing that they had been granted their freedom, fought long and hard with elements of the French army against the British army. For a spirited account of this insurgency, see David Barry Gaspar, "La Guerre des Bois: Revolution, War, and Slavery in Saint Lucia, 1793–1838," in *A Turbulent Time: The French Revolution and the Greater Caribbean,* ed. David Barry Gaspar and David Patrick Geggus (Bloomington: Indiana University Press, 1997), 102–30.

111 Kendel Hippolyte, "The Master Drummer," in Auguste and Gill, eds., *Oral and Folk Traditions of St. Lucia.* The master drummer referred to here was Lennards John, from the community of Piaye, Choiseul.

112 Erna Brodber, "Making a Living in Jamaica, 1923–1980" (Ph.D. diss., University of the West Indies, Mona, Jamaica, 1987), 147.

FOUR   POWER IN POSTCOLONIAL PERFORMANCE

Earlier versions of this essay were presented at the twenty-fifth annual Caribbean Studies Association conference, Belize City, Belize, May 25–31, 2003, and at the University of Chicago "Decentering Globalization" conference: The Transnationalism Project, April 26–27, 2003.

1 Achille Mbembe, *On the Postcolony* (Berkeley: University of California Press, 2001), 8.

2 Achille Mbembe, "Provisional Notes on the Postcolony," *Africa* 62, no. 1 (1992): 22.

3 Interview with Achille Mbembe by Christian Hoeller, *Chimurenga: Who No Know Go Know*, http://www.chimurenga.co.za.

4 Mbembe, "Provisional Notes on the Postcolony," 9.

5 Mikael Karlström, "On the Aesthetics and Dialogics of Power in the Post-colony," *Africa* 73, no. 1 (2003): 73.

6 Mbembe, *On the Postcolony*, 107.

7 Ibid., 110.

8 Ibid.

9 Mbembe, "Provisional Notes on the Postcolony," 4.

10 Renate Lachmann, "Bakhtin and Carnival Culture as Counter-Culture," Centre for Humanistic Studies, *Occasional Papers* (Minneapolis: University of Minnesota, 1987), 5.

11 Karlström, "On the Aesthetics and Dialogics of Power in the Postcolony," 63.

12 Bruce Janz, review of Mbembe, *On the Postcolony*, *H-Net Reviews*, March 2002, 2 (http://www.h-net.org/reviews).

13 Mbembe, *On the Postcolony*, 241.

14 David Scott, *Refashioning Futures: Criticism after Postcoloniality* (Princeton, N.J.: Princeton University Press, 1999), 214. Scott's reading of Fanon's colonized native comes up against Ato Sekyi-Out's more favorable analysis of Fanon's writings, "Fanon and the Possibility of Postcolonial Critical Imagination" (paper prepared for Codesria Symposium on Canonical Works and Continuing Innovations in African Arts and Humanities, University of Ghana, Legon, Accra, September 17–19, 2003).

15 See Adrian Fraser, "Colourful Tales of "Rude Boys" and Cops," http://www.jamaica-gleaner.com.

16 Scott, *Refashioning Futures*, 214.

17 See Saskia Sassen, *Losing Control? Sovereignty in an Age of Globalization* (New York: Columbia University Press, 1996); and Robin Balliger, "Popular Music and the Cultural Politics of Globalisation among the Post-Oil Boom Generation in Trinidad," in *Identity, Ethnicity and Culture in the Caribbean*, ed. Ralph R. Premdas (St. Augustine, Trinidad: School of Continuing Studies, 1999), 54–79.

18 Nestor García Canclini, "Popular Culture: From Epic to Simulacrum," *Studies in Latin American Popular Culture* 15 (1996): 61.

19 Another study which explores this approach is F. Mitchell Land, "Reggae, Resistance and the State: Television and Popular Music in the Côte d'Ivoire," *Critical Studies in Mass Communication* 12 (1995): 438–54.

20 Referencing here the Irish poet William Butler Yeats's "The Second Coming."

21 Jorge I. Dominguez, "The Caribbean Question: Why Has Liberal Democracy (Surprisingly) Flourished," in *Democracy in the Caribbean: Political, Economic and Social Perspectives*, ed. Jorge Dominguez, Robert Pastor, and R. DeLisle Worrell (Baltimore: Johns Hopkins University Press, 1993), 14.

22 For example, Anthony Bogues, "Politics, Nation and PostColony: Caribbean Inflections," *Small Axe* 11 (March 2002): 1–30.

23 This array is represented by the variety of capital accumulation processes, which attend this general unevenness. See Ray Kiely, "Globalization, Post-Fordism and the Contemporary Context of Development," *International Sociology* 13, no. 1 (March 1998): 95–115.

24 Mahmood Mamdani, *Citizen and Subject: Contemporary Africa and the Legacy of Late Colonialism* (Princeton, N.J.: Princeton University Press, 1996).

25 Stuart Hall, "The Local and the Global: Globalization and Ethnicity," in *Culture, Globalization and the World System*, ed. Anthony D. King (Minneapolis: University of Minnesota Press, 1997), 19–40. See also Raymond Williams, *Marxism and Literature* (Oxford: Oxford University Press, 1977).

26 Victor Marquis, "The Night of Slapstick Politics," *Weekend Voice*, December 1, 2001, 4–5.

27 Terry Nichols Clark, "The City as Entertainment," forthcoming in *The City as an Entertainment Machine*, vol. 9 of *Research in Urban Policy* (New York: JAI Press). This follows from Clark's work on the rise of a new political culture, by which he means the shift from class- and clientilism-based politics to lifestyle issues, and the role of consumption in this new lifestyle. Clark's work deals primarily with industrial cities of Europe and the United States. See Terry Nichols Clark and Vincent Hoffman-Martinot, eds., *The New Political Culture* (Boulder, Colo.: Westview Press, 1998).

28 According to George Steinmetz, "A structure-changing policy is one that alters the state in a way that systematically affects the production of subsequent policies; a structure-producing policy expresses and affirms the existing form." See Steinmetz, ed., *State/Culture: State-Formation after the Cultural Turn* (Ithaca, N.Y.: Cornell University Press, 1999), 9.

29 Michaeline Crichlow interview with Hunte, in Vigie, Castries, St. Lucia, December 5, 2003.

30 When asked about this, Hunte says that the people on the ground have a better sense of "Lucians": they get it. The name Lucians is short for St. Lucians. He is referring to St. Lucians as a whole.

31 Benedict Anderson, *Imagined Communities: Reflections on the Origin and Spread of Nationalism* (London: Verso Books, 1991).

32 I use the idea of "echo" here in the sense of Louis Chude-Sokei, in terms of the cross-cultural fertilization that is taking place quite intensely because of the time compression of geographies. Sokei speaks of sound and its relation to the creation of alternative public spheres in relation to "African culture." I believe that this fertilization is not limited to any ethnicity or geography, nor is there a fundamental African anything in that sense. Moreover, I find uncompelling the view that nation-states are being "relentlessly undermined." See Louis Chude-Sokei, *Dr. Satan's Echo Chamber: Reggae, Technology and the Diaspora Process* (Mona, Kingston: Institute of Caribbean Studies, Reggae Studies Unit, 1997). For an example of this echoing, see F. Mitchell Land, "Reggae, Resistance and the State: Television and Popular Music in the Côte d'Ivoire," *Critical Studies in*

Mass Communication 12, no. 4 (1995): 438–54. It is not simply a passive echo but also embraces clashes of creolization processes and sovereignties, state sovereignties and individual sovereignties, and the mobilization of nontraditional musics to facilitate a cultural politics of meaning and signification. The case of Alpha Blondy, the subject of Land's article, highlights these processes of struggling within the terms of the structures of larger state projects.

33 In a brief telephone conversation with Michaeline Crichlow, the St. Lucian journalist Jason Sifflet referred to the group as representing counter-counter-protest. What Jason was alluding to was the group's reproduction of the symbols of order into their subversions and disorders of the state crisis.

34 Interview with Michaeline Crichlow, in Vigie, Castries, St. Lucia, January 5, 2003,

35 Selwyn Ryan and Taimoon Stewart, eds., *Power: The Black Power Revolution, 1970, a Retrospective* (St. Augustine, Fla.: Institute of Social and Economic Research, 1995); Herman Bennett, "The Black Power February Revolution in Trinidad," in *The Modern Caribbean*, ed. Franklyn Knight and Colin Palmer (Chapel Hill: University of North Carolina Press, 1989): 129–46.

36 The St. Lucia Labour Party referred to itself as the "new" Labour Party, following Tony Blair's British Labour Party in 1996.

37 Sonia E. Alvarez, Evelina Dagnino, and Arturo Escobar, eds., *Cultures of Politics: Politics of Cultures* (Boulder, Colo.: Westview Press, 1998), 7.

38 Ibid.

39 Mahmood Mamdani, *Citizen and Subject*; also see García Canclini, *Consumidores y ciudadanos: Conflictos multiculturales de la globalizacion* (Mexico City, Grijalbo, 1995). Canclini's argument is that contemporary Latin American popular culture relies on consumption as a primary strategy for achieving citizenship. Certainly I do not believe that situation holds for the Anglophone Caribbean, where I believe consumption—which is a dense concept and needs to be unpacked—is only one in a series of routes to engender alternative forms of belonging to the nation-state, territorialized or deterritorialized. See Laura Podalsky, "Consuming Passions: Popular Urban Culture in Mexico," *Studies in Latin American Popular Culture* 15 (1996): 325–32.

40 Statement attributed to Norman Manley at a political party meeting in Kingston during the 1930s, a period of social unrest. See Ken Post, *Arise Ye Starvelings: The Jamaican Labour Rebellion of 1938 and Its Aftermath* (The Hague: Martinus Nijhoff, 1978), 292.

41 Anne McClintock, "The Angel of Progress: Pitfalls of the Term 'Post-Colonialism,'" *Social Text* 10, nos. 2–3 (1992): 92.

42 Hayden Herrera, *Frida: A Biography of Frida Kahlo* (New York: Harper and Row, 1983).

43 Interview with Michaeline Crichlow, early December 2003.

44 *Mirror* columnist David Vitalis reported one minister advising a neophyte, "If your opponent gives you a punch on your chin, give him a harder punch on the

nose . . . if he throws a rock at you, throw a boulder at him." This meanspirited-
ness must have been what was at play in the attack on the STAFF party by
incumbent politicians and government ministers.

45 Reported by the columnist Victor Marquis, "The Night of Slapstick Politics,"
Voice of St. Lucia, December 1, 2001, 4–5.

46 "STAFF Party under Fire," http://www.montserratreporter.org, 1.

47 Ibid.

48 Zadie Smith, *White Teeth* (New York: Random House, 2000); idem, *The Autograph Man* (New York: Random House, 2002).

49 Chantal Mouffe, "Hegemony and New Political Subjects: Toward a New Con-
cept of Democracy," trans. Stanley Gray, in *Marxism and the Interpretation of
Culture,* ed. Cary Nelson and Lawrence Grossberg (Champaign: University of
Illinois Press, 1988), 94.

50 Ibid., 96.

51 Homi Bhabha, "The Third Space: Interview with Homi Bhabha," in *Identity:
Community, Culture and Difference,* ed. Jonathan Rutherford (London: Law-
rence and Wishart, 1990), 207–21. Also see Stuart Hall, "Cultural Identity and
Diaspora," in *Diaspora and Visual Culture: Representing Africans and Jews,* ed.
Nicholas Mirzoeff (London: Routledge, 2000), 21–33.

52 James Ferguson and Akhil Gupta, "Spatializing States: Toward an Ethnography
of Neoliberal Governmentality," *American Ethnologist* 29, no. 4 (November
2002): 981–1002.

53 Mbembe, *On the Postcolony,* 16.

54 For example, railing against the failure to explore the production of hemp,
because of U.S. regulations and prejudices against the holy herb, marijuana, and
addressing issues pertaining to the production of national identity and of
course subversion.

55 Annie Paul, "Emancipating Ourselves in Post-Slave Societies of the New World,"
Axis: Journal of the School of Caribbean Architecture 7 (June 2004): 122–35. As
well, see the debates in *Small Axe* 16 (September 2004): 137–98, for a discussion
of these emancipation monuments. Petrina Dacres, "An Interview with Laura
Facey Cooper," *Small Axe* 16 (September 2004): 125–36. Laura Facey Cooper is
the sculptress who produced the provocative *Redemption Song,* Jamaica's mon-
ument commemorating slave emancipation.

56 See *Saint Lucia: National Cultural Policy-Government of St. Lucia* (Castries:
Ministry of Social Transformation, Culture and Local Government, ca. 2000).

57 These quotations are from televised interviews conducted by Hunte on St.
Lucian streets.

58 Sassen, *Losing Control?*

59 Virginia R. Dominiguez, "The Politics of Heritage in Contemporary Israel," in
Nationalist Ideologies and the Production of National Cultures, ed. Richard Fox,
American Ethnological Society Monograph Series, no. 2 (Washington: Ameri-
can Anthropological Association, 1990), 130–47.

60 Ibid., 132.

61 I draw on the work of Kara Zugman, "Building the Alter/Nation: A Meditation on Zapatismo, Race and Nationalism in the Age of Globalization" (paper presented at the American Sociological Association, Chicago, August 2003). Zugman's work shows the complexity of the antistate position of the Zapatistas and their engagement of the state to negotiate their autonomy. Moreover, the concepts like democracy and autonomy are redeployed by them to construct an alter/nation. This is akin to the double operationalization of Gilroy's politics of fulfillment and that of transfiguration.

62 Michael Omi and Howard Winant, *Racial Formation in the United States* (New York: Routledge, [1988] 1991). Using the concept of racial formation, Omi and Winant demonstrate a history of the ways in which the U.S. state reproduces racialisms even as its institutions grapple with popular resistance against them. See also Derek Bell, *Faces at the Bottom of the Well: The Permanence of Racism* (Boston: Beacon Press, 1999). There are many other important texts which show compellingly how racisms are reproduced and recycled differentially through the national body politic, institutionally or routinely, in popular form.

63 Briefly put, the digital activists use cyberspace "in a performance that combine(s) political protest with conceptual art" to "send thousands of messages through the 'barbed wire' of ports open to the cyber network." For a discussion of the workings of Electronic Disturbance Theater implemented by Digital Zapatistas, see Jill Lane, "Digital Zapatistas," *Drama Review* 47, no. 2 (summer 2003): 129–44; quote on p. 130.

64 Massey argues against the tendency to give places single identities and fixed meanings, as well as enclosing them; see Doreen Massey, "Double Articulation: A Place in the World," in *Displacements: Cultural Identities in Question*, ed. Angelika Bammer (Bloomington: Indiana University Press, 1994): 14.

65 Sassen, *Losing Control?*

66 I invoke the idea of multi-accentuality here because it can be supposed that Lucians operates as a multisign and like signs proffer different readings. Interfaced with the concept of "time of entanglement," one could argue that multiple meanings are embedded within these various temporalities but also that multiple messages flow from Lucians' various performances, as actors enact different types of consciousness and identities. Consider Stuart Hall, "Old and New Identities," in King, ed., *Culture, Globalization and the World System*.

67 See Sassen, *Losing Control?*; Linda Weiss, *The Myth of the Powerless State* (Ithaca, N.Y.: Cornell University Press, 1998).

68 See Ferguson's and Gupta's formulation about these spatial aspects of states in "Spatializing States."

69 Stuart Hall, "The Local and the Global: Globalization and Ethnicity," in King, ed., *Culture, Globalization and the World System*.

70 Quotes are from Daniel Segal, "Nationalism in a Colonial State: A Study of Trinidad and Tobago" (Ph.D. diss., University of Chicago, 1989), 175. Re Sin-

gapore: author's interview with the then former prime minister of St. Lucia, Honorable John Compton, for whom Singapore was his economic model for the island. He was a friend of Singapore's prime minister, Lee Kuan Yew, who he said felt that St. Lucia could be far more modernized (ca. June 1998).

71 The state's relation to culture is taken up by several contributors in George Steinmetz, ed., *State/Culture: State-Formation after the Cultural Turn* (Ithaca, N.Y.: Cornell University Press, 1999).

72 Interview with Peter Serieux, 1998. See also P. Serieux, "Marketing Strategies for Small Windward Producers" (paper presented at the International Banana Conference, Brussels, May 4–7, 1998); Michaeline Crichlow, "Neo"-Liberalism, States, and Bananas in the Windward Islands," *Latin American Perspectives* 30, no. 3 (May 2003): 37–57.

73 William Connolly, quoted in Scott, *Refashioning Futures*, 216–17. The context is Scott's appeal for a different set of questions asked about the present and about the imagining of a postcolonial future built on critical democratic pluralities.

74 A St. Lucian Creole expression, implying pure spectacle and nonsense, deriving from "poppy show." The permanent Secretary of Education reportedly demanded that the television show's concept be changed "before we are forced to call on government to address the airing of such shows." The Ministry of Education deemed "Lucians" "a degradation of our national character and image," http://www.st.lucia.com (visited January 30, 2001). Also see *Saint Lucia: National Cultural Policy* (Castries: Ministry of Social Transformation, Culture and Local Government, ca. 1999, 2000), which outlines the official approaches to the island's culture.

FIVE "GENS ANGLAISES"

I presented a version of this chapter at the conference "Rethinking Caribbean Culture," at the Cave Hill Campus in Barbados, June 4–7, 2001. Carolle Charles of CUNY Charles Carnegie of Bates College made valuable comments on that version. I thank Jolien Harmsen of the Reef in St. Lucia, an anthropologist, for helping me track down references and for suggesting sources.

1 Kamau Braithwaite, "The Emigrants," *Rights of Passage* (London: Oxford University Press, 1967).

2 Statement by Dr. John Samuel, chairperson, the Caversham Center for Artists and Writers, Balgowan, South Africa, *The HourGlass Project: BAGGAGE* (Johannesburg: South Africa: National Arts Council of South Africa, 2001).

3 Ulf Hannerz, "Scenarios for Peripheral Cultures," in King, ed., *Cultures, Globalization and World-Systems*, 107–28.

4 Personal correspondence with my colleague Hilbourne Watson.

5 Ibid.

6 See, for example, the very informative article by Krista Angelique Thompson, "Passage through the Islands of Shallow Water: An Exploration of Migration in

Contemporary Bahamian Art," in *Marginal Migrations: The Circulation of Cultures within the Caribbean*, ed. Shalini Puri (Oxford: Macmillan, 2003), 109–37.

7 Winston James, "The History of Afro-Caribbean Migration to the United States," 13 (http://www.inmotionaame.org); but also see David Griffith, "Peasants in Reserve: Temporary West Indian Labor in the U.S. Farm Labor Market," *International Migration Review* 20, no. 4 (fall 1986): 875–98.

8 See Ramón Grosfoguel, " 'Cultural Racism' and Colonial Caribbean Migrants in Core Zones of the Capitalist World Economy," *Review: Fernand Braudel Center* 22, no. 4 (1999): 409–34. The video *Salsa* chronicles the underside of the migration of Puerto Rican people to the United States and highlights the effect of Operation Bootstrap. See Jeremie Marre, *Salsa: Latin Music of New York and Puerto Rico* (Newton, N.J.: Shanachie, [1979] 1988).

9 Homi K. Bhabha's comment in response to James Clifford's "Traveling Cultures," in Clifford's *Routes: Travel and Translation in the Late Twentieth Century* (Cambridge: Harvard University Press, 1997), 42.

10 I refer here to nation-states, states, as well as the relation of the individual(s) to these transformed states.

11 Dale Tomich, *Slavery in the Circuit of Sugar*, 266. I am grateful to the Jamaican writer Olive Senior for her idea of a protolinking of movement and grounds, presented in a talk she gave at St. Lawrence University ca. 1994.

12 Dany Laferriére, "America, We Are Here," in *The Butterfly's Way*, ed. Edwidge Danticat (New York: Soho, 2001), 53–56. Laferriére implicates the United States in Caribbean migration.

13 Carolle Charles, "Different Meanings of Blackness: Patterns of Identity among Haitian Migrants in New York City," *Cimarron* 3 (1990): 129–39.

14 Irit Rogoff, *Terra Infirma: Geography's Visual Culture* (London: Routledge, 2000), 43.

15 Stuart Hall, "Cultural Identity and Diaspora," in *Diaspora and Visual Culture: Representing Africans and Jews*, ed. Nicholas Mirzoeff (London: Routledge, 2000), 21–33.

16 Mary Chamberlain, *Narratives of Exile and Return* (New York: St. Martin's Press, 1997), 9.

17 Maude Heurtelou, "My Suitcases," in Danticat, ed., *The Butterfly's Way*, 89–90.

18 Ibid., 90–93.

19 By "travelers" I include those who choose to leave and those who have no such choices.

20 Desperate for a place of her own, because of older sibling rivalry, and a desire for privacy nót allowed her by her mother, Audre Lorde idealizes Carriacou, her parents' original home, referring to it as her "private paradise." Her knowledge of Carriacou was conveyed to her through her parents' recollections. It is apparently Lorde's first claiming of her Caribbean identity. See Audre Lorde, *Zami: A New Spelling of My Name* (Watertown, Mass.: Persephone Press, 1982; reprint, Freedom, Calif.: Crossing Press, 1994), 14.

21 Hall, "Cultural Identity and Diaspora."

22 See chapter 2.

23 Homi K. Bhabha, "DissemiNation: Time, Narrative and the Margins of the Modern Nation," *The Location of Culture* (London: Routledge, 1994).

24 From informal interviews conducted in 1987 and 1998 and in September 2003.

25 Michaeline A. Crichlow, "An Alternative Approach to Family Land in the Anglophone Caribbean: The Case of St. Lucia," *New West Indian Guide/Nieuwe West-Indische Gids* 68, nos. 1–2 (1994): 77–99.

26 These are based on preliminary findings, but as in 1987 I believe these coincide with the trends in the country, intense commodification of land leading to the rise in individually held as opposed to family held land. No doubt a significant number refuse to sell or have not sold. One Yonkers Town resident told me that the family would willingly sell unused portions of family land. In recent times, the practice has been the buying out of other family members and the development of land. Several real estate development schemes (including those for hotels) have come about in this fashion. Clearly, the issue of family land is complex and varies from parish to parish and from island to island. My visit to the land registry in September 2003 was fraught with difficulty. Since 1987, when the University of Wisconsin team conducted the survey, much has changed, including the rules of access to information. Researchers like myself are allowed access only if they can be supervised at all times. Legal clerks and lawyers have full access to the registry. Apparently this is in the wake of incidents of stolen identities and the resultant land loss.

27 The *Daily News* editorial went on to say that Britain's emigration situation was not Barbados' problem. "As far as we are concerned, anything which contributes to the welfare of Barbados and Barbadians suits us fine. The only point that causes some worry is the fact that, by and large, the emigrants are some of our best artisans, but even there, we cannot blame them for wishing to do better for themselves, and good luck to them." *Barbados Daily News*, quoted in *Voice of St. Lucia*, December 31, 1960, 4.

28 Referenced in Frank K. Abernaty, "St. Lucians and Migration: Migrant Returnees, Their Families and St. Lucian Society" (Ph.D. diss., South Bank University, England, 2000), 79; idem, "The Dynamics of Return Migration to St. Lucia" (Twenty-second Annual Conference of the Society for Caribbean Studies, University of Warwick, Coventry, July 7–9, 1998).

29 "The Budget Address," *Voice of St. Lucia*, January 2, 1960, 9.

30 Ibid.

31 Reported in the *Voice of St. Lucia*, November 12, 1960, 1. Reference is to British West Indian dollars (BWI), at the time the currency used by members of the West Indian Federation (with the exception of Jamaica and the Cayman Islands, which retained the pound sterling), a political organization that lasted from 1958 to 1962.

32 In BWI dollars.

33 *Voice of St. Lucia*, October 15, 1960.

34 Harry V. Atkinson, in a letter to the editor of the *Voice* refuting the claims of the last editorial, which lamented the advent of bananas, asked: "What other industry has in so short a time contributed so much to the island's economy? Do you know that St. Lucia's export trade increased from a value of $2,095,606 in 1950 to $4,459,356 in 1958 and that bananas contributed $1,946,087 of the increase? And that in 1959 the contribution was further increased to $3,990,990? *Voice of St. Lucia*, July 23, 1960, 5, 7. Currency referred to is in federal dollars.

35 After the island became independent in 1979, dual citizenship was possible for those who had been resident in Britain for at least ten years prior to independence, or for those whose father "was born or became a British citizen by naturalisation or registration." Others could apply for citizenship like any other individual. See, for example, "St. Lucians Worried Despite Commissioner's Circular: Citizenship: Nationals in U.K. Want Both Immediately," *Voice of St. Lucia*, October 26, 1978, 5.

36 Abernaty, "St. Lucians and Migration," 89.

37 C. Peach quoted in ibid., 135.

38 Ibid.

39 Interview with Michaeline Crichlow, #5, Yonkers Town, August 29, 2003.

40 Interview with Michaeline Crichlow, #5, Yonkers Town, August 29, 2003.

41 Interview with Michaeline Crichlow, #4, Yonkers Town, August 29, 2003.

42 Interview with Michaeline Crichlow, #2, Carre Vieux Fort, August 29, 2003.

43 Interview with Michaeline Crichlow, #1, Carre Vieux Fort, August 27, 2003.

44 Correspondence with colleague Hilbourne Watson.

45 Interview with Michaeline Crichlow, Yonkers Town, August 28, 2003.

46 I have in mind Margaret Somers's discussion of class formation, where she states: "Ontological narratives make identity and the self something that one *becomes*. Public, cultural and institutional narratives are those narratives attached to 'publics,' to structural formations larger than the single individual, to intersubjective networks or institutions, however local or grand, micro or macro-stories about American social mobility, the 'freeborn Englishman,' the emancipatory story of socialism and so on." See Margaret R. Somers, "Narrativity, Narrative Identity, and Social Action: Rethinking English Working-Class Formation," *Social Science History* 16, no. 4 (winter 1992): 604.

47 Interview with Michaeline Crichlow, #1, Yonkers Town, August 27, 2003.

48 This notion of core as Caribbeans' periphery I adopt from an article by Stephan Palmié, "Adjusting Lenses: Discourse, Power, and Identity, at Home and Abroad," *New West Indian Guide* 68, nos. 1–2 (1994): 113.

49 Jonathan Schwartz, " 'Roots' and 'Mosaic' in a Balkan Border Village: Locating Cultural Production," in *Siting Culture: The Shifting Anthropological Object*, ed. Karen Fog Olwig and Kirsten Hastrup (London: Routledge, 1997), 262.

50 "En Passant," *Voice of St. Lucia*, November 21, 1978, 5.

51 Interview with Michaeline Crichlow, Cachilet, August 27, 2003.

52 I use pseudonyms for all people and places, as it is a small island and individuals and situations are easily recognizable. Interview with Michaeline Crichlow, # 4, Yonkers Town, August 29, 2003.

53 Karen Fog Olwig, "Cultural Sites: Sustaining a Home in a Deterritorialized World," in Olwig and Hastrup, eds., *Siting Culture*, 33.

54 Karsten Pærregarrd, "Imagining a Place in the Andes: In the Borderland of Lived, Invented, and Analyzed Culture," in Olwig and Hastrup, eds., *Siting Culture*, 42.

55 Interview with Michaeline A. Crichlow, #5, Yonkers Town, August 28, 2003.

56 Interview with Michaeline A. Crichlow, # 1, Yonkers Town, August 27, 2003.

57 Caryl Phillips, *A State of Independence* (New York: Farrar, Straus and Giroux, 1986), 136.

58 Customs Duties (Amendment) Order: Saint Lucia Statutory Instrument, 1998, no. 2 (Castries: Government of St. Lucia, January 31, 1998), 7.

59 Ibid., 9–12.

60 Ibid., 2.

61 The idea of flexible citizenship has been popularized in Aiwa Ong's *Flexible Citizenship: The Cultural Logics of Transnationality* (Durham, N.C.: Duke University Press, 1999).

62 Ahmed Gurna, "Elvis in Zanzibar," in *The Limits of Globalization*, ed. Alan Scott (New York: Routledge, 1997), 116–42; see also Manthia Diawaru, *In Search of Africa* (Cambridge: Harvard University Press, 2000), esp. chap. 4. The *lambwaza* are Zambian youth who have affected an urban style that is cosmopolitan. James Ferguson defined cosmopolitanism not "in relation to international mobility, say, or by a cultural orientation to 'the West,' but specifically in relation to the pressures I have identified for 'cultural compliance' with the demands of localism. That is, given a set of localizing social pressures applied to urban Copperbelt dwellers by their rural allies, I call cosmopolitan those stylistic modes that refuse or establish distance from those pressures." Ferguson, *Expectations of Modernity* (Berkeley: University of California Press, 1999), 211–12.

63 Abrams suggests that "we should recognize that cogency of the *idea* of the state as an ideological power and treat that as a compelling object of analysis. But the very reasons that require us to do that also require us not to *believe* in the idea of the state, not to concede, even as an abstract formal-object, the existence of the state." Philip Abrams, "Notes on the Difficulty of Studying the State," *Journal of Historical Sociology* 1, no. 1 (1977): 79. See also Ferguson and Gupta, "Spatializing States."

64 Jorge Duany, *Quisqueya on the Hudson: The Transnational Identity of Dominicans in Washington Heights*, Dominican Research Monographs, CUNY Dominican Institute, 1994, quoted in Milagros Ricourt, *Dominicans in New York City: Power from the Margins* (New York: Routledge, 2002).

65 Linda Basch, Nina Schiller, and Cristina Szanton-Blanc, eds., *Nations Unbound: Transnational Projects, Postcolonial Predicaments and Deterritorialized Nation-States* (Amsterdam: Gordon, Breach, 1994), 114.

66 Referring to "systems of durable transposable dispositions" and behavioral patterns which are a product of people's environment and their collective experience that includes the unexamined wisdom or notions of the group, its myths, and ethical precepts, its rhythms of living, and its division of labor between the sexes and age cohorts. See chapters 1 and 2 and Bourdieu, *The Logic of Practice*.

67 Carolle Charles, "Gender and Politics in Contemporary Haiti: The Duvalierist State, Transnationalism, and the Emergence of a New Feminism, 1980–1990," *Feminist Studies* 21, no. 1 (1995): 150, 152.

68 Ibid.

69 Ricourt, *Dominicans in New York City*.

70 Basch, Schiller, and Szanton-Blanc, *Nations Unbound*.

71 Antonio Gramsci, *Prison Notebooks* (New York: International Publishers 1987). I am referring here to at least one deployment of the concept of hegemony. Also see Raymond Williams, *Marxism and Literature* (Oxford: Oxford University Press, 1977), 108–14.

72 See, for example, the work of Philip Corrigan and Derek Sayer, *The Great Arch: English State Formation as Cultural Revolution* (Oxford: Basil Blackwell, 1988), 205.

73 Of course such ideas mask the impossibilities that migration entails. The unfulfilled dreams and dire frustrations of migrant West Indians to London are succinctly captured in Sam Selvon's *The Lonely Londoners* (London: Longman Caribbean Writers, [1956] 1999).

74 Mary Chamberlain, "Family Narratives and Migration Dynamics: Barbadians to Britain," *New West Indian Guide* 69, nos. 3–4 (1995): 259.

75 Ibid.

76 I should add that noting the social construction of the modern in this way does not negate the idea of survivalisms from whatever group, for example, Africa or India, that were clearly artifacts of an earlier entangled precapitalist or emergent capitalist era elsewhere. It accommodates John Thornton's geographic and cultural folding forward of the creative cultural processes in Africa to the American continent, where several encounters between diverse groups of Africans and Europeans and others occurred (some in a freer context than others) and accounts for a more complex evolution of modern American cultures, and the modernity of Atlantic economies. Indeed, if one considers his compelling argument that more African(isms) survived than hitherto accounted for, one can argue that this is precisely what the fashioning and refashioning of modernity entailed. Thus, broadly speaking, *Africanisms* and *Indianisms,* however fragmented and unsystematic their forms, connected the imaginary of the past to modernity's New World representations encountered in socioracial structures emanating from the master/slave dynamic, which also entailed the discursive, material, and symbolic refashioning of "true" Indian culture in the face of "African" and "European" identities, themselves offline versions of "Creole" truths.

77 What I want to stress here is that Europeans' sociocultural presence (though numerically small numbers of them) in many parts in the smaller Caribbean islands was, as many scholars note, given the racialisms embedded in the global socioeconomic and cultural processes, effectively localized, more pervasive, and more "normalized" than any other presence.

78 Laurier Turgeon, "Beads, Bodies and Regimes of Value: From France to North America, c. 1500–c.1650," in *The Archaeology of Contact in Settler Societies*, ed. Tim Murray (Cambridge: Cambridge University Press, 2004), 19–47.

SIX AN EBAY IMAGINARY IN AN UNEQUAL WORLD

1 Chantal Mouffe, "Radical Democracy: Modern or Postmodern?" *Universal Abandon: The Politics of Postmodernism,* ed. Andrew Ross (Minneapolis: University of Minnesota Press, 1988), 44.

2 "Creolization is not a fusion. It requires that each component endure while it is already going through a process of change" (translation of epigraph by Anny Curtius); Édouard Glissant, *Traité du Toute-monde* (Paris: Gallimard, 1997), quoted in Nicholas B. Coates, "Garden in the Sands: The Notion of Space in Recent and Contemporary Writing from the French Antilles," http://web.mac .com/nick.coates.

3 Dr. Seuss, *One Fish, Two Fish, Red Fish, Blue Fish* (New York: Random House, 1960).

4 Democratic Socialism was the ideological frame for the policies adopted by the Michael Manley–led government of the Peoples National Party during the 1970s (see note 5). Jamaica's political parties set up garrison communities to control the political culture in inner city communities, or parts of them. The ultimate aim is to ensure the homogenization of the vote. I use "garrisons" as a way of masking the name of the community but also to point out that it was indeed politically barracked. According to the excerpts of the *Report of the National Committee on Political Tribalism* published in the *Jamaica Daily Gleaner,* Garrison communities are created by: "(i) the development of large-scale housing schemes by the State and the location of the houses therein to supporters of the party in power; (ii) homogenisation by the dominant party activists pushing out the minority from within and guarding against invasion from outside; and (iii) the expelled setting up a squatter community." See http://www.jamaica-gleaner.com/pages/politics/.

5 There are several texts which analyze the 1970s in Jamaica. See, for example, Olive Senior, *The Message Is Change: A Perspective on the 1972 General Elections* (Kingston: Kingston Publishers Limited, 1975); Michael Manley, *Jamaica: Struggle in the Periphery* (London: Third World Media Limited. Writers and Readers Publishing Cooperative Society, 1982); Evelyn Huber Stephens and John D. Stephens, *Democratic Socialism in Jamaica: The Political Movement and Social Transformation in Dependent Capitalism* (Princeton, N.J.: Princeton University

Press, 1986); George Beckford and M. Witter, *Small Garden, Bitter Weed: The Political Economy of Struggle and Change in Jamaica* (Morant Bay: Maroon Publishing House, 1980).

6 This image was used to advertise the first issue of the journal *Small Axe: A Caribbean Journal of Criticism* in 1997 and was reproduced in Patricia Mohammed, "Taking Possession: Symbols of Empire and Nationhood," *Small Axe* 11 (March 2002): 47.

7 I refer here to the embrace of structural adjustment policies followed by the state's facilitation of the neoliberal globalization project. An example of this is in Crichlow, *Negotiating Caribbean Freedom*, especially chaps. 5 and 7.

8 Dick Hebdige, *Subculture: The Meaning of Style* (New York: Routledge, [1979] 1993); Hebdige, *Cut 'n' Mix: Culture, Identity and Caribbean Music* (New York: Routledge, 1987).

9 Quoted in Coates, "Garden in the Sands," 219.

10 Ibid., 218.

11 Ibid., 213.

12 As Michel de Certeau argued, any effort to discern the dynamics of lived experience must address not just the "problematics of enunciation" but also the ways in which power enters into those efforts and procedures for sustaining expressive capacity, or in de Certeau's terms, for realizing "space"—"a practiced place." Thus, one "must pass from a linguistic frame of reference to a polemological one. We are concerned too with the battles between the strong and the weak, and with the 'actions' which remain possible for the latter." See Michel de Certeau, *The Practice of Everyday Life* (Berkeley: University of California Press, [1984] 1988), 117, 34.

13 Doreen Massey, "Double Articulation: A Place in the World," in *Displacements: Cultural Identities in Question*, ed. Angelika Bammer (Bloomington: Indiana University Press, 1994), 114. See also Doreen Massey, *For Space* (London: Sage, 2005).

14 The concept of Plantation America is Charles Wagley's: "Plantation America: A Culture Sphere," in *Caribbean Studies—A Symposium*, ed. Vera Rubin (Seattle: University of Washington Press, [1960] 1988), 3–13. According to Wagley, "This culture sphere extends spatially from about midway up the coast of Brazil into the Guianas, along the Caribbean coast, throughout the Caribbean itself, and into the United States (South). In Wagley's scheme, the rest of the New World consists of two other culture spheres: Euro-America and Indo-America, reflecting the character of the dominant races," 5. The concept also is foundational in George L. Beckford, *Persistent Poverty: Underdevelopment in Plantation Economies of the Third World* (Oxford: Oxford University Press, 1972), 18.

15 Fredric Jameson, "Fear and Loathing in Globalization," *New Left Review* 23, (September/October 2003): 108.

16 Ibid.

17 Charles Stewart, "Syncretism and Its Synonyms: Reflections on Cultural Mixture," *Diacritics* 29, no. 3 (1999): 40–62.

18 Sidney Mintz and Richard Price, *The Birth of African American Culture: Anthropological Perspectives* (Boston: Beacon Press, 1976).

19 Melville J. Herskovits, *The Myth of the Negro Past* (Boston: Beacon Press, [1958] 1970).

20 Ulf Hannerz, "The World in Creolization," *Africa* 57 no. 4 (1987): 546–59.

21 Ibid.

22 Hannerz, "The World in Creolization," and "Scenarios for Peripheral Cultures," in King, ed., *Cultures, Globalization and World-Systems*. Also see Ulf Hannerz, "Cosmopolitans and Locals in World Culture," in *Global Culture: Nationalism, Globalization and Modernity*, ed. Mike Featherstone (London: Sage, 1987), 237–51.

23 James Clifford, *The Predicament of Culture: Twentieth Century Ethnography, Literature, and Art* (Cambridge: Cambridge University Press, 1988), 173.

24 Espelencia M. Baptiste, "Creolization and the Development of Creole Cultures," paper presented at the International Conference on Cultural Exchange and Transformation in the Indian Ocean World, UCLA, April 5–6, 2002, 5.

25 Mimi Sheller, "Theoretical Piracy on the High Seas of Global Culture: Appropriations of 'Creolization' in the Discourses of Globalization," paper presented at the conference "Rethinking Caribbean Culture," University of the West Indies, Barbados, June 4–8, 2001; idem, *Consuming the Caribbean: From Arawaks to Zombies* (New York: Routledge, 2003); and idem, "Creolization in Discourses of Global Culture," in *Uprootings/Regroundings: Questions of Home and Migration*, ed. Sarah Ahmed et al. (London: Berg, 2004), 273–94.

26 Sheller, "Theoretical Piracy on the High Seas of Global Culture," 2. See also: Harvey Neptune, "Moving History in the Aftermath," review of Sheller's *Consuming the Caribbean*, *Small Axe* 19 (September 2004): 214–21.

27 Sheller, "Theoretical Piracy on the High Seas of Global Culture," 2.

28 See Aisha Khan, "Journey to the Center of the Earth: The Caribbean as Master Symbol," *Cultural Anthropology* 16, no. 3 (2001): 271–302. See also the assorted commentaries following Viranjini Munasinghe's article "Theorizing World Culture through the New World," *American Ethnologist* 33, no. 4 (2006): 549–62. Also see Stephan Palmié, "Creolization and Its Discontents," *Annual Review of Anthropology* 35 (2006): 433–56.

29 By pluralism I am referring to the perspective offered by Michael G. Smith, *The Plural Society in the British West Indies* (Berkeley: University of California Press, 1965).

30 Mintz and Price, *The Birth of African American Culture*, 27–28.

31 Stuart Hall, "Thinking the Diaspora: Home-Thoughts from Abroad," *Small Axe* 6 (September 1999): 6.

32 See Sean Lokaisingh-Meighoo, "The Diasporic Mo(ve)ment: Indentureship and Indo-Caribbean Identity" (originally CERLAC/CRP Working Paper, September 1998), in *Nation Dance: Religion, Identity and Cultural Difference in the Caribbean*, ed. Patrick Taylor (Bloomington: Indiana University Press, 2001), 171–92.

33 Brian Axel, *The Nation's Tortured Body: Violence, Representation and the Formation of a Sikh "Diaspora"* (Durham, N.C.: Duke University Press, 2001).

34 Brent Hayes Edwards, *The Practice of Diaspora: Literature, Translation, and the Rise of Black Internationalism* (Cambridge: Harvard University Press, 2003), 13.

35 Dwayne E. Williams, "Rethinking the African Diaspora: A Comparative look at Race and Identity in a Transatlantic Community, 1878–1921," in *Crossing Boundaries: Comparative History of Black People in Diaspora*, ed. Darlene Clark Hine and Jacqueline McLeod (Bloomington: Indiana University Press, 1999), 116.

36 See Gilroy, *The Black Atlantic*; Hall, "Cultural Identity and Disapora."

37 Michael Hanchard, "Afro-Modernity: Temporality, Politics and the African Diaspora," *Public Culture* 11, no. 1 (1999): 245–68.

38 Bonnie J. Barthold, *Black Time: Fiction of Africa, the Caribbean and the United States* (New Haven, Conn.: Yale University Press, 1981), 18.

39 I am reminded here of Richard Wright's statement at the First World Congress of Black Writers and Artists in 1956, which alluded to the conference's focus on Africa's Heritage—the sliding signification of Africa and black: "This is not hostility; this is not criticism. I am asking a question of *brothers*. I wonder where do *I*, an American negro, conditioned by the harsh industrial, abstract force of the Western world that has used stern political prejudice against the society which Senghor has so brilliantly elucidated—where do I stand in relation to that culture?" quoted in David Macey, *Frantz Fanon: A Biography* (New York: Picador, 2001), 286.

40 Barthold, *Black Time*, goes on to say that "if neither rebellion nor resistance was totally successful, they were nevertheless sufficient to bring into question the slave master's ownership of time and with it his capacity to dispossess others" (18, 27). Of course, I do not share Barthold's binary notion of time, as in Western and linear versus "traditional" African and nonlinear and mythic. Yet I think this text is one of the earliest comparative writings on diaspora to grapple consciously with the idea of temporality and its meaning for the spatial materiality of blacks.

41 See in this regard Holt's insightful article on slavery and freedom in the Atlantic world, which calls for a recognition of the interstitial struggles of Creole subjectivities, which were at once "tortured and creative," "rooted in a particular place, but dreams of an 'elsewhere,' . . . always looking to a future time." Thomas Holt, "Slavery and Freedom in the Atlantic World: Reflections on the Diasporan Framework," in Hine and McLeod, eds., *Crossing Boundaries*, 37.

42 Flora Anthias, "Evaluating 'Diaspora': Beyond Ethnicity?" *Sociology* 32, no. 3 (August 1998): 580. But see also Paul Gilroy's *Against Race: Imagining Political Culture beyond the Color Line* (Cambridge: Harvard University Press, 2001). Gilroy's provocative link between racial purity and fascism has raised alarm, but it was his intention to show the tendencies of racial nationalisms to slip into various separatisms that may have genocidal tendencies. See, for example, Nick Nesbitt, "Antinomies of Double Consciousness in Aimé Césaire's *Cahier d'in*

Retour au Pays Natal," *Mosaic: A Journal of Interdisciplinary Study of Literature* 33, no. 3 (September 2000): 107–28. Here Nesbitt discusses the fascistic underpinnings of Césaire's thought, even as the text itself spoke directly to issues of black emancipation.

43 Tiffany Ruby Patterson and Robin D. G. Kelley, "Unfinished Migrations: Reflections on the African Diaspora and the Making of the Modern World," *African Studies Review* 43, no. 1 (April 2000): 19.

44 Edmund T. Gordon, *Disparate Diasporas: Identity and Politics in an African-Nicaraguan Community* (Austin: University of Texas Press, 1998).

45 Bill Maurer, "Creolization Redux: The Plural Society Thesis and Offshore Financial Services," *New West Indian Guide* 7, nos. 3–4 (1997): 249–64. Maurer was referring to the ways in which British Virgin Islanders tout their Britishness as a marketing tool to secure their position as a bona fide offshore financial location. In short, "British Virgin Islander nationalist discourse empties out 'the BVI' as a signifier, leaving nothing 'original' behind—much like the uninhabited islands of the tourist brochure." Idem, *Recharting the Caribbean: Land, Law, and Citizenship in the British Virgin Islands* (Ann Arbor: University of Michigan Press, 2000), 263.

46 Gordon, *Disparate Diasporas.*

47 As Homi K. Bhabha notes in his discussion of the emergence of diverse subjectivities, multiple subject positions that cut across the categories of race, gender, generation, class, etc. These interstitial spaces "provide the terrain for elaborate strategies of selfhood and communal representations that generate new signs of cultural difference and innovative sites of collaboration and contestation." See "Frontlines/Borderposts," in Bammer, ed., *Displacements,* 269.

48 Bhabha, *The Location of Culture,* 10, 26.

49 Jeffrey Skoller, "Space Is the Place," *Afterimage* 25, no. 3 (November–December 1997): 14.

50 Commentary in John Akomfrah's *The Last Angel of History,* video (45 minutes), 1996.

51 Paul Tiyame Zeleza argues that African intellectuals had complex identities missed by the binaries of colonizer and colonized. "Take the question of racial nationalism, for example. Pan Africanism, a movement that antedated territorial colonial nationalism and sought to promote the interests of changing idioms and organizational forms. At least six versions of Pan-Africanism emerged: trans-Atlantic, Black Atlantic, continental, sub-Saharan, Pan-Arab and global." See Zeleza, "Imagining and Inventing the Postcolonial State in Africa," *Contours: A Journal of the African Diaspora* 1, no. 1 (spring 2003): 103.

52 Skoller, "Space Is the Place." See also the film *Sankofa* (Negod, Gwod Productions, Haile Gaima-Ghana National Commission on Culture, Diproci of Burkina Faso, NDR/WDR Television in association with Channel 4, Washington, D.C.: Myphedu Films, ca. 1993).

53 Michel-Rolph Trouillot, *Silencing the Past: Power and the Production of History* (Boston: Beacon Press, 1995).

54 Ibid.

55 See Garth White, "The Development of Jamaican Popular Music, Part 2: The Urbanization of the Folk," *African Caribbean Institute of Jamaica Research Review* 1 (1984): 72.

56 Gilroy, *The Black Atlantic*, 37–38.

57 Louis Chude-Sokei, *Dr. Satan's Echo Chamber: Reggae, Technology and the Diaspora Process* (Kingston: Institute of Caribbean Studies, 1997), 8. See also Dick Hebdige, *Cut and Mix: Culture: Identity and Caribbean Music* (London: Comedia, 1987); and Carolyn Cooper, "Hip-Hopping across Cultures: Crossing over from Reggae to Rap and Back," in *Questioning Creolization*, ed. Verene A. Shepherd and Glen L. Richards (Kingston: Ian Randall Press, 2002), 265–80; Gilroy, *The Black Atlantic*.

58 Joshua Mitnick, "Israeli Hip-Hop Takes on Mid-East Politics," special for *USA Today*, November 6, 2003. Mitnick writes of a rapper (Kobi Shimoni) called Subliminal who preaches a Zionist nationalism. "The angry lyrics and Subliminal's right-wing political convictions have drawn fire from Israeli cultural critics, who call him a militarist and a fascist. Subliminal, whose fluent English is peppered with slang imported from the USA, rejects the labels." He says "his songs reflect the daily realities and feelings of Israeli youth. 'In America, hip-hop is the fastest way to get rich, to talk about the "bitches, cars and money" ' . . . 'In Israel the words are very militant, like the situation we're living in. You open the newspaper in the morning in Israel, and this is what you get.' " Mitnick writes that "the appeal of hip-hop has crossed the country's ethnic boundaries. Young Israeli Arabs alienated by the Jewish majority glorify African-American rappers as kindred spirits in the struggle against discrimination. Tamer Nafer, an Israeli Arab from the Tel Aviv suburb of Lod, was one of the first to begin rhyming in Arabic after years of listening to Tupac Shakur. 'I said, "Damn, if we removed the word——-and you put (in) the word Arab, it's like singing about us," ' says Nafer, whose hybrid Hebrew and Arabic lyrics challenge Jewish stereotypes of Arabs as terrorists. 'It's delivering the message to a younger generation. Politicians don't talk to our generation. But politics is the way of our life, so I'm bringing the way of our life in their language.' " http://www.usatoday.com/news/world/.

59 See the notion of mimesis taken up in chapters 1 and 2 that incorporates but exceeds mimicry. Also, Stuart Hall says that it is mimicry "active and constitutive," "New Ethnicities," in *Race Culture and Difference*, ed. James Donald and Ali Rattansi (London: Sage, 1992), 254, quoted in Alan Seinfield, "Diaspora and Hybridity: Queer Identities and the Ethnicity Model," in *Diaspora and Visual Culture: Representing Africans and Jews*, ed. Nicholas Mirzoeff (London: Routledge, 2000), 101. See also Stuart Hall, "Cultural Identity and Diaspora," in

Identity, ed. Jonathan Rutherford (London: Lawrence and Wishart, 1990), 222–37. This essay is reproduced elsewhere, for example, in Mirzoeff, ed., *Diaspora and Visual Culture*, 21–33.

60 I am appropriating Patterson's and Kelley's (2000) arguments in "Unfinished Migrations" vis-à-vis diaspora.

61 To be sure, this multiple rooting and routing texture of creolization is well recognized in the work of Glissant, who speaks of "submarine roots: that is, free-floating, not fixed in one position in some primordial spot, but extending in all directions of our world through its network of branches," Édouard Glissant, *Caribbean Discourses: Selected Essays*, trans. M. Dash (Charlottesville: University Press of Virginia, 1989). For a comparison of Glissant's meaning and an extended discussion of its appropriation by the latter-day Creolistas in Martinique, and the content of their contribution, see Richard Price, "Shadowboxing in the Mangrove," *Cultural Anthropology* 12, no. 1 (1997): 23. Also see Richard Burton, *Afro-Creole: Power, Opposition, and Play in the Caribbean* (1997) and Paul Gilroy, *There Ain't No Black in the Union Jack* (1987). See also Richard Price, *The Convict and the Colonel: A Story about Colonialism and Resistance in the Caribbean* (Boston: Beacon Press, 1998).

62 Dipesh Chakrabarty, "The Time of History and the Time of Gods," in *The Politics of Culture in the Shadow of Capital*, ed. Lisa Lowe and David Lloyd (Durham, N.C.: Duke University Press, 1997), 36–60. Chakrabarty questions the Eurocentric notion of historical time. This critique is extended later in his book, *Provincializing Europe: Postcolonial Thought and Historical Difference* (Princeton, N.J.: Princeton University Press, 2000).

63 Karen McCarthy Brown, *Mama LoLa: A Vodou Priestess in Brooklyn* (Berkeley: University of California Press, 1991).

64 Hannerz, "Scenarios for Peripheral Cultures," in King, ed., *Culture, Globalization and the World-System*, 107–28.

65 http://programaderemesas.org.

66 See Michaeline A. Crichlow, "Living under the Long Shadows of Capital," in *Informalization: Process and Structure*, ed. Faruk Tabak and Michaeline A. Crichlow (Baltimore: Johns Hopkins University Press, 2000), 166–86.

67 Nicole Polier, "A View from the 'Cyanide Room': Politics and Culture in a Mining Township in Papua New Guinea," *Identities: Global Studies of Culture and Power* 1 (1994): 64. See also Bill Maurer's account of the role of the British Virgin Islands state in shaping the identities of BVI islanders in *Recharting the Caribbean: Land, Law, and Citizenship in the British Virgin Islands* (Ann Arbor: University of Michigan Press, 1997).

68 I borrow from the title of the interview of the renowned Caribbean writer George Lamming, who at the time was being interviewed by David Scott. Both Scott and Lamming raised this issue of sovereignty, distinguished from the limited sovereignty that we associate with nation-states. David Scott, "The Sovereignty of the Imagination: An Interview with George Lamming," *Small Axe* 12 (2002): 147.

69 Immanuel Wallerstein, "Social Conflict in Post-Independence Black Africa: The Concepts of Race and Status Group Reconsidered," chap. 10 in *The Capitalist World-Economy* (Cambridge: Cambridge University Press, 1979); also, "The National and the Universal: Can There Be Such a Thing as World Culture?" in King, ed., *Culture, Globalization and the World-System*, 91–105.

70 Roland Robertson, "Social Theory, Cultural Relativity and the Problem of Globality," in King, ed., *Culture, Globalization and the World-System*, 69–90.

71 Paul Gilroy, *The Black Atlantic*; C. L. R. James, *The Black Jacobins* (New York: Vintage, [1939, 1963] 1989); Sidney Mintz, *Caribbean Transformations* (New York: Columbia University Press, 1974); Eric Williams, *Capitalism and Slavery* (Chapel Hill: University of North Carolina Press, [1944] 1994).

72 George Orwell, *Animal Farm* (New York: Plume, 2003).

EPILOGUE

1 Irit Rogoff, in an exchange following several essays debating creolization and other matters, "Open Sessions," in Okwui Enwezor et al., eds., *Creolité and Creolization* (Ostfildern, Germany: Hatje Cantz, 2003), 102.

2 Edward Brathwaite, "Caliban," *The Arrivants: A New World Trilogy* (Oxford: Oxford University Press, 1973), 194–95.

3 Kathleen Balutansky and Marie-Agnès Sourieau, *Caribbean Creolization: Reflections on the Cultural Dynamics of Language, Literature and Identity* (Gainesville: University Press of Florida, 1998), 3.

4 Erna Brodber's work is animated by Zora Neale Hurston's almost caricatured view of Jamaican males of the 1930s. The absent male was also the perspective of Edith Clarke, *My Mother Who Fathered Me: A Study of the Family in Three Selected Communities in Jamaica* (London: George Allen and Unwin, 1957). Also, Mary Chamberlain, *Narratives of Exile and Return* (London: St. Martin's Press, 1997). John Western, *A Passage to England: Barbadian Londoners Speak of Home* (Minneapolis: University of Minnesota Press, 1992). Erna Brodber's "A Profile of Jamaican Men" (unpublished manuscript, ca. 1970s, 1987) consists of 200 interviews with male migrant returnees born between 1893 and 1900. Brodber's study was a response to Zora Neale Hurston's and Edith Clarke's anthropological observations about absent Jamaican males in rural households (personal conversation, 2000). See also Erna Brodber, *Standing Tall: Affirmations of the Jamaican Male: 24 Self-Portraits* (Kingston: Sir Arthur Lewis Institute of Social and Economic Research, 2003); unfortunately, it does not foreground or interweave Hurston's or Clarke's anthropological assumptions to provide much-needed rationale for its focus. Idem, *The Second Generation of Freemen in Jamaica, 1907–1944* (Gainesville: University Press of Florida, 2004).

5 Janet Wolff, "The Global and the Specific: Reconciling Conflicting Theories of Culture," in King, ed., *Culture, Globalization and the World System,* 161–73.

6 Ibid., 167.

7 Stephen White, *Sustaining Affirmation: The Strengths Of Weak Ontology in Political Theory* (Princeton, N.J.: Princeton University Press, 2000).

8 See the critiques of John Tagg and Janet Wolff in King, ed., *Culture, Globalization and the World-System*, 154–73.

9 Saskia Sassen uses the concept of assemblages to highlight the spaces of globalization that exist within the nation-state but are not of it. See Sassen, *Territory, Authority and Rights: From Medieval to Global Assemblages* (Princeton, N.J.: Princeton University Press, 2006).

10 In analyzing the multiple labor bargaining strategies that slaves used in the Leeward Islands involving withdrawal of labor, the appeal to outside mediation, and collective representation, Glen Richards notes some of the conditions and strategies, the imagination of creating locales: labor bargaining strategies signaled the increasing social investment of enslaved Africans and their descendants in plantation society and their emerging Creole sensibilities and commitment to the only home they knew. It is this feature of plantation society which best explains how a "transitory and alienated nucleus of [white] workers, sharing no common economic ground with the ownership, was able to hold in subjection a massive body of restless slaves. It was the enslaved worker and his/her free descendant who, both in trying to 'make life' and to remake the world anew, expressed the strongest commitment to a new Creole existence which would embrace enslaved and enslaver, black and white." Glen Richards, " 'Driber Tan Mi Side': Creolisation and the Labour Process in St. Kitts and Nevis, 1810–1905," in *Questioning Creole: Creolisation Discourses in Caribbean Culture,* ed. Verene Shepherd and Glen Richards (Kingston: Ian Randle Publishers, 2002), 218–19. However, Richards does not consider the global context of St. Kitts, Nevis, and the global and accounts for these diverse labor strategies only in terms of the driver's dual roles. What was the role of transatlantic communication in the formation of such labor relationships in those places? Even so, the connection as an explanation is problematic.

11 Aijaz Ahmad, "The Politics of Literary Postcoloniality," *Race and Class* 36, no. 3 (January 1995): 11.

12 For nuanced perspectives on the idea of state retreat, see Linda Weiss, *The Myth of the Powerless State* (Ithaca, N.Y.: Cornell University Press, 1998); Saskia Sassen, *Losing Control?*

13 During that early nationalist phase, citizens invested variously in that "spirit" of the nation-state. As Norman Manley put it, "There is a tremendous difference between living in a place and belonging to it and feeling that your own life and destiny is irrevocably bound up in the life and destiny of that place. It is that spirit which is the most hopeful thing in Jamaica today. It is that spirit which alone encourages the development of our national consciousness." Quoted in Petrine Archer-Straw, "Paradise, Primitivism and Parody," in Enwezor et al., eds., *Creolité and Creolization*, 70.

14 Gerard Aching, "On Masking and Carnival Time: Some Methodological Con-

siderations," keynote address given at the summer symposium "The Arts and Cultural Politics of Carnival," Obermann Center for Advanced Studies, University of Iowa, July 12, 2005. See also Aching, *Masking and Power: Carnival and Popular Culture in the Caribbean* (Minneapolis: University of Minnesota Press, 2002).

15 See Pelton, *The Trickster in West Africa*. While deployed in the context of discussions of ritual practices and drawn from the literature interpreting folklore tales, as noted earlier, the idea of liminality has crossed over to social and cultural theory and analysis and has been a productive concept for addressing the problem of opening up relations of power or conditions of hegemonic overdetermination. Robert Pelton has produced a remarkable study of the trickster figure in West African societies, in particular examining the Ashanti, Fon, Yoruba, and Dogon trickster figures in their social and mythical contexts, exploring their meaning for these peoples and also critically reflecting on secularized cultures' view of them.

16 Ibid., 35.

17 Diane Austin-Broos, *Jamaica Genesis: Religion and the Politics of Moral Orders* (Kingston: Ian Randle Publishers and University of Chicago Press, 1997), 47.

18 Aching, "On Masking and Carnival Time"; and *Masking and Power*.

19 Austin-Broos, *Jamaica Genesis*, 47.

20 See David Harvey, *A Brief History of Neoliberalism* (Oxford: Oxford University Press, 2007).

21 Paul Tyambe Zeleza, "Imagining and Inventing the Post-Colonial State in Africa," *Contours: A Journal of the African Diaspora* 1, no. 1 (spring 2003): 101.

22 Achille Mbembe, "Provisional Notes on the Postcolony," *Africa* 62, no. 1 (1992): 5. For a general discussion of the postcolonial condition in Africa, see also Richard Werbner and Terence Ranger, eds., *Postcolonial Identities in Africa* (London: Zed Books, 1996).

23 Stuart Hall, "Créolité and the Process of Creolization" in Enwezor et al., eds., *Creolité and Creolization*, 32.

24 Roger Ebert, *Chicago Sun-Times*, August 9, 1991.

25 Michaeline A. Crichlow, "An Alternative Approach to Family Land in the Anglophone Caribbean: The Case of St. Lucia," *New West Indian Guide/Nieuwe West-Indische Gids* 68, nos. 1–2 (1994): 77–99.

26 David Scott, "The Sovereignty of the Imagination: An Interview with George Lamming," *Small Axe* 12 (September 2002): 147.

27 Susan Broadhurst, *Liminal Acts: A Critical Overview of Contemporary Performance and Theory* (London: Cassell, 1999).

28 To paraphrase the Trinidadian artist Ken Crichlow, "The past, therefore, really is a preparation for tomorrow, and the work that we do, even though it is today and rooted in the past, is really about tomorrow." Interview with Ken Crichlow by a St. Lawrence University team, ca. June 5, 2002.

29 Carolle Charles, "Gender and Politics in Contemporary Haiti: The Duvalierist

State, Transnationalism, and the Emergence of a New Feminism (1980–1990)," *Feminist Studies* 21, no. 1 (spring 1995): 135–64.

30 Juan Flores, "The Diaspora Strikes Back: Créolité in the Hood," in Enwezor et al., eds., *Créolité and Creolization*, 174.
31 Gerardo Mosquera, "From," in Enwezor et al., eds., *Creolité and Creolization*, 146.
32 Ibid.
33 Rogoff, "Open Sessions," in Enwezor et al., eds., *Creolité and Creolization*.
34 Flores, "The Diaspora Strikes Back." Paul Gilroy, in *Against Race: Imagining Political Culture beyond the Color Line* (Cambridge: Belknap Press of Harvard University Press, 2001), though offering problematic readings of popular culture, nonetheless raises productive questions that are fundamental to understanding the perils of dwelling in fixed racial identities.

Boy, Henry, 92

Brathwaite, Edward Kamau: "Caliban," 201, 281 n.2; "Caribbean Man in Time and Space," 1, 222 n.1; creolization as seen by, 178; *The Emigrants,* xi, 135, 268 n.1; imaginations of geographies in work of, 44; on Lembe, 252 n.115; pluralist view of plantation of, 30–31; on relation of space and time, 232 n.29

Brazil: first blacks in, 30; high-tech jobs combined with Afro-Creole religion in, 12; ideology of racial democracy in, 8

Breen, Henry, 98, 99–100

Brewer, Benjamin D., 35–36

Bricolage, 19, 77, 231 n.26

Bridging, 19, 231 n.26

Britain: British black identities, 70–71, 216; Caribbean migrants to, 148–49; Queen Elizabeth, 173; welfare state of, 158; West Indian settlement patterns in, 150

British Virgin Islands, 278 n.45

Brodber, Erna, 104, 227 n.55, 281 n.4

Brown, Katherine, 223 n.14

Brubaker, Roger, 232 n.30

Burton, Richard, 74–75, 180, 181

Butler, Judith, 247 n.73

Butler, Octavia, 190

Calhoun, Craig, 232 n.30

"Caliban" (Brathwaite), 201, 281 n.2

Calibrations, 243 n.22

Cameroon, 108

Canada, 137

Caribbean, the: ambivalencies in cultural practices in, 95–97; antagonistic indebtedness to West, 81, 254 n.21; Caribbean-Western problematic, 2; as central to modern Atlantic economy, 176; creolization's rhizomic rootings in, ix; creolizing techniques of free-dom in, 81; decentering plantation in creolization discourses, 202; as economically inconsequential, 43–44; emigration to Britain, 148–49; free African migrants to, 260 n.85; globalization's shadier side in, 196–97; informal sector in, 4, 196–97, 223 n.14; in international division of labor, 36; as international locale, 137; locating the global in creolization, 15–40; migration from, 44; mobility of population of, 160–61; modernity of, xii–xiii; neoliberalism insinuates itself into, 4; oppositional culture of, 75; as outside and inside spaces of the modern, 81; pan-Caribbean identity, 150; "peasant folk" as central figures in culture of, xiii; as peripheral, 181; as pivotal location for global economic forces, 198; plural uneven temporalities and spaces of, 1; racialization of Caribbeans, 141; tourism industry in, 138. *See also* Dominican Republic; Haitians; Jamaica; Martinique; St. Lucia; Trinidad and Tobago; *and other islands by name*

Carnegie, Charles V., 29, 161, 237 n.66

Carnivalesque: in flower festivals, 100–101; of Lucians group, 119, 124, 126, 127, 130, 133, 134; Mbembe on Bakhtin's view of, 108–9

Cartesian conception of space, 44, 45, 58

Cartesian conception of time, 49, 277 n.40

Castaway, The (Cozier), ii, x–xi, xii

Catholics: anti-Catholic violence in St. Lucia, 12, 227 n.49; flower festivals associated with Church, 99–100; Portuguese black, 30

Chakrabarty, Dipesh, 195, 227 n.47, 280 n.62

Chamberlain, Mary, 142–43, 165–66

Chaos, 174, 214

Charles, Carolle, 163–64, 214–15

Christianity, violent episodes in, 226 n.45. *See also* Catholics

Chude-Sokei, Louis, 194, 264 n.32

Citizenship: achieving citizenness as public venture, 102; alternative conceptions of, 122; citizenness, 77–78, 81, 104, 105, 116, 207; complexity of resistance and citizenness, 84; complexity of struggle for citizenness, 79; consumption as strategy for, 265 n.39; creolization influenced by and influencing, 28; of decolonization, 7, 128–29; desire for, 210–11; development and cultural constructs of, 117; flexible, 161; as gendered, 84; globalization redefines, 34–35, 43; Lucians group and grasp for citizenship, 128; middle-class youth demand more democratic practice of, 9; nation and development triangulated in West Indies, 131–32; negotiating imaginings of, 3; older traditions of, 209–10; pursuit as socially textured, 100; qua S/s/ objects, 19, 231 n.25; state elites ignore differences in meaning of, 8; for thwarting enslavement, 29; working peoples' construction of, 81

City-citizen game, 13, 62, 63, 211

Clark, Terry Nichols, 119, 264 n.27

Clarke, Edith, 281 n.4

Class: diaspora studies and, 187; differentiation among smallholders, 90; dress and, 97–98; flower festivals and, 98, 99; as fundamentally unstable phenomenon, 42; inequalities in land of opportunity, 141

Clifford, James, 138–39, 140, 167, 179

Clinton, George, 190

Coates, Nicholas, 174

Colonialism: Afro-Creoles under colonial rule, 73–106; coloniality of power, 56, 62, 106; decolonization, 7,

10, 115, 122, 128–29; dialogic relationship of colonized and colonizer, 183; exclusionary policies during, 80; indigenous interaction with, 238 n.83; peasant resistance to, 82; plantation practices of, 78–79, 85–86; power in postcolonial period versus, 10; reconfiguration of creolization and, x; resistance strategies of working people and smallholders, 90–95; working peoples' resentment of, 80. *See also* Postcolonial condition

Comité Feminin, 163

Commonwealth Immigrants Act (1962), 148–49

Condition of Postmodernity (Harvey), 57

Consumption, 265 n.39

Cooper, Frederick, 232 n.30

Cooper, Laura Facey, 266 n.55

Cosmopolitanism, 2, 272 n.62

Cozier, Christopher, ii, x–xi, xii

Craig, Susan, 7–8

Crane, Hart, 231 n.27

Creoles: concept as free-floating signifier, 180; "Creole time on the move," 58; experiences of Creole subjects, 18; intertwinement of economic and cultural in, 4; negotiation within histories of diverse but linked places, 2; Nicaraguan, 188–89; overlapping and competing forms of, 75, 180. *See also* Afro-Creoles; Creolization; Post-Creole imaginations

Creolization: African developments in shaping of, 27; context of oppression of, 10; as creative cultural evolutionary process, 21; "creolization-in-the-world," 21–23, 28, 181–82, 205; debate over globality or specificity of, 175; decentering Caribbean plantation in discourses of, 202; dialogic relationship of diaspora and creolization studies, 177–78; diasporas and, 190–

93, 194–95; double articulating practices of, 33, 67–68, 69, 168, 176; duality of space entailed by, 175; dynamized, xiii, 3, 41; eBay imaginary in deployment of concept, 178; as emancipatory, 19, 33, 184; generalized, xiii, 28–33; globalization and Creole identities, 1–14; globalization refurbishes and undermines, 201–2; governmentality in processes of, 24–25, 236 n.49; as harbinger of cultural fusion, 177; historical contamination of term, 18; historicized, xiii, 25–28, 211; as homing of modern freedom, 19, 33, 63, 184, 199, 202, 219, 250 n.102; as journeying from place to place, 63, 250 n.102; as linked to the plantation, 11–13, 180, 181, 182; locating the global in, 15–40; making places in, 19, 219; as morphogenetics of cultures of power, 24, 65, 66–69; on the move, 171–99; as ongoing, xiv, 3; as ontological conditioning process, 44; as politics of the cross, 70; polycultural practices in, 29; in post-plantation world, 11–13, 176–78; as projects, 1–2, 6–14; in redux, 13, 188; resurgence of concept of, 178–79; rethinking through multiple *présences,* 201–19; rhizomic rootings in Caribbean, ix; as selective creation and cultural struggle, ix, xiv, 1, 3, 21, 22, 23, 24, 25, 33, 49–50, 51, 56, 63, 70, 204; space in discourses of, 44–45; as subject and problematic, 20–21; as symbolic refractions of mapping of the present, x, 183–84; transportation of peoples seen as crucial for, 179–80; unequal power in, 5–6; in an unequal world, 207; as universalizable, xiii
Crichlow, Ken, 283 n.28
Critical realism, 66, 206, 250 n.108
Cross, politics of the, 70–71, 115, 197, 215
Crowley, Daniel, 101, 102, 262 n.108

Cuba, 42, 106, 260 n.86
Culture: binaries in typologies of, 179; complexity of cultural development as social process, 50; culturalization of social life, 35; cultural hybridity replaces political geography in identity, 162; cultural policy and politics of governable space, 128–29; cultural politics, 121–24, 127, 211; cultural styles, 85, 174; cultural "suitcases," 140, 141–44; "culture building" concept, 225 n.26; cultures of power, 24, 44, 59, 61, 65, 66–69, 73, 165, 184, 185, 199, 202, 206; development's effect on, 132; doubly articulated production of, 128; fixedness associated with, 138, 139, 167; incoherencies in, 217–18; limitations of, 81; mimetic manipulation of cultural space, 104; oppositional Caribbean, 75; polycultural practices in creolization, 29; rural space privileged as site of constructing, 7–9; seen as possession and end product, x; systems of, 24, 44, 235 n.48, 243 n.20. *See also* Popular culture
Culture, Globalization, and the World-System (King), 205–6
Cyberprotests, 130, 267 n.63

Dagnino, Evelina, 121–22
"Dark Complete World of a Caribbean Store, The" (Price), 2
Dasein, 22, 51, 52
Davies, Omar, 243 n.17
Dean, Mitchell, 61
De Certeau, Michel, 75, 208, 253 n.3, 275 n.12
Decolonization, 7, 10, 115, 122, 128–29
Deindustrialization, 190, 191
Deleuze, Gilles, 18, 206, 221 n.3, 231 n.22, 232 n.29
Democracy: alternative conceptions of, 122; cultural politics and, 122; demo-

Democracy (*continued*)
cratic antagonism, 126–27; Lucians group's vision of, 130; middle-class nationalists and workers in construction of West Indian, 114–15; racial democracy in Brazil, 8
Democratic Socialism, 3, 172, 274 n.4
Denationalization, 36–37
Dennet, R. E., 252 n.115
Dependency theory, 37
Derrida, Jacques: on becoming-space of time, 48; on becoming-time of space, 48; on *différance*, 17, 33, 47–48, 51; on the ineluctable, 247 n.73; influence on this study, 206; on relation of space and time, 232 n.29; on scenes of presence, x; on trace, 47, 245 n.36
"Desistance," practices of, 58
Deterritorialization, 10, 29, 35, 154, 157
Development: end of, 43, 242 n.15; Lucians group's different vision of, 132; and the nation and citizenship triangulated in West Indies, 131–32; seen in terms of fleeing the plantation, 16; state divestment limits commitment to, 34; sustainable, 16; (un)making nation-states in processes of, 114–17
Developmentalist state, 9, 18, 113–14, 127
Dialectics: liminal, 21, 207, 210, 233 n.36; of resistance, 73–106
Diasporas: African, 185, 186; characteristics attributed to creolizing New World, 183; creolization and, 190–93, 194–95; cultures along shifting national lines, 160; decentering of nation-state and, 184, 186; dialogic relationship of creolization and diaspora studies, 177–78; diaspora temporality, 48; diasporic habitus, 31–33, 53, 105, 141, 165, 185, 203, 207, 238 n.77, 239 n.85; diasporic identity, 144; diasporic mo(ve)ment, 145, 249 n.101;

(dis)articulating, 184–89; home and, 250 n.102; as methodology rather than condition, 185, 189; movements remixing the world with post-Creole imaginations, 135–70; Muslim *Umma* seen as political diaspora, 239 n.90; pervasiveness of spatial and political, 35; Puerto Rican, 216, 218; as signifying practices, 184
Diawara, Manthia, 161
Différance, 17, 33, 47–48, 51, 70, 76, 186, 194
Discrimination, opposition to, 80
Distanciamento, 164
Domesticity, foreign-ness within, 62
Domestic labor schemes, 137
Domestic violence, 123
Dominguez, Jorge, 114–15
Dominguez, Virginia, 129
Dominican Republic: Dominican community in New York City, 164; Haitian cane workers in, 11–12; migrants to U.S. from, 137; neoliberalism's effect on, 34; settlement patterns in Britain, 150
Doubling processes, 17, 33, 67–68, 69, 168, 176
Dress, 97–98
Drewal, Margaret Thompson, 33, 239 n.85
Duany, Jorge, 162
Dube, Saurabh, 1, 28, 57, 58, 222 n.1
Du Bois, W. E. B., 259 n.73
Dwelling: disruption of former, 77, 78; involves imaginative movement, 2; limboing struggles for, 74; in migratory movements, 237 n.66; modes of, xi, 79, 81; politics of, 73, 74, 77, 78, 138; politics of the cross sustains hope for homely, 70; promise of development and sovereignty and belief in possibility of homely, 116–17; "proper dwelling places," 53; travel overemphasized in relation to, 138, 140. *See also* Home

eBay imaginary, 178; global and local place making subject to, 202; as increasing across world, 177, 198

Ebert, Roger, 214

Edensor, Tim, 52, 62

Edwards, Brent Hayes, 185–86

Eisner, Gisela, 257 n.47

Elden, Stuart, x, 19, 20, 22, 232 n.29

Electoral politics, 9

Elizabeth II, 173

Ellison, Ralph, 47

Emergent conditions of existence, 17, 230 n.14

Emigrants, The (Brathwaite), xi, 135, 268 n.1

Enclaves, 25, 37

England. *See* Britain

Escobar, Arturo, 121–22

Ethnicity: diaspora studies and, 187; dress and, 97; essentialisms of, 185; flexible, 50; as fundamentally unstable, 42; hierarchical organization of, 76. *See also* Race

Family: as grounding and rooting the individual, 137; land, 146–48, 155, 157; practicing national belonging through, 148–54

Fanm D'Ayiti (Women of Haiti), 163

Fanon, Frantz, 8, 95, 232 n.29, 254 n.15, 263 n.14

Farm labor schemes, 137

Fashion, 97–98

Ferguson, James, 84–85, 98, 127, 161, 249 n.100, 261 n.90, 272 n.62

Festivals: A-bwé songfest, 102–4; flower festivals, 98–102

Few Small Nips, A (Kahlo), 124

Filipinas, 5

Fischer, Sibylle, 46, 47, 56, 245 n.35

Fixity: culture associated with, 138, 139, 167; in diasporic mo(ve)ments, 145; fixed identities, 176; locale privileging

in creolization studies, 181; the nation as fixed and unfixed, 165; returning migrants and, 157, 158; unthinking, 140–41

Fleeing the plantation, 34–35; as critical to rethinking creolization, 20, 184, 215; development seen in terms of, 16; diasporas and, 185, 189; duality of space and, 204; nondeterminatism of social being in, xiv; *ruud bwai* self-fashioning contrasted with, 111; two dimensions of, xiv

Flores, Juan, 43, 216, 218, 219

Flower festivals, 98–102; African dimension of, 98–99, 100; Catholic connections of, 99–100; class characteristics of, 98, 99; as mimicking status quo, 99; political character of early, 98; respectability and, 101, 102; royal and aristocratic symbols in, 100–102, 105; seen as mindless imitation, 213

Folding processes, 17–18, 22, 33, 56, 77, 168, 206

Forum, The, 121

Foucault, Michel: on "chains of power," 55; decolonization and governmentality and, 10; on discourse, 236 n.48; on entry of forces, 230 n.14; on governmental effects, 68; on governmentality, 59–61, 247 n.75; influence on this study, 206; on knowledge-power episteme, 56, 115; Mbembe on, 110; on power as way of acting upon a subject, 248 n.80; on the present as prisoner of the passage, 48, 245 n.46; on refusal of what we are, 41, 241 n.2; on relation of space and time, 232 n.29; Scott's analysis of *ruud bwai* and, 110, 111; "The Subject and the Power," 235 n.41; on versatile power equilibrium, 250 n.107; on writing history of the present, 233 n.33

Freedom: Burton's social model of, 75; creolization as emancipatory, 19, 33, 184; homing of modern freedoms, 19, 33, 63, 184, 199, 202, 203, 207, 219, 250 n.102, 252 n.114; land-based and working peoples' practices of, 77, 80; practicing within prevailing relationships of power, 111–12; resistance as fundamental to Caribbean places and, 74–75; and sovereignty as inseparable from formation of Creole nation-state, 116

French Creole, 103, 147, 148

Friendly societies, 80, 93, 94

Frontiers, 25, 37

Gaines, Kevin, 93–94

García Canclini, Néstor, 113, 265 n.39

Garrison communities, 274 n.4

Garvey, Marcus, 172, 186, 188

Gaspar, D. Barry, 29, 237 n.67, 262 n.110

Gebauer, Gunter, 249 n.89

Geertz, Clifford, 259 n.76

Gens anglaises: on disjuncture between St. Lucian government and people, 158; family land and, 146–48; "Jack and Judith," 146–47, 167, 169; jobs of, 151; lack of state support for returning, 159–60; locals' resentment toward returned, 155, 156, 216; practicing national belonging through family, 148–54; returning home to St. Lucia, 10–11, 152, 153, 154–58, 217; sending money home, 152; settlement patterns in Britain, 150; as students, 151, 152

Gilroy, Paul: on antagonistic indebtedness of Caribbean to West, 81, 254 n.21; *The Black Atlantic*, 13, 44, 234 n.40; on Caribbean region as modern transnational space, 205; on crises within modernity, 44; on cultural nationalism, 234 n.40; on de-essentializing black identity, 186; on diasporas, 185; on double consciousness, 56; on liminal dialectics, 234 n.36; on living memories, 76; on politics of transfiguration, 193; on popular culture, 284 n.34; on racial purity and fascism, 277 n.42; on relation of space and time, 232 n.29; on sensibility of shared community, 203; on sounds creating alternative public spheres, 194; on space as product and rhythm, 46, 47; on syncopated temporality, 47, 48; on transnationalized community, 13, 14

Glissant, Édouard: on Caribbean as worlding phenomenon, 198; on Caribbeanness as dream, 15, 228 n.3; concern with space of, 44, 232 n.29; on creolization as not a fusion, 171, 274 n.2; influence on this study, 206; on nature of Creole form, 210; on openness, 174, 175; on poetics of relation, 57, 174; on rhizome concept, 174, 221 n.3; on submarine roots, 31, 280 n.61

Globalization: beyond local and global, 176–78; characteristics of, 35; citizenship redefined by, 34–35, 43; creole identities and, 1–14; creolization in studies of, 179; cultural politics and, 122; decentering dialectics of resistance in globalizing modern, 73–106; facilitation and engagement of, 134; fleeing the plantation as critical to rethinking, 184; in formation of new spatialities and temporalities, 36–38, 43; inequalities of, 195–97; limitations of, 81; locating the global in creolization, 15–40; Lucians' expressive culture in context of, 113–14, 130; mechanisms for elites and populace to maneuver within, 115–16; the present as apparent time of, 20–21; as project, 1–2

Gomes, Flávio, 238 n.70

Gordimer, Nadine, 47

Gordon, Edmund, 188

Governable space: cultural policy and politics of, 128–29; ontology of, 64–66; reconstitution of, 131

Governmentality, x; as conduct of conduct, 59; in creolization processes, 24–25, 236 n.49; decolonization and, 10; economy of power, 44; Foucault on, 59–61, 247 n.75; governmentalization of the state, 63; as guidance, 60; knowledge-power episteme in, 56; as law of tendency, 59; politics of modern, 59–61, 198, 202; politics of neoliberal, 197; racialized modes of, 186; spatial history and, 58; tactical limboing of modern, 211

Gramsci, Antonio, 75, 165

Gray, Obika, 12

Grenada, 121, 150, 162

Griffin, Glenn A. Elmer, 227 n.49

Grosfoguel, Ramón, 138

Guadeloupe, 26

Guattari, Félix, 221 n.3

Gupta, Akhil, 84–85, 127, 249 n.100

Guyana, 87, 88, 106

Habermas, Jürgen, 109

Habitus: agency and, 53; conditioning of, 226 n.36; diasporic, 31–33, 53, 105, 141, 165, 185, 203, 207, 238 n.77, 239 n.85; pluralist Atlantic, 14; postcolonial, 108; tangled, 130; U.S. racialized sociocultural relations in immigrant experience of, 163

Haile Selassie, 172, 173

Haitians: in Dominican Republic, 11; migration to Bahamas and Florida Keys, 137; multiple attachments of migrants, 162; on racial and class inequities in United States, 141; "suitcase" contents of transnationals, 143–44; women's organizations in diaspora, 163–64, 214–15

Hall, Douglas, 87

Hall, Stuart, 11, 131, 142, 144, 183, 186, 216, 232 n.29, 255 n.33, 256 n.34

Hanchard, Michael, 186–87

Hannerz, Ulf, 38, 136, 179, 232 n.32

Haraksingh, Kusha, 254 n.14

Harder They Come, The (film), 111

Hardt, Michael, 247 n.65

Harris, Wilson, x, 15, 44, 56, 206, 228 n.1, 230 n.15, 232 n.29

Harvey, David, x, 1, 57, 58, 230 n.12, 244 n.26

Hebdige, Richard, 174

Hegemony, 165

Heidegger, Martin, 18–19, 51, 57, 206, 232 n.29

Heritage tourism, 196

Herskovits, Melville, 6, 179, 234 n.40

Hesse, Barnor, 70–71

Heurtelou, Maude, 143–44

Heywood, Linda, 30

Hintzen, Percy, 16, 225 n.30

Hip-hop, 194, 279 n.57

Hippolyte, Kendel, 103, 262 n.111

History: conventional notions of, xii; creolization historicized, xiii, 25–28; disruption of histories, 77; embodied, 9; habitus as product and producer of, 32; historicizing space, 48; as open-ended, 213; of the present, 21, 233 n. 33, 233 n.34; relational histories, 204; world systems analysis' tendency to universalize, 44. See also Spatial hi/story

Holt, Thomas, 88–89, 93, 258 n.71, 277 n.41

Home: in analysis of diasporic movements, 250 n.102; gens anglaises return to St. Lucia, 10–11, 154–58; in Greek mythology, 250 n.102; making, 62, 136, 211; migrants' idea of return-

Home (*continued*)
    ing, 151–52, 153, 217; as mode for pro-
    ducing space, 52; stakes in, 74, 81,
    105–6; unhomeliness, 51, 74, 250
    n.102. *See also* Homing
Homeland, 157–58, 185, 186
Homing: as analytical register for
    rethinking creolization, 215; of Carib-
    bean New World movements, xi; Cre-
    ole practices under coloniality of
    power and, 62; creolization's specific-
    ity and, xiv; limboing struggles for,
    74; of modern freedoms, 19, 33, 63,
    184, 199, 202, 203, 207, 219, 250 n.102,
    252 n.114; "otherwise," 56; of place, 63;
    politics of, 73, 74, 203; proper pres-
    ence and, 211; (re)homing place, 74,
    78, 80, 81, 105–6, 136, 145, 203, 207,
    208, 209, 212, 214
Hoy, David, 17, 231 n.25
Hunte, 118, 120, 121, 124, 125, 264 n.30
Hurricane Katrina, 240 n.97
Hurston, Zora Neale, 227 n.55, 281 n.4
Hutton, Clinton, 92
Hybridity, 37, 162, 178, 179, 193, 197
Hysterical realism, 126

Identity: as always under construction,
    185; black, 185–89; citizenness and
    creolized, 78; cultural mobility and
    hybridity in, 162; diasporic, 144; dual
    sense of, 162; elusiveness as analytical
    category, 232 n.30; fixed, 176; flower
    societies for, 99; as incoherent and
    pragmatic, x; local versus global, 13–
    14; manipulability of Creole, 12;
    mobility in formation of, 136; pan-
    Caribbean, 150; of place, 85; shared,
    188; silencing power of, 180; as social
    garment, 50. *See also* National
    identity
Imafuku, Ryuta, 251 n.114
Imagination: coloniality of power and

geographies of, 56; different versions
of imagining, 129–33; in fleeing the
plantation, xiv; of geographies, 44;
imagined communities, 21–22, 120–
21, 135, 136, 192, 211; imagining utopian alternatives, 109; of places in
traveling, 140–41; sovereignty of, 130–
31, 197, 214, 217; unfinished genesis of,
133–34. *See also* Post-Creole
imaginations
Indo-Caribbeans, 7, 161, 180, 254 n.13
Industrialization: deindustrialization,
190, 191; as ineffectual means of economic advancement, 35–36
Ineluctable, the, 247 n.73
Inequalities: creolization in unequal
world, 207; globalized, 195–97; semiotics of inequality and struggle, 3
Informal, the: creolization studies contribute to debate on, 28; growing levels of, 35; as intrinsic to Creole culture, 223 n.14; nationalisms, 237 n.66;
supersedes formal sector in Caribbean, 196–97; term as used in this
study, 237 n.63; women in informal
economy, 4–5
Ingold, Tim, 51
Israel, 129, 194; 279 n.57

Jamaica: Afro-American influence on
music of, 193; Brodber's study of male
migrants from, 227 n.55; decline as
sugar producer, 79, 92–93; domination practices in, 85–86; export of
skilled labor from, 5, 224 n.19; garrison communities, 274 n.4; King
Arthur, 171–74; land-based working
people in, 255 n.23; land reform
workers in, 3; Manley's attitude
toward working people, 122–23;
migrants to United States, 137; Morant Bay Rebellion, 91, 92, 258 n.63;
Nicaraguan Creoles descended from,

188; plantations in, 26, 79; *ruud bwai* in, 110–11; settlement patterns in Britain, 150; smallholders in, 87–88, 88–89; vestry politics in, 93

James, C. L. R., 56, 74, 152, 232 n.29

James, Clifford, 250 n.102

James, Winston, 137

Jameson, Fredric, 113, 178, 226 n.40

Jordan, Glenn, 243 n.20

Kahlo, Frida, 124

Karlström, Mikael, 109

Kay Fanm, 163

Kelley, Robin D. G., 187–88

Khan, Aisha, 180

King, Anthony D., 205–6

King Arthur, 171–74, 185, 198

Kolar, Ernestine, 261 n.97

Konte dancing, xii–xiii, 222 n.13

Lacoue-Labarthe, Philippe, 247 n.73

Lamming, George, 214, 280 n.68

Land, F. Mitchell, 264 n.32

Land ownership, 104

Land registration program, 145–46, 148

Land Use and Land Tenure Patterns in the Windward Islands (Crichlow), 223 n.8

Last Angel of History, The (Akomfrah), 190–93

Law of tendency, 59, 248 n.80

Leeward Islands, 282 n.10

Lefebvre, Henry: Harvey influenced by, 57; influence on this study, 206; on power and space, 54–55; on present space, 46, 49, 245 n.50; on relation of space and time, 232 n.29; on space as product, 45, 46, 48–49; on time and emancipation, 41, 241 n.3; on triangulations of space, 52, 53, 54

Lembe, 69, 252 n.115

Lemke, Thomas, 59

Lewis, Arthur, 16

Limbo, 251 n.114; citizenness as strategy of, 78; "limbo gateway," x; limboing strategy of making place, 68, 69, 74, 202; tactical limboing of modern governmentality, 211

Liminality: of Anansi, 210; Caribbean's lived experiences as liminal, 167–68; of double articulating creolization practices, 67–68; limbo and, 252 n.114; liminal dialectics, 21, 207, 210, 233 n.36; liminal genesis, 58; liminal politics, 48, 74, 80–81, 105–6, 184; liminal transformation, x; limit point experiences, 58; space as liminal, 48, 49, 58

Lorde, Audre, 144, 269 n.20

Louis, Michael, 96–97, 99, 258 n.61, 260 n.84

Lovejoy, Paul, 27

Lucians: ambivalent oppositional expressive culture of, 112–13; appropriations of *Saturday Night Live* styles by, 120, 213; context of, 113–14; as counter-counter-protest, 265 n.33; criticism of, 124–25; cultural entanglement characteristic of, 127; cultural politics of, 121–24, 127; democratic antagonism of, 126–28; different versions of belonging and imagining of, 129–33; masculinism of, 123; as multisigns, 267 n.66; as not antiliberal, 130; as "pappyshow," 125, 133, 268 n.74; political reform urged by, 119–21; politicians lampooned by, 117–19; popularity of, 121; recurring refrains of, 132; represent grasp for citizenness, 128; St. Lucian imagined communities criticized by, 120–21; seriousness of, 124–26; STAFF party of, 118, 123, 124–25; Zapatistas compared with, 129–30

Manley, Michael, 274 n.4

Manley, Norman, 122–23, 172, 282 n.13

Mapping the present: "creolization-in-the-world" process entangled in, 28; creolization processes as symbolic refractions of, x, 183–84; cross-cultural fertilization and, 168, 169; de Certeau's "une place propre" and, 253 n.3; erasure of freedom in hegemonic, 77; inclusionary citizenship versus exclusionary, 210; Lefebvrian panopticon for, 54; making and unmaking historically specific, 68; ontology of governable space in, 64–66; politics of, 22, 57, 202, 219; remapping, 63, 65–66, 184, 209; triangulations of space in, 52–54; virtual, 206; as vital condition of creolization, 56; will to place in, 49–51

Maroons, 96, 161, 260 n.83

Marshall, Woodville, 90, 257 n.57

Martinique: Cuban sugar industry compared with that of, 42; informal sector in, 223 n.14; local and international interwoven in, 79; smallholder Creole life in, 2–3

Marx, Karl, 19, 57, 86, 177

Marxism, 121

Masking and masquerade, 61–63; in flower festivals, 100–101; maintaining, 210; politics of, 203

Massey, Doreen, 41, 73, 176, 206, 241 n.1, 253 n.1, 267 n.64

Matos Rodríguez, Felix V., 26

Maurer, Bill, 188, 278 n.45

Mbembe, Achille: on Africa as constrained by West, 50; on exercising existence, xii, 70, 110, 112, 133; on freedom within relationships of power, 111–12; on getting from colony to what comes after, 73, 253 n.2; influence on this study, 206; on logic of conviviality, 109, 130; pessimism of, 109; on plurality of postcolony, 212–13; on postcoloniality, 107–10; on

power, 108; on social theory and collapse of worlds, 107, 262 n.2; on time of entanglement, 12, 67, 127, 173, 183; "time on the move," 41, 241 n.4

McClintock, Anne, 123

McMichael, Philip, 44, 213

Meighoo, Sean Lokaisingh, 184, 186, 249 n.101

Memory, as fixing people at certain locations, 140

Messianicity, 17, 214

Mestizaje, 210

Metayage: coloniality accommodated by, 90, 258 n.61; planter attitude toward, 257 n.57; in St. Lucia, 79, 89–90

Midgett, Douglas, 149

Migdal, Joel, 62, 127

Migration: from Caribbean, 44; Caribbean emigration to Britain, 148–49; as central to state formation and disruption in Caribbean, 137; cultural "suitcases" in, 140, 141–44; dread associated with return to "motherland," 137; idea of returning home, 151–52, 153; pervasiveness of, 208; state encouragement of, 137; transportation of peoples crucial for creolization, 179–80. See also Diasporas; Gens anglaises

Mimesis: masking and masquerade and, 61–63; mimetic appropriation of proper presence, 103; mimetic manipulation of cultural space, 104; mimetic signifying practices, 85; mo(ve)ments of, 63, 68, 69, 71, 85, 203, 209, 211, 249 n.101, 252 n.114; as more than imitation, 61, 249 n.89; politics of accommodation, dwelling, or homing seen as critical, 74; smallholders employ transitional mimetic props, 78; in West Indian nationalism, 131; working-class mimicry of elite culture, 80

Mimicry: in labor strategies of enslaved and indentured, 214; refabricates and reinvents post-Creole culture, 194; staging of different but similar truth and, 119–21; in West Indian nationalism, 131. *See also* Mimesis

Mintz, Sidney: on Caribbean region as modern, 56, 205; on Caribbeans as Westernized subjects, 74; on creolization in creation of New World identities, 178, 234 n.40; on cultural development as social process, 50; culture-building concept of, 225 n.26; master/slave dynamic dismissed by, 182; on monolithic notions of resistance, 84; randomization argument of, 27; on relation of space and time, 232 n.29; on world-systems theory, 39

Mitnick, Joshua, 279 n.58

Modernity: Afro-Creoles interweave modern ideas with Creole notions of respectability, 4; Caribbean as outside and inside spaces of the modern, 81; contestation of, 169; contingency and plurality of, 57; countercultural modernities, 77; crises within, 44; decentering dialectics of resistance in the globalizing modern, 73–106; domination practices and, 85–86; "flight to," 4, 76, 77, 78, 84, 91, 96, 117–19, 168; homing of modern freedoms, 19, 33, 63, 184, 199, 202, 203, 207, 219, 250 n.102, 252 n.114; "inaugural regime of violence" of, 6, 77; making and unmaking of modern space, 56–58; making modern subjects, 21–25, 59–61; modernist context for study of creolization, 25–26; on place-time relationship, 52; politics of modern governmentality, 59–61, 198, 202; slaves' constitutive presence in, 46, 47; spatiality of, 16, 230 n.12; temporality in articulating concept of, 229 n.10;

United States' hegemonic power in economy of, 76–77; vernacular, 217

Modes of production analysis, 41, 42, 44, 204, 242 n.6

Moore, Donald, 46, 61, 246 n.65

Morant Bay Rebellion, 91, 92, 258 n.63

Morphogenesis of cultures of power, 24, 65, 66–69, 73, 202

Mosquera, Gerardo, 217

Mouffe, Chantal, 9, 126, 171, 274 n.1

Multilateral Agreement on Investment (MAI), 38

Multinational corporations, 11, 37–38

Munasinghe, Viranjini, 18

Music: Afro-American influence on Jamaican, 193; hip-hop, 194, 279 n.57; techno, 190–93

Myal, 99

My Son's Story (Gordimer), 47

Nation: citizenship and development triangulated in West Indies and, 131–32; cultural "baggage" representing, 142; denationalization, 36–37; as fixed and unfixed, 165; as grounding and rooting the individual, 137; making, 161–62; as mode for producing form of space, 52; movement forces reimagining, 135; multiple attachments of nationals, 162; practicing national belonging through family, 148–54; reworking through transnationalizing, 145–48; transnational experiences reshape national lives, 204; transnationalism in remaking the national, 144–45, 169; "writing," 144–45. *See also* Citizenship; National identity; Nationalism; Nation-state

National identity: belief in possibility of, 116; cannot be essentialized, 169; cultural "baggage" and, 142; disparate, 12; Lucians group on St. Lucian, 120, 127; in state of crisis, 9

Nationalism: alternative, 130; becomes irrelevant, 191; creolization influenced by and influencing, 28; elites seek to rehabilitate, 116; informal, 237 n.66; intersection with transnationalism, 159–68; without the nation-state, 136–37; of 1960s, 1970s, and 1980s, 183; performative, 168; privileged men as leaders of, 122–23; racial, 277 n.42, 278 n.51; (un)making nation-states and, 114–17. *See also* Transnationalism

Nation-state: belief in leaders who can "do something," 10, 226 n.39; diasporas and decentering of, 184, 186; elites seek to rehabilitate, 116; freedom and sovereignty inseparable from formation of Creole, 116; globalization in transformation of, 34–35, 239 n.89; as grounding the individual, 137; imagined community associated with, 136; multinational corporations require concessions from, 38; nationalism without, 136–37; "poétique de la Relation" within, 215; popular culture in questioning, 9–10; returning migrants' relation to, 10–11, 154–58; rural space privileged as site of constructing, 7–9; as site of symbolic and cultural production, 62; transnationalism disturbs, 136; transnationals in rehabilitating, 169; (un)making in processes of development, 114–17

Negotiating Caribbean Freedom: Peasants and the State in Development (Crichlow), xiii, 222 n.14

Negri, Antonio, 247 n.65

Negritude, 175

Neo-Chinese culture, 106

Neo-Indian culture, 106

Neoliberalism: biopolitics of, 208; Creole traditions restructured by, 34–35; cultural politics and, 122; in formation of new spatialities and temporalities, 36–38, 43; insinuation into Caribbean, 4; as latest global context of creolization, 27–28; Lucians' expressive culture in context of, 114, 130; plural temporalities and, 195–96; politics of neoliberal governmentality, 197; post-Creole imagination conditioned by, 35–40

New Guinea, 197

Newness, 11, 20, 22–23, 175, 184

New World theorists, 11

New York City, 164, 196

Nicaraguan Creoles, 188–89

Nicholls, Grace, ix, 221 n.1

Northover, Patricia, xiii–xiv, 224 n.15

North-South divide, 35–36

Olwig, Karen Fog, 76, 96, 157

Omeros (Walcott), 250 n.102

Omi, Michael, 267 n.62

Ong, Aihwa, 60

Osborne, Thomas, 233 n.34

Pærregarrd, Karsten, 157–58

Palmer, Colin, 236 n.57

Palmié, Stephan, 13, 18, 153

Pan-Africanism, 10, 152, 172, 186, 191, 278 n.51

Paris Is Burning (documentary), 213–14

Parker, David, 238 n.77

Pastiche, 19

Patterson, Orlando, 5, 224 n.19

Patterson, P. J., 5

Patterson, Tiffany Ruby, 187–88

Peach, C., 150

Peasants. *See* Smallholders

Pelton, Robert, 210, 234 n.36, 251 n.114, 283 n.15

People's National Movement (PNM), 7, 8

People's National Party (PNP), 172, 174

Pérotin-Dumon, Anne, 26

Perry, Lee, 190

Phillips, Caryl: *The Atlantic Sound*, 13, 14, 203; on contemporary cultural parochialisms, 13–14, 203; on returning West Indian migrants, 159

Pile, Steve, 6

Place: circuits of, 70; complexity of resistance and making, 84; creolization as politics of making, 213; development and politics of, 117; diasporas and making of, 189; as essentialized, 176; flight into modernity and sense of, 117–19; for grasping being-modern-in-the-world, 16; homing of, 63; how imagination of places travels, 140–41; identity of, 85; journeying from place to place, 63, 250 n.102; limboing strategy of making, 68, 69; limboing struggles for, 74; locale privileging in creolization studies, 181; making in the Atlantic and beyond, 70–71; multiple ontological grounding of, 50; open-endedness in making of, 174; "placing and journeying," 57; politics of making, 14, 24, 54, 105–6, 175, 182; power and space and, 54–55; (re)homing, 74, 78, 80, 81, 105–6, 136, 145, 203, 207, 208, 209, 212, 214; resistance as fundamental to Caribbean places, 74–75; sovereignty of, 210; spacing and, 45, 49; spatialized, place-based racism, 14, 203; staking of, 207, 212; in time, 49, 52, 53, 54, 208, 209; typographies of, 64–65; will to, 18–19, 49–51, 68, 76, 117, 184, 202, 207, 208

Plantation: as characteristic of the Americas, 29–30; as context for study of creolization, 25, 26; counter-plantation system, 95; creolization linked to, 11–13, 180, 181, 182; decentering Caribbean plantation in creolization discourses, 202; diverging memories of, 13; diversity among, 26–

27; domination practices on, 85–86; former slaves reluctant to function as wage labor after emancipation, 86–87; as labor intensive, 86; master/slave power dynamic on, 182; post-plantation era, 1-14, 34–35, 176–78; provision grounds on, 139; seen as prototype of modern factory, 74; varieties of colonial practices of, 78–79; violence of, 189. *See also* Fleeing the plantation

Pocomania, 12

Polanyi, Karl, 223 n.12

Politics: of accommodation, 73, 74, 76, 77, 79–80, 94, 104, 105, 208; biopolitics, 63, 208, 209, 211; creolization as politics of making place, 213; of the cross, 70–71, 115, 197, 215; cultural, 121–24, 127, 211; cultural mobility and hybridity replace political geography in identity, 162; development and politics of place, 117; of dwelling, 73, 74, 77, 78, 138; electoral, 9; fashion and, 97–98; in flower festival origins, 98; of fracturing imagined communities of the nation, 21–22; of governable space, 128–29; of homing, 73, 74, 203; leftist, 121; liminal, 48, 74, 80–81, 105–6, 184; Lucians group lampoons politicians, 117–19; Lucians group urges reform of, 119–21; of making place, 14, 24, 54, 105–6, 175, 182; of mapping the present, 22, 57, 202, 219; of masking and masquerade, 203; of modern governmentality, 59–61, 198, 202; of neoliberal governmentality, 197; of "othering," 211; of poesis, 56; political theater, 125; vestry, 93. *See also* Democracy

Pons Te Te (Bridge of Tits), xii–xiii

Popular culture: concerns about overuse of "popular," 113; Lucians' ambivalent oppositional expressive culture in,

Popular culture (*continued*)
112–13; as multi-accentuated, 131; the state questioned by, 9–10; transnational flows of, 208. *See also* Music

Portugal, Africans in, 30

Postcolonial condition: in Africa, 212; cultural practices within, 43; liminal politics of, 48; plural temporalities of, 187; power and its subjects in post-colonial performance, 107–34; power in colonialism versus, 10; uncertainty of, 211; unhomeliness in, 250 n.102; women in, 123–24

Postcolonial studies, 21, 107

Post-Creole imaginations: Akomfrah's *The Last Angel of History* and, 190–93; ambivalencies of cultural practices in, 96; creolization experiences as affir-mations of, 184; "creolization-in-the-world" and, 22, 23; desire for citizen-ness in, 81; in development project, 117; diasporic habitus and, 32–33; diasporic movements remixing the world with, 135–70; global and local place-making subject to, 202; in global interweaving of economies and societies, 112; historicizing strat-egies of, 211; for homing modern free-doms, 19, 199, 202; interrogation of being-modern-in-the-world for understanding, 16–17; in making place in present time-spaces, 19; neo-liberal conditioning of, 35–40; oper-ate without guarantee of a specific kind of community, 218; of proper presence, 70, 79, 207; racial time and, 187; triangulations of space in map-ping the present, 53, 54; violence and disruptiveness in world of, 77; will to place and, 51

Power: banality of, 108; "chains of," 16, 55, 69; coloniality of, 56, 62, 106; in colonialism versus in postcolonial-ism, 10; creolization studies, of un-equal power, 5–6; cultures of, 24, 44, 59, 61, 65, 66–69, 73, 165, 184, 185, 199, 202, 206; of economy, 44, 205; econ-omy of, 44, 201–2, 205; freedom within relationships of, 111–12; hege-mony of, 165; informality and, 197; of investor class, 38; and its subjects in masking and masquerade, 61–63; and its subjects in postcolonial perfor-mance, 107–34; knowledge-power episteme, 56, 60, 115; mappings of, 49; master/slave dynamic of, 182; ontol-ogy of governable space and, 64–66; of postcolonial state, 108–9; in shap-ing creolization, 180, 181; sovereign, 60; space and place and, 54–55; space as particularized by, 49; spaces of, 64, 68; subjects as embedded in, 110; ver-satile equilibrium of, 65, 250 n.107; as way of acting upon a subject, 248 n.80

"Power and Its Subjects" (Crichlow and Northover), 224 n.15

Practice of Everyday Life, The (de Cer-teau), 253 n.3

Présence, 106; *américaine*, 216; continual refashioning of, 214; creation of new, 215; *neo-Africaine*, 84, 255 n.33; *neo-Europeene*, 84, 255 n.33

Present, the: as apparent time of global-ization, 20–21; Caribbean as symbolic refractions of a particular mapping of, x; "history of the present," 21, 233 nn. 33, 34; modern governmentality and emergence of forms of, 60; nego-tiating terms and conditions of, 209; power and differing journeys in, 199; present space, 46, 49, 245 n.50; provi-sion grounds and, 139; reconfiguring, 58; rehoming, 203; unhomeliness of present space, 51; wombs of present space, 17, 24, 32, 51, 56, 206, 230 n.15. *See also* Mapping the present

Price, Richard: on Caribbean region as modern transnational space, 205; on Creolité in Martiniquan intelligentsia, 223 n.7; on creolization in creation of New World identities, 178, 234 n.40; on cultural development as social process, 50; culture-building concept of, 225 n.26; on Martiniquan store, 2; master/slave dynamic dismissed by, 182; randomization argument of, 27; on relation of space and time, 232 n.29; on specificities of history and place, 49

Price, Sally, 232 n.29

Proper presence: belief in possibility of, 116–17; Caribbean struggle for, 33; homing and, 211, 212; mimetic appropriation of, 103; post-Creole imaginations of, 70, 79, 207; re/mappings of the present that promise, 63; triangulation of space in mapping the present and, 53, 54; wish to return home as step in line of escape for, 217; will to place and, 19, 51

Provision grounds, 139

Puerto Rico: competing nationalisms in, 136–37; encouraged to migrate to United States, 137–38; recreolization of Puerto Ricans in United States, 215–16; slaves in, 26

Puri, Shalini, 74, 95, 259 n.78

Quayson, Ato, 45, 61, 243 n.22, 249 n.90

Quijano, Aníbal, 4, 56, 76, 84, 106, 167, 256 n.33

Race: alternative conceptions of, 122; black diaspora literature's focus on, 32; black racial connectedness, 192; categorizations in America, 84; inequalities in land of opportunity, 141; racial democracy in Brazil, 8; racialization of Caribbeans, 141;

racialization of work, 35; racialized domination, 56; racialized sites, 45–46; racialized subjectivity, 186–87; racial nationalisms, 277 n.42, 278 n.51; racial time, 186–87; spatialized place-based racism, 14, 203. *See also* Ethnicity

Race Space Place project, xvi, 222 n.16

RAFA (Rally of Haitian Women), 163

Ranger, Terence, 259 n.76

Rastafarians, 10, 12, 172, 179, 188, 227 n.49

Realism: critical, 66, 206, 250 n.108; hysterical, 126

Realist Social Theory (Archer), 66

Reed, Ishmael, 190

Regulatory fractures, 1, 37

(Re)homing. *See* Homing

Relationality: of Atlantic geographies and histories, 50; of experiences and hi/stories through optic of global and local, 182, 183, 184; poétique de la Relation, x, 11, 57, 174–75, 177, 181, 204, 207, 209, 215, 219; relational histories, 204

Religion: of Rastafarians, 10, 12, 172, 179, 188, 227 n.49; voodoo, 196. *See also* Christianity

Remittances, 152, 196–97

Reputation, 95

Resistance: Caribbean peasantry and, 82–83; complexity of, 84; creolization practices make present moment sensitive to, 58; decentering dialectics of, 73–106; as fundamental to Caribbean places and freedoms, 74–75; as layered process, 105; opposition contrasted with, 75; on plantation, 85–86; political forms of, 105; in post-colonies, 108; spaces of, 6; strategies of working people and smallholders, 90–95; transnational studies focus on, 136

Respectability: dress and, 97; flower festivals and, 101, 102; in formation of Caribbean nation-state, 116; French Creole lack of, 103; Lucians group pokes fun at middle-class, 118, 128; reputation contrasted with, 95; in St. Lucian society, 102; sought by poor, 101; working peoples engage with elite definitions of, 4, 80

Richards, Glen, 94, 282 n.10

Ricourt, Milagros, 164

Rizvi, Ali Muhammad, 233 n.33

Roberts, George, 257 n.51

Robertson, Roland, 38, 138–39, 198

Rodney, Walter, 87

Rogoff, Irit, x, 140, 141–42, 201, 207, 217–18, 281 n.2

Rohlehr, Gordon, 103

Rose, Nikolas, 64, 233 n.34

Roseberry, William, 38

Rural space, 7, 45, 244 n.28

Ruud bwai, 110–11

Saint Domingue, 26

St. Lucia: A-bwé songfest, 102–4; anti-Catholic violence in, 12, 227 n.49; banana production in, 149, 271 n.34; as British colony, 150, 152; dress in, 97–98; dual citizenship for, 150, 271 n.35; enduring communal ties on, 96–97; family land in, 146–48, 155, 157, 270 n.26; flower festivals in, 98–102, 105; French Creole's status in, 103; governmentality practices disturbed by transnationals in, 63; land registration program in, 145–46; *metayage* system in, 79, 89–90; migrants to England who returned to, 10–11, 154–58; migration to Britain, 149; migration to United States, 137, 149; national cultural policy of, 128; political independence delayed, 155; popular culture protest by middle-class youth, 9; racial

homogeneity of, 129; rebellion of 1849, 91–92; respectability's social importance in, 102; slaves fight with French against British in, 262 n.110; sugar industry in, 79, 89, 149; working class in, 80. *See also* Gens anglaises; Lucians

St. Lucia Association, 153

St. Vincent, 137

Saldaña-Portillo, María Josefina, 238 n.83

Samuel, John, 135, 268 n.2

Sankofa (film), 191

Sassen, Saskia, 1, 36–37, 112, 205

Sayyid, S., 239 n.90

Scenes of presence, x, 182, 195, 206

Schiller, Nina, 162–63

Schouten, Swithin, 149

Schwartz, Jonathan, 154

Scott, David, 46, 56, 110–11, 183, 236 n.49, 247 n.65, 263 n.14, 280 n.68

Scott, James, 261 n.101

Scott, Rebecca, 235 n.45

Sekyi-Out, Ato, 263 n.14

Self-fashioning of *ruud bwai,* 110–11

Sheller, Mimi, 74, 178, 180, 181, 249 n.102

Shepherd-flock game, 62, 63, 211

Sifflet, Jason, 265 n.33

Silver, Beverly J., 35–36

Simmons, Harold, 102–3, 262 n.108

Simonsen, Kristen, 45

Singapore, 131, 267 n.70

Skoller, Jeffrey, 191

Slaves: abolition of British slave trade, 79; Caribbean smallholders originate from, 82; constitutive presence in modernity, 46, 47; Creole nation-states forged in slavery, 116; creolization as result of slavery, 178–79; cultural groupings among, 27, 237 n.61; experiences differing by place and time, 50; labor bargaining strategies of, 214, 282 n.10; master/slave power dynamic, 182; "miracle of creolization" of, 21; provision grounds for, 139; reluctant to function as wage labor after emancipation, 86–87; urban slavery, 176; variations in conditions of, 26, 236 n.56

Smallholders: become contract farmers, 88–89; Catholic Church supported by St. Lucian, 100; class differentiation among, 90; colonial rule protested by, 80; domination practices and, 85–86; European versus Caribbean, 82; forced into wage work, 89; in *metayage* system, 89–90; resistance strategies of, 90–95; struggle to participate in world accumulation processes, 86–88; transitional mimetic props employed by, 78

Small Islands and Huge Comparisons (Tomich), 42

Smith, Michael G., 96

Smith, Zadie, 126

Soja, Edward, 244 n.27

Somers, Margaret, 271 n.46

Sourieau, Marie-Agnès, 15

Sovereignty, 60; and freedom as inseparable from Creole nation-state, 116; of the imagination, 130–31, 197, 214, 217; of place, 210

Space: abstract, 54–55; appropriated, 54, 55, 64; as (ar)rhythm, 45, 47–48; becoming-space of time, 48; becoming-time of, 48; Cartesian conception of, 44, 45, 58; closed system of, 53; in discourses of creolization, 44–45; duality of, 54, 65, 175, 204; globalization in new spatialities, 36–38, 43; governable, 64–66, 128–29, 131; for grasping being-modern-in-the-world, 16; historicizing, 48; lived as liminal, 48, 49; making and unmaking of modern, 56–58; as particularized by power, 49; power and place and, 54–55; present space, 46, 49, 245

n.50; production of, 45–49; representations of, 45, 48–49, 52; spatial designs of places, 45; spatialization of time, 57–58; triangulations of, 52–54, 64; unhomeliness of present space, 51; wombs of present space, 17, 24, 32, 51, 56, 206, 230 n.15. *See also* Place; Spatial hi/story

Spatial hi/story, 21–25; "creolization-in-the-world" and, 21–23, 205; diasporas and making, 189; governmentality and, 58; historicizing space and spatializing history, 20; as making place in the world, 175; relational, 184; will to place and, 51

Spaulding, Anthony, 171, 172

STAFF party, 118, 123, 124–25

State: African postcolonial, 212; Caribbeans look to, 10; Caribbeans' response to, 81; carnivalesque perpetrated by, 108–9; developmentalist, 9, 18, 113–14, 127; governmentalization of, 63; Lucians group challenges to, 112, 119, 127; migration encouraged by, 137; mobility challenges primacy of, 136; as not in decline, 131, 169; "state in society," 62–63, 209, 211. *See also* Governmentality; Nation-state

State of Independence (Phillips), 159

Steinmetz, George, 264 n.28

Stewart, Charles, 178

Structural Emergent Powers (SEPS) model, 66–67, 251 n.111

Style, 85, 174

Subjects: black, 186–87; as embedded in power, 110; making modern, 21–25, 59–61; power and its subjects in masking and masquerades, 61–63; power and its subjects in postcolonial performance, 107–34; racialized subjectivity, 186–87; subject-being-in-the-world, 23, 70; subject space, 45

Sun Ra, 190

Surplus value chains, 68

Syncopated temporality, 47, 48

Syncretism, 178, 179, 181

Szanton-Blanc, Cristina, 162–63

Tapeño culture, 157

Tate, Greg, 190

Techno music, 190–93

Tenant farmers, 89

Territorialization, 154, 207

Theory, 48–49, 229 n.11

Thomas, Nicholas, 1–2

Thornton, John, 27, 77, 237 n.61, 273 n.76

Time: becoming-space of, 48; becoming-time of space, 48; Cartesian notion of, 49, 277 n.40; "Creole time on the move," 41, 58; of entanglement, 12, 67, 79, 127, 139, 173, 181, 183, 209, 202, 209, 267 n.66; globalization in formation of new temporalities, 36–38, 43; place in, 49, 52, 53, 54, 208, 209; plural temporalities, 1, 187, 195–96, 199, 208; racial, 186–87; spatialization of, 57–58; syncopated temporality, 47, 48. *See also* Present

Tomich, Dale, 15, 23, 24, 41–43, 44, 79, 139, 204, 206, 228 n.2, 232 n.29

Tourism, 138, 196, 203

Trace, 47, 245 n.36

Transformational Model of Social Activity (TMSA), 66

Transnational corporations, 36

Transnationalism: black transnational community, 186; British black identities and, 70–71, 216; of Caribbean traders and runaways, 29; conservative influences in, 136; creolization influenced by and influencing, 28; cultural "baggage" represents, 142; disjuncture and transience attributed to, 157; forces reimagining the nation,

135–36; intersection with nationalism, 159–68; local skepticism regarding returned transnationals, 155; mutable ideas of homelands of transnationals, 157–58; national lives reshaped by, 204; Puerto Rican, 216–17; as re-grounding the individual, 139–40; in remaking the national, 144–48, 169; as rhizome, 161, 168; transnational flows of popular culture, 208. *See also* Gens anglaises

Travel: how imagination of places travels, 140–41; overemphasized in relation to dwelling, 138, 140; personal advancement associated with, 150; and rituals of rootedness, 168; tourism, 138, 196, 203; unthinking, 140–41; in order to work, 5. *See also* Migration

Trinidad and Tobago: army mutiny of 1970s, 121; Best Village Competition, 7–8; East Indians in, 180, 254 n.14; French Creole gives way to English in, 103; neo-Indian and neo-Chinese cultures in, 106

Trotman, David, 27

Trouillot, Michel-Rolph: on authenticity, 192; on contexts for historical study of creolization, 25–27; on creolization, ix, xiii, 11, 21, 23, 58; on former slaves leaving plantations, 256 n.39; on globalization in the Caribbean, 34; on histories as open-ended, 213; influence on this study, 206; on modernity and place-time relationship, 52; on past in relation to present, 13, 191; on relation of space and time, 232 n.29; on systematic articulations of process, 24; on time, 12, 226 n.44; on working for capital, 3

Truth, Sojourner, 130

Turgeon, Laurier, 170

Turner, Victor, 252 n.114

UFAP (Union of Patriotic Haitian Women), 163

Unhomeliness, 51, 74, 250 n.102

United States: black condition in, 190–93; Caribbean migration to, 44; farm labor schemes of, 137; Grenada invasion by, 121; Haitians in, 141, 214–15; immigrant political communities in, 162–63; Lucians group on influence of, 120, 121, 127, 266 n.54; modern economy shaped by, 76–77; New York City, 164, 196; Puerto Rican migrants in, 136–37, 215–16; Puerto Rican nationalism and, 136–37; St. Lucian migration to, 149; smallholders produce export crops for, 88

Uplift strategies, 93–94, 259 n.73

Urban space, 45

USAID (United States Agency for International Development), 145–46

Utopian alternatives, 109

Valiant Women, 163

Vergès, Françoise, 231 n.26

Vestry politics, 93

Village councils, 7–8

Virgin Islands, 96, 278 n.45

Vitalis, David, 265 n.44

Voice of St. Lucia (newspaper), 213

Voodoo religion, 196

Wagley, Charles, 176, 275 n.14

Walcott, Derek, ix, 221 n.1, 232 n.29, 250 n.102

Wallerstein, Immanuel, 4, 76, 84, 167, 198, 256 n.33

Watson, Hilbourne, 136

Weedon, Chris, 243 n.20

Welfare state, English, 158

White, Garth, 193

White, Stephen, 206

White Teeth (Smith), 126

Williams, Brackette, 99, 105, 261 n.96

Williams, Raymond, 165, 243 n.20

Will to place, 18–19, 49–51, 68, 76, 117, 184, 202, 207, 208

Wilmot, Swithin, 86, 93, 256 n.40

Wilson, Peter, 95

Winant, Howard, 267 n.62

Wolf, Eric, 38–39

Wolff, Janet, 205

Wombing, 57, 168

Wombs of present space, 17, 24, 32, 51, 56, 206, 230 n.15

Women: alternative conceptions of, 122; gens anglaises, 152; in informal sector, 4–5; land ownership by, 148; organizations of Haitian, 163–64, 214–15; postcolonial state and, 123–24; in village councils, 8; work as necessary for Caribbean, 5

Workers Revolutionary Movement, 121

World systems theory, 38–39, 41, 42, 44, 205, 242 n.6

Wright, Richard, 277 n.39

Wulf, Christoph, 249 n.89

Wynter, Sylvia, 17, 232 n.29, 234 n.36

Yeats, William Butler, 114

Yonkers Town Association, 155–57

Yoruba, 33, 239 n.85

Zambos, 26, 236 n.57

Zapatistas, 129–30, 267 n.61

Zeleza, Paul Tiyambe, 212, 278 n.51

Zionism, 129

"Zombification," 108, 130

Zugman, Kara, 267 n.61

MICHAELINE A. CRICHLOW is an associate professor of African and African American Studies at Duke University. She is the author of *Negotiating Caribbean Freedom: Peasants and the State in Development* (2005). She coedited, with Faruk Tabak, *Informalization: Process and Structure* (2000).

PATRICIA NORTHOVER is a fellow at the Sir Arthur Lewis Institute of Social and Economic Studies, University of the West Indies, Mona.

Library of Congress Cataloging-in-Publication Data

Crichlow, Michaeline A.
Globalization and the post-Creole imagination:
notes on fleeing the plantation / Michaeline A. Crichlow;
with Patricia Northover.
p. cm.
"A John Hope Franklin Center book."
Includes bibliographical references and index.
ISBN 978-0-8223-4427-8 (cloth : alk. paper)
ISBN 978-0-8223-4441-4 (pbk. : alk. paper)
1. Cultural fusion. 2. Creoles. 3. Globalization.
I. Northover, Patricia. II. Title.
HM1272.C74 2009
305.5'633089960729—dc22   2009003599